6/1/77

Methodology of Social Impact Assessment

COMMUNITY DEVELOPMENT SERIES

Series Editor: Richard P. Dober, AIP

TERRAIN ANALYSIS: A Guide to Site Selection Using Aerial Photographic Interpretation/Douglas S. Way
URBAN ENVIRONMENTS AND HUMAN BEHAVIOR: An Annotated Bibliography/Edited by Gwen Bell et al.
APPLYING THE SYSTEMS APPROACH TO URBAN DEVELOPMENT/Jack LaPatra
BEHAVIORAL RESEARCH METHODS IN ENVIRONMENTAL DESIGN/Edited by William Michelson
STRATEGY FOR NEW COMMUNITY DEVELOPMENT IN THE UNITED STATES/Edited by Gideon Golany
PLANNING URBAN ENVIRONMENT/Melville C. Branch
LANDSCAPE ASSESSMENT: Values, Perceptions, and Resources/Edited by Ervin H. Zube et al.
THE URBAN ECOSYSTEM: A Holistic Approach/Edited by Forest W. Stearns
URBAN PLANNING THEORY/Edited by Melville C. Branch
COMMUNITY PLANNING FOR AN AGING SOCIETY/Edited by M. Powell Lawton et al.
ENVIRONMENTAL KNOWING: Theories, Research, and Methods/Edited by Gary T. Moore and Reginald G. Golledge

MIXED LAND USE: From Revival to Innovation/Dimitri Procos
THE URBAN NEST/Anne-Marie Pollowy
HOUSING MESSAGES/Franklin D. Becker
METHODOLOGY OF SOCIAL IMPACT ASSESSMENT/Edited by Kurt Finsterbusch and C. P. Wolf

EDRA Conference Publications
EDRA 1/Edited by Henry Sanoff and Sidney Cohn
EDRA 2/Edited by John Archea and Charles M. Eastman
ENVIRONMENTAL DESIGN RESEARCH, Vol. I: Selected Papers/Edited by Wolfgang F. E. Preiser (EDRA 4)
ENVIRONMENTAL DESIGN RESEARCH, Vol. II: Symposia and Workshops/Edited by Wolfgang F. E. Preiser (EDRA 4)
MAN-ENVIRONMENT INTERACTIONS: Evaluations and Applications, Parts I, II, and III/Edited by Daniel H. Carson (EDRA 5)
RESPONDING TO SOCIAL CHANGE/Edited by Basil Honikman (EDRA 6)
THE BEHAVIORAL BASIS OF DESIGN, BOOK 1/Edited by Peter Suedfeld and James A. Russell (EDRA 7)

CDS/32

Methodology of Social Impact Assessment

EDITED BY

Kurt Finsterbusch
UNIVERSITY OF MARYLAND

C. P. Wolf
CITY UNIVERSITY OF NEW YORK

Dowden, Hutchinson & Ross, Inc.
STROUDSBURG, PENNSYLVANIA

Copyright © 1977 by **Dowden, Hutchinson & Ross, Inc.**
Community Development Series, Volume 32
Library of Congress Catalog Card Number: 76-54656
ISBN: 0-87933-273-5

All rights reserved. No part of this book covered by the copyrights hereon may be reproduced or transmitted in any form or by any means —graphic, electronic, or mechanical, including photocopying, recording, taping, or information storage and retrieval systems—without written permission of the publisher.

76 77 78   5 4 3 2 1
Manufactured in the United States of America.

Library of Congress Cataloging in Publication Data

Main entry under title:
Methodology of social impact assessment.

(Community development series ; v. 32)
"Originally presented at a workshop held in conjunction with the sixth annual conference of the Environmental Design Research Association (EDRA), Lawrence, Kansas, in May, 1975."
Includes index.
1. Social sciences—Methodology—Congresses. 2. Evaluation research (Social action programs)—Congresses. I. Finsterbusch, Kurt, 1935–   II. Wolf, Charles Parker, 1933–   III. Environmental Design Research Association.
H61.M4926   300'.1'8   76-54656
ISBN 0-87933-273-5

Foreword

Those concerned with physically developing communities at all levels now recognize, and fully welcome, assistance in establishing the important links between social and cultural behavior and the creation of physical forms. The state of the art has even advanced so that some measurement can be given to probable impact in advance of construction, particularly the natural environment, and plans can be adjusted accordingly. In a similar vein, there now emerges an interest in evaluating the social dimensions with the hope of immediately ameliorating plans where possible and effecting long-range public policy wherever necessary.

The recognition and interest is neither new nor without historic precedent. After all, what did Queen Elizabeth I have in mind but "social impact assessment" when she asked Parliament to legislate against further settlement in seventeenth-century London.

What is new, however, is the systematic approach to the subject, including conceptual frameworks, methodologies, and application. All this has advanced sufficiently to yield an important reference work that Kurt Finsterbusch and C. P. Wolf have intelligently assembled in *Methodology of Social Impact Assessment*—a book timely, pertinent, helpful.

In putting together the material for this book, it is obvious that Finsterbusch, Wolf, and their colleagues see the importance of practitioners in the field sharing their expertise with those other professionals seeking such information and advice. This is a fundamental proposition in publishing the Community Development Series.

Here then is a book that offers planners, architects, landscape architects, engineers, and those in related disciplines beneficial knowledge in a readily convenient form. Those wishing to move from the rhetoric of good intentions to the reality of genuinely improved environment will find the editors' pioneering efforts immediately useful both for the insights offered and the techniques made available. In George L. Peterson's words "it lengthens all our studies."

Richard P. Dober, AIP

Preface

This book is a partial inventory of methodologies for social impact assessment (SIA). While conspicuous gaps occur at numerous points, it does present a fairly representative sampling of methods applied in this area. Conceivably, any methodology or technique of social research could be enlisted in the service of SIA, though not with equal success. The methods presented here were intended to demonstrate appropriateness to this specific context.

Most contributions to the volume were originally presented at a workshop held in conjunction with the Sixth Annual Conference of the Environmental Design Research Association (EDRA), Lawrence, Kansas, in May, 1975. Based on workshop discussion and subsequent criticism, papers were extensively revised for publication here. The workshop objective of compiling brief descriptions of field-tested methods for relatively inexperienced assessors has not been fulfilled to date, although a number of similar efforts are becoming available. In all cases, further technical refinement and translation to user needs is necessary to produce an operational methodology for SIA. Following that, an extended period of feasibility testing under actual field conditions will be required to establish reliability and validity. This book is one initial step in that direction.

The EDRA 6 workshop and this book were structured according to the main sequence of steps outlined in U.S. Army Corps of Engineers guidelines for the assessment of economic, social and environmental impacts: profiling, projection, assessment, and evaluation. A final step, mitigation of unavoidable adverse impacts, is implied in many of the papers. Our intention was to identify various methodological approaches and associate them with each assessment step, keying specific techniques to their procedural and information requirements. While considerable smoothing and meshing remain to make this an integrated methodological schema, there has emerged a general consensus on several main methodological points:

1. The conduct of SIA should proceed in an iterative fashion adding depth and detail as assessments proceed through a first-round "mini-assessment," intensive study of the full set of plausible alternative proposals, policy adjustments, and mitigation measures.
2. Earlier approaches that relied on *checklists* are being superseded by more sophisticated efforts at casual modeling. In turn, these should be grounded in social indicator systems.
3. In addition to retrospective and current studies, longitudinal studies are required for the assessment of longer-term, higher-order impacts. Recognizing that we are dealing with dynamic systems, the one-shot study must be supplanted by periodic reassessments and, ideally, continuous quality-of-life monitoring.
4. In light of the complexity of the analytic situation, pluralistic approaches and multiple measures such as triangulation should be employed. We are far from that stage of methodological development where any one best way can be prescribed, but the achievement of greater methodological determinancy is possible within the state of the art.

5. Along with community and regional studies, SIA must focus increasing attention on individuals, organizations, and institutions as units of impact analysis. Both macro- and micro-level analyses are required, including an effective means for bridging between them, to achieve a fully-integrated assessment methodology.
6. As an interdisciplinary undertaking, SIA must draw widely from the range of conceptual and methodological tools of disciplines from ecology to ethnography. The interdisciplinary character of SIA poses both problems of multidisciplinary teamwork and possibilities for fruitful collaboration.
7. Policy decisions, between *action* and *no action* as well as the choice of planning alternatives, hinge in part on the projection of future system states with and without the contemplated intervention. The methodological basis for such projections appears both highly important and problematic.

Although we have attempted to give broad coverage to the diverse interests of SIA, methodological completeness in this field will depend on many further innovations and applications. Areas in which methodological developments must occur include:

Social Profiling	Projection Techniques
Archival Research	Social Forecasting
Social Indicators	Trend-Impact Analysis
Observational Methods	Cross-Impact Analysis
Interaction Analysis	Sensitivity Analysis
Model Building	Multivariate Analysis
Demographic Analysis	Social Graphics
Institutional Analysis	Public Participation
Input-Output Analysis	Heuristic Approaches
Matrix Methodologies	Evaluation Research
Ethnographic Methods	Risk Analysis
Computer Methods	Impact Monitoring
Remote-Sensing Techniques	Psychological Assessment

Developments in these areas must be deployed to the substantive topics of SIA interest, such as:

Housing and Urban Renewal	Population Displacement and Relocation
Energy Development	Rural Development
Highway and Mass Transportation	Weather Modification
Facility Siting	Health and Community Services
Community Development and Land Use	Water Resources Planning and Management
Coastal Zone Management	Boom Towns
Community Cohesion	Architecture and Buildings

The catalogue of methodological and substantive areas of concern to SIA is practically inexhaustible. In proportion as these are developed the need for methodological integration and codification will increase.

Throughout this book the relevance of SIA to policy formulation, program planning, and project implementation will be a primary concern, as the introduction by Finsterbusch makes explicit. SIA is addressed to real problems of real life. The social—and especially the political—context of SIA is part of the analytic problem social impact assessors must resolve. It cannot be done without the active collaboration of colleagues in many professions and disciplines, the sponsorship and support of socially concerned and informed officials, and the cooperation and encouragement of the people they serve.

We gratefully acknowledge the assistance received in preparing this book from Vonda Harper and Lisa Jacobson; the patience and encouragement of Community Development Series Editor Richard P. Dober and Publisher Charles S. Hutchinson; and, of course, the worthy contributions of colleagues whose efforts made this book possible.

C. P. Wolf

Contents

Series Editor's Foreword   v
Preface   vi

I Social Impact Assessment and Public Policy   1

    The Potential Role of Social Impact Assessments in Instituting Public Policies   2
    Kurt Finsterbusch

    Estimating Policy Consequences for Individuals, Organizations, and Communities   13
    Kurt Finsterbusch

II Methodological Approaches to Social Impact Assessment   21

    A Framework for Community Impact Assessment   24
    Audrey Armour, Beate Bowron, Earl Miller, and Michael Miloff

    Development of a Social Impact Assessment Methodology (SIAM)   35
    George A. Watkins

    Toward a Methodology for Conducting Social Impact Assessments Using Quality of Social Life Indicators   43
    Marvin E. Olsen and Donna J. Merwin

    Grounded Theory Construction in Social Impact Assessment   64
    Mark Shields

    Social Impact Assessment and Cost-Benefit Analysis   74
    Peter G. Sassone

    Using Cost-Benefit Analysis in Social Impact Assessment: Hazards and Promise   83
    Jeff V. Conopask and Robert R. Reynolds, Jr.

Macro and Micro Levels of Analysis in the Social Impact Assessment of a Reservoir Development   91
Raghu N. Singh

Combining Ethnographic and Survey Research   102
Raymond L. Gold

Comprehensive Values and Public Policy   108
Ruth P. Mack

The Social Psychological Level of Analysis in Social Impact Assessment: Individual Well-being, Psychosocial Climates, and the Environmental Assessment Scale   132
Donald H. Deane and Jeryl L. Mumpower

III Profiling   153

Yaquina Bay: A Case Study in Social Impact Assessment   155
William T. White

Leadership Generated Community Social Profiles   160
Pamela Dee Savatsky and Elva Dianne Freilich

Computer-Assisted Social Profiling: Some Uses of Computerized Data Banks in Social Impact Assessment   167
James V. Aidala, Jr.

Center for Census Use Studies Small Area Data Technology: Potential Tools for Social Impact Assessment in Urban Areas   172
Harold C. Wallach

A Quality of Life Production Model for Project Impact Assessment   182
Ben-chieh Liu

IV Projecting   200

Methods for Estimating Societal Futures   202
David C. Miller

The Use of Scenarios for Social Impact Assessment   211
Evan Vlachos

Community Structure, Resources, and the Capacity to Respond to Environmental Problems: New Concepts for Social Impact Assessment   224
Donald R. DeLuca

Correlational Tools for Predicting Community Acceptance of Nuclear Power Plant Sites   235
J. F. Byrne and E. W. Sucov

Gaming and Simulation in the Service of Social Impact Assessment: An Exploration   245
Joseph D. Ben-Dak

V Assessment   263

Toward an Assessment of the Potential Social Impacts of a Nuclear Power Plant on a Community: Survey of Residents' Views   265
John W. Lounsbury, Eric Sundstrom, C. Richard Schuller, Thomas J. Mattingly, Jr., and Robert DeVault

A Strategy for Using Survey Questionnaires in Planning Nonstructural Flood Control Programs   278
L. Douglas James

The Use of Mini Surveys in Social Impact Assessments   291
Kurt Finsterbusch

Methodologies for Assessing the Social Impact of Projects Necessitating Forced Relocation of Rural People   297
Ted L. Napier

Assessing Toward Social Impacts: The Diachronic Analysis of Newspaper Contents   303
Annabelle Bender Motz

VI Evaluation   314

Identifying Publics in Social Impact Assessment   317
Gene E. Willeke

Evaluation of a Proposed Residential Development Policy   324
Henry E. Gregori, Elliot B. Reiff, D'Ann L. Roch, William M. Rohe, John L. Street, and Lawrence A. Swanson

Quality of Life Assessment: The Harvard Square Planning Workshops   331
Lajos Heder and Mark Francis

Policy Capturing in Energy   341
Jean M. Johnson

Probing Complexity in Social Systems Through Interpretive Structural Modeling   347
Kazuhiko Kawamura and David W. Malone

Overcoming Obstacles to Agency and Public Involvement: A Program and Its Methods   355
Kenneth E. Hornback

Social Impact Assessment: A Survey of Highway Planners   364
Lynn G. Llewellyn

VII Epilogue   373

Social Impact Assessment: Comments on the State of the Art   374
George L. Peterson and Robert S. Gemmell

I Social Impact Assessment and Public Policy

The Potential Role of Social Impact Assessments in Instituting Public Policies

Kurt Finsterbusch
University of Maryland

I. Introduction

The primary goal of social impact assessment (SIA) and assessments generally is to facilitate decision making by determining the full range of costs and benefits of alternative proposed courses of action. The most important secondary goal is to improve the design and administration of policies in order to ameliorate the disbenefits and to increase the benefits. Policy design involves policy specification, supplementation and modification. Policy administration involves implementation, mitigation, monitoring and revision. The SIA elements which assist these policy processes are outlined in Table 1.

It should be stressed that SIAs are mainly oriented to serving decision making needs. The traditional research standards of analytic perceptiveness and precision, data completeness and reliability, and depth of causal understanding apply only insofar as they serve the purposes of policy selection, design and administration. For example, only modest amounts of data may suffice for choosing between two or three alternative courses of action, and the information needs of decision makers may be satisfied long before analytic closure is approached.

Assessment entails the analytical operations of research design, data collection, data analysis, interpretation and the application of findings in policy recommendations. More than analysis and advising, however, research design and data collection lend themselves to procedural codification and explication; they are the operations emphasized in this discussion.

II. Policy Selection

Policy selection usually entails two decisions: the decision to act and the choice between alternative course of action. Current SIAs generally focus on the choice between alternatives. In large part this is because government sponsors request research only after they have already decided to act. Policy makers often "know" that something should be done. They feel no need to invite researchers to advise them on the choice between action and no action. Government officials are elected and employed to enact and administer government programs. They naturally feel that identified problems call for government actions. The "do nothing" option is included in policy studies mainly because of legal requirements and generally is not given a fair review. This construction of reality is also likely to become the perspective of the research team. A conscious effort should be made, therefore, to identify and neutralize this perspective of the research sponsor and to explore

TABLE 1: THE ELEMENTS OF SOCIAL IMPACT ASSESSMENTS

I. Policy Selection
   A. Selection of Alternatives for Assessment by Means of:
      1. First round SIA
      2. Delphi interviewing of experts
      3. Workshops for interested parties.

   B. Descriptions of Policy Alternatives in Terms of:
      1. Actions authorized, required, or encouraged
      2. Allocation of responsibilities and jurisdictions
      3. Enforcement incentives and sanctions
      4. Implementation schedule and plan
      5. Capabilities of agencies for performing their roles.

   C. Research Design
      1. Selection of evaluation criteria
      2. Conceptual framework
      3. Measures for variables
      4. Sources of data and methods of mining them
      5. Information sought
      6. Analytical techniques to be employed
      7. Organization and selection of research team.

   D. Research Operations
      1. Identification of impacts by means of:
         a. relevance tree
         b. literature survey
         c. delphi interviewing
         d. iterative interviewing
         e. contextual analysis
         f. contingency trees
         g. model construction.
      2. Selection of impacts for analysis on the basis of:
         a. extent (number of people affected)
         b. intensity (seriousness or extent of impact)
         c. duration
         d. irreversibility
         e. higher-order impacts (magnitude and severity)
         f. political sensitivity.
      3. Measurement of impacts by means of:
         a. surveys (including small sample surveys)
         b. informant interviews
         c. ethnographic studies
         d. census and other data banks
         e. documents and other records.

   E. Data Analysis Using Standard Procedures in the Social Sciences

   F. Conclusions and Recommendations

TABLE 1 continued

II. Policy Design
   A. Specification of Provisions of the Policy

   B. Modification of Provisions of the Policy (sensitivity analysis: changing a policy parameter and observing the changes in the impact parameters)

   C. Supplementation of the Policy to Ameliorate Disbenefits

III. Policy Administration
   A. Implementation of the Policy by Administrators

   B. Monitoring the Policy by Identifying its Consequences

   C. Revision of the Harmful Features of the Policy

---

alternative perspectives. Citizen participation, perhaps institutionalized in a review committee, can be very helpful for this purpose.

There are six basic analytical operations involved in assessing a set of alternative courses of actions. The first step is to narrow the range of alternatives for more careful assessments. Some method must be used to pare the feasible options down to a small number for intensive study. One is to proceed as though one is conducting a full assessment, but to substitute informed judgments for all time-consuming and costly operations. The result is a "first round" SIA which is useful in determining data needs of the subsequent full-scale SIA.

An alternative method is interviewing experts by means of the delphi technique. This involves several rounds of interviews, with feedback of the aggregated results to the interviewees between rounds. The experts are asked to propose the most promising alternatives or to evaluate the relative importance of a list of alternatives. Results using the delphi technique identify the degree of expert consensus about the various alternatives. Another method allows the interested parties to select the alternatives for the full assessment. Workshops with varying interest groups represented are useful for generating interaction over candidate alternatives.

Two general strategies can be used in selecting alternatives for intensive analysis: one is to select the most likely candidates; the other is to select alternatives which differ widely. The latter strategy is advisable when it is difficult to eliminate candidates a priori or when the assessment is more exploratory.

The second step is to fully _describe_ the selected alternatives, including the actions to be authorized, the mechanisms of enforcement, the implementation schedule and program, the responsibilities of the involved agencies, and the capabilities of the agencies for performing their roles. Each of these aspects will affect the kinds of impacts which the alternatives may have and needs to be taken into account in the assessment.

The third step is to design the research strategy by proposing the criteria for evaluation, the conceptual framework to guide analysis, measures for the relevant variables, sources of data, information to be obtained, analytic techniques to be employed, and the organization of the research team. The research design can benefit from the examples of previous studies of similar types, with a view to improving upon past performance. Many SIAs which have produced considerable social profile data on communities and groups provide almost no analysis to help determine the best alternative or point out negative features of a policy which need to be corrected. Ideally, the variables to be measured in a SIA should be evaluative criteria, which can indicate the superiority of one alternative over others, recognizing however their political nature and the need for participation by the sponsor and interested parties in their selection.

Selecting an appropriate conceptual framework is another research design action which greatly affects the utility of the research. SIAs often proceed on a common sense, ad hoc basis and overlook important considerations as result. Because a conceptual framework maps a system of variables, it highlights the interrelationships among them and the importance of tracing through their systemic linkages. Use of similar conceptual frameworks will facilitate the development of cumulative knowledge in the field of SIA.

The fourth step in policy selection is systematic data collection. All of the significant impacts of each alternative, including the consequences of the no action policy, should be identified and their extent and magnitude estimated.

Identification of significant impacts is facilitated by a scanning device such as the relevance tree presented in Figure 1.[1] This enables the researcher to systematically question whether the proposed alternative would have any potential impacts across a broad range of social categories. Possible subjective bias can be reduced by using several analysts with different backgrounds to identify impacts. Other methods for improving these judgments are surveys of similar past cases, delphi interviewing of experts, iterative interviewing of impactees, contextual analysis, contingency trees, and model construction. The literature survey brings past experience to bear on the analysis. Delphi interviewing requires assessors to reevaluate their judgments in the light of the opinion and criticism of others. Iterative interviewing solicits information and judgments from groups, agencies, and organizations that are likely to be impacted and judiciously uses information already obtained from informants in probing subsequent informants. Contextual analysis adds information on the community, organizational and institutional settings of a project to the analysis of impacts. A contingency tree permits the systematic mapping of possible first-, second-, and higher-order impacts. This approach involves listing an exhaustive set of possible direct impacts along with their estimated probabilities and intensities and continuing the procedure using the second-order impacts so identified for estimating higher-order impacts. As a practical matter, however, contingency trees are not exhaustive and include only the more probable impacts for each order. The scenario is a single path on a contingency tree. Finally, in its most sophisticated form, model construction programs mathematical relationships among a fairly large system of variables which are used to calculate the cross-impacts of a policy alternative.

---

1. See Finsterbusch (1975) for an extended discussion of the use of the relevance tree.

FIGURE 1. IMPACT RELEVANCE TREE FOR SOCIAL IMPACT ANALYSIS

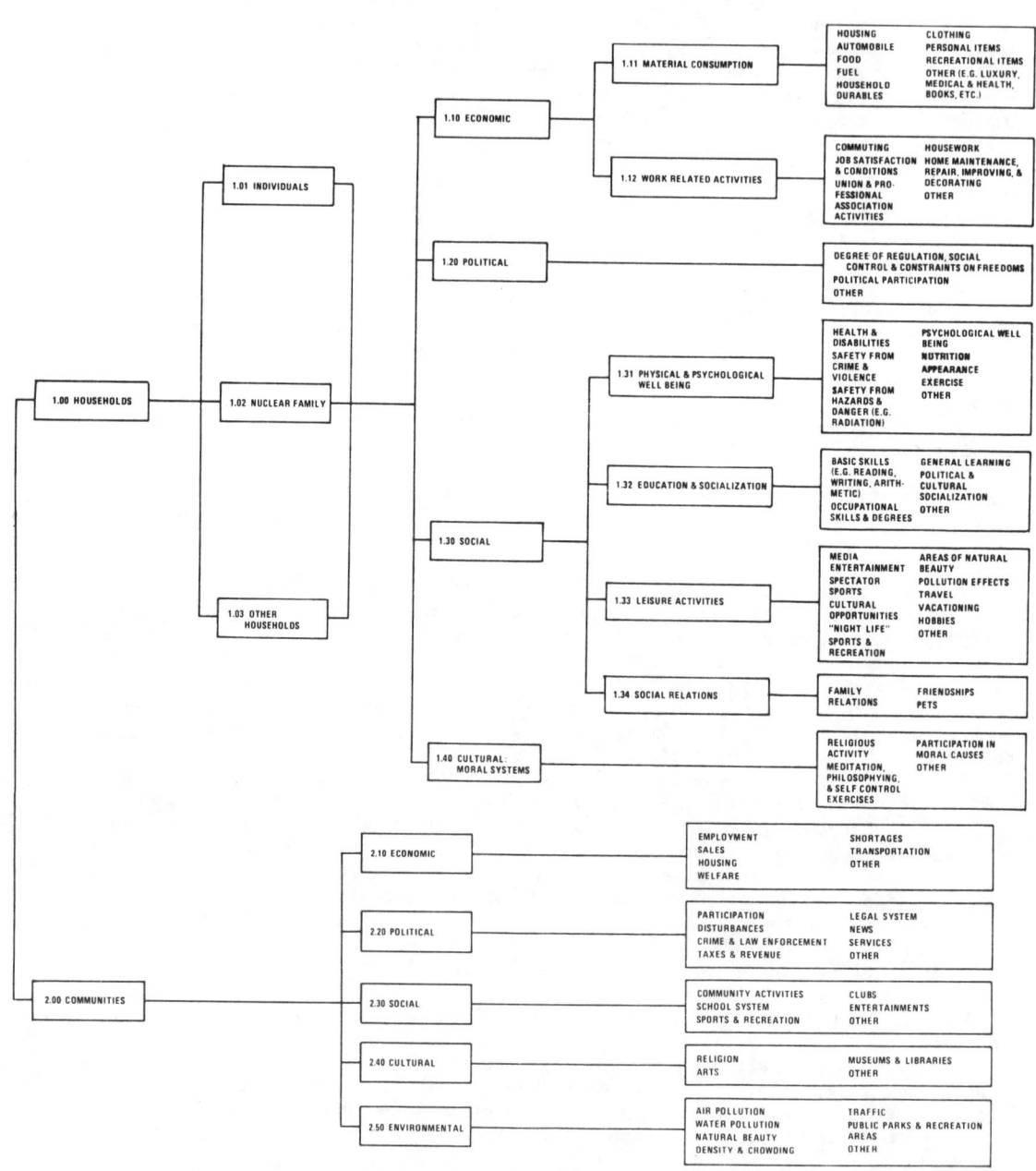

FIGURE 1. Continued

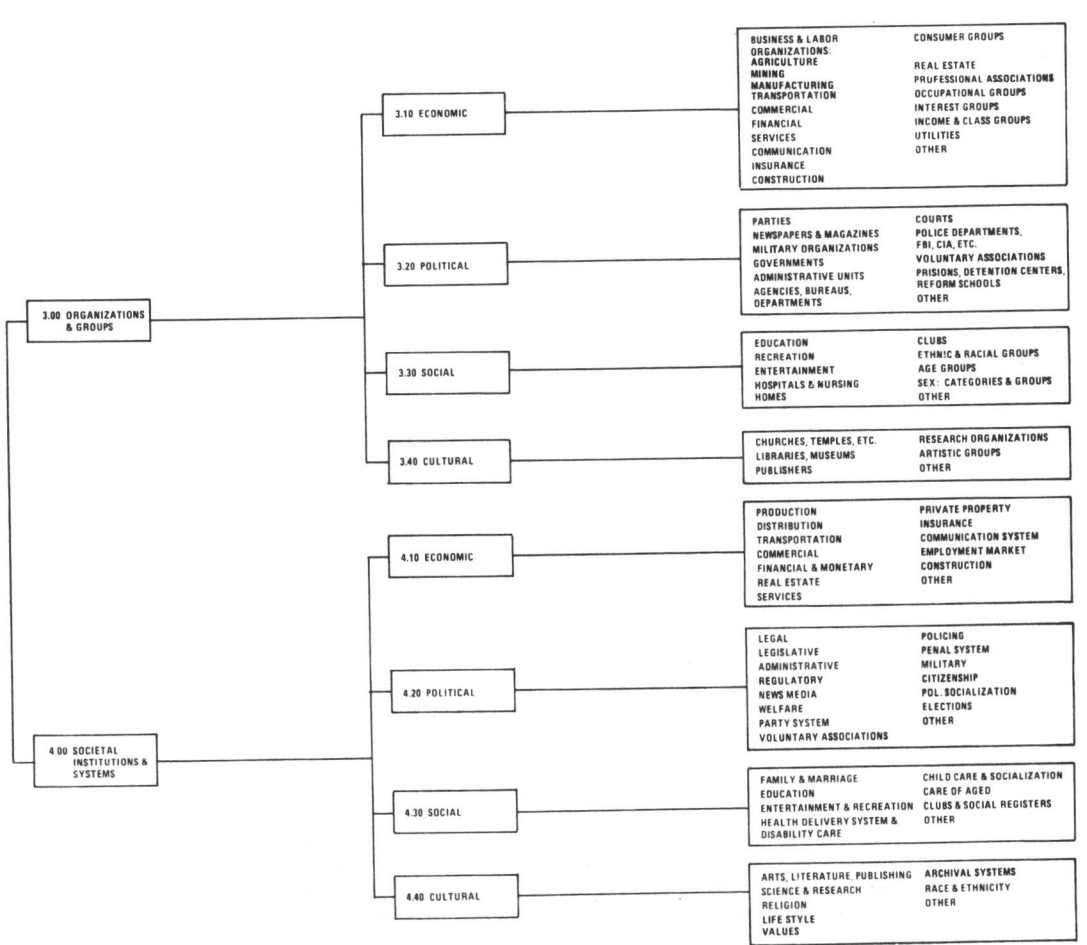

Once impacts have been identified the more significant ones must be isolated for study. Commonly used criteria of significance are: intensity, probability, irreversibility, political sensitivity, duration, higher-order impacts, and the number of persons affected. Inevitably, considerable subjective judgment enters in this process.

The major problem in identifying impacts is inclusiveness; no significant impact should be overlooked. The major problem in estimating the extent of impacts is measurement. SIAs fall heir to all of the measurement problems of the social sciences generally, with the addition of having to estimate future as well as existing impacts. Improvement in the scientific quality of SIA will necessarily depend upon major improvements in measurement.

The basic operation in impact measurement is to compare the situation which will result from policy A with the situation which would result if policy A were not implemented. The crucial question is whether and to what extent the situation will remain "the same" if policy A were not implemented. Constructing a beltway around Central City, say, would change traffic patterns, downtown business activity, perimeter land values and land use, motel development, etc., from the no beltway situation. These comparisons appear relatively straightforward, assuming present trends continue unchanged if the beltway is not built. Often, however, the no action option would not result in the continuation of present trends but rather would produce a series of adaptations by local groups and organizations, even resolving the "problem" without governmental action. For example, if the city decides not to build a second hospital on the west side of town, the private Presbyterian Hospital on the west side may build a new 100 bed wing or the westsiders may start a volunteer ambulance service. These adaptations should be estimated before the no action case can be compared to other alternatives, and such estimates have wide margins of error.

Since impacts vary considerably in type, a variety of research tools is necessary for their estimation. While the choice of research tools is dependent on the research design selected for a particular impact situation, a few general comments are in order. The survey, perhaps the sociologist's favorite research tool, should be used more widely in SIAs. Too often budgetary decisions have eliminated surveys from SIAs which would have benefited from them. Surveys can provide specific, detailed information on the people in a target area and surface their concerns, attitudes and perceptions. In conjunction with research on similar prior cases, this information can assist in estimating the extent of potential impacts and likely responses to them. On the other hand, one can also err by depending too much on surveys. Especially when estimating future impacts, surveys require confirmation from other sources. Since multiple research techniques are required in SIAs and budgets are constrained, the survey sample may have to be relatively small (Finsterbusch 1976).

Informant interviewing is the backbone of SIAs. Estimating impacts frequently requires the artful piecing together of expert opinions, claims of potentially impacted parties, official judgments and objective information. Delphi interviewing of experts, iterative interviewing of impacted parties, and informant interviewing of government personnel are current techniques for doing the necessary social detective work, but SIA does not stop there. Social impact assessors must hunt for relevant information by making endless inquiries, following leads and checking out what people tell them. Experience in SIAs teaches skepticism of what people say, even when the people are experts without axes to grind. After all, experts too must form their judgments on the basis of a limited range of past experiences and a limited set of criteria.

Ethnographic studies also depend heavily on informant interviewing and should definitely have a larger role in SIAs. The ethnographer combines interviewing with extensive field observations and attempts to know a community inside and out. Most SIAs cannot afford such complete knowledge of the community, however, especially if an ethnographic study can only moderately improve the accuracy of estimates by other means. On the other hand, most SIAs suffer from too little immersion in the potentially impacted community and fail as a result to secure a sure grasp of its inner workings.

Informant interviewing should also be supplemented by a wide range of research techniques. All sources of information should be expertly tapped. Documents, records, reports, newspapers, data banks, etc., provide vital information. Probably the most generally helpful are census data. Until recently the major barrier to using census data files was the dissimilarity between the units of social analysis and the units of reporting census data, e.g., tracts. To overcome this, the Center for Census Use Studies has recently developed a method for translating census tracts into other units and vice versa.

Another use of documents is in historical analysis which, in our judgment, is too often neglected in SIAs. For example, the history of the public discussion of a project as reported in the newspapers can indicate shifts in public opinions which provide perspective on current opinion surveys and identify the events leading to opinion formation.

The fifth analytical step in the process of selecting the policy for implementation is to <u>analyze</u> the information collected in the fourth step. Analysis involves putting all the information together in a way that "tells the story." It involves classification, synthesis, comparison of cases, measurements of the association among variables, and other data manipulation techniques. For this step SIAs can borrow heavily from the current array of analytic techniques in the social sciences. The differences in objectives between SIAs and social science analyses should be borne in mind, however. SIA is generally less interested in measures of association and complex techniques for partialling out causal influences than in measuring the extent of potential impacts and determining the variables that can be effectively manipulated.[1]

The sixth step in the process of policy selection is deducing <u>conclusions</u> from the analysis and formulating <u>recommendations</u>. The major difficulty in this step is the summing up of positive and negative impacts into an overall evaluation. Estimating tradeoffs in social utilities for different groups has not reached a high stage of development. Most SIAs evade the issue by only reporting their impact estimates, without summing up to a net balance. The readers of the report must draw their own

---

1. For extensive discussions of the differences between academic and policy research see Coleman (1972), Etzioni (1971) and Scott and Shore (1974).

conclusions from a personal summation, using weights determined by their own implicit criteria and values. A different approach is to systematically construct a value system or set of weights which enables choice between alternatives on the basis of net benefits. Policy capturing and interpretive structural modeling are two value-eliciting techniques for performing this operation.

The above analytical steps apply both to the action vs. no action decision and to the choice between alternative courses of action. These two decisions tend to have important differences which should be taken into account in selecting and applying various research techniques. Four important differences are:((1) salience of value questions, (2) length of the evaluative time frame, (3) uncertainly of probability estimates of impacts, and (4) measureability of crucial dimensions. These differences are briefly described below.

The action vs. no action decision requires the selection of criteria for evaluating alternatives. What values are to be maximized? What is a good state of affairs and what a bad state? The choice between action and no action generally focuses on ultimate values, whereas choice between alternative courses of action generally focus on instrumentalities. For example, the decision to build or not build a highway might involve tradeoffs between reduced traffic congestion and increased accessibility (which translates into increased land values) on the one hand with the displacement of residents, reduced mass transit ridership, increased suburban sprawl, and reduced accessibility for pedestrians on the other hand. Such decisions raise major value questions about what ways of life are preferable. Once the decision to build is made, however, attention shifts to the simpler questions of which route displaces the fewest persons and costs least in acquisition and construction. Of course, value considerations are not ignored completely in choosing between alternatives, but they do not occupy a central focus of attention as in the choice between action and no action.

Another difference between the action vs. no action decision and the choices between alternatives is the longer time frame required for the former, since some of the most significant differences in impacts may not surface in the short run. For example, a long time frame is required to compare the situations which would evolve if a city did or did not build low-income housing. The major conclusion of Forrester's (1969) model of urban dynamics is that most government actions, including building low-income housing, have long run negative effects, e.g., increasing the shortage of such housing.

The third contrast between the two types of decisions is the greater uncertainty of probability estimates for the action vs. no action decision. It contrasts very different situations, each having many possible consequences with uncertain probabilities. The dam vs. no dam decision involves social impacts (e.g., settlement patterns, community life style) having greater uncertainties than those associated with decisions whether to build a 100-foot or 150-foot dam and whether to locate it 4 miles or 8 miles above Mudville. For the action vs. no action decision the analyst is, therefore, obliged to advise not only on possible outcomes whose probabilities can only be roughly surmised but also on the confidence interval within which such outcomes may fall, itself highly uncertain.

Finally, the outcome of the no action decision is extremely hard to predict. As mentioned earlier, no action by Federal or State Governments often results in unpredictable actions by lower governmental levels and by numerous other interested parties. Government action is usually considered when a situation is sufficiently troubling to affect people's behavior. One cannot assume therefore that the no action situation will result in more of the same. If the government does not act, other organizations will act on the problem or individuals will alter their behavior patterns. If a city does not build a badly needed expressway to the downtown area, the city might increase the number of rush hour one-way streets, bus companies might expand their services, or commuters might increasingly car pool. Because adaptive changes are likely the analyst cannot simply extrapolate present trends in such cases. Often it is almost impossible to predict which set of adaptive changes will occur, however.

III. Policy Design

SIAs not only aid in the selection of policy alternatives but also can contribute to the design of the selected policy. Once an alternative has been selected, detailed provisions for implementation need to be specified. When guided by an SIA, the specification of provisions should improve the societal benefits from the policy. The SIA can also demonstrate the need for modifications in specifications to avoid or reduce negative impacts. Finally, the SIA might suggest ways in which the policy should be supplemented with programs for ameliorating the disbenefits. For example, a special program may be needed for retraining displaced workers.

Most SIAs contribute little to policy design. Usually policy design recommendations are more afterthoughts than they are logical outcomes of study. If the various kinds of possible policy provisions are identified before impact estimation begins, then the provisions can be assessed as part of the SIA. SIA's special contributions to policy design are mainly in reporting the hardships that people will experience, suggesting ways to ameliorate these hardships, and designing modifications which do not interfere with project goals but which make the policy more congruent with public attitudes. Simple actions like communicating to the public, slightly altering the implementation schedule or using local contractors whenever possible can often improve the program's benefits and generate good will at very little cost. The possibility of manipulative or "public relations" uses of SIA again calls attention to its political nature in a political context.

IV. Policy Implementation and Monitoring

After the policy is specified, modified and supplemented the next step is program implementation. Once the program is set up its effects should be monitored and evaluated, requiring further application of SIA. Now impacts are actual rather than potential and measurement can replace much of the expert judgment previously exercised. The analytic problem now becomes one of determining whether the measured changes result from the policy, exogeneous factors, or some combination of both. This is a problem for which standard techniques of quasi-experimental design and multiple regression are available.

Monitoring impacts involves the measurement of change against an established set of evaluative criteria for defining whether the policy is succeeding or failing. If it is failing, SIA can help determine the revisions which are necessary to correct its defects and achieve greater success. Candidate revisions are selected and the SIA helps decide among the alternatives and the no revision option in the same way it assisted in the policy selection stage.

This article has outlined the potential role that social impact assessments can play in the development and implementation of public policies. Political forces may cause SIAs to deviate from the ideal type described here or nullify the influences of SIAs on policy decisions. Nevertheless, our underlying thesis is that properly conducted SIAs can increase the social utility of policy decisions.

Bibliography

Coleman, James S. (1972) Policy Research in the Social Sciences. New York: General Learning Press.

Etzioni, Amitai (1971) "Policy Research," The American Sociologist, 6, 8-12.

Finsterbusch, Kurt (1975) A Methodology for Analyzing Social Impacts of Public Policies. Vienna, Va.: BDM Corporation.

Finsterbusch, Kurt (1976) "The Mini Survey: An Underemployed Research Tool," Social Science Research, 3, (March), 81-93.

Forrester, Jay W. (1969) Urban Dynamics. Cambridge, Mass.: M.I.T. Press.

Scott, Robert A. and Arnold Shore (1974) "Sociology and Policy Analysis," The American Sociologist, 9, 2 (May), 51-79.

Estimating Policy Consequences for Individuals, Organizations, and Communities

Kurt Finsterbusch
University of Maryland

The most difficult operation in social impact assessment (SIA) is the measurement of social impacts. In contrast to measurement, the identification of potential impacts is relatively easy. Brainstorming, interviewing experts and interested parties, and reviewing similar past cases will identify a multitude of potential impacts with considerable assurance that the most serious and probable impacts are included in the list. But how valuable is a list of impacts if they are poorly measured? In our judgment, improved measurement is currently the most needed methodological development in SIA. In this paper the problem of social impact measurement is explored. (Of course, in assessing potential impacts, rather than ones that have actually occurred, the measurement operation required is one of estimation, properly speaking.) A classification of social impacts is presented which sorts impacts into sets that require different measurement techniques, and research strategies are devised for each category of impacts. We differentiate impacts by the social unit being impacted because different social units require different analytic operations. Our focus here will be on three major social units for SIA, individuals, organizations and communities; other social units might be institutions, regions, states, counties, SMSAs, census tracts, neighborhoods or families.

It should be noted that impacts on individuals are usually analyzed in terms of status categories, e.g., residents, tourists, the elderly, black working women. Impacts on organizations and communities are similarly analyzed for particular types or categories of these units, e.g., rural towns, oil companies, restaurants in Chicago, etc.

I. Impacts on Individual Quality of Life

In general, survey research is the tool used to determine how changes in people's lives affect them personally. Quality of life is the concept which stands for the overall conditions of the individual relative to his/her values. Objective social conditions are observable and therefore measureable by quantitative indicators such as income, size of house, age of car and calories consumed per day. Quality of life assessments, however, should go beyond objective social conditions and ascertain the meaning of these conditions for the individual. Because the quality of life of individuals is partly subjective, individual attitudes, perception and values should be surveyed in quality of life assessments. Since it is nearly universal that people want more rather than less income, housing, friendships, accessibility, goods and services, health, safety, etc., objective information can determine the direction of change in individual quality of life. The interpretation of increases or decreases, however, depends upon subjective states of the impacted individuals and must be estimated in terms of their subjective evaluations.

Individuals are impacted by policies in seven major ways:

1. Economically, as employees who loose or gain income or jobs;

2. Environmentally, as residents whose habitat is altered or confiscated;

3. Commercially, as consumers who are affected by changing prices of goods and services;

4. Transportation-wise, as drivers, riders or pedestrians who gain or loose accessibility;

5. Socially, as relatives, friends, members, participants, viewers and tourists whose social and leisure patterns may be altered;

6. Biologically, as organisms which are vulnerable to disease, injury and other bodily insults; and

7. Psychologically, as persons who experience stress, esteem, love, fear, deprivation, self-realization, etc.

This list does not exhaust the significant quality of life categories, but it does indicate some major modes of impacts on individuals and provide a basis for discussing specific research methods addressed to them.

1. Economic Impacts

The social impact assessor examines the distribution and determines the social consequences of economic impacts on specified categories of individuals. The distribution of economic impacts involves the question of equity, increasingly a major criterion for policy decision. Inequitable economic losses suggest the need for compensation. The distribution of economic consequences should also be studied to ascertain the capacity of impacted groups to deal with their losses. Of particular concern are the elderly, disabled, poor, and workers with several dependents.

The social consequences of economic impacts can be crudely measured by surveys after the fact, but can only be vaguely estimated beforehand on the basis of past research. The most relevant research is on unemployment and the consumer behavior of income losers. Studies of unemployment depict severe hardships for the long-term unemployed, including serious losses in self-esteem (Komarovsky 1973; Tiffany, Cowan and Tiffany 1970; Wilcock and Franke 1963). Studies of consumer behavior in households experiencing reduced income portray a pattern of increased indebtedness, the suspension of luxury and leisure expenditures and a shift to cheaper foods and other essentials.

2. Environmental Impacts

Another common way in which policies impact individuals is by affecting their habitat (housing and environment). The major impact on housing is displacement. Considerable research indicates that displacement is a crisis for some and a nuisance for most, although people **generally adjust** to it over time. In situations where compensatory payments allow relocation in better housing, some people welcome the move. Most people regret moving even into better quarters, however, because their previous social relations are disrupted. In general, the elderly, poor, long-time residents and minorities are the most adversely affected because the social ties and familiar surroundings of the old neighborhood are irreplaceable.

Whenever displacement results from a policy, the degree of the resulting hardships should be assessed. Census data are helpful for determining the social characteristics--e.g, age, income, length of residence and minority status--of residents of census tracts or minor civil divisions in which displacement occurs. Generally, a survey is necessary to ascertain the number of people to be displaced who are in the categories likely to experience the greatest hardships. In addition to information on social characteristics, the following are examples of questions which can be helpful in estimating the hardships of displacement:

- How would you rate your neighborhood as a place to live?

- What do you like about this neighborhood?

- What do you dislike about this neighborhood?

- If you were forced to move because a fire damaged your home, would you want to relocate in this neighborhood?

- Of your three closest friends how many live in this neighborhood?

The other impacts on habitat that require assessment are air, water and noise pollution levels; visual changes; and maintenance costs. In addition, if a policy decision results in a population influx the availability of housing should be determined. Both the facts and the people's attitudes toward the facts should be examined. Surveys are the accustomed method for obtaining the latter.

3. <u>Commercial Impacts</u>
After economic analysis of expected price changes in goods and services, the social impact assessor may estimate their impact on individual's lifestyle. For example, increasing gas prices may reduce driving, encourage purchases of smaller cars and the selection of housing closer to work and shopping areas. Interviewing car and home buyers is one way to establish some of these connections, but statistics on the sales of cars and homes may have to suffice when assessment budgets are small. For assessing first-order impacts, market research and family budget analysis techniques should be explored. The assessment of higher-order impacts of changes in purchasing patterns requires more complex methodologies.

4. <u>Transportation Impacts</u>
Transportation changes are constantly taking place, affecting accessibility to jobs, schools, churches, stores, recreation, friends and relatives, etc. Destination surveys in conjunction with mapping techniques provide the descriptive material for assessing project impacts on transportation patterns.

5. <u>Social Impacts</u>
House location and transportation facilities affect visiting and leisure patterns

since greater or lesser time, expense and energy are required to visit friends and relatives, attend functions, and reach recreational sites. But social patterns are affected in many additional ways that are often difficult to measure, such as changes in overtime work, public participation, housing turnover, increasing density and status loss from unemployment. Questionnaires, sociometric ranking techniques, field observation of public places and public gatherings, time budgets, audience surveys and participant observation are among the techniques for tracing these ellusive impacts.

6. <u>Biological Impacts</u>

Health and safety hazards are estimated by engineers and medical researchers but assessing the attitudes toward, perceptions of and responses to these hazards is the responsibility of the social impact assessor. The literature of medical sociology contains some information on each of these social factors and on the higher-order impacts of sickness and injury on the families of patients.

7. <u>Psychological Impacts</u>

Quality of life assessment requires a review of social conditions as discussed above, but also one of the psychological impacts of changes in the external conditions of individuals. Attitude surveys attempt to discover potential or actual psychological impacts. The respondents can estimate whether the impacts are positive or negative in sum and whether they are great, moderate or slight. In addition, value rankings, scenario rankings, tradeoff analysis, and even projective techniques can probe psychological impacts more deeply.

II. <u>Impacts on Organizations</u>

Formal organizations are created to achieve specific purposes. When the purpose is completely fulfilled or the organization can no longer serve that purpose, the organization should atrophy according to this view. But in fact organizations frequently outlive their usefulness in terms of their original goals. For example, the conquest of polio fulfilled the purpose of the March of Dimes and should have resulted in its demise. Instead, the March of Dimes took up a new cause and persisted. It is as though the organization develops goals of its own which are different from the goals of its founders or owners. The two principal organizational goals of this type are survival and autonomy. Of course, organizations are not people and cannot have goals, strictly speaking. The members of the organization, especially its leaders, have a stake in its survival and autonomy, and their actions are conveniently summarized by referring to the goals of survival and autonomy. The assessment of impacts on organizations should therefore examine impacts on their survival and autonomy, as well as on their formal goals.

The analysis of organizational impacts becomes more complicated when the reactions of the organization must be considered in estimating higher-order impacts. Sometimes organizations are predictable because they have standard responses to standard problems. But non-standard problems require inventing, evaluating and choosing alternative courses of actions. Sometimes the choice can be predicted on the basis of organizational goals; at other times, knowledge of the way organizations operate (organizational theory) and of the way that the particular organization operates (case history) are required for predicting responses. The analysis becomes even more uncertain when the interactive responses of several sets of organizations must be predicted in the impact analysis.

Informant interviewing is the major research technique for measuring impacts on organizations. Interviewing informants is different from surveying respondents. the latter asks interviewees to report their opinions and circumstances but informants should be capable of providing facts about an organization or social system. Since informants respond from the perspective of their position inside or outside the organization, their reports should be cross-checked with those persons in different positions. This technique can correct for bias and increase the reliability of the findings. It is, therefore, often useful to interview members of competing or conflicting organizations for another view of potential organizational impact and organizational response.

Business organizations evaluate their own circumstances in terms of profitability, so the assessment of policy impacts on their profit position is essential. In addition, changes in employment levels should be predicted because employment usually has the most important higher-order impacts. Obviously we are talking about standard economic analyses for which there are numerous tested techniques. While more difficult to perform, economic analysis is also germane to non-economic organizations since most of them must also operate on financial resources. Loss of income almost always limits their ability to pursue their goals.

Analyzing a non-economic organization should be done in terms of both the mobilization of its resources and the realization of its goals. In addition to economic resources discussed above, non-economic organizations mobilize symbolic or coercive resources. All organizations depend upon the actions of individuals who must be motivated to contribute to organizational goals. Three major types of rewards or sanctions for motivating individuals to act are money, symbols and coercion.[1] Most non-economic organizations depend upon monetary and symbolic rewards to motivate participants and to influence the public or significant non-member groups. Symbolic resources vary with the degree of normative consensus and personal attraction among members and with the normative support of non-members. The policy of "divide and conquer" is one of many tactics for reducing the symbolic resources of organized groups. The social impact assessor should evaluate both the intended and unintended impacts of policies on the symbolic resources of organizations.

The above discussion has focused on direct policy impacts on organizations. For many SIAs this is only the beginning, however. Policies may start chain reactions and the SIA methodology must be adapted to dynamic interactive processes. Three possible techniques for estimating the likely results of such interactive process are surveys of case histories, simulations and interactive interviewing techniques. These techniques can be used effectively in combination.

The survey of case histories attempts to establish the patterns of development of interorganization interactions from past experience (Yin and Heald 1975). Obviously, this technique can be utilized only when a standard set of interacting organizations is confronted with a relatively standard stimulus. If the parameters are fairly standard then the survey of case studies can generate the statistical basis for estimating probabilities of outcomes.

---

1. See Etzioni (1961) for an extended discussion of a typology of organizations based on mechanisms for motivating organizationally prescribed actions.

Simulation is a technique for reproducing the actions of organizations to explore possible outcomes of the interaction process. The participants should be members of the actual organizations when an insider's knowledge is necessary for predicting how it will act in the simulated situation. For greater precision, several key positions in each organization are assigned so that both intra- and interorganizational interactions are simulated. The simulation should be rerun several times with different participants to test the reliability of results. Because it is a simulation and not the real world, there is always a question of validity; but other techniques have similar problems to some degree.

Lastly, the iterative interview can be used for assessing the likely actions of interacting organizations. A sample of all of the directly impacted organizations is interviewed about the likely effect and organizational response. All organizations which are believed affected by the response of directly affected organizations are then interviewed for estimates of their own impacts and responses. These steps are repeated as often as necessary, including reinterviewing the first organizations for their response to the probable reactions of other organizations. By this means, the final assessment can take account of both direct and interactive impacts on organizations.

The social impact assessor must be concerned about reliability when depending heavily upon informants. As suggested earlier, multiple informants and informants from competing or conflicting organizations are necessary for cross-checking the reports. With iterative interviewing one can return to an earlier informant and give him/her the doubts and criticisms of others. The informant is then given a chance to revise or defend his/her estimates. Finally, challengers can be given an opportunity to revise their estimates. This process reduces discrepancies, but some conflicting opinions are likely to remain in the final analysis.

III. Impacts on Communities

A major problem in assessing impacts on communities is how to select impacts for analysis. Communities are not goal-oriented social units, hence the techniques for organizational analysis are inappropriate. Community impact analysis can be related to individual quality of life assessment, however. One approach is to study impacts in terms of their effects on the capacity of the community to provide a high quality of life for its citizens. To guide this analysis involves a systems framework of inputs, structures, activities, and outputs. First, impacts on inputs into the community system are analyzed in terms of increases and decreases of community resources and demands on those resources (assets and liabilities). Second, impacts on community structures are analyzed in terms of changes in the overall organization of the community and in its institutions and organizations. Third, impacts on activities are analyzed in terms of changes in the amounts of activities of various types. Finally, impacts on community outputs are analyzed in terms of changes in the quality of life which a community can provide for its citizens.

Table 1 presents a number of dimensions for community impact assessments. The Table reads from right to left for assessing existing policies and from left to right for estimating the potential impacts of policies. For existing policies, changes in outputs are in evidence; thus the assessor seeks to identify the activity changes which altered the community outputs. Next, impacts on community structure and resources are sought to explain the activity changes. If the potential impacts

TABLE 1. SELECTED RESOURCES, STRUCTURAL CHARACTERISTICS, ACTIVITIES AND OUTPUTS OF COMMUNITIES

Resources Inputs	Structural Characteristics	Activities	Quality of Life Outputs
Human resources	General structural dimensions	Economic activities	Economic
Workers	Degree of gov. centralization	Production and construction	Standard of living
Producers of goods	Degree of citizen participation in policy decisions	Commerce and finance	Employment
Providers of services	Pluralistic or monolithic leadership	Services, etc.	Housing & habitat
Volunteers	Degree of equality of income, wealth, privileges & opportunities	Government services	Transportation accessibility
Entrepreneurs	Degree of diversity of econ. base	Legislation & admin.	Availability of goods & services
Natural Resources	Degree of econ. & political autonomy	Educ. & socialization	Job satisfaction
Land	Degree of homogeneity or integration of groups	Law enforcement & judicial review	Political
Productive	Community complexity & specialization	Health & welfare services	Public participation
Residential	Concrete social structures	Political activities	Freedoms & civil rights
Recreational	Government	Citizen participation	Public services
Water	Local economy	News coverage	Equality & justice
Exportable resources	Labor market	Social & cultural activities	Law & order
Scenery	Commodity & service market	Recreation & entertain.	Government responsiveness
Economic facilities including	Credit market	Socializing	Social & cultural
Primary industry	Housing industry & market	Religious activities	Social relations
Secondary industry	Education system	Ceremonies & community events	Education
Utilities	Health & welfare systems	Travel, tourism & communications	Health, safety & nourishment
Commercial & financial	Transportation systems	Migration & turnover	Mental health & well-being
Community facilities	Communication systems	Conflicts & disturbances	Recreation & entertainment
Educational	Recreation & entertainment	Crime & delinquency	Cultural opportunities
Government	Religious institutions	System activities	Quality of environ.
Health	Cultural institutions	Institute new organizations	Air
Transportation	Status system	Reorganize organizations	Water
Communication	Personal social networks		Noise
Recreation	Voluntary associations		Areas of natural beauty
Cultural	Planning & zoning system		
Social			
Religious			
Housing			
Psychological identification with community			
Location			
Accessibility to major centers			
Accessibility to resorts			
Federal & state assistance			
Tax base			
Demand on resources			
Population			
Catastrophies			
Federal & state taxes			

of policies are being estimated, the assessor predicts impacts on inputs or resources and on structures in order to estimate activity and output changes. The causal chain tends to go from left to right.

Obviously, if resources are reduced one should expect outputs to be reduced. Some output changes may flow directly from the resource changes; for example, if seepage of dangerous gases causes a mine to be shut down, the loss of this economic resource to the community will result in unemployment and reduced income. Other output changes result from the structural and activity changes which the policy or the resource changes produce. For example, an economixing policy which closes neighborhood clinics may reduce the accessibility of health services and affect the health quality of life factor.

IV. Summary and Conclusion

This paper has explored various methods for measuring social impacts. The first step is to classify impacts by the social unit being affected. Then methods for analyzing impacts on individuals, organizations and communities are presented. No general methodology can be applied to all assessments within these three categories of impacts; any SIA will require some improvisation to fit a unique situation.

A general framework for assessing each type of impact can be conceived, however. Quality of life is the assessor's focus for impacts on individuals. Organizational resources and goal attainment, survival and autonomy are the foci for impacts on organizations. Community resources, structure, activities, and quality of life outputs are the foci for impacts on communities. In addition to describing this framework, the paper suggests a number of specific research techniques for designated purposes. It should be apparent however that techniques for measuring social impacts require considerable further development.

References

Etzioni, Amitai (1961) A Comparative Analysis of Complex Organizations. New York: Free Press of Glencoe.

Komarovsky, Mirra (1973) The Unemployed Man and His Family. New York: Octagon.

Tiffany, Donald W., James R. Cowan and Phyllis M. Tiffany (1970) The Unemployed: A Socio-Psychological Portrait. Englewood Cliffs, NJ: Prentice-Hall.

Yin, Robert K. and Karen A. Heald (1975) "Using the Case Survey Method to Analyze Policy Studies," Administrative Science Quarterly, 20 (September), 317-81.

Wilcock, Richard C. and Walter H. Franke (1963) Unwanted Workers. London: Free Press of Glencoe.

II Methodological Approaches to Social Impact Assessment

Section I focused on public policy issues and implications of social impact assessment (SIA). The present section emphasizes general methodological approaches for carrying out SIA in the context of public policy. The main pattern of SIA--profiling, projection, assessment and evaluation--will be amplified and illustrated by specific techniques and applications in later sections.

The ten articles in Section II span a wide range of methodological approaches. The Section begins with a delineation and discussion of five basic features of SIA: design, identification, prediction, evaluation of options and recommendations. Next are two conceptual frameworks which suggest a number of crucial variables and dimensions. The fourth article describes one approach to theory building in SIA, and the balance of the Section presents a variety of methodological arguments and approaches.

The article by Armor and others provides a framework for assessing impacts at the community level. However it's general categories lend themselves to the assessment of impacts on other social units as well. The authors urge that primary attention be directed to persons directly impacted by planned interventions, especially at the neighborhood level, in contrast to the planning bias that gives precedence to "large community" interests. In analyzing the political aspects of intervention decisions, they emphasize the important role of informed public participation.

An integral part of any research design for SIA is a conceptual framework which relates public policies and projects to a set of impact categories and their measures. The next two papers, by Watkins and Olsen and Merwin, are impressive efforts to establish such frameworks. These general frameworks will be too broad for many specific assessments, but the social indicator models they contain are <u>specifiable</u> to any impact situation.

The Watkins' conceptual framework seeks a theoretical basis in the combination of Warren's locality-relevant community functions and the general systems framework of Laszlo. Like that of Armour and others, Watkins' framework focuses on community impacts. It specifies a relatively inclusive set of community impact categories (state variables) which are derived from social goals and social processes. Following Warren, Watkins selects five community processes as the main elements of his framework: social control, mutual support, production-distribution-control, socialization and social participation. These are termed "functional pathways" because they are means by which communities achieve their goals or meet their system needs. A special feature of Watkins' framework is its inclusion of the concept of "feedback" from general systems theory. Communities are perceived as actors which purposefully respond to changes in order to maintain state variables at desireable levels. In this context, Watkins sees SIA as a feedback mechanism to assist community administrators in the attainment of community goals.

Olsen and Merwin concentrate their effort on specifying variables for a system of social indicators to measure the "quality of life". Their theoretical model posits resource scarcities, policy decisions and development projects as the "inputs" which cause demographic and economic changes and which in turn cause social structural changes and public service alterations. All these impacts cause social problems and all, with the addition of values, elicit collective responses. The authors concede that their system needs further refinement and testing. For example, in the three-step deduction from the quality of life concept to social indicators collective responses have positive significance for the quality of life; political activities have positive meaning for collective responses; and the number of political protests and demonstrations have positive meaning for political activities. But is it true that the number of political protests and demonstrations have positive meaning for the quality of life? Despite such difficulties in conceptualization, and severe measurement problems, few would doubt the value of a social indicators approach to SIA.

Shields, in the fourth article, describes a methodology for grounded theory construction in SIA. His first step is to review systematically a broad range of SIAs in order to generate a set of appropriate theoretical concepts and empirical generalizations. The literature is not surveyed exhaustively or sampled randomly; rather it is theoretically sampled. A case is coded and analyzed, and the next case is selected in light of its potential contribution to building cumulative knowledge. When one category is theoretically "saturated", the sampling shifts to another category. By this procedure of conceptual elaboration and the recasting of empirical relationships into meaningful generalizations, a theoretical basis for SIA can be laid.

The last six papers present a variety of methodological approaches to SIA. Sassone argues for the utility of cost-benefit analysis in SIA, while Conopask and Reynolds propose that "appropriate" economic analysis must extend to regional impact assessment. Singh argues for combining both macro and micro levels of analysis in SIA, and Gold makes a similar argument for ethnographic and survey research. Mack provides a model for individual well-being in policy assessment and design, and Deane and Mumpower present a case for strengthening the social psychological level of analysis in SIA, particularly in regard to organizational analysis.

Sassone's general description of cost-benefit analysis (CBA) covers the stages of problem definition, research design, data collection and analysis. CBA attempts to assess project impacts in monetary terms, as the aggregated value to each member of the nation, region or community. Sassone depicts SIA as attempting the same assessment but without converting all impacts into monetary values. This difference makes CBA and SIA appropriate for different types of impacts: CBA is most effective for impacts that affect many people superficially, while SIA is appropriate for impacts that affect few people more deeply. He concludes that the two approaches complement one another when suitably combined. Conopask and Reynolds are more critical in detailing the limitations of CBA and the questionable assumptions upon which it is based. They opt for a less aggregated, regionally-based CBA which identifies more precisely who benefits from and who pays for the costs of development planning.

Singh is also concerned with scale, contrasting the macro and micro levels of analysis in SIA. Both are illustrated in his SIA of a dam project. The macro level was a river basin studied through broad indicators of economic, social and environmental conditions. The micro level analysis examined past and expected future impacts on a nearby community. By means of a random sample survey and other techniques, the temporal sequence of the behavior of individuals and organizations in the various project stages was analyzed.

Gold proposes the complementary use of ethnographic and survey research, but warns that the two approaches construe social reality quite differently and are likely to result in contrasting interpretations of social behavior. Gold's preference for ethnographic research sharply diverges from the current methodological preoccupation with quantitative research methods. Nevertheless, following his approach can produce results that are highly effective in communicating with officials and publics alike.

Mack also recognizes the "urgent need to construct an adequate mapping of the micro entity--the consumer, the experiencing unit--and its efforts to optimize the necessities and satisfactions of life." This leads her to develop a model for individual well-being and to apply it in policy analysis and project design. While its origins can be traced to marginal utility theory, the inclusion of traditionally nonmarket values is a notable departure.

Insufficient attention has been paid in SIA to the social psychological level of analysis. Most SIAs have a macro level focus; impacts on individuals are often measured by quality of life indicators like unemployment, air quality and educational opportunity, but the relationship of these indicators to peoples' actual experiences go unexamined. The paper by Deane and Mumpower argues for inclusion of the social psychological level of analysis in SIAs and illustrates this approach in the study of residential treatment centers.

A Framework for Community Impact Assessment

Audrey Armour, Beate Bowron,
Earl Miller, and Michael Miloff
York University

Planning and decision-making processes for urban areas increasingly are coming under pressure to widen the consideration given to environments, both socio-cultural and natural. An emerging institutionalized solution to this problem is environmental impact assessment. As a form of project evaluation it directs explicit attention to the consequences of human intervention. It is now generally recognized that if built into the earlier phases of planning and policy formation, impact assessment offers considerable potential for improving decisions and the environmental quality of their results. Contention arises however in discussions of how this integration is to be accomplished. To some, "integration" is accomplished through the addition of impact assessment procedural requirements to the project review stage of the planning process: it is an administrative problem. To others, this is not "integration" but a simple grafting on of impact assessment: integration requires reforming decision processes (which planning merely serves) in such a way that they confront explicitly the effects of proposed actions, who is affected, how to resolve conflicting perceptions of what is important, and how to balance larger and local interests. Building such processes, which are evaluative in an ongoing way and which are more adaptive to changing community values and goals, transcends the routine design of procedures.

This paper takes as its starting point the latter perspective on integration of impact assessment into planning and policy decision-making processes. Community impact assessment (CIA) as conceptualized here, is more than another set of analytical tools employed to generate environmental information that will subsequently be fed into an urban planning process. Information derived from project evaluation alone does not insure the development of environmentally sensitive and responsive planning and management organizations and processes. Emphasis in this paper is placed more on the information exchange needs of the CIA process than on the information generation needs: where to exchange information, to whom, in what form, etc. are questions which directly address the potential of CIA to reform the decision-making processes of urban planning and management.

THE NATURE AND PURPOSE OF COMMUNITY IMPACT ASSESSMENT

Community Impact Assessment can be defined as:

A process	sequence of interrelated activities over time
of assessing	includes identification and prediction
the effects	describes changes expected to be generated
and impacts	evaluates the desirability of such changes
of proposed interventions	buildings, services, etc., but also policies and plans
at the neighborhood scale	from the perspective, first of the people who experience the changes directly and then of interests outside the neighborhood.

There are several key principles underlying this definition which bear directly upon its operationalization:

1. CIA is necessarily interdisciplinary in its approaches and requires the participation of specialists from various fields to uncover linkages between ecological, social and economic effects.

2. CIA must be a participative process. The distinction between effects and impacts emphasizes the likelihood that for any given effect (e.g. removal of trees) there will be a range of legitimate viewpoints concerning impact (depends on how much importance you attach to trees themselves, shade, birds that rest in them, etc.). From a practical point of view, obtaining a full understanding of "impact" necessitates adding personal knowledge of community members to the technical knowledge of the study team. From an ethical point of view, people have a right to be involved in a meaningful way in decisions which affect their lives and their environment.

3. Impacts are to be assessed <u>first</u> from the perspective of those directly affected and <u>then</u> from the larger-interest perspective, a turn around of the usual urban planning approach based on the concept of "the public interest." Local "public interest" and municipality-wide "public interest" must be continually tested and balanced. Neither should automatically take precedence over the other.

A COMMUNITY IMPACT ASSESSMENT FRAMEWORK

There are several "orders" of concern for which differing strategies or guidelines for Community Impact Assessment can be devised:

1. This area/this issue: An on-the-spot reactive concern triggered by an "emergency," requiring <u>specific study</u> guidelines.

2. This area/any issue: A concern for advance preparation, involving the systematizing of institutional response and the preparation of <u>process</u> guidelines.

3. Any area/this issue: A concern for advance preparation, and involving the analysis of the substantive aspects of the issue and the preparation of <u>class of issue</u> guidelines.

4. Any area/any issue: A concern for an all-inclusive, cover-every-angle approach requiring the development of the fundamental principles of both procedural and substantive aspects of CIA in a <u>framework</u>.

Presented below is a general methodological <u>framework</u> within which specific planning and control processes may be designed.

Three major and interrelated functional components of the Community Impact Assessment Framework are: an analytical component, an urban management component and a strategic/contextual component.

ANALYTICAL COMPONENT

The analytical component is concerned with how the assessment or study process is conducted. Consideration is given to such aspects as the scope and nature of information required to determine the project's potential consequences and a community's potential responses, and to the kind of process required to produce recommendations which will allow decisions to be made on whether a project should be approved or rejected, and whether or how it should be modified. The analytical component contains five distinct activities which occur in a non-linear, iterative fashion, continuously adjusted as information accumulates: Design, Identification, Predictions, Options and Recommendations (see Figure 1).

FIGURE 1: THE ANALYTICAL COMPONENT

Stage of CIA Study Process	Concerns			
Design	Process Rules	Criteria for Evaluation	Typology of Information to be Collected	
Identification	Project Characteristics	Community Activity Systems	Community Concerns	Agency Jurisdictions
Predictions	Effects		Impacts	
Options	Project Without Mitigations	Project With Mitigations	No Project	
Recommendations	Best Option(s)			

1. __Design__
   During this preparation stage three aspects of the assessment process must be dealt with.

   First, formulation of process rules: who is to be involved in the assessment process and at what point(s), what roles are to be assumed by those involved, and how are decisions to be made during the assessment activity?

   Next, criteria for evaluation of effects: this may involve determining the extent to which community values are reflected in municipal minimum standards. Should these standards be expanded, modified or traded-off? For example, in neighborhoods where many of the recreational activities are street-oriented rather than park-oriented, the minimum standard for parkland becomes a flexible bargaining point. A "neighborhood" criterion for evaluation would likely __not__ be extent of loss of parkland and violation of minimum standards; rather, extent of loss of street space for recreation would be more relevant and constitute an undesired effect. Such information early in the process assists in providing directions for in-depth study in the identification stage. Evaluating effects in terms of their desirability is one criterion for setting priorities for decisions regarding the project. Other criteria by which effects can be evaluated (and by which, therefore, degree of impacts can be determined) include reversible/irreversible changes in community and natural systems; number of avoidable/unavoidable effects; duration of effect--short-term/long-term; magnitude; commitment of community and natural resources and opportunity costs of such commitments; distribution of effects--who benefits/who pays.

   Third, the type of information to be collected: focus is on such areas of investigation as general project characteristics (e.g. high density residential), classes of effects which have been associated with the introduction of the project into other communities, general community activity patterns, community concerns regarding the project, and agencies involved in the community. A community inventory could be the vehicle for obtaining some of the above information. Its preparation would not necessarily consume a large amount of time since it would not be a comprehensive overview. Using McHarg's (1971) technique of map overlays, the community inventory could present a preliminary overview of current conditions by identifying community problems and resources, thus assisting in setting priorities for information gathering.

2. __Identification__
   This is the actual data collection phase of the study process. Utilizing the directions formulated in the design phase, the four main areas requiring detailed identification are project

characteristics (impacting), community activity systems, community concerns (the impacted), and agency jurisdiction (ameliorative actions possible).

Project characteristics refer to the information which a proponent of a project would be required to supply. Using a high-density housing project as an example, the type of information required would include: physical design aspects, especially those relating to general land use (e.g. traffic flow); number and size of residential units; micro-climate; utilities and servicing facilities; potential air, soil, water and noise pollution; demographic information relating to marital status, income range, tenure, and possible ethnic composition of prospective inhabitants of the project; projected demands on community services and facilities.

Community activity systems refers to the uses made of the human and natural environment in the area being examined; information required would include who can be observed where and at what times of the day or night; obvious satisfactions/dissatisfactions with particular aspects of the environment; distribution of opportunities for use of community services and facilities.

Community concerns brought forward during the design phase may require information to be gathered regarding such issues as level of accessibility and adequacy of various community facilities; desirability of development trends; preservation of certain physical or social features of the community; and who appears to benefit/pay.

Agency jurisdiction refers to the capability of governmental and similar institutions to respond to effects created by the project. Various types of information to be collected concern jurisdictions: policies and goals; constraints; programs/services/facilities, present and projected; and clientele.

3. Predictions
The prediction phase of the process focuses on the changes to be expected in community activities and the environmental systems. It is in this phase that the results of investigations are tabulated. Linkages are made between effects and those affected. The extent of (or impact of) effects in relation to criteria for evaluation is presented.

4. Options
In this phase, consideration is given to the specific community responses possible and required if predicted changes are to be dealt with satisfactorily. The study process thus far has focused on the project with no mitigation. Further studies are under-

taken at this stage with the intent of articulating the benefits/
costs of two other options: no project and project with mitigations.

5. Recommendations
Following the evaluation criteria established in the design phase
and evolved during the identification/prediction/option phases,
existing options are assessed and recommendations made either to
approve or reject the proposal, to suggest modifications in line
with the community's capability to respond, or to repeat part or
all of the assessment in light of new evidence which has surfaced
during the assessment.

URBAN MANAGEMENT COMPONENT

The urban management component is, in effect, the broader context for the analytical component. It refers to the organizational dimensions of Community Impact Assessment and includes: participation requirements, the monitoring and dissemination of information in both the assessment and post-assessment periods, and decision-making aspects.

1. Participation Aspects
In the organizational aspects of Community Impact Assessment, concern centers on participation by affected interests. Present "community impact assessment" processes have little involvement by members of the public, and then usually only after commitments have been made. Ideally there should be a broad spectrum of involvement: first, because to uncover the qualitative aspects of the affected environment it is necessary to complement technical knowledge with the personal knowledge of those experiencing the environment directly; second, because varying perceptions of the importance of effects are legitimate; third, because involvement is an educative process assisting in community development, here considered desirable; and fourth, because those affected by a proposal have a right to contribute to its assessment.

Also to be considered is the identification of interest existing outside the physical boundaries of the community but nevertheless affected by the proposal, or outside the time-frame of the study (e.g. future residents), or within the community but normally excluded from the planning/decision process.

The relative capacity of participants varies; their ability to contribute adequately is dependent on disclosure of information and sharing of resources. Presently, some participants (mainly planning staff and developers) have most of the required information and resources while other participants (mainly citizens) are inhibited by being mis- or uninformed and by lack of access to expertise and money.

The amount of influence exerted varies similarly in the present process. Some parties (mainly Council, Planning Board, planning staff members and developers) exercise the most influence in determining the criteria for impact assessment and decision. Influence has many dimensions, including both formal powers to make decisions and informal powers to prevent certain decisions or issues from being examined. Influence rests upon instruments and resources such as money and access to information, skilled personnel, and media. In an ideal process, it could be argued that every participant should have equal access to such instruments and resources, and further that there should be substantive change in the pattern of influence to insure equal access to the channels through which influence is exerted. Both aspects would have to be developed: to educate without providing access to exert influence at the critical decision points, or to invite involvement without insuring the quality of that involvement, will merely create frustration.

Public participation in a disjointed, narrowly-conceived planning and assessment process leads to alienation, discouragement and frustration. Ideally, the process should provide a rewarding experience for all involved, an opportunity which promotes the satisfaction of exercising democratic responsibilities. The process should also provide a learning experience, revealing the variety of perspectives on community values and goals, the factors influencing the quality of life in the urban environment, the need for the channels of cooperative actions in dealing with environmental problems, and the limitations of our knowledge and abilities for dealing with environmental issues. Ideally, the process should provide an opportunity to "close the circle" on people--to confront them with the full implications (social and environmental) of the decisions, leading to changes in behavior and values and, thereby, future individual and collective action more sensitive to human and non-human environmental concerns.

2. <u>Information Aspects</u>

Community involvement in the assessment process is necessary and fundamental to Community Impact Assessment. To insure in some measure the involvement of individuals, groups and organizations, proper management of the information flow is essential. This includes sufficient advance notification to allow those concerned to mobilize their resources, notification and dissemination of information to all affected interests, and information presented in a format suited to the needs of the recipients.

Timeliness and relevance of information are critical. Needed is a cumulative <u>environmental data base</u> utilizing the information built up through current planning processes and previous project assessments.

In the assessment process monitoring of analytic activities is important to provide feedback concerning the changes in perspectives of the participants in the assessment as they acquire more information and understanding of their community, of project implications, of knowledge limitations and of organizational constraints. Monitoring also provides feedback concerning the effectiveness of the assessment process, documenting where difficulties occur and where shortcuts can be taken.

In the _post-assessment_ period monitoring is similarly important to provide feedback concerning possible changes in the demographic characteristics of the project (should it be accepted). Since recommendations concerning the facilities, programs, and/or services to be provided by the community and/or project proponent are based on an expected population configuration, it is necessary to insure that recommendations are not outdated by demographic changes. Post-assessment monitoring also provides feedback concerning the effects of the physical design of the project (thereby facilitating adjustments such as the location of tot lots or the erection of wind and noise barriers); changes in the community (thus allowing recommendations of the project assessment to be re-evaluated and enabling unexpected effects to be uncovered and dealt with); and the effectiveness of the recommendations accepted and implemented.

Continuous monitoring in the post-assessment period can lay a firm foundation for a coordinating function of Community Impact Assessment. By gathering and feeding back information concerning the community's human and non-human environmental conditions and by evaluating the effectiveness of implemented recommendations, Community Impact Assessment can assist in decisions regarding further policy adjustments. As well, the assessment period, with its emphasis on interdisciplinary and community involvement processes, provides the opportunity not only for sharing of information but also contact with other participants. In this way both the community residents and the agencies operating within the community learn more about their environments--where important resources (human and non-human) are located, and where problems are occurring (e.g. redundancy or lack of agency involvement).

3. Decision or Value Aspects
   Ultimately, a decision concerning the proposal must be made. Although this aspect of the framework is the least developed of the CIA process, three parameters can be identified: control, community response and importance.

   Control refers to what the community can do to effect corrective actions. Control may be formal (e.g. legal) or informal (e.g. economic or political influences). It exists in many sectors of the community, such as public or quasi-public agencies, political bodies, voluntary associations, media and the private sector. Knowing the nature and extent of workable control assists in assessing and implementing recommendations.

Community response capabilities, discussed briefly earlier, refers to the willingness and/or ability of interests involved (agencies, citizens, private developers) to mobilize their resources to effect corrective actions and to accommodate the opportunity costs involved. In the design activity of the analytical component participants engage in a period of bargaining to determine assessment criteria which are acceptable to all involved. During this period, indications of the willingness and/or ability of participants to respond to anticipated changes will emerge. For example, in considering criteria regarding recreational space and facilities, citizen groups may indicate a dissatisfaction with present facilities and thus considerable unwillingness to tolerate even minimal adverse changes in recreational space and facilities; or agencies may indicate concern with budget limitations and thus a severe constraint on their ability to respond at this point in time to further financial demands created by adverse effects. Community response capabilities will be a significant factor in making decisions regarding recommendations forwarded as a result of the study process.

Importance varies according to the various perspectives existing in the community regarding the desirability of identified effects. In most cases the recommendations concerning effects which are presented to the decision-maker are based on a mixture of objective evaluation and subjective reactions. Community Impact Assessment widens the input of the community in the determination of the "desirability" of effects. The decision-maker needs to have documentation regarding who and how many hold to a perspective and the basis by which the perspective was formulated (empirical evidence, professional judgment, personal knowledge, speculation, etc.).

STRATEGIC/CONTEXTUAL COMPONENT

The strategic component is concerned with examining the organizational and contextual factors which influence the nature and practice of Community Impact Assessment. Understanding their factors allows practitioners to capitalize on opportunities for improving current practice and preventing the potential misuse of CIA.

1. <u>Costs</u>
   At the same time, it is recognized that Community Impact Assessment will cost money, require valuable staff from various agencies, take up citizens' time, and generally create many of the same headaches now present in any organizational activity. Obviously, it is essential to maximize the possible benefits of Community Impact Assessment in order to justify its costs. Such maximization could be accomplished through a multiple purpose approach: use of the monitoring function to assist in coordination of agency activities; use of the collection of information to assist in a community information function; use of the involvement process to provide information to assist in identifying and mobilizing

community resources; and use of the process as a whole to assist in the development of capacities for responsible participation.

2. Negative Side-Effects

   Possible negative side-effects of Community Impact Assessment (in addition to time and money) cannot be ignored. The involvement process may result in the frustration of the citizens involved; more may be demanded of them than they are able to deliver or they may demand more of the process than it can deliver. It is important to avoid raising excessive expectations with possible disillusionment and subsequent abandonment of Community Impact Assessment. A pragmatic maneuver would be to provide information to community participants concerning the context in which the rules of the game are set, i.e. the legal, political and organizational constraints which will present possible sources of friction in the practice of CIA. As well, to improve the practice of CIA, it is necessary to study the study process itself as it operates in the community, monitoring the effectiveness of the type, form, timing and amount of information which is being disseminated and critically examining those stages of the process perceived as most stressful by the participants.

   Another problem is the danger of misuse of CIA process to force developments on other localities which are poorly organized, thereby perpetuating the inequalities within and between communities. To overcome this problem, an impact assessment that recommends rejection of a project ought to have the responsibility of proposing alternate means of meeting the need to which the project was addressed.

   Community Impact Assessment information may be misused by influential participants to bias the presentation of issues. Overcoming this difficulty will be dependent to a degree on the abilities of the participants to sort out fact from fiction. The community (citizens and agencies) must be "prepared" for involvement through the provision of information identifying the many perspectives on the issue, points of agreement and conflict, and the basis for the various perspectives.

3. Knowledge Limitations

   Community environmental data are usually lacking, and this presents some major difficulties for Community Impact Assessment. Knowledge limitations in dealing with the quantitative and qualitative aspects of the environment should be made explicit with the classification of information needs; categories may include the known and unknown, and within the latter, the knowable (through further study) and the unknowable.

IN CONCLUSION

As stated earlier, the framework addresses the fundamental principles of both the procedural and substantive aspects of Community Impact Assessment. The underlying perspective of the framework is that Community Impact Assessment can be more than merely a technique for revealing the consequences of a proposed action. It also provides an opportunity for responsible participation of elected representatives, administrators, planners and citizens in the examination and evaluation of environmental decisions affecting the community. Within that framework considerable work remains to be done, particularly with respect to the development of methods for assessing the impacts of classes of projects and the development of procedural guidelines applicable to a given context.

Reference

McHarg, Ian (1971) Design with Nature. Garden City, NY: Doubleday.

Development of a Social Impact Assessments Methodology (SIAM)

George A. Watkins
Battelle Columbus Laboratories

INTRODUCTION

This concept paper represents an effort to develop a comprehensive social impact assessment methodology (SIAM). SIAM is the result of combining the work of Roland L. Warren (1973) on locality-relevant functions with a general systems framework (Laszlo, Levine and Milsum 1974; Buckley 1967; Easton 1957) and a social indicators approach. Such a conceptual framework for performing comprehensive social impact assessments is intended to assist social scientists and interested others in analyzing the probable impacts which might accrue to a given community through various social interventions.

PROBLEM

The National Environmental Policy Act of 1969 requires that any proposed resource development activity by a Federal agency be assessed for social impacts (Liroff 1976: 286). To date, much of this social impact assessment has been largely descriptive, unsystematic, and seldom comprehensively analytical. There are methods of the identification of social impacts, methods for prediction, and methods for interpretation (Munn 1975), but seldom are the various methods combined into a systematic and comprehensive framework.

One commonly used method for the identification of social impacts is the "screening matrix." Essentially this amounts to a checklist of possible impact areas with some probability and/or value attached. Commonly used prediction methods usually share the same criteria, namely, (a) the assessment of the baseline condition, (b) the estimate of the future of the community without the proposed action and (c) the estimate of the future with the proposed action. Methods for interpretation usually are characterized by the display of value sets for impact areas and the ranking of alternatives within impact categories. Such procedures have some utility in assessing the probable social impacts which might be associated with a proposed action. None combines in any systematic fashion a comprehensive analytical framework with acceptable methods of measurement of social impacts, however.

Currently there are two major trends developing in an attempt to perform better social impact assessments: social indicators and systems modeling. The strong interest in social indicators as a way to make social impact assessment more empirical and to allow for the documentation of change is widespread (Fox 1974; Schoenfield and Shaw 1972; Thomas 1972). Yet the use of social indicators will yield little improvement in social impact assessment in the absence of a comprehensive analytical framework. Additionally, there is a growing interest in the development of specific models for "arenas" of social concern (Klir 1972), such as health care subsystems (Belanger and others 1974). Such models are often costly to develop because they require the generation of much original data and cumbersome to deploy because of their site-specific nature. It is my purpose to demonstrate that the principles underlying the social indicators approach, when combined with those of the general systems framework, offer a sound basis for developing a comprehensive social impact assessment methodology.

The Community Social System

The utility of social indicators is to measure the magnitude of social impacts associated with a proposed development. To apply such measures, the unit of impact analysis must first be defined. For our purpose this will be the community system.

There are a number of ways in which "community" has been defined. Such definitions usually include the following criteria: (a) territoriality, (b) psychological identification, and (c) other measures of commonality such as shared interests and functions (Minar and Greer 1969; French 1969). The working definition used in SIAM is that offered by Warren (1973: 9): "Community is that combination of social units and systems which perform the major social functions needed to afford people daily local access to those broad areas of activity which are necessary for day-to-day living." Given this definition of community, Warren (1973: 153 et passim) suggests five leading questions:

First, what units make up the community system? The community social system is comprised of social units (e.g., groups, agencies, organizations) and their interrelationships. The concept as developed here differs from Warren's in that the definition of community depends on the level of analysis. For some purposes, "community" may be defined as a region comprising several Standard Metropolitan Statistical Areas (SMSAs). For other purposes, "community" may be defined as a single geopolitical entity, such as an SMSA. This flexibility is required if SIAM is to be applicable to a broad range of proposed actions.

Second, to what extent can the community as a social system be distinguished from its surrounding environment? Again, this distinction is a function of the level of abstraction (i.e., level of aggregation of geopolitical entities). If one is concerned with an entity such as an SMSA, then major social functions having locality relevance must be conceptualized and operationalized on that level. The level of aggregation appropriate to any specific proposed action must be scaled to area of probable impacts associated with that action.

Third, what is the nature of structured interaction of units within the community social system? Generally this is characterized by the inputs and outputs of each social unit as they systematically relate to others. The way in which these social units interact in a systematic manner over time denotes the internal or horizontal patterning of relationships. In addition, many of these same units interact systematically with other social organizations and agencies outside of the community being assessed for social impacts. This is referred to as the external or vertical patterning of relationships. The distinction is important since there appears to be a general tendency for the locus of functional control to shift from local to extralocal (e.g. Federal) auspices.

Fourth, what are the tasks which the community performs as a social system? Communities at all levels of abstraction are assumed to perform at least five generic tasks. These are Warren's locality-relevant functions: social control, mutual support, production-distribution-consumption, socialization, and social participation.[1] Though common to any community, specification of these locality-relevant functions will differ at different levels of aggregation. Moreover, there are alternative auspices under which the locality-relevant functions may be carried out in the community social system.

Finally, by what means are the structured relationships among these interacting units of a community social system maintained? Warren suggests the following: (a) local political and governmental systems, (b) local press, (c) organizations specifically instituted to effect horizontal integration, (d) organizations which bring people together because of specialized interests, and (e) the family. These provide the cultural, normative, communicative, and functional integration necessary among the interacting social units.

It is assumed in SIAM that communities have overarching social aims such as "promotion of the general welfare." Intermediate to these are actionable social goals, such as the maintenance of security and the enhancement of opportunity. In turn, goal achievement takes place along functional pathways, represented by Warren's locality-relevant functions and their components, through the purposeful actions of structural elements in the community system (individuals, groups, organizations). In this way, the community is conceptualized as a goal-oriented and goal-seeking system. The potential impacts of proposed developments can impinge on any element or linkage in the system, creating secondary impacts on system parts interrelated with it. However useful this may be as conceptual framework, little direct measurement of the state of the system can thus far be performed. It is now necessary to establish a systematic framework for measuring the baseline social condition from which deviations in the form of development impacts can be estimated.

THE GENERAL SYSTEMS FRAMEWORK

Figure 1 shows the basic framework used in the general systems approach. For SIAM the system state may be defined as existing structured relationships of social units in terms of their locality-relevant functions (functional pathways). The system state is characterized by inputs deriving from horizontal and vertical relationships and outputs issuing to them. Should a proposed development result in measureable changes in the system state, the system will require some adjustment through the feedback process if it is to maintain the patterned interaction

---

[1] Social control is characterized by those activities through which a social group or organization influences the behavior of its members. Mutual support is help provided in those instances where individual needs are not satisfied by the usual pattern of social behavior. Economic needs and opportunities are served through the system of production-distribution-consumption. Socialization is the process through which individuals acquire the knowledge, values and behavior patterns of their community and society, and learn behavior appropriate to their various social roles. Social participation is the opportunity for individuals to associate, both formally and informally, with others having common interests.

FIGURE 1. GENERAL SYSTEMS FRAMEWORK

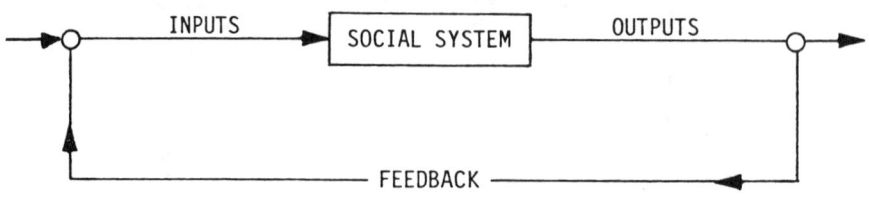

of units. Thus, the general systems framework requires the systematic recognition of the inputs and outputs of any community social system for both the baseline condition and the probable condition of the community social system should the proposed development occur. The general systems approach thus assumes that the community social system's baseline condition is a function of the flow of activities within the community and between it and the external environment.

Components of community social systems: In the community social system identified in Figure 2, (a) represents the principal functional pathways and social units. The measurement of the probable impacts of any proposed action on a community entails identifying the state elements (b), their component variables (c) and state variable metrics (d).

State elements: These are the immediate goal-orientations of a given community. Health care quality, for example, is one of the several state elements related to mutual support.

State variables: These are measurable dimensions of a state element. For instance, three state variables related to the state element of health care quality are health facilities, health services, and population/morbidity characteristics. Through appropriate state variable metrics one can construct an index of health care quality from the measurement of state variables related to it. Health facilities, for example, can be measured by considering the distribution of facilities in the impacted area, the types of facilities, and the cost to the community of building and maintaining the facilities.

State variable metrics: These are commonly referred to as "social indicators." They are constructs which allow for the quantification and measurement of a state variable. According to Moriyama (1968: 593), such state variable metrics:

- Should be meaningful and understandable
- Should be sensitive to variations in the state variables
- Should have underlying assumptions which are theoretically justifiable and intuitively reasonable

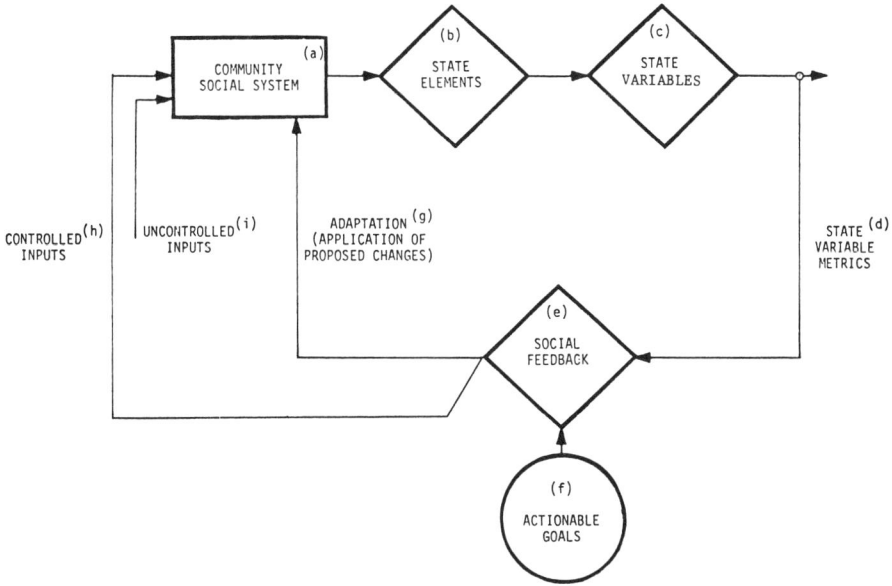

Figure 2. Components of Community Social Systems

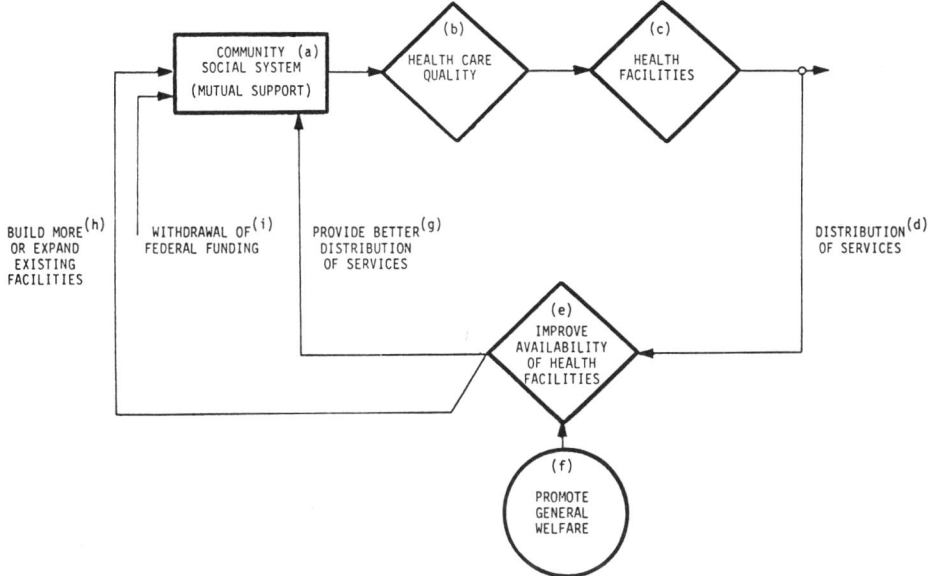

Figure 3. Selected Components of the Mutual Support Pathway

39

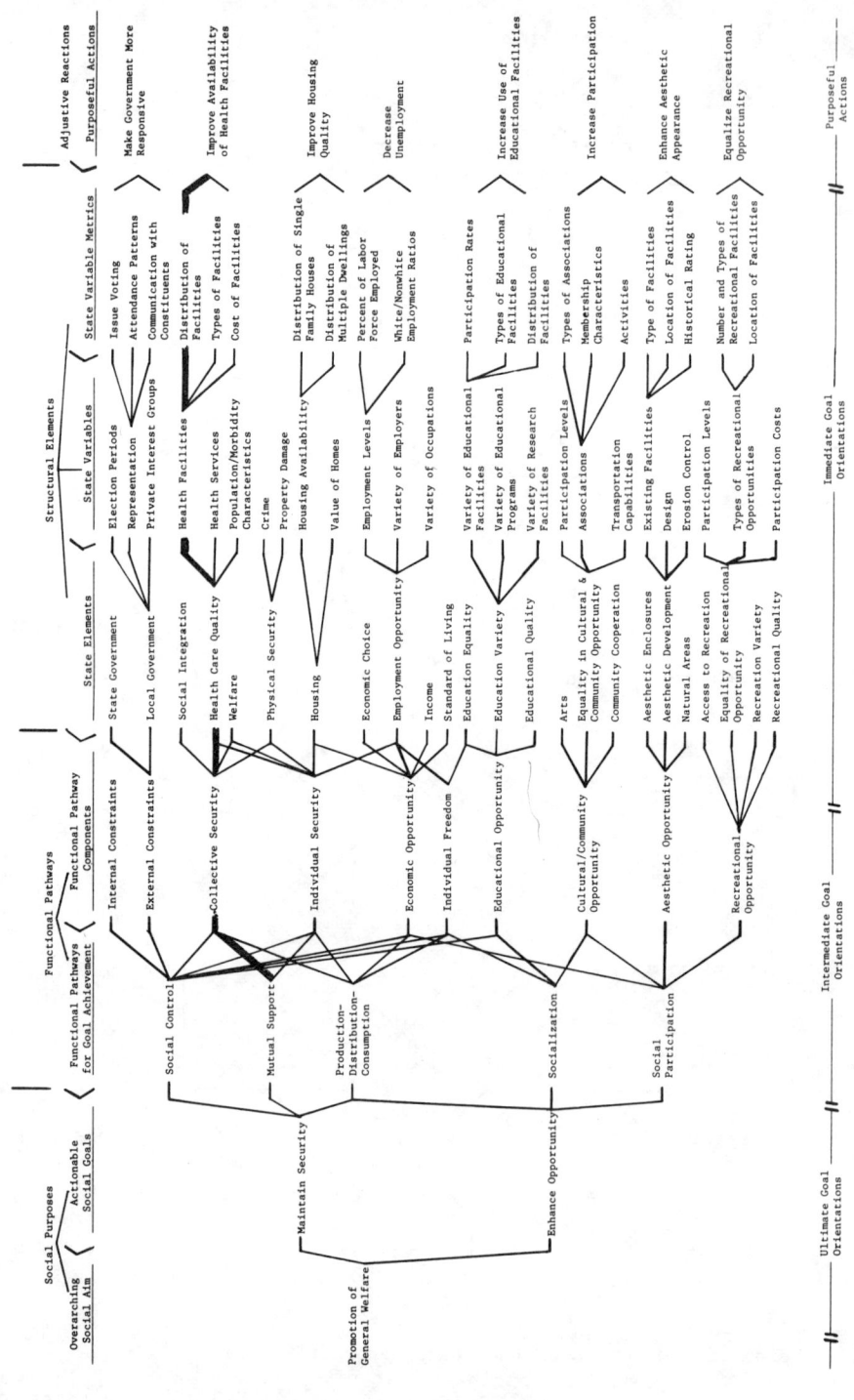

Figure 4. Representative Components of the Social Impact Assessment Methodology

- When used to construct indexes, each component part should make an independent contribution to variations in the state variable being measured
- Should be derivable from data that are available or feasible to obtain.

Within the general systems framework such state variable metrics provide the information necessary for the feedback loops (e), most often represented as the decision-making function concerned with "ultimate goal orientations" and actionable goals (f). The feedback loop represents that process by which the output of a given system state is evaluated. Therefore, as Culyer, Lavers and Williams (1972) note, it is necessary that state variable metrics also:

- Measure the output of social policies as reflected in the system state-- or in those units by which policy objectives are to be defined
- Provide a means of deriving the social valuation placed upon different outputs--or allow for value increments in those units appropriate to each objective
- Measure the technical possibility of affecting output--that is, provide specifics so that trade-offs can be reasonably evaluated.

Social Feedback

Depending upon the intensity and type of induced change and upon the actions of decision-making bodies, inputs are fed back into the community social system. These inputs are typically one or more of three types: changes which result in adaptation by the community social system (g), controlled inputs which may or may not result in changes in the community (h), and inputs over which the feedback process has no control (i). The social feedback elicited by the decision-making bodies in a given community in response to a proposed action represents a purposeful action to change. Thus, should a community determine that a proposed action will cause a population influx adversely affecting the availability of health services, an explicit decision could be made to mitigate that anticipated impact.

Figure 3 represents a general systems approach to measuring the impact of a proposed action on a community social system with emphasis on the mutual support pathway. Note that only one pathway, one state element, one state variable, and one state variable metric are being operationalized in this example.

Figure 4 shows a more comprehensive model of SIAM, with selected components of mutual support highlighted by a heavier line. Hopefully this will serve to illustrate the usefulness of SIAM as a methodology for considering a broad range of planning alternatives and potential impacts within a comprehensive analytic framework.

References

Belanger, P., and others (1974) "On the Modelling of Large-Scale Health Systems," Behavioral Science, 19, 6 (November) 407-414.

Buckley, Walter (1967) Sociology and Modern Systems Theory. Englewood Cliffs, NJ: Prentice-Hall.

Culyer, A. J., R. J. Lavers and Alan Williams (1972) "Health Indicators," pp. 94-118 in Andrew Schonfield and Stella Shaw (eds.), Social Indicators and Social Policy. London: Heinemann.

Easton, David (1957) "An Approach to the Analysis of Political Systems," World Politics, 9, 3, (April) 383-400.

Fox, Karl A. (1974) Social Indicators and Social Theory. New York: John Wiley.

French, Robert M. (ed.) (1969) The Community: A Comparative Perspective. Itasca, IL: F. E. Peacock.

Klir, George J. (1972) Trends in General Systems Theory. New York: John Wiley.

Laszlo, C. A., M. D. Levine and J. H. Milsum (1974) "A General Systems Framework for Social Systems," Behavioral Science, 19, 2 (March) 79-92.

Liroff, Richard A. (comp.) (1976) The Environmental Impact Statement Process under NEPA. Washington, DC: Environmental Law Institute

Minar, David W. and Scott Greer (eds.) (1969) The Concept of Community: Readings with Interpretations. Chicago: Aldine.

Moriyama, Iwao M. (1968) "Problems in the Measurement of Health Status," pp. 573-600 in E. B. Sheldon and W. E. Moore (eds.) Social Change. New York: Russell Sage Foundation.

Munn, R. E. (ed.) (1975) Environmental Impact Assessment; Principles and Procedures. SCOPE Report 5. Toronto: International Council of Scientific Unions.

Schonfield, Andrew, and Stella Shaw (eds.) (1972) Social Indicators and Social Policy. London: Heinemann.

Warren, Roland L. (1973) The Community in America. 2nd ed. Chicago: Rand McNally.

Toward a Methodology for Conducting Social Impact Assessments Using Quality of Social Life Indicators*

Marvin E. Olsen and Donna J. Merwin
Battelle Human Affairs Research Centers

I. INTRODUCTION

Considerable attention is currently being directed toward the process of social impact assessment by social scientists, social planners, and public officials. This work is severely hampered, however, by the lack of a standardized methodology. Thus far, virtually all social impact assessments have been made on an ad hoc (and often haphazard) basis, with no attempt to ground the work on any kind of theoretical foundation or to employ a methodology that could be replicated by others. Two serious consequences of this condition have been the absence of any continuity among social impact assessments that would render their findings comparable or cumulative, and the lack of any attempts to perform social impact research on current or completed projects to ascertain their actual social consequences. As a result, we do not at the present time have a sound empirical base from which to derive social impact assessments.

The methodological approach employed in most previous social impact assessments has been some version of cost-benefit analysis, as borrowed from economics. Although this methodology may be fully appropriate for assessing the likely economic consequences of a proposed policy or project, it is often inadequate for assessing social impacts, as noted by several writers: (1) most social phenomena cannot be specified in monetary terms, (2) what is beneficial to one group or set of people may be detrimental to another, (3) often those who receive the benefits are not those who pay the costs, and (4) there is usually a considerable time lag between the imposition of costs and the realization of long-term benefits (Dunning 1974:61). More generally, since straightforward balancing of social costs and benefits is never possible, one's evaluation of any expected social impacts is always affected by one's social values. As expressed by Wolf (1974:6), "Social impacts may be beneficial as well as detrimental, and often both at the same time. Who decides, on what rational basis and legal authority, and which...values and interests are served, are questions for major consideration." Use of the cost-benefit format for social impact assess-

---

*The research reported in this paper was supported by the Pacific Northwest Regional Assessment Program of the Division of Biomedical and Environmental Research, Energy Research and Development Administration.

ments has often resulted in environmental impact statements designed to demonstrate that the benefits to be gained from a proposed project will undoubtedly outweigh the expected costs, rather than to ascertain the full nature and extent of the probable impacts (Wolf 1974:9).

The purpose of this report is to propose a new methodology for conducting social impact assessment, which we call "Quality of Life Indicators of Social Impacts." Although this methodology still requires considerable refinement and testing, its main features can be described in enough detail to be of practical use to social researchers and planners. Conceptually, the methodology is grounded on a unifying theoretical perspective and integrated around a general analytical model. Empirically, it utilizes a wide variety of standardized quality of social life indicators that are measured with objective data, weighted according to subjective value judgments, and combined into factor indexes. The resulting methodology should be useful both for measuring the actual effects of ongoing programs or projects, and for forecasting the likely consequences of proposed policies or developments.

Section II of this paper discusses the nature of social impacts, followed in Section III by a sketch of the theoretical model underlying our proposed methodology. The quality of social life indicators and factors to be measured with this approach are described and listed in Section IV. Sections V and VI then explain how these indicators and factors would be utilized in performing social impact research and preparing social impact forecasts.

II. SOCIAL IMPACTS

There is no standard definition of the nature or scope of social impacts. As this topic has received increasing attention in recent environmental impact statements, social impact analysis has been approached in numerous ways. Among these have been the following, all of which Peelle (1974:114) argues are totally inadequate: (a) creating an economic balance sheet of monetary costs and benefits, (b) collecting unevaluated demographic and related data, (c) compiling a few observations and opinions on "aesthetics," and (d) asserting in the absence of any respectable data that "no further social or land-use impacts are expected."

Broadly conceived, social impacts refer to all changes in the structure and functioning of patterned social ordering that occur in conjunction with an environmental, technological, or social innovation or alteration. Impacts are dynamic processes, not static conditions, and must therefore be continually measured through time. They may be judged to be either desirable or undesirable in nature. And although impacts are often described as caused by prior innovations or alterations, in reality they always interact with their original causes in a reciprocal process, either immediately or after some time lag. Hence the above definition speaks of impacts as occurring in conjunction with an innovation or alteration, rather than resulting from it. For instance, the interactive process between a construction project and its impacts, as well as other related factors that must be examined in any thorough social impact analysis (SIA), has been diagrammed and described by Wolf (1974:11) in the following manner:

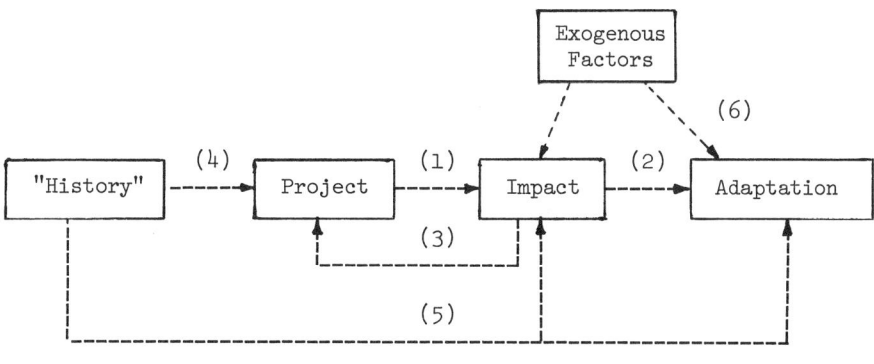

The direct impact (1) is a deformation in the state variables describing initial conditions, but if analysis were to end there it would severely distort the reality situation of SIA. The continuing effects of readjustment and adaptive change represent a sort of "feed-forward" (2). We can further hypothesize a <u>differential</u> social responsiveness on the part of impacted units. Conversely, in the planning phase the direct image may result in a kind of "reaction formation" which impinges on project planning itself (3), in the form of public opposition and plan modification. Moreover, the project itself may be regarded as the social effect of a social cause--its "history" as a prospective solution to preexisting concerns, problems and issues residing in the affected area (4), and this history conditions public receptiveness at the points of impact and subsequent adaptation (5). Finally, the intrusion of exogenous variables (6), whether randon or systematic, compounds the problem of attributing measured effects to planned interventions.

It is also important to distinguish between two forms of social impact assessment: impact research and impact forecasts. These two activities are closely interlinked, however, and the methodology proposed here is applicable to both. Impact <u>research</u> examines current or completed projects to identify and measure the impacts they actually are producing or have produced. It is, in effect, the study of ongoing social change processes. Knowledge gained through such research in turn provides a factual base for making impact forecasts. An impact <u>forecast</u> is a prediction of the consequences that will most likely result from a proposed policy, program, or project. Ideally, it should be based on detailed knowledge of both (a) existing social, economic, and policial conditions in the area affected, and (b) processes of social change and development. Although forecasts always involve considerable margins of error, when properly done they become vital inputs to decision-making and long-range planning.

The methodology described in this report uses quality of social life indicators to measure both predicted and actual impacts of new projects and developments of all kinds. A proposal to use social indicators to measure social impacts was recently put forth by Finsterbusch and others (1975), but their "methodology for analyzing social impacts of public policies" consists only of an elaborate "relevance tree" classificatory scheme, and they have not quantified any of their suggested indicators. Several attempts have been made in recent years to construct sets of quality of life indicators (e.g., Liu 1975), although most of this work has (a) lacked any sound theoretical basis, (b) involved only one-time static measurements, and (c) not been applied to social impact assessment. Consequently, there is presently an unequivocal need to develop a set of quality of social life indicators that can be incorporated into a standardized methodology for conducting social impact assessment. These indicators should be quantitative in nature (on at least an ordinal scale); they should adequately represent the real phenomena of which they are measures; and they should be accessible from existing governmental or organizational records and documents as far as possible.

III. THEORETICAL MODEL

The methodology proposed here is grounded in the theoretical perspective of human ecology. This viewpoint essentially argues that humankind is inexorably dependent on the natural environment, and that collective social life is always constrained and shaped by the basic ecological factors of natural resources, population characteristics, material and social technology, and the economic order which satisfies peoples' sustenance needs (Micklin 1973). To this ecological perspective we add two further assumptions: (1) collective social activities are generally aimed at the attainment of goals which reflect the values and interests of the participants, so that social impact assessment must reflect both the ecological conditions prevailing in a community and the values, interest, and goals of the community members; and (2) a community can be viewed as a problem-solving social system, in which (a) challenges such as new environmental or technological conditions initially disrupt existing social processes and patterns of social ordering, which (b) creates temporary problem conditions and activities, which in turn (c) generate collective responses to cope with these problems, which finally (d) act back (as either positive or negative feedback) on the initial disruptive conditions.

These perspectives and assumptions are reflected in the General Social Impact Model shown in Figure 1, which provides a basic theoretical framework for our proposed social impact assessment methodology. The inputs to this model are (a) such disruptive innovations or alterations as growing resource scarcities (e.g., oil depletion), governmental policy decisions (e.g., limiting economic growth), or technological development projects (e.g., nuclear energy centers); and (b) values and interests of the people in the affected area. Whatever the precise nature of the outside disruption, it can be expected to have direct and relatively immediate impacts on the basic ecological factors of the local population and economy. Since these two factors are highly interrelated, any change in one of them will likely also produce a corresponding change in the other. These direct impacts will in turn lead to numerous indirect secondary effects on the social structure and public services of the surrounding area, and may also generate a variety of social problems that affect the social well-being of the community. All of these direct and indirect impacts together may--though not inevitably--give rise to collective responses of one kind or another by persons in the impacted area. These responses will also be affected, however, by prevailing values and interests. Finally, these outputs from the overall impact process may act as feedback on the initial changes, with the effect of either sustaining or altering them.

FIGURE 1. GENERAL SOCIAL IMPACT MODEL

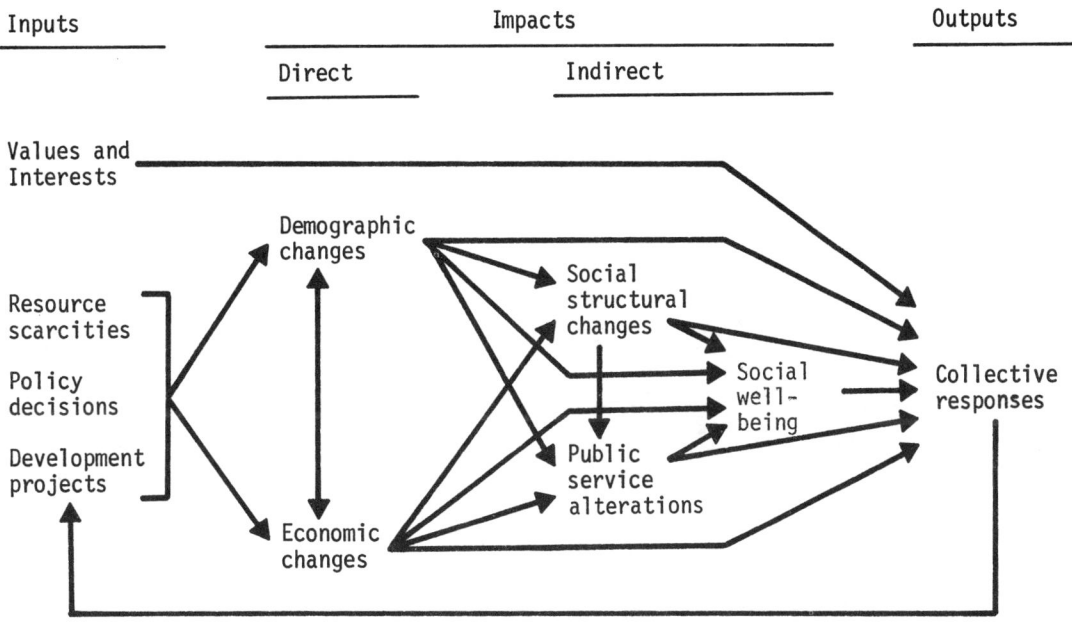

IV. QUALITY OF SOCIAL LIFE FACTORS AND INDICATORS

The General Social Impact Model provides a basic framework for integrating the social impact methodology proposed here, but it does not contain any specific quality of life factors, empirical measures of those factors, or causal linkages among them. The first step in developing this methodology, therefore, is to construct sets of factors and indicators for measuring the quality of social life.

The concept of "quality of life" has no commonly accepted meaning, beyond the vague notion of the "general welfare." In his recent review of the existing literature on quality of life indicators, Liu (1975: Ch. 2) mentions a number of attempts to define this concept, but does not offer a precise definition of his own. Perhaps the best we can do, therefore, is to note that all conceptualizations of "quality of life" refer in one way or another to what people think is important in life. In short, (a) whatever contributes to the quality of life of a population of people is ultimately determined by them, not by elites or experts of any kind, and (b) people's notion of life quality is thoroughly infused with normative values concerning what is good and right in life. Hence, there is probably no point in trying to construct a single definitive concept of "quality of life," since its meaning is highly realtive and valuative.

Because the purpose of this paper is to propose a methodology for studying social impacts, we deal here with the quality of social life. We therefore exclude several other facets of the overall quality of life, including psychological perceptions of satisfactions or well-being, the condition of the natural environment, and the level of technological development. On the basis of a thorough review of the existing literature on social indicators, we identified 50 factors, or community characteristics, that are essential components of the quality of social life in the United States and other western societies. These factors would be of direct concern to policy makers in evaluating virtually any innovation. The factors are categorized under the five headings previously shown in Figure 1: demography, economy, social structure, public services, and social well-being. We also identified five kinds of collective responses that citizens, organizations, or public leaders may make to social impacts affecting their community. These responses, labeled as "impact outputs" in Figure 1, represent efforts to maintain or improve the quality of social life in a community. In addition, in any actual impact research or forecast it will also be necessary to collect data on the nature of the initial innovation or alteration, prevailing public values and interests, and other exogenous variables, but these are not conceptualized as quality of social life indicators or responses.

Each quality of social life factor and collective response is measured with an index composed of one or more (preferably two or three) empirical indicators. The index for the factor of "residential stability," for instance, is composed of these two indicators: (a) mean length of occupancy of all dwelling units in the community, and (b) the proportion of all dwelling units that are owner-occupied. An index score for a particular quality of social life factor or collective response in a particular community at a particular point in time is constructed by transforming the observed value of each of its component indicators into a standardized score that expresses the degree to which the indicator approaches its preferred value, and then computing the mean of these standardized indicator scores. The preferred value for each indicator may be specified either by a set of qualified experts (e.g., the ideal ratio of .80 primary care physicians per 1000 population established by the American Medical Association), or by the public as a whole (e.g., a sex ratio of 1.0). With many of these indicators, the preferred value is simply as high or low a figure as possible, as illustrated by educational expenditures per child or number of violent crimes per capita. In a number of these cases there is an upper or lower limit beyond which further increases or decreases would be meaningless--such as one television channel for every 100 people or one policeman for every three citizens. In practice this is not a serious problem, however, since rarely (if ever) are these limits approached in real life. We are presently in the process of obtaining these preferred values for each indicator.

More specifically, the standard scores are computed with the following formula:

$$SS = 1 - \left| \frac{OV - PV}{PV} \right|$$

where SS = standard score for an indicator, OV = observed value for that indicator, and PV = preferred value for that indicator. The absolute value of this ratio is utilized in order to include deviations both above and below the preferred value. The resulting standard scores have a maximum possible value of 1.00 when the observed value equals the preferred value. In most cases the minimum possible value of a standard score is 0, but if the observed value can be a negative number (as in the case of a negative growth rate), then the resulting standard score could be any negative number. The index score for a quality of social life factor or collective response is then the mean of all its indicator standard scores. This index construction procedure can be illustrated by continuing the above example of residential stability. A hypothetical index score for this factor might be computed for community Z at time T as shown below:

	Observed Value	Preferred Value	Standard Score
Mean occupancy length	15 years	10 years	.50
Units owner-occupied	50%	60%	.83
Index score			.665

Appendix 1 lists these 55 quality of social life factors and collective responses, arranged into the previously mentioned categories. All of the items are stated in implicitly or explicitly positive terms. For instance, the term "residential stability" implies that greater stability contributes positively to the quality of life in a community. In other cases, such as "lack of crime," the positive nature of the term is quite explicit.

Under each item in the appendix is listed one or more empirical indicators to be used in measuring it. These indicators are stated in terms of both their quantitative measurement and their qualitative contribution to the quality of social life. Some of these qualitative evaluations--such as the assumptions that high educational attainment or low infant mortality contribute to the quality of social life--would undoubtedly be accepted by most people. Other evaluations--such as associating length of residential occupancy with quality of social life--are open to considerable debate, and will likely vary from one community to another according to prevailing social values. Hence the qualitative evaluations attached to the indicators should be considered only provisional, to be altered later as necessary to reflect the values of specific communities. For the present, all the indicators of a given factor are weighted equally, although eventually it may become desirable to weight them differentially. This listing of indicators in the appendix should therefore not be taken as definitive, but merely as an illustration of the kinds of data that can be used to measure each quality of social life factor.

Virtually all previous efforts to measure the quality of social life have assigned equal weights to all the component factors and then simply added the factor scores together to obtain one or more composite scores. This procedure in effect assumes that all factors are equally important in contributing to the quality of social life. That assumption is highly questionable, however. We shall therefore assign different weights to the various factors, according to their perceived importance for the quality of social life. These weightings will be derived from subjective judgments obtained from a variety of respondents, including (a) citizens within different demographic and social categories (e.g., males and females; young, middle-aged, and old; black and white; blue-collar and white-collar workers; poor, middle-income, and rich; elementary, high school, and college graduates); (b) various kinds of professionals (e.g., planners, social workers, social scientists), and (c) community leaders (e.g., public officials, business elites, organizational leaders).

We are presently in the process of obtaining these subjective evaluations and assigning weightings to the quality of social life factors. Tentatively, these factor weightings will range from -5 (strongly negative) through 0 (irrelevant) to +5 (strongly positive). Each factor score will be multiplied by its weighting before being combined with other factor scores to form overall quality of social life assessments. For example, if residential stability were weighted "3", its index score of .665 computed above for community Z would become 2.0. This residential stability factor score could either be reported by itself or else combined with the weighted scores for all the other social structural factors to obtain an overall score for that category.

V. SOCIAL IMPACT RESEARCH

The purpose of developing indicators of the quality of social life is to provide standardized measures of social change--in this case, impacts caused by a new policy or project. Before we can predict with any accuracy the likely impacts of a proposed innovation, however, we must thoroughly study past and current change processes to determine what kinds of effects do in fact result from various kinds of new policies and projects. That is, we must conduct extensive social impact research utilizing our quality of social life indicators. Where the necessary information is already available, we can do this research on past events or utilize the results of previous research studies. Since the concept of social indicators is relatively new, however, much of the currently existing social science literature is not directly relevant to this task. Hence there is a pressing need for numerous studies of ongoing programs and projects to determine how they are actually affecting the quality of social life in surrounding areas.

Although the geographical size of the area affected by any particular innovation will be heavily influenced by its nature and scope, most social impacts are generally experienced within the community or communities closest to where the innovation occurs. And even though a large project or broad new program might have discernable impacts throughout a region or even the total society, most of these effects are nevertheless experienced most intensely in the immediately surrounding area. We propose, therefore, that as a general rule social impact research should take the community as the basic unit of analysis. In urban areas, community boundaries will likely coincide with either the total urban place or the encompassing county. In rural areas, the functioning community may consist of two or more towns that are relatively close in location and economically interdependent. In addition, some social indicators pertain to the whole county in which the community is located.

The basic purpose of social impact research is to determine how much change occurs in each social indicator (and hence each factor index) between $time_1$ (before the innovation) and $time_2$ (after the innovation), and perhaps also at subsequent intervals of $time_3$, $time_4$, etc.:

$$\Delta A = A_{time_2} - A_{time_1}$$

In addition, however, we want to determine how much of that observed change is actually caused (either directly or indirectly) by the particular innovation under investigation, as opposed to all other events and social trends occurring in the community. Hence our ideal social impact research model would be as follows:

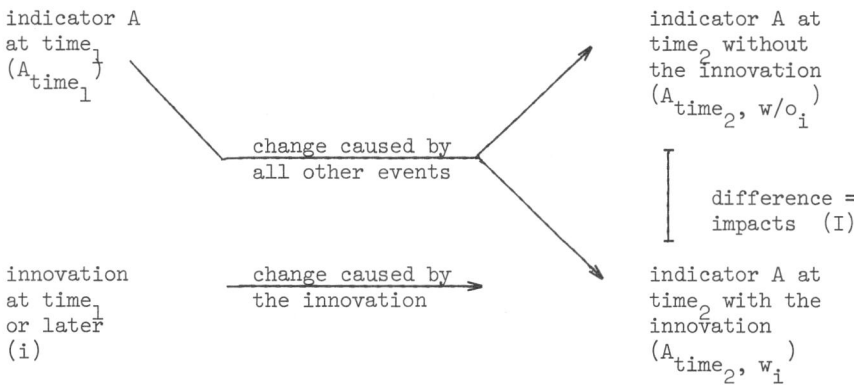

In this model, the magnitude of the impacts resulting from the innovation under investigation is determined by comparing the value of each indicator (such as A) at $time_2$ with what that value would have been at that time had the innovation not occurred. In short:

$$I = (A_{time_2}, w_i) - (A_{time_2}, w/o_i)$$

The main difficulty with this model, obviously, is estimating the hypothetical value of A_{time_2} without the effects of the innovation. There are three ways of estimating this figure, all of which provide at best only crude approximations: (1) If a time trend can be established for variable A during the years preceding $time_1$, this trend (whether it be linear, curvilinear, exponential, etc.) can be extrapolated to $time_2$ with fair accuracy, especially if the time period involved is not too great. (2) The community or county being studied can be matched (on as many variables as possible) with another community or county not experiencing the innovation, and the value for indicator A at $time_2$ in the control community or county taken as an estimate of $A_{time_2, w/o_i}$ in the area being studied. (3) The national mean (or median) for A_{time_2} can be applied to the community or county under investigation as an estimate of $A_{time_2, w/o_i}$ in that area.

The procedure described above is particularly relevant to the two categories of direct impacts--demographic changes and economic changes--which are closely linked to the innovation being studied. The researcher has more methodological flexibility, however, with the three categories of indirect impacts--social structural changes, public service alterations, and social well-being--as well as with collective response outputs. The causal linkages from demographic and economic changes to these latter sets of factors, and also among these sets, can be examined apart from any policy or project innovations. As one example, the effects of rising socio-economic status on the quality of medical care or the crime rate can be studied in almost any community. In point of fact, these kinds of relationships have long been a central concern of sociological research, although our knowledge of most of these relationships is still extremely limited and fragmentary.

The fundamental purpose of social impact research is to determine the patterns, directions, strengths, and lags of the causal relationships existing among all the variables relevant to one's concern. That is, we need to determine--usually in the following order of increasing methodological sophistication-- (a) which variables are related to which other variables, (b) the causal directions of these relationships (both recursive and nonrecursive), (c) regression coefficients for the strengths of these relationships, and (d) any temporal lag effects that occur in this causal process. Although much social science research is still dealing with the first of these tasks, and only recently has any significant headway been made on the second and third tasks, these limitations can at least temporarily be circumvented by specifying hypothetical patterns of causal relationships in one's theoretical model, and then asking the question: If these hypothetical sets of causal relationships did in fact exist, what kinds of impacts would a particular innovation have on the quality of social life in this community?

VI. SOCIAL IMPACT FORECASTS

The ultimate goal of this entire process of social impact assessment is to improve our ability to predict the likely impacts of any anticipated or porposed new policy, program, or project. Thus far, the usual way of making these forecasts has been merely to project (usually on a linear basis) whatever trends were known to be occurring and then to add onto them the expected (or guessed or estimated) effects of the innovation. In terms of the methodological model sketched in the previous section, both $A_{time_2, w/o_i}$ and A_{time_2, w_i} have been at best crude estimates with little or no basis in empirical knowledge. Moreover, this current practice does not take into account the ways in which one impact may affect others throughout the entire social system. Several methods, such as cross-impact forecasting (Bloom (1975), have been developed to identify these interrelated indirect impacts, but they rely heavily on subjective judgments by presumed experts.

The principal benefit of our proposed social indicator methodology, in contrast, is that when fully developed it will enable social scientists to use dynamic system modelling to predict the most likely impacts of any specified innovation. Once we can measure--at least crudely--the causal effects of each variable in the system upon every variable, it becomes possible, using a computer, to identify all the impacts likely to result from a specified alteration in any one part of that system. Although such dynamic system modelling can never perfectly predict the future-- since it cannot take into account unforeseen future events that may change the system in other ways--it nevertheless can greatly improve our ability to forecast future social impacts of all anticipated and proposed innovations. Moreover, the "collective problem solving" theoretical perspective underlying this methodology focuses attention on the ways in which affected communities will likely respond to the impacts of an innovation in a feedback process.

To perform dynamic systems analysis, one must first design a system model to represent the total process being investigated (or at least its most important components). The "Process Model of Social Impacts of Development Projects" shown in Figure 2, which depicts the general process through which a major construction project might affect the local surrounding area, is a simplified illustration of the kind of detailed system model that would be constructed for this purpose. When applied to an actual situation, the model would be elaborated to include relevant unique features of that situation, as well as observed measurements of all variables, regression coefficients for connecting paths among the variables, and additional feedback loops. In general, however, this illustrative model could be applied to most innovations with only minor modifications. Dynamic system models such as this will provide a means for predicting with considerable accuracy the most probable consequences that would result from any proposed development project or other innovation.

The model in Figure 2 begins with the scope and duration of the construction project, plus a number of conditions already existing in the affected area, including the size, socioeconomic status distribution, and other characteristics of the population; the availability of unemployed qualified manpower; the extent of unoccupied housing; existing public service capabilities of all kinds; current tax rates and total financial resources of the area; and prevailing public values and interests. Some of the more significant direct demographic and economic impacts of the project would include the number and nature of jobs provided by the project, as well as secondary economic growth in the area generated by the project; the resulting total population growth and changes in various population characteristics; the resulting overall economic growth produced by the project; the willingness of the public to approve new taxes or bonds to fund expanded public services and the resulting increase in public revenues; and other sources of additional revenues such as taxes paid by the project or governmental assistance.

Included under the heading of indirect social structural, public service, and social well-being impacts are a wide variety of potential social consequences of the construction project. Social structural factors include changes in the occupational,

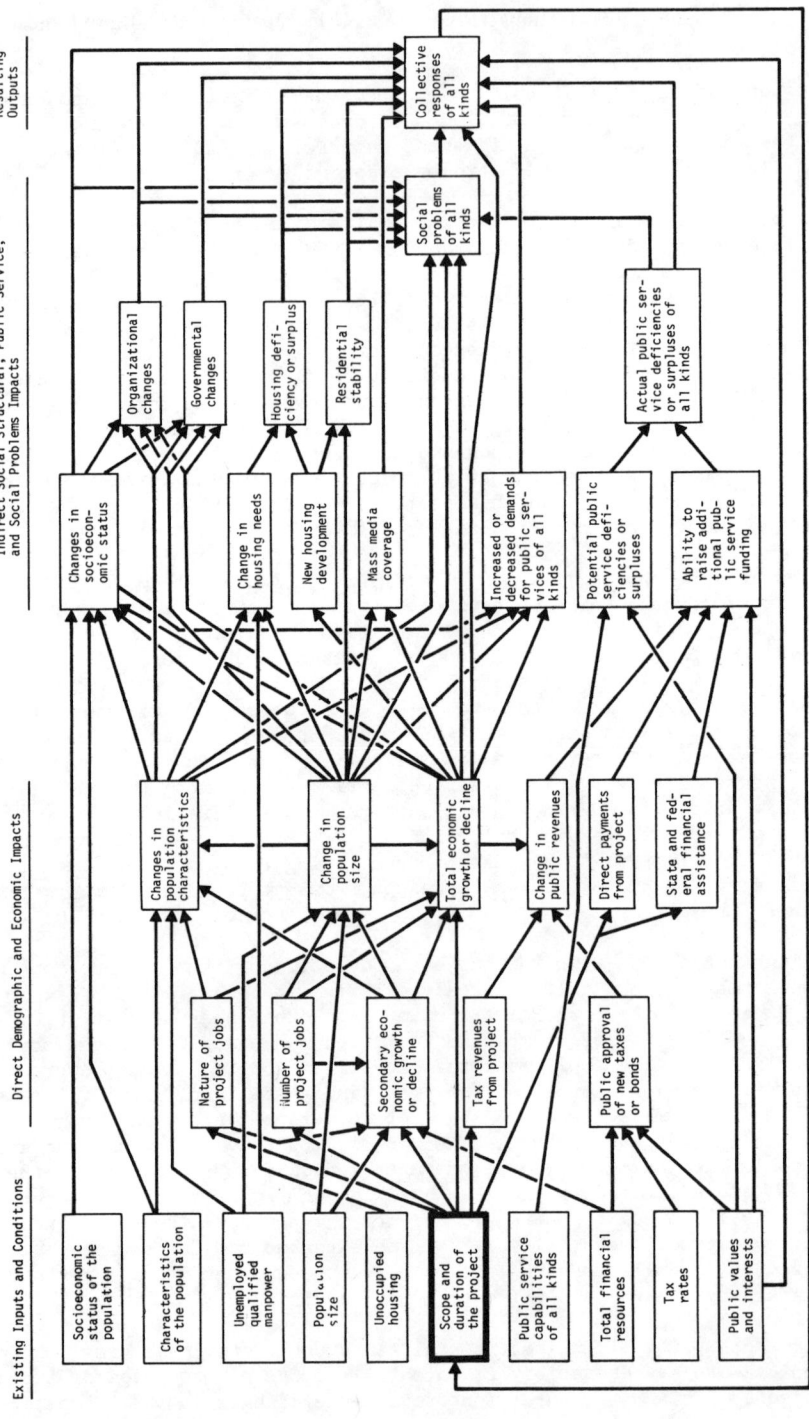

Figure 2. Process Model of Social Impacts of Development Projects

educational, and income distributions of the affected populations, housing deficiencies and residential stability; changes in the number of voluntary associations such as civic or occupational organizations, as well as rates of involvement in them; changes in both political participation and the size and scope of local government; and changes in the extent of mass media coverage. Additional demands for, or recognized deficiencies in, public services might involve education, medical care, public health, public transportation, police and fire protection, legal services, social services, recreation, or cultural facilities. The list of social problems that might be aggravated or otherwise influenced by social changes resulting from the project is virtually limitless, but could include crime and juvenile delinquency, physical and mental illness, alcohol and drug abuse, racial and sexual discrimination, family disruption, unemployment and poverty, inadequate housing, and collective violence.

The collective responses that might be stimulated by any of the preceding conditions could take the form of actions by civic or special-interest organizations; all kinds of political efforts by individuals or groups or parties; initiation or expansion of governmental programs of all kinds; and increased attempts at comprehensive community planning.

As elaborate system models are designed, quantified and analyzed, they will provide extensive sets of data on which to base forecasts of likely future impacts, as well as knowledge about the process through which these changes occur as they spread throughout an entire social system. This factual knowledge will not, however, provide answers to the ultimate valuative question that policy makers must eventually face: Will this anticipated or proposed innovation contribute to or detract from the quality of social life? When making these basic valuative decisions, policy makers must take into account the amount of change likely to result from the innovation, its specific nature, the rate at which this change will occur, and the overall configuration of conditions that will probably exist after these changes have transpired. With this information in hand, they must then evaluate the overall social value of the innovation and decide whether or not to instigate it.

A unique feature of our proposed use of quality of social life indicators to measure social impacts, however, is that the evaluation process is broken down into many relatively small and manageable segments. Whereas the usual procedure in the past has been to collect all relevant data in a value-neutral manner and then attempt to make a single overall value judgment that hopefully considered all this information at once, our proposed procedure places much of this evaluative process in the initial stage of specifying empirical indicators. For each indicator, the researcher using this method must ascertain which possible trends will contribute to the quality of social life and which will detract from it in that situation. These judgments will also be quite subjective in nature, but since each one pertains only to a fairly small and delineated facet of life, each one can be discussed and defined with considerably more rationality than can a single global subjective judgment. A final evaluative decision must still be made by policy makers, but the base of knowledge on which their decision rests will be considerably deeper and richer with our proposed quality of social life approach to social impact assessment. An adequate knowledge base does not insure wise decisions, but hopefully, our proposed social impact methodology will help improve the quality of future policy decisions in many realms of contemporary society.

Appendix 1. Quality of Social Life Factors and Indicators

A. Demography

1. Population size of the community
   a. Number of inhabitants
      + = positive relationship up to 500,000; negative above that*
2. Amount of population growth in the community
   a. Annual amount of growth through natural increase during the past 10 years
      + = cannot be specified at the present time
   b. Annual amount of growth through net migration during the past 10 years
      + = cannot be specified at the present time
3. Rate of population growth in the community
   a. Annual percentage rate of growth during the past 10 years
      + = the closer to 1%
4. Degree of urbanization of the county
   a. Proportion of population in cities of 20,000 or more
      + = the closer to 60-75%
5. Population density of the county
   a. Number of persons per square mile
      + = the closer to 100
6. Population concentration of the county
   a. Proportion of the total population in the largest urban place
      + = the closer to 20-50%
7. Age dependency in the community
   a. Proportion of the population under 18 and over 65
      + = the smaller the proportion
8. Sex ratio of the community
   a. Ratio of males to females
      + = closer to 1.0
9. Ethnic composition of the community
   a. Percent of the population nonwhite
      + = the closer to 13%
10. Family size in the community
    a. Number of persons per household
       + = the closer to 2.0

B. Economy

1. Job opportunities
   a. Proportion of available unskilled jobs that are vacant
      + = higher proportion
   b. Proportion of available semi-skilled jobs that are vacant
      + = higher proportion
   c. Proportion of available skilled jobs that are vacant
      + = higher proportion

---

* + for each indicator specifies that condition we provisionally judge most favorable for the quality of social life.

d. Proportion of available clerical/sales jobs that are vacant
      + = higher proportion
   e. Proportion of available managerial jobs that are vacant
      + = higher proportion
   f. Proportion of available professional jobs that are vacant
      + = higher proportion
2. Job distribution
   a. Proportion of available jobs that are unskilled
      + = lower proportion
   b. Proportion of available jobs that are semiskilled
      + = lower proportion
   c. Proportion of available jobs that are skilled
      + = higher proportion
   d. Proportion of available jobs that are clerical/sales
      + = lower proportion
   e. Proportion of available jobs that are managerial
      + = higher proportion
   f. Proportion of available jobs that are professional
      + = higher proportion
3. Gross county product size
   a. Gross county income per year
      + = greater amount
4. Gross county product growth
   a. Annual percentage rate of growth in gross county income during past 10 years
      + = higher rate
5. Employment level
   a. Proportion of the labor force that is employed
      + = greater the proportion
6. Participation in the labor force
   a. Proportion of women in the labor force
      + = greater the proportion
   b. Proportion of persons age 65 or older in the labor force
      + = greater the proportion
7. Property tax base
   a. Total value of assessed real property
      + = higher amount
   b. Total value of assessed personal property
      + = higher amount
8. Financial inflow from federal government
   a. Amount of federal revenue sharing funds received per year
      + = greater amount
   b. Amount of direct federal aid to impacted areas received per year
      + = greater amount
   c. Amount of other federal monies received per year
      + = greater amount
9. Price level
   a. Consumer price index for the community
      + = lower the index
10. Public revenues
    a. Total revenues collected by all community governmental units in past year

+ = greater amount

C. Social structure

1. Educational attainment
   a. Median educational attainment of persons age 25 or older
      + = higher attainment
2. Socioeconomic status
   a. Mean occupational status of the work force
      + = high status
   b. Median gross family income
      + = high income
3. Housing availability
   a. Number of unoccupied dwelling units per 1000 population
      + = greater number
4. Housing space
   a. Mean dwelling unit size (sq. ft.) per person
      + = greater space
   b. Proportion of dwelling units that are single-family detached
      + = high proportion
5. Residential stability
   a. Mean length of occupancy of all dwelling units
      + = greater length
   b. Proportion of all dwelling units that are owner occupied
      + = higher proportion
6. Mass media coverage
   a. Combined circulation per capita of all local newspapers
      + = high circulation
   b. Number of television channels in the area
      + = greater number
7. Civic association extensiveness (e.g., business, professional, fraternal, service, educational, ethnic, and political associations)
   a. Number of associations per 1000 poulation
      + = greater number
8. Civic association participation
   a. Total memberships per capita in all such associations
      + = higher number
9. Political participation
   a. Proportion of eligible persons who are registered
      + = higher proportion
   b. Turnout rate in local elections during previous year
      + = higher rate
10. Local government size
    a. Total number of community governmental employees per 1000 population
       + = higher number
    b. Total program budget of all community governmental units per capita
       + = greater amount

D. Public Services

1. Public education

a. Mean class size (students per classroom)
      + = low number
   b. Mean student-teacher ratio
      + = low ratio
   c. Mean educational level of teachers
      + = high level
   d. Total educational expenditures per student per year
      + = greater amount
2. Medical care
   a. Hospital beds per 1000 population
      + = greater number
   b. Total hospital expenditures per capita per year
      + = greater amount
   c. Number of mental health clinics per 1000 population
      + = greater number
   d. Number of physicians per 1000 population
      + = greater number
   e. Number of dentists per 1000 population
      + = greater number
   f. Number of psychiatrists and clinical psychologists per 1000 population
      + = greater number
3. Public health
   a. Total local governmental expenditures on public health per capita per year
      + = greater amount
   b. Number of public health workers (excluding sanitation) per 1000 population
      + = greater number
   c. Number of sanitation employees per 1000 population
      + = greater number
4. Fire protection
   a. Number of five employees per 1000 population
      + = greater number
   b. Total local government expenditures on fire protection per capita
      + = greater amount
   c. Fire protection classification of the community
      + = higher the classification
5. Police protection
   a. Number of police employees per 1000 population
      + = greater number
   b. Total local government expenditures on police protection per capita
      + = higher proportion
   c. Proportion of all cases cleared by arrest
      + = higher proportion
6. Public transportation
   a. Total expenditures for public transportation of all kinds per capita per year
      + = greater amount

   b. Number of miles of scheduled bus routes per capita
      + = greater number

            c. Number of buses per capita
                + = greater number
            d. Total expenditures for street maintenance per capita per year
                + = greater amount
        7. Legal services
            a. Number of attorneys per 1000 population
                + = greater number
            b. Total budgets of legal services centers per capita
                + = greater amount
            c. Median months to trial in criminal cases
                + = lower number
            d. Median months to trial in civil cases
                + = lower number
        8. Social services
            a. Total number of professionals in all social service agencies per 1000 population
                + = greater number
            b. Total budgets of all social service agencies per capita per year
                + = greater amount
            c. Number of social service agencies per 1000 population
                + = larger number
        9. Recreational facilities
            a. Number of movie theaters per 1000 population
                + = greater number
            b. Acres of public parks per 1000 population
                + = greater number
            c. Total governmental expenditures for parks and recreational facilities per capita per year
                + = greater amount
            d. Total governmental expenditures for recreational programs and activities per capita per year
                + = greater amount
        10. Cultural facilities
            a. Number of books in municipal public library per 1000 population
                + = greater number
            b. Total budgets of all major museums per capita per year
                + = greater amount
            c. Number of publicly sponsored cultural courses per 1000 population per year
                + = greater number

E. Social Well-Being

    1. Lack of crime and delinquency
        a. Number of violent crimes per 1000 population per year
            + = low number
        b. Number of property crimes per 1000 population per year
            + = low number
        c. Number of serious delinquency violations per 1000 population per year
            + = low number
    2. Lack of alcohol and drug abuse

    a. Number of people treated for alcoholism or drug abuse by hopitals per 1000 population per year
       + = low number
    b. Number of contacts made with alcohol and drug abuse programs per 1000 population per year
       + = low number

3. Lack of physical and mental illness
    a. Hospitalization rate for physical or mental illness per 1000 population per year
       + = low number
    b. Number of disability days per year per capita
       + = low number
    c. Suicide rate per 1000 population per year
       + = low number

4. Lack of racial or sexual discrimination
    a. Ratio of black to white unemployment rates
       + = 1.0 ratio
    b. Ratio of black to white family income
       + = 1.0 ratio
    c. Ratio of female to male unemployment rates
       + = 1.0 ratio
    d. Ratio of female to male income
       + = 1.0 ratio

5. Lack of family disruption
    a. Number of divorces filed for per 1000 population per year
       + = low number
    b. Proportion of all families with only one adult
       + = low number

6. Lack of educational difficulties
    a. Rate of school dropouts per 1000 students per year
       + = low rate
    b. Mean score of all students on national achievement tests, compared to national averages
       + = ratio of 1.0 or higher
    c. Functional illiteracy (less than 5 years of education) rate per 1000 population
       + = low rate

7. Lack of employment difficulties
    a. Gross labor turnover rate per year
       + = low rate
    b. Proportion of unemployment compensation recipients exceeding maximum benefits
       + = low proportion

8. Lack of poverty
    a. Proportion of all families below the official poverty line
       + = low proportion
    b. Proportion of all families receiving public welfare
       + = low proportion

9. Lack of substandard housing
    a. Proportion of housing units classified as dilapidated
       + = low proportion

b. Proportion of housing units without plumbing
+ = low proportion
10. Lack of public violence
a. Number of riots or similar events per year
+ = low number
b. Number of deaths and serious injuries due to riots or similar events per 1000 population per year
+ = low number
c. Amount of property damage due to riots or similar events per capita per year
+ = low amount

F. Collective Responses (directly or indirectly related to the event being investigated)

1. Public issues
a. Number of public issues that receive extensive mass media attention per year
+ = greater number
b. Number of public interest lawsuits filed per 1000 population per year
+ = greater number
c. Number of appeals to governmental decisions per 1000 population per year
+ = greater number
2. Organizational activities
a. Number of organizations making public statements on issues or problems per 1000 population per year
+ = greater number
b. Amount of financial contributions by organizations to programs or other activities per capita per year
+ = greater amount
c. Number of programs or other activities initiated by organizations per 1000 population per year
+ = greater number
3. Political activities
a. Number of petitions and initiatives filed per 1000 population per year
+ = greater number
b. Number of political movements or <u>ad hoc</u> political groups created per 1000 population per year
+ = greater number
c. Number of political protests and demonstrations per year
+ = greater number
4. Governmental programs
a. Number of new governmental programs or activities initiated per 1000 population per year
+ = greater number
b. Number of existing governmental programs or activities expanded per 1000 population per year
+ = greater number
c. Amount of increased expenditures for new or expanded governmental programs or activities per capita per year

+ = greater amount
5. Community planning
   a. Existence of a planning department in the local government
      + = yes
   b. Number of employees in local planning department per 1000 population
      + = greater number
   c. Total budget of local planning department per capita per year
      + = greater amount

References

Bloom, Metchel F. (1975) "Deterministic Trend Cross-Impact Forecasting," Technological Forecasting and Social Change, 8, 1, 35-74.

Dunning, C. Mark (1974) "A Systemic Approach to Social Impact Assessment," pp. 59-64 in C. P. Wolf (ed.), Social Impact Assessment. Milwaukee, WI: Environmental Design Research Association.

Finsterbusch, Kurt and others (1975) A Methodology for Analyzing Social Impacts of Public Policies. Vienna, VA: BDM Corporation, May.

Liu, Ben-Chieh (1975) Quality of Life Indicators in U.S. Metropolitan Areas, 1970: A Comprehensive Assessment. Washington, DC: Washington Environmental Research Center, U. S. Environmental Protection Agency, 7 May.

Micklin, Michael (ed.) (1973) Population, Environment, and Social Organization: Current Issues in Human Ecology. Hinsdale, IL: Dryden.

Peelle, Elizabeth (1974) "Social Effects of Nuclear Power Plants," pp. 113-20 in C. P. Wolf (ed.), Social Impact Assessment. Milwaukee, WI: Environmental Design Research Association.

Wolf, C. P. (1974) "Social Impact Assessment: The State of the Art," pp. 1-44 in C. P. Wolf (ed.), Social Impact Assessment. Milwaukee, WI: Environmental Design Research Association.

Grounded Theory Construction in Social Impact Assessment

Mark Shields
Oak Ridge National Laboratory

Introduction
The field of social impact assessment (SIA) is characterized better by its practitioners and what they study than by any distinct theoretical perspectives. In spite of the large and growing body of empirical research on social impacts, little attention has yet been given to its systematic theoretical development. There is a prevailing tendency for social impact studies to be atheoretical or for theoretical stance to function implicitly as hidden "background assumptions" (Gouldner 1970). The reasons for this have as much to do with the rather disorderly condition of social theory as with the typical constraints on most social impact studies--shortages of personnel, time and money that make it difficult to obtain even adequate descriptive data. There are, certainly, many varieties of substantive and formal theory to draw on in conducting social impact research. However, it would appear that what is needed now is not an eclectic blend of theoretical ideas, but an approach to theory construction in SIA that is closely connected to the cumulative empirical findings of social impact studies.

Whatever the obstacles, it is apparent that a firmer theoretical basis for SIA is likely to lead to many practical payoffs in doing impact assessments. Theories, in fact, may be viewed as assessment strategies: they propose different ways of interpreting the social world and different propositions about how individuals and social systems respond and adapt to change.[1] Different analysts could very well arrive at competing interpretations of the same data, simply on the basis of having analyzed the data from alternative theoretical standpoints. Theoretical orientations not only influence judgments about "acceptable" magnitudes of impact, but also affect decisions as to what variables are considered and how they are related. Theory intervenes at every operational phase of impact assessment--in "profiling," through the selection of baseline indicators and in the determination of probable loci of impact; in "projecting," through modeling the anticipated effects of alternative plans; in "assessing," through the delineation of "significant" effects; and in "evaluating," through differential criteria for judging "costs" and "benefits," selective identification of publics and interpretations of their preferences and values.[2]

Grounded Theory Construction
This paper proposes a strategy for strengthening the relationships between theory and research in SIA. It is an inductive strategy which seeks to generate theoretical concepts and generalizations through the systematic comparative analysis of a broad range of empirical studies. I call it a "grounded theory" approach because it is similar to the rationale proposed by Barney Glaser and Anselm Strauss in The Discovery of Grounded Theory: Strategies for Qualitative Research (1967).

Grounded theory is a method of inductive, comparative analysis for discovering theory from the data of social research. It is inductive because it starts with the empirical findings of social impact studies[3] and attempts to "discover" theoretical concepts and generalizations from the data, rather than starting with a particular theory or group of propositions which are then tested against the available evidence. It is comparative because it calls for the analysis of a wide range of social impact studies for the purpose of obtaining a variety of "slices of data" for developing theoretical categories.[4] While it would be naive to think that existing theories could be excluded entirely from the analytical process, the aim of grounded theory is to reduce as much as possible the role of existing theories in interpreting data. By controlling the influence of preconceived theoretical ideas and by insisting on constant interaction and shifting between the empirical and conceptual levels of analysis, this strategy increases the likelihood that the theory thus generated will have rather high empirical validity and be credible to social scientists and laypersons alike. Beyond being just a _method_ of theoretical analysis, grounded theory is an _attitude_ toward the purposes and uses of empirical research: it insists on the reduction of the intellectual division of labor between theory and research. It is best adapted to building theories of the "middle range" (Merton 1968) and thus stands in contrast to both _ad hoc, post factum_ and "logico-deductive" theorizing. Given the present state of social impact research, grounded theory appears well-suited to fulfilling the theoretical requirements of SIA.

The core of the grounded theory approach rests on a technique Glaser and Strauss call "theoretical sampling."

> Theoretical sampling is the process of data collection for generating theory whereby the analyst jointly collects, codes, and analyzes his data and decides what data to collect next and where to find them. The process of data collection is _controlled_ by the emerging theory. The initial decisions for theoretical collection of data are based only on a general sociological perspective and on a general subject or problem area....(p. 45)

This technique differs, of course, from probability sampling where one seeks to insure that cases are statistically representative of the population from which they are drawn. Grounded theory, on the other hand, calls for an _ongoing inclusion of cases_ throughout the research process--not arbitrarily chosen cases, but cases selected for particular theoretical purposes.[5] Sampling continues until a category has been theoretically "saturated."

> _Saturation_ means that no additional data are being found whereby the sociologist can develop properties of the category. As he sees similar instances over and over again, the researcher becomes empirically confident that a category is saturated. In trying to reach saturation he maximizes differences in his [units] in order to maximize the varieties of data bearing on a category, and thereby develops as many diverse properties of the category as possible. The criteria for determining saturation, then, are a combination of the empirical limits of the data, the integration and density of the theory, and the analyst's theoretical sensitivity.[6] (pp. 61-62)

In the rest of this paper I shall describe an operational procedure for applying the general rationale of grounded theory to SIA. An illustration of the procedure will be given for each step, using examples from social impact studies of displacement and relocation of populations. Although I focus the discussion on grounded theory construction from existing social impact research, the strategy may also be applied to most types of field research and case studies. The diagram below outlines the three steps involved. A fourth--verification--is logically implied in theory construction, but is not conceived as a function of the discovery process itself.

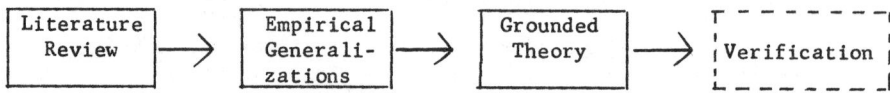

Literature Review. The procedure begins with a systematic search and review of available empirical studies.[7] The purpose of this step is to create an "analytic bibliography" consisting of a selective but representative detailing of the contents of each study reviewed. The format of the analytic bibliography is designed to provide a common organizational framework for presenting the salient contributions of the research and provides an effective way of classifying a large amount of information in an easily retrievable form. This format, illustrated in Table 1, enables users to make comparative appraisals of studies in a consistent, systematic manner.

TABLE 1. FORMAT OF THE ANALYTIC BIBLIOGRAPHY*

Citation: Title, author(s), place and date of publication, other identifying information.

Abstract: Brief summary of study.

Descriptors: Key words describing broad subject areas and specific contents of each source; these can be combined in a single list in the style of a conventional index for quick reference.

Locators: Indicate physical setting of research; these too can be combined in a single list.

Methods/Techniques: Indicate the general analytic procedures and specific techniques of data manipulation; these can be combined in a table listing all studies and the methods, techniques and data sources (see Shields 1974: 37-39).

Data/Indicators: Sources and types of data and measures used in study.

Findings: Main results and conclusions of study.

Interpretive Points: Comments, reactions, criticisms and references to related studies.

*From Shields (1974)

The analytic bibliography goes well beyond an annotated bibliography. It aims for a level of completeness and detail short only of the original studies themselves. This is accomplished by classifying the contents of sources according to the categories described in Table 1. The analytic bibliography thus becomes the organized data base for theory construction.

Empirical Generalizations. In the second step, findings from the analytic bibliography are separately entered into an inventory of empirical generalizations. But instead of classifying a finding by its original source (as in the first step), findings are grouped according to their bearing on various categories of social impacts--e.g., displacement and relocation, community cohesion, lifestyles, taxes, services, employment, etc. The delineation of appropriate categories emerges in the process of analyzing the empirical research, as particular findings are related to each other and to their common conceptual bases. The density, or degree of elaboration, of a category guides the analyst in deciding what type of information to collect next, the objective being to "saturate" each category as fully as possible by identifying its underlying properties. This process may be considered as analogous to factor analysis. Table 2 illustrates this procedure. The category "displacement and relocation" is first characterized by three separate dimensions (or "properties")--susceptibility, attitudes and consequences--and under each of these dimensions are listed a series of empirical findings found in selected studies (noted in parentheses). These findings are grouped together to form empirical generalizations pertaining to the defined properties of displacement and relocation. As additional studies are analyzed, other properties may emerge and existing properties may be further refined. Apart from its importance in constructing grounded theory, the inventory is a useful accounting of the type and amount of empirical research devoted to various areas and, along with the analytic bibliography, can serve as a reference source in all subsequent and related research.

Grounded Theory. The purpose of this step is to consider the theoretical significance of the empirical generalizations. This entails more conceptual elaboration of the variables, further specification of their operational indicators and a recasting of empirically established relationships as theoretically meaningful generalizations. "The scope of the original empirical findings is considerably extended, and several seemingly disparate uniformities are seen to be interrelated..." (Merton 1968: 151). It is worth emphasizing that this step, like the previous two, is only _analytically_ separate from the others; in practice, and in accord with the logic of grounded theory, the researcher interested in generating theory operates at all three levels interchangeably throughout the research process.

Two types of theoretical analysis are joined at this step. The first involved the generation of grounded theory as described above. At the same time, the emerging grounded theory's plausible relationship to other substantive and formal theory should be considered. This does not mean _fitting_ the grounded theory to other theories any more than it means that those theories will directly correspond to the grounded theory. Instead, we ask in what ways the grounded theory is compatible with alternative existing theories. In this respect, other theories are as much a source of concepts as the empirical research on which grounded theory is based.[8] In its early stages, the form of the theory will consist primarily of scattered notes, comments and tentative propositions as in Table 3. Later on, as categories

TABLE 2. DISPLACEMENT AND RELOCATION: SOME EMPIRICAL GENERALIZATIONS

<u>Susceptibility</u> (differential exposure to probability of being displaced)

    The poor, elderly, minorities and those of low educational attainment are most likely to be displaced and relocated (Burdge and Johnson 1973; Llewellyn 1974).

    Higher socioeconomic status facilitates separation from place (Burdge and Ludtke 1973; Ludtke and Burdge 1970).

<u>Attitudes</u> (prior to displacement; "anticipatory migration")

    Positive attitudes are likely when people perceive real benefits for themselves or their community. Negative attitudes arise from the feeling that they will lose something because of the project (Burdge and Johnson 1973; Burdge and Ludtke 1973; Ludtke and Burdge 1970).

    People with favorable attitudes toward reservoir projects tend to be young, have high vested interests in the project, and have an extremely low identification with their place of residence. Because of these factors, they tend to be less apprehensive about relocating than others (Burdge and Ludtke 1973).

<u>Consequences</u> (impact of relocation)

    A major problem for most relocatees is the financial costs of moving. These include loss of income due to the move, litigation costs, low market value of land sold and the high costs of replacement housing (Burdge and Johnson 1973; Llewellyn 1974; Mack 1974; Williams, Jr. 1969).

    The difficulty of forming new personal and community associations, coupled with loss of or separation from established friends, are among the most important social-psychological costs of relocation (Burdge and Johnson 1973; Booth and Camp 1974; Llewellyn 1974).

    Relocatees tended not to be alienated from their community, but from the agency responsible for carrying out the relocation program. The ability to maintain group associations was a factor which worked against alienation from community (Napier 1972).

Source: Shields (1974)

(<u>Note</u>: This illustrative inventory of empirical generalizations is compiled from only eight studies.)

TABLE 3. GROUNDED THEORY: NOTES ON CONCEPTS AND TENTATIVE PROPOSITIONS

Susceptibility

Those most likely to be relocated tend to have poor life chances. In general they have low social status, low incomes and lack political power and influence. This suggests that they are not likely to be able to organize effectively in protection of their interests--i.e., they have low organizational potential. Some observers have argued that public agencies charged with planning projects attempt to locate them in areas where organized resistance is improbable--at least this is one siting criterion. As a tentative proposition, susceptibility is inversely related to life chances and organizational potential. But further comparisons need to be made with cases where (1) groups with relatively high life chances and organizational potential are targeted for relocation, if indeed such a case can be found and (2) groups with poor life chances are able to resist and reverse relocation decisions.

Attitudes

Attitudes toward projects are, not surprisingly, strongly associated with the degree of personal dislocation expected. This is apt to be most severe for potential relocatees, whose interests are seldom served by projects. Do those groups also tend to have strong identification with place? If so, there is an important link between attitudes and life chances, which are both "maladaptive" in this context. Their joint effects could produce great stress. Even more basically, what underlies a strong identification with place? The findings assembled thus far suggest that if people perceive their capacity to adapt to change as generally high, then they are also likely to be less apprehensive of moving and to have more favorable attitudes toward projects.

Consequences

A significant effect of relocation is its tendency to work toward the further disadvantage of the disadvantaged, in spite of compensation programs by official agencies. The economic effects of relocation are seldom offset by these programs and since the overall adaptive capacity of these relocatees is low anyway, this transition is analogous to downward mobility. The social-psychological effects of relocation are frequently severe stress and role disorganization. However, when group continuity is maintained, these effects seem less severe. Overall, though, displacement and relocation due to construction projects create a class of involuntary benefactors (Smith and Hogg 1971) who are forced to pay disproportionately for the costs of project-induced change while getting few, if any, benefits. The impact of displacement and relocation on the social integration of small communities is a problem of considerable policy importance.

are more densely developed, as relationships between categories are established and as its various parts are integrated, the theory can be stated in a more testable form.[9]

<u>Verification</u>. The information needed to verify grounded theory in SIA is of the same kind that was used to generate it: single and comparative case studies. The criteria for verification shift, however, to research designs and methods that are consistent with the specifications for controlled verificational studies. The decision about what research designs and methods are appropriate depends on the circumstances of the research and the informed judgment and training of the researcher. As I have explained it, grounded theory emphasizes theory construction as a continuing <u>process</u>, even though the theory may be taken as provisionally complete when it reaches a certain level of closure. Thus particular areas of the theory may be well developed while the connections between areas may be weak. This would have a bearing on the testability of the theory. The more a theory is elaborated and integrated, the greater the possibilities for testing it.

The logic of verification demands that empirical statements derived from a theory be tested through observation. If those observations are inconsistent with the empirical derivations from the theory, then we have good reason to believe the theory is wrong. If, however, our observations are compatible with the theory, we have reason to believe the theory is more plausible or more credible than it was before. But the crucial test of a theory is its capacity to provide a better explanation than an alternative theory (Stinchcombe 1968: 13-28).

The logic of verifying grounded theory is no different from that described above. That is, there are no "unique" ways to test grounded theory. It should be noted, however, that the process of grounded theory construction has an internal verificational logic insofar as the constant comparative analysis of cases results in the theory's extension or revision. This sense of "verification" should not be confused with the more formal procedure described above. Yet it does point to a way in which theory construction and verification can be simultaneously advanced.

<u>Conclusion</u>
The strategy proposed in this paper is intended as a practical, immediately useable approach to discovering the theoretical implications of social impact studies. It can be applied to both primary and secondary data analysis. The strategy is incremental and cumulative and places strong emphasis on the importance of theory which is consistently in contact with empirical research. On these accounts, grounded theory promises to be a most feasible solution to ordering the theoretically inchoate field of social impact assessment.

<u>Footnotes</u>

1. The theoretical significance of SIA is that it constitutes a strategic focus in social science for developing a paradigm for the study of planned social change.

2. These phases are the crucial sequence of the eleven "assessment steps" outlined in Section 122 Guidelines (Office of the Chief of Engineers 1972). These steps are discussed more fully in Wolf (1974: 21-28).

3. Impact _studies_ are distinguished from impact _statements_ in this paper. A study is any piece of research that reports on _observed_, verifiable impacts--in effect, a type of evaluation research. A statement, on the other hand, is typically produced at the behest of governmental body or private concern _prior_ to the construction of a project and in accordance with the mandate of the National Environmental Policy Act and other legal requirements. Thus, a statement is a social _forecast_ of anticipated impacts. Grounded theory is generated from impact studies, even though the practical payoffs come through improved forecasting capabilities and more reliable impact statements.

4. "In theoretical sampling, no one kind of data on a category nor technique for data collection is necessarily appropriate. Different kinds of data give the analyst different views or vantage points from which to understand a category and to develop its properties; these different views we have called _slices of data_..." (Glaser and Strauss 1967: 65). Denzin (1970: 301-3) takes a similar position.

5. As Glaser and Strauss argue, "Since accurate evidence is not so crucial for generating theory, the kind of evidence, as well as the number of cases, is also not so crucial. A single case can indicate a general conceptual category or property; a few more cases can confirm the indication" (p. 30). This argument does not, of course, apply to verification of the theory.

6. There are some interesting similarities between grounded theory and "analytic induction." Analytic induction is a qualitative method which employs an intensive and extensive case study approach for discovering universal causal generalizations. It seeks to formulate relationships that are unexceptionably true--i.e., it allows no exceptions to a proposition. According to Manning (1971), this is a disadvantage of the method since it is unable to deal with degrees of magnitude and variation in phenomena, a criticism which cannot be leveled at grounded theory. Manning maintains that there are four advantages to analytic induction: its capacity (1) for generating conceptual formulations, (2) for inducing revision in theories, (3) for integrating sampling models (through "judgment" or theoretical sampling) and (4) its potential for creating processu**al theories.** These strengths are all present in grounded theory.

7. The domain of studies includes research on nuclear power plants, highways, dams, reservoirs, flood plain management, new and renewed towns, large installations (such as military bases and industrial plants), etc. They may pertain to social units of various types, but typically focus on community and regional impacts and different groups in these areas.

8. Bensman and Vidich (1970) speak of the "heuristic" functions of theories in field research. By this they mean that a variety of theories which seem relevant to particular analytical problems arising in field work can be used as critical perspectives from which to judge empirically grounded research hypotheses. "Each of the theories provides a set of questions asked of the

data, and the data lead to the continuous destruction of unproductive theories whenever the theories no longer yield new data or fail to solve the original problem. The reverse is also true: the theory may lead to the evocation of new data by focusing observation and its assessment" (p. 332).

9. One problem which is not addressed in this paper is that of combining theory statements of different types and at different levels into an integrated summary. A recent provocative contribution to the solution of this problem is Mullins (1974).

References

Bensman, Joseph and Arthur Vidich (1970) "Social Theory in Field Research," pp. 328-39 in William J. Filstead (ed.), Qualitative Methodologies. Chicago: Markham.

Booth, Alan and Henry Camp (1974) "Housing Relocation and Family Social Integration Patterns," Journal of the American Institute of Planners, 40, 2 (March), 124-28.

Burdge, Rabel J. and K. Sue Johnson (1973) Social Costs and Benefits of Water Resource Construction. Research Report No. 64. Lexington: Water Resources Institute, University of Kentucky.

Burdge, Rabel J. and Richard L. Ludtke (1973) "Social Separation among Displaced Rural Families: The Case of Flood Control Reservoirs," pp. 85-108 in W. R. Burch and others (eds.), Social Behavior, Natural Resources and the Environment. New York: Harper and Row.

Denzin, Norman K. (1970) The Research Act--A Theoretical Introduction to Sociological Methods. Chicago: Aldine.

Glaser, Barney G. and Anselm L. Strauss (1967) The Discovery of Grounded Theory: Strategies for Qualitative Research. Chicago: Aldine.

Gouldner, Alvin W. (1970) The Coming Crisis of Western Sociology. New York: Basic Books.

Llewellyn, Lynn G. (1974) "The Social Impact of Urban Highways," pp. 89-108 in C. P. Wolf (ed.), Social Impact Assessment. Milwaukee: Environmental Design Research Association.

Ludtke, Richard L. And Rabel J. Burdge (1970) Evaluation of the Social Impact of Reservoir Construction on the Residential Plans of Displaced Persons in Kentucky and Ohio. Research Report No. 26. Lexington: Water Resources Institute, University of Kentucky.

Mack, Ruth P. (1974) "Criteria for Evaluation of Social Impacts of Flood Management Alternatives," pp. 175-95 in C. P. Wolf (ed.), Social Impact Assessment. Milwaukee: Environmental Design Research Association.

Manning, Peter K. (1971) "Analytic Induction," Paper presented at the 66th Annual Meeting of the American Sociological Association, Denver, CO, 1 September.

Merton, Robert K. (1968) Social Theory and Social Structure. New York: Free Press.

Mullins, Nicholas C. (1974) "Theory Construction from Available Materials: A System for Organizing and Presenting Propositions," American Journal of Sociology, 80, 1 (July), 1-15.

Office of the Chief of Engineers (1972) "Guidelines for Assessment of Economic, Social and Environmental Effects of Civil Works Projects" ER 1105-2-105. Washington, DC: U.S. Army Corps of Engineers, 15 December.

Napier, Ted I. (1972) "Social-Psychological Response to Forced Relocation Due to Watershed Development," Water Resources Bulletin, 8, 2 (August), 784-95.

Shields, Mark S. (1974) Social Impact Assessment: An Analytic Bibliography. IWR Paper 74-P6. Fort Belvoir, VA: U.S. Army Engineer Institute for Water Resources, October.

Smith, Courtland L. and Thomas C. Hogg (1971) "Benefits and Beneficiaries: Contrasting Economic and Cultural Distinctions," Water Resources Research, 7, 2(April), 254-62.

Stinchcombe, Arthur L. (1968) Constructing Social Theories. New York: Harcourt, Brace and World.

Williams, J. Allen, Jr. (1969) "The Effects of Urban Renewal upon a Black Community: Evaluation and Recommendations," Social Science Quarterly, 50, 3(December), 703-12.

Wolf, C. P. (1974) "Social Impact Assessment: The State of the Art," pp. 1-44 in C. P. Wolf (ed.), Social Impact Assessment. Milwaukee: Environmental Design Research Association.

Social Impact Assessment and Cost-Benefit Analysis

Peter G. Sassone
Georgia Institute of Technology

The purpose of this paper is to sketch out, from an economist's viewpoint, the relation between two approaches to project evaluation: social impact assessment (SIA) and cost-benefit analysis (CBA).[1] The central theme is the essential complementarity between the two. This complementarity is no historical accident. The argument is easily made that the recent ascension to prominence of SIA was nourished by the shortcomings of traditional CBA. That is, SIA and CBA initially stood in dialectical contrast. Today, the synthesis is well under way; particularly, as seems most fitting, in a revision of traditional approaches to CBA (Prest and Turvey 1965: 684-85). The term, "CBA," remains; its content, however, has steadily evolved in response to the pressure of SIA.

Three points are covered: Section I briefly reviews CBA methodology. The next section discusses the specific areas of divergence and complementarity between SIA and CBA, and the final section describes an approach which has been employed to weave together CBA and SIA approaches.

I. COST-BENEFIT METHODOLOGY

Following is a brief outline of what has come to be recognized as cost-benefit methodology. The methodology is then compared with and contrasted to the more loosely defined approach of SIA. CBA proceeds in four steps: (1) Defining the Problem, (2) Designing the Analysis, (3) Collecting the Data and (4) Performing the Analysis.

Step 1. Defining the Problem
Although defining the problem to be analyzed may appear to be an almost trivial task, any CBA veteran will testify otherwise. This first step gives direction to the remainder of the analysis. It is here that the decision maker plays a critical role, communicating to the analyst precisely what he wishes to be done. It is the analyst's task to record these desires and elicit whatever information is needed to exactly define the problem. While each project has its own unique features, many aspects of problem definition are common to most. Though such a listing can never be complete, it forms a basic checklist for both the analyst and decision maker.

A. Project scenario: A technical description and a detailed scenario definition of the projects to be analyzed are obviously important initial steps. The main point here is that explicit recognition should be given to all resource inputs and final outputs of the projects, and the calendar time in which they will occur.

B. Base-line scenario: Similarly, a technical description and detailed scenario of the universal alternative--the status quo--should be constructed. Every project has an alternative, even if it is to "do nothing." For to "do nothing" implies a time stream of costs and benefits to society just as a positive project does. Of course, it's exactly this "do-nothing" or <u>base-line</u> scenario with which each project is compared. CBA focuses on how a project will change the <u>base-line</u> time stream of social well-being. Thus, only the <u>differences</u> between the <u>base-line</u> and the <u>with-project</u> time stream are considered in CBA. The "good" differences are the benefits of the project, the "bad" differences are the costs. Since the <u>difference</u> that the project will make is of prime importance, it is essential to have the base-line scenario with which to compare the project scenario.

C. Definition of society: CBA attempts to assess social costs and social benefits; that is, CBA takes the public point of view (see Coase 1960). The value of a project is the sum of its value to each member of society. Clearly then, costs and benefits depend on who is included in "society." For projects at the national level, the usual definition is that society consists of all U.S. citizens. At the regional, state, and local levels, the operational definition of society is not so easily posited. For there are often benefit and cost spillovers (externalities) beyond the stipulated geographical bounds of the project.[2]

D. Constraints on the problem: It may be necessary that a chosen project satisfy a number of diverse constraints. Such constraints may be budgetary, legal, social, political, or institutional.[3] These, of course, must be communicated to the analyst at the start of the CBA. This early communication will enable the analyst to quickly exclude alternative projects which obviously are not feasible.

E. Control variables: Often, all the technical details of a project will not be initially specified by the decision maker. Rather, the analyst will be charged with choosing optimal values for some variables, such as scale, location, start-up time, number of installations, etc. In a strict sense, optimization falls outside the domain of CBA and generally into the domain of operations research. The variables to be optimized, if any, should be clearly distinguished from those to be parameterized. Ordinarily, the latter (sometimes called "state variables") are outside the control of the decision maker and the former are not.

F. Discount rate: The discount rate, the rate at which present and future effects are traded off, is best considered a policy variable, to be set by the decision maker. A single rate may be used, or several values may be considered. The choice of the proper discount rate to employ in a CBA has stimulated a very lively discussion among economists--one which is likely never to be resolved. The fundamental issue revolves around whether the opportunity cost of public investment should be the controlling factor, or whether the social rate of time preference should determine the proper rate. Baumol (1968) presents a persuasive case for the former while Feldstein (1964) argues for the latter. Operationally, the debate has significant consequences, for while Baumol's reasoning leads to rates on the order of 10-12%, Feldstein's leads to rates half as large.

G. Time horizon: The time horizon is also a policy variable, though it is not as volatile an issue as the discount rate. The decision maker must decide how far into the future that costs and benefits are to be projected and thus counted into the net present value of the project. Ordinarily, most costs of a public project are incurred in its early years, so a truncated time horizon has the effect of excluding more benefits than costs from consideration. The discounting process is such that values occurring far into the future add little to present value. Clearly, the higher the discount rate chosen, the shorter the time horizon that need be considered.

Step 2: Designing the Analysis
Formally designing the cost-benefit analysis should be done during the early stages, prior to plunging into data collection and cost and benefit estimation. Six basic points are involved in carrying out the design stage.

A. The problem structure: Determining the analytic structure of the problem follows directly from defining the problem. The purpose here is to determine which measure (e.g., net present value or benefit-cost ratio) to employ in comparing alternatives. The main aspects of structure are the dependence or independence[4] of projects, the type of constraints, and the variables to be optimized. At this stage of the design, the analytic structure of the problem should be written out as carefully as possible and all ambiguities should be uncovered and eliminated.

B. Preliminary identification of costs and benefits: Basically, there are two ways of discovering costs and benefits: searching for affected goods and services or searching for affected persons. In practice, it is useful to employ both of these approaches, remembering however that each is a different way of arriving at the same costs and benefits. That is, either the commodities or the persons approach is a good way to discover effects, but only one can be used to count a cost or benefit. Using both approaches results in double counting.[5] How are the affected commodities and persons to be discovered? A number of complementary ways can be used to suggest what interrelationships exist between the project and the rest of the economy:

- Economic and social theory

- Professional literature dealing with previous similar projects

- The scenarios developed in defining the problem

- Introspection

- Brainstorming with colleagues

- Interviews with interested persons, including the decision maker.

Thus, the result of this step is a list of costs and benefits which are likely to be incurred by each project under consideration.

C. Assessment of the listed costs and benefits: This assessment is with respect to validity and quantifiability. With regard to the former, the analyst must be wary of including transfer payments[6] or sunk costs as social benefits or costs. He must also be sure that true values are not being double counted. It must then be determined whether, to what extent, and in what dimensions each valid cost and benefit can be quantified. This determination requires a cursory survey both of data availability and of the potential for gathering new data.

D. Scope and dimensions of the quantitative analysis: In principle, a CBA should deal with all the costs and benefits of a project. Some of these will be quantified, the others treated in a qualitative fashion. Of necessity, some costs and benefits can be treated only qualitatively, as "intangibles." Among the quantifiable costs and benefits, some may not be quantified in the CBA because of time and budgetary restrictions. Of those which are quantified, some will be put in money terms and others in their own dimensions (incommensurables). However, by no means is there a well-defined boundary between incommensurables and the costs and benefits which have ready dollar values. It is probably best to consider the costs and benefits of a project as lying along a spectrum of "quantifiability," ranging from intangibles through incommensurables to market goods. Intangibles would include the project's effects on such things as social justice, social harmony, personal freedom, democracy, aesthetics, etc. These all involve values beyond the economic and do not exhibit even likely dimensions for measurement, much less actual numerical values. Incommensurables would include lives lost, injuries and illnesses sustained, national defense, other public goods such as recreation facilities, and some externalities. Evidently, incommensurables may involve economic or non-economic values. Their distinguishing characteristic is that they may be readily quantified, but not in money terms. For example, measurements can easily be made of number of lives lost, number of work days lost due to illiness, or number of user-days of a recreation facility. Measurements can even be made of national defense as a <u>probability</u> of forestalling pre-emptive nuclear attacks, or as a <u>percentage</u> of population survival after an enemy's first strike. Of course, to a greater or lesser extent, these measurements are not easily converted into dollar values.

Market goods are agricultural products, textiles, electricity, auto servicing, etc.--any good or service exchanged through a market. The most important feature of a market good is the existence of a corresponding market price which, subject to some important qualifications, directly measures social value in money terms.[7]

Thus, with regard to a spectrum of "quantifiability," all nonquantifiable costs and benefits fall into the intangibles range and all quantifiable effects are in the incommensurable to market goods range. Only effects in the market goods range, however, are readily measured in money terms. There is no clearcut boundary between any of the ranges in the spectrum and it often happens that some cost or benefit will appear to lie somewhere between incommensurables and market goods. Such an effect will be readily measurable in nonmonetary terms but will also appear convertible into a meaningful dollar value. One of the major problems faced by the analyst is determining how far to go in converting apparent incommensurables into dollar **values**. Some observers would argue that the analyst should convert all effects into dollar values, even intangibles. This notion--total conversion into dollar values--has probably been the greatest source of criticism for CBA. Fortunately, the advocates of that notion seem to be waning in strength.

On the other hand, a CBA which fails to convert very many effects into dollars will not be a successful decision aid. For the decision maker will then be forced to compare projects on the basis of two- or three-dozen dimensions, a situation not too far removed from eyeballing raw data. Once again, then, how far is the analyst to go in converting seeming incommensurables into dollar values? Although there is no categorical answer, the decision maker can specify to the analyst those apparent incommensurables for which he can accept dollar conversions and those for which he cannot. The decision maker and the analyst can jointly determine the dimensionality of the results. In effect, with the technical aid of the analyst in elucidating relevant tradeoffs, the decision maker determines the cut-off point in the cost-benefit spectrum between effects usefully measured in dollars and those better measured in their own dimensions. This process would appear to be the only way an analyst can insure that his approach to quantification will be acceptable to the decision maker and the results will be credible and thus useful as a decision aid.

Step 3: Collecting the Data
Although it is not necessary to go into a detailed discussion on collecting data, a few common sense considerations deserve mention. Planning the format of the collected data is extremely important. The format should specify the number of significant figures for each entry and should allow easy access to any part of the data, and should be capable of quick updating. The data should be gathered from original sources when possible. Using original sources minimizes the risk of recording errors which creep into transcribed data. All the qualifications to the data should be accurately recorded. Finally, the sources of all data should be recorded for eventual reference in preparing footnotes and bibliography.

Step 4: Performing the Analysis
The essence of this task is the use of raw data and economic and social theory to make good estimates of social costs and benefits. Market prices or "shadow prices" form the basis for these estimates.[8] If a thorough job of designing the analysis (discussed above) has been done, the analyst hopefully will encounter no major problems at this stage. Performing a thorough job does not mean that every estimate will be precise, only that any lack of precision will be acknowledged either verbally or in a formal sensitivity analysis. The quantitative analysis includes finding "best" point estimates of the social value of a project along with a sensitivity analysis. Sensitivity analysis is an imposing term under whose rubric common sense analytics are carried out. As the name suggests, sensitivity analysis attempts to discern the sensitivity (or robustness) of results to the various underlying assumptions, parameter estimates or structural forms. Essentially this is accomplished by varying the assumptions, etc., and observing the effect on the results. In this manner "crucial" assumptions, etc., are discovered, and further attention may be given to improving their quality.

Performing the qualitative analysis, defined to include an examination of non-economic effects, was discussed under 2.D above. In this part of the analysis, all nonquantified effects are described as clearly as possible.

These four steps, then, summarize the essential ingredients of cost-benefit methodology.

II. COMPARISONS

A principal difference between SIA and CBA lies not in their respective scopes but in their stage of development. SIA is a problem area without a well-defined and widely accepted methodological approach. Indeed, it is an aim of this volume to further the search for, and development of, a consistent methodology. In stark contrast, CBA embodies a comparatively well-defined and widely accepted methodology. Advancing CBA to this state of development has been neither easy nor costless. Uniformity and rigor take their toll in myopia and undue rigidity. Nonetheless, a consistent framework for analysis has emerged.

Both SIA and CBA address the selfsame question: given some proposed action (typically governmental and often involving advanced technology), is that action in the best interests of society? CBA assumes that a meaningful answer can be formulated by valuing the good and bad effects in monetary terms. One assumes not that all effects can be monetized, but that those that can are a reasonable guide for the decision maker. Further, one assumes that market, or market-like, values are meaningful quantities. SIA, I believe, will never settle on a single measure of worth to the extent that CBA has adopted market, or market-like, valuation. Rather, at least several widely accepted measures will always be in view, with new measures constantly arising and occasionally supplanting the established ones. The important problems of the day will shape SIA.

The most crucial difference between CBA and SIA, and simultaneously the reason for their harmony, is the nature of the problems each is suited to handle. CBA is designed for problems where the impact is broad but shallow. SIA's forte is the narrow and deep impact. By this is meant that a project which impacts many people, but none substantially, is efficiently and realistically evaluated through CBA. A project which affects relatively few people substantially calls for SIA.

To see this, recall that economics is a study of "marginalism." In particular, even under ideal circumstances, a market price measures only the value of the marginal units of a good or service consumed. To the extent that effects are intra-marginal, the methods of economics become less precise and, in many cases, less applicable. Thus, a substantial impact on a person does not lend itself to economic valuation. Further, economics draws its inferences about values to particular persons, not by observations of those persons, but by observations of the prices they face. Thus, it is not difficult to extend economic analysis across a broad group of individuals, since the specific individuals need never be observed. On the other hand, the methods of SIA are far more individual-oriented. Survey research, community studies, social network analyses, etc., demand the researcher give attention to the personal circumstances of the individual. Clearly, research of this type is best applied to a limited group.

In addition to CBA's inability to adequately cope with valuing substantial effects on the individual, CBA is equally incapable of comparing the severity of impacts across different individuals. Economics' traditional difficulty in objectively evaluating alternative distributions of income is a serious liability in project analysis. The approach of CBA is to value any given dollar loss (and let's assume that a dollar valuation may be found) at its face value, independent of the financial circumstances of the impacted person. Thus, a $100 loss to a $50,000 per year executive is counted equally with a $100 loss to a $5,000 per year laborer. Since the problem here lies in finding a way to adequately take account of the individuals' circumstances, I believe the sociologist's more intimate concern with the individual is more likely to result in an acceptable approach than the economist's abstraction of homo economicus. The making of interpersonal comparisons is an area ripe for breakthrough in SIA.

Two final points of complementarity between SIA and CBA are the likely areas of intangibles and effect identification. As discussed above, intangibles are those effects which do not even exhibit reasonable dimensions for quantification. They are often effects with values beyond the economic. Thus, the socially oriented measures of SIA can prove valuable in handling those aspects of a project analysis.

In complex projects, the _identification_ of impacts is the most important part of the analysis, and the part least amenable to coverage by a single methodology. Economic methodology, the foundation of CBA, has a peculiarly narrow range in impact search. The varied and important ties of individuals to neighborhood, family, community, institutions, etc., receive only passing notice. Yet these may be the area of greatest impact in many project types.

In sum, SIA and CBA are, if properly used, completely complementary. The rigorous and well-defined procedures of CBA are reasonable and efficient valuation techniques for broad and shallow impacts. The individual-oriented approaches of SIA are necessary and proper for evaluating the narrow and deep impacts.[9] How can both of these approaches be integrated in a single, consistent, project analysis?

III. A TENTATIVE STEP TOWARD UNIFICATION

As part of a recent study of CBA methodology for NASA, the following approach was suggested as a tentative first step toward unified project analysis. As will be evident, a great deal remains to be done. The approach hinges on extensive interaction with the decision maker along with an iterative procedure. The approach is readily integrated with the step-by-step CBA methodology outlined above.

Step 1. Specify the set of benefit and cost impacts, S.

Step 2. Choose S', a subset of S, which includes the expected most significant impacts.

Step 3. As part of the research design, determine those impacts (from S') which will be evaluated via CBA, and those via SIA.

Step 4. Perform the CBA and the SIA.

Step 5. Present the results to the decision maker. Assuming the CBA is performed in terms of present value analysis, the situation is:

Present Value of CBS Benefits + Favorable Social Impacts

+ Other Benefits in S-S' = Present Value of CBA Costs

+ Unfavorable Social Impacts + Other Costs in S-S'.

Step 6. Decision maker determines whether the present state of information is sufficient for a decision, or whether additional analysis is required. If the former, STOP. If the latter, do at least one of the following:

(a) Expand the scope of S' to more fully account for all impacts;

(b) Use CBA to evaluate an impact previously analyzed via SIA;

(c) Use SIA to evaluate an impact previously analyzed via CBA.

The proper choice of a-c depends on the analyst and decision maker's joint determination of where the hope for greatest progress lies.

Step 7. Go to Step 4.[10]

Of course, this is merely a hueristic approach, and there is no assurance of convergence to a correct solution. Nonetheless, in some preliminary applications, progress toward better solutions appears to have been made. This approach was used in an evaluation of potential wind energy projects for NASA. In that application at least, the approach appeared fruitful. More importantly, it carries monetary quantification only as far as necessary for a decision.

Footnotes
1. We prefer the term "cost-benefit analysis" to "benefit-cost analysis" mainly because the former does not suggest the benefit-cost ratio, a criterion academic economists have long since abandoned but which persists in Federal circles. In addition, cost-benefit analysis appears to be the preferred term among academicians. See, e.g., Dasgupta and Pearce (1972), Feldstein (1964), Mishan (1971), Musgrave (1969), Prest and Turvey (1965).

2. A good discussion of the complexities surrounding this point is contained in Rothenberg (1970).

3. A typical budgetary constraint, for example, might be that the initial cost of the project cannot exceed a given amount. A legal constraint could be the preclusion of output pricing which would discriminate against certain classes of project users. A political constraint might be that a majority of affected persons are favorably affected.

4. When two or more projects may be chosen for implementation, it is important to know whether the projects are dependent on, or independent of, each other. One project is independent of another if the net present value of the first is invariant with respect to whether the second project is implemented or not. Projects are dependent otherwise. The significance of this distinction is that when dependence prevails, all combinations of projects must be evaluated as single projects. This increases the difficulty of the evaluation since, for example, an original set of six projects gives rise to 64 combinations.

5. In general, the more complex the effects of a project, the easier it is to overlook costs or benefits, and the more likely it is that both the goods and persons approaches will prove helpful. Unfortunately, it also seems to be the case that the more complex the effects of a project, the more difficult it will be to unravel "goods" effects from "persons" effects.

6. Transfer payments are transfers of funds from one agent to another without a corresponding increase in current production. Examples of transfer payments are food stamps, social security, and unemployment compensation.

7. The principle qualification is the absence of external economies or diseconomies (or simply, externalities). An externality exists when an economic agent does not bear the full costs or gain the full benefits of his decisions.

That is, others are incidentally harmed or favored. The classic example, of course, is pollution. The polluter harms others by his own actions. He, himself, does not pay the costs of his polluting the environment. Thus the market price of waste disposal (into the atmosphere or into a water course) is zero while the actual cost is positive.

8. Unfortunately, even a cursory discussion of shadow pricing is beyond the scope of this paper. See Mishan (1971) or Sassone and Schaffer (forthcoming).

9. C. P. Wolf comments, "I accept that SIA should study impacts in depth, but it does not follow that their treatment in that fashion is individualistic (as opposed to collective)--indeed, a main criticism of CBA from the sociological viewpoint would be its social atomism."

10. The iteration through steps 4, 5, 6 sharpens the decision maker's view of the scope and magnitude of project impacts. We are not necessarily convinced that iteration produces "better numbers," but we are convinced it leads to better decisions. It has been stated (Prest and Turvey 1965) that CBA is simply "a way of setting out the factors which need to be taken into account in making certain economic choices." To the extent that this "setting out" is the crucial consideration, the different facets of the problem exposed by iteration seem sure to be a decision aid.

References

Baumol, W. J. (1968) "On the Social Rate of Discount," American Economic Review, 58 (September), 788-802.

Coase, H. (1960) "The Problem of Social Cost," Journal of Law and Economics, 3, 1-44.

Dasgupta, P. and D. W. Pearce (1972) Cost Benefit Analysis. New York: Harper and Row.

Feldstein, M. S. (1964) "The Social Time Preference Discount Rate in Cost-Benefit Analysis," Economic Journal, 74, 2 (June), 360-379.

Mishan, E. J. (1971) Cost-Benefit Analysis. London: Allen and Unwin.

Musgrave, R. A. (1969) "Cost-Benefit Analysis and the Theory of Public Finance," Journal of Economic Literature, 7, 797-806.

Prest, A. R. and R. Turvey (1965) "Cost-Benefit Analysis: A Survey," Economic Journal, 300 (December), 683-735.

Rothenberg, Jerome (1970) "Local Decentralization and the Theory of Optimal Government," pp. 31-64 in Julius Margolis (ed.), The Analysis of Public Output. New York: National Bureau of Economic Research.

Sassone, P. G. and Schaffer, W. A. (forthcoming) Cost-Benefit Analysis: A Handbook. New York: Academic Press.

The proper choice of a-c depends on the analyst and decision maker's joint determination of where the hope for greatest progress lies.

Step 7. Go to Step 4.[10]

Of course, this is merely a hueristic approach, and there is no assurance of convergence to a correct solution. Nonetheless, in some preliminary applications, progress toward better solutions appears to have been made. This approach was used in an evaluation of potential wind energy projects for NASA. In that application at least, the approach appeared fruitful. More importantly, it carries monetary quantification only as far as necessary for a decision.

Footnotes

1. We prefer the term "cost-benefit analysis" to "benefit-cost analysis" mainly because the former does not suggest the benefit-cost ratio, a criterion academic economists have long since abandoned but which persists in Federal circles. In addition, cost-benefit analysis appears to be the preferred term among academicians. See, e.g., Dasgupta and Pearce (1972), Feldstein (1964), Mishan (1971), Musgrave (1969), Prest and Turvey (1965).

2. A good discussion of the complexities surrounding this point is contained in Rothenberg (1970).

3. A typical budgetary constraint, for example, might be that the initial cost of the project cannot exceed a given amount. A legal constraint could be the preclusion of output pricing which would discriminate against certain classes of project users. A political constraint might be that a majority of affected persons are favorably affected.

4. When two or more projects may be chosen for implementation, it is important to know whether the projects are dependent on, or independent of, each other. One project is independent of another if the net present value of the first is invariant with respect to whether the second project is implemented or not. Projects are dependent otherwise. The significance of this distinction is that when dependence prevails, all combinations of projects must be evaluated as single projects. This increases the difficulty of the evaluation since, for example, an original set of six projects gives rise to 64 combinations.

5. In general, the more complex the effects of a project, the easier it is to overlook costs or benefits, and the more likely it is that both the goods and persons approaches will prove helpful. Unfortunately, it also seems to be the case that the more complex the effects of a project, the more difficult it will be to unravel "goods" effects from "persons" effects.

6. Transfer payments are transfers of funds from one agent to another without a corresponding increase in current production. Examples of transfer payments are food stamps, social security, and unemployment compensation.

7. The principle qualification is the absence of external economies or diseconomies (or simply, externalities). An externality exists when an economic agent does not bear the full costs or gain the full benefits of his decisions.

That is, others are incidentally harmed or favored. The classic example, of course, is pollution. The polluter harms others by his own actions. He, himself, does not pay the costs of his polluting the environment. Thus the market price of waste disposal (into the atmosphere or into a water course) is zero while the actual cost is positive.

8. Unfortunately, even a cursory discussion of shadow pricing is beyond the scope of this paper. See Mishan (1971) or Sassone and Schaffer (forthcoming).

9. C. P. Wolf comments, "I accept that SIA should study impacts in depth, but it does not follow that their treatment in that fashion is individualistic (as opposed to collective)--indeed, a main criticism of CBA from the sociological viewpoint would be its social atomism."

10. The iteration through steps 4, 5, 6 sharpens the decision maker's view of the scope and magnitude of project impacts. We are not necessarily convinced that iteration produces "better numbers," but we are convinced it leads to better decisions. It has been stated (Prest and Turvey 1965) that CBA is simply "a way of setting out the factors which need to be taken into account in making certain economic choices." To the extent that this "setting out" is the crucial consideration, the different facets of the problem exposed by iteration seem sure to be a decision aid.

References

Baumol, W. J. (1968) "On the Social Rate of Discount," American Economic Review, 58 (September), 788-802.

Coase, H. (1960) "The Problem of Social Cost," Journal of Law and Economics, 3, 1-44.

Dasgupta, P. and D. W. Pearce (1972) Cost Benefit Analysis. New York: Harper and Row.

Feldstein, M. S. (1964) "The Social Time Preference Discount Rate in Cost-Benefit Analysis," Economic Journal, 74, 2 (June), 360-379.

Mishan, E. J. (1971) Cost-Benefit Analysis. London: Allen and Unwin.

Musgrave, R. A. (1969) "Cost-Benefit Analysis and the Theory of Public Finance," Journal of Economic Literature, 7, 797-806.

Prest, A. R. and R. Turvey (1965) "Cost-Benefit Analysis: A Survey," Economic Journal, 300 (December), 683-735.

Rothenberg, Jerome (1970) "Local Decentralization and the Theory of Optimal Government," pp. 31-64 in Julius Margolis (ed.), The Analysis of Public Output. New York: National Bureau of Economic Research.

Sassone, P. G. and Schaffer, W. A. (forthcoming) Cost-Benefit Analysis: A Handbook. New York: Academic Press.

Using Cost-Benefit Analysis in Social Impact Assessment: Hazards and Promise

Jeff V. Conopask*
United States Department of Agriculture

Robert R. Reynolds*
United States Environmental Protection Agency

INTRODUCTION

In recent years, criticism of traditional economic cost-benefit analysis (CBA) has intensified due to the need for environmental impact statements and increasing evidence of adverse, unforeseen consequences of public sector policy and investment decisions. Other social sciences, notably sociology, have responded to a concern for the distributive, higher-order and extra-economic effects of public programs with a broader-based analysis called "social impact assessment" (SIA). Unfortunately, an integrated mode of analysis which neatly interfaces economics and sociology has not yet been developed. This paper will explore the use of "appropriate" economic analysis in establishing a valid base for SIA and will identify economic linkages (points of transition) to social impact issues.

A COMMON DILEMMA

CBA is utilized for assessing the profitability of a public project or a change in government policy. Conceptually, CBA is applied welfare economic theory. This means the analyst makes the following simplifying assumptions about society: (1) full employment, (2) perfect resource mobility, (3) perfect knowledge, and (4) no external economies or diseconomies. The test of the validity of CBA must rest with the extent to which the assumptions fit reality because, by definition, simplifying assumptions enable the analyst to eliminate certain issues from empirical consideration.

At its simplest, CBA is a ratio of benefits to costs, which, if greater than unity, indicates a net economic return to society. The denominator of the ratio reflects the costs of the project--not only investment costs, but also annual operating costs. These costs must be placed into a temporal perspective with an appropriate social discount rate. The costs utilized are the market prices of the inputs in the project. The benefits may or may not be estimated using market prices. If a flood control project will produce irrigation benefits to farmers, then the net income from the increased agricultural production can be considered a benefit. Project benefits (e.g., recreation) are not always directly valued in the market-

---
*Views expressed in this paper are the authors' and do not necessarily reflect those of the U.S. Department of Agriculture or the U.S. Environmental Protection Agency.

place, however. In this case, an indirect method must be utilized. Since market prices reflect a buyer's willingness to pay, surveys or related procedures are often used to estimate the upper limits of "willingness."

Assessment of secondary effects is especially critical where the neo-classical assumptions cited previously are not met. But in practice CBA usually only includes primary, direct effects. Indirect, secondary effects on the regional economy are not included, nor are environmental externalities and interregional effects of impacted economic sectors.[1] To the extent these changes occur, important shifts in social structure and population dynamics can occur on a local basis.

Equilibrium Analysis
Long-standing conventions within the CBA approach account for the neglect of secondary effects. As Prest and Turvey (1965) have noted:

> ...C/B analysis as generally understood is a technique for making decisions within a framework which has to be decided upon in advance, and which involves a wide range of considerations, many of them of a political or social character. If investment decisions are so large relative to a given economy . . . that they are likely to alter the constellation of relative outputs and prices over the whole economy, the standard technique is likely to fail us, for nothing else than some sort of general equilibrium approach would suffice in such cases.

One must also use caution in utilizing the equilibrium concept, however. Both sociological and economic perspectives which subscribe to equilibrium analysis of social decision-making introduce certain biases in their assessment due to preoccupations with the integrity of the "whole" system.

Vilfredo Pareto was a key transitional figure between classical positivist equilibrim analysis in both modern sociological and economic theory. Subsequently there have been variations in approach to equilibrium conceptions within each discipline, but there are major similarities which have important implications for impact analysis. A notion of "balance" lies at the heart of the matter. "Equilibrium" as defined by Pareto (1935, IV: 1432-53) refers to some state in society such that, if subjected to some modification at variance from those it usually undergoes, a reaction at once occurs tending to restore its "normal" state. The problem with this formulation is that a precise definition of what the system is and what constitutes a "normal" state are generally lacking. The result is a tendency to see almost any disturbance in an economic or the large social system as touching off reciprocal adjustments in system parts that will utlimately return the system to normalcy. This view of course has been frequently criticized for its static biases by modern social theorists.

---

1. According to Long (1970), regional benefits result from the following conditions: (1) employed resources are shifted to more productive use, (2) employed resources are employed closer to optimum capacity and (3) unemployed resources are employed as a result of the project. Similarly, regional costs may be created for essentially opposite reasons. Interregional effects are normally considered as Pareto irrelevant (see below), but may well be significant in a grants economy, or if they result in a change in interregional competitive advantage.

Dynamic equilibrium and open system variants of equilibrium theories attempt to counteract criticism of the static bias in Pareto equilibrium approaches by allowing systems to undergo change over time--achieving balance or stability without necessarily re-establishing initial conditions. Although the static criticism has been overcome to some extent, the process of focusing analysis on change at various points in time has produced only limited results. Successful impact forecasting (and retrospective analysis) depends on the ability of the analyst to define the manner in which the social or economic units are articulated in the system, what the boundaries of the system are, and what an equilibrium level is, i.e., what a "restored system" looks like at another point in time. Fulfillment of these criteria has yet to be realized by social analysts. Ironically, it would appear dynamic conceptions of equilibrium have introduced fewer constraints into the process of defining a system in order to meet the static criticism, but at the cost of rendering tenuous the process of differentiating altered forms of the original system from totally "new" systems.

Despite these conceptual difficulties, the tendency has been to assume a homeostatic or self-equilibrating tendency in society and to proceed without much concern for internal consequences that may adversely affect selected components and participants as the system undergoes realignment through time. Practitioners of dynamic systems approaches still tend to ignore the question of the extent to which non-focal or "secondary" goals and objectives of the system are actually satisfied by the system's adjustments to inputs such as policy actions.

To its credit, the equilibrium balance notion draws explicit attention to the interrelationships and interdependencies between social system parts. In practice, however, because of the implicit concern for the integrity of the whole and the belief that disruptions within society are either appropriately constrained by the system or that they ultimately produce a new level of equilibrium, the consequences of change over time for system parts or individuals are frequently ignored. Thus, there is a tendency to ignore unplanned change; to approach planned change with a single-minded concern for efficiency of resource allocation and use; and to focus this concern on the system at its most general (i.e., national) level.

Pareto Optimality
Another failing of conventional CBA results from strict adherence to Pareto welfare criteria. These criteria state that a social policy measure (such as a pesticide restriction) is desirable if it results in either (1) everyone being made better off, or (2) someone being made better off without anyone being made worse off.[2] It is generally assumed, however, that positive economics states nothing about equity and is concerned solely with efficiency; thus, the theory tacitly takes the prevailing wealth, income and property right distribution as given and, implicitly, as socially acceptable. If however a social policy measure has uncounted, unintended, secondary effects (quantitative or qualitative) which result in changes in the formal and informal property right bundles (citizen control of material and

---
2. The literature has been witness to a large controversy over the composition and construction of the social welfare function. Our tentative approach is to rely on goals socially legitimated through the legislative process.

symbolic resources) previously accepted as appropriate, then the Pareto criteria may be unfulfilled.[3]

Of course, the more familiar version of secondary benefits and costs are the pecuniary ones stemming from relative price changes of inputs and outputs in a general equilibrium world. Those changes originate from a change in the quantity supplied or price of a service, and the concept of economic linkages is utilized to explain this result. In a conventional CBA these changes are usually considered monetary transfers which net to zero in the aggregate and hence are not subject to Pareto criteria. In this analysis, however, the question of real relevance--who pays the cost and who benefits--may be ignored.

The result of acceptance of narrowly-interpreted Pareto criteria for public program managers is a dangerous complacency in believing the program to be good without full cognizance of implicit assumptions and consideration of unintended secondary effects. Mishan (1972: 24) has stated, in reference to externalities, legal arrangements, and welfare distribution, that "in the absence of any systematic research into the question, one can say only that it is not implausible to believe that the introduction of significant disamenities into a large area is likely to reduce the welfare of the more mobile rich less than that of the poor."

Insufficiency of CBA for SIA

Traditional CBA fails then to provide a sound base for assessing social impacts due to insufficient detailing of interactions among various classes of economic units (producers and consumers) and the failure to distinguish those who pay the costs from those who receive the benefits. These omissions result from short cuts in analysis which are acceptable only under extraordinary circumstances. Both problems are once again a function of terminating the analysis with highly aggregated primary impacts and not exploring regional impacts. In fact, the question of who pays, who benefits has been a perennial problem in public program evaluation and has been criticized in the literature on the basis of concerns for equity (Bonnen 1970; Clawson 1975). The equity considerations which prompted the present exploration were mainly the result of concern over environmental externalities and the apparent lack of social decision-making capabilities at the public manager level. As Mishan (1972: 26) observes:

> Many of the spillover considerations do not lend themselves easily to analytic elegance. With respect to environmental spillover--the most urgent economic problem of our fragile civilization--they are more pertinent than those arising from traditional allocative analysis. It is not, of course, hard to understand the somewhat exaggerated weight attached by economists to allocative aspects of an economic problem as distinct, say, from those connected with equity. For the former aspects lend themselves nicely to formal theorizing and, with patience and a little finesse, impressive measures of social losses

---

3. Dales (1972: 58-76) states that "ownership always consists of (1) a set of rights to use property in certain ways (and a set of negative rights or prohibitions, that prevent its use in other ways); (2) a right to prevent others from exercising, or to set the terms on which others may exercise them; and (3) a right to sell your property rights." Property rights are defined also in the Marxian sense of access to and control of resources.

and gains can be foisted on credulous civil servants and a gullible public.

Currently, SIA does not have a culling mechanism to pinpoint the most significant social impacts likely to occur. Properly executed, CBA can provide important assistance to this effort by identifying specific population classes subject to economic shocks. In order to derive this level of sensitivity the thrust of CBA must be directed initially to a determination of both primary and secondary impacts on various classes of economic resources. Differential economic impacts of interest to SIA practitioners include changes in economic diversity, income, employment (quantity, quality, and utilization), public service complexion/demand, tax base, land base, the stock of housing, etc. With this type of focus, the analysis begins to get at economically stimulated social impacts which are otherwise obscured through aggregation in conventional CBA.

REGIONAL ANALYSIS

Since CBA as often practiced merely assesses first order impacts, there is an obvious need for redirection in analytic approach. Unfortunately, second order effects frequently occur in different geographic locations and are separated in time. A pragmatic operational methodology sensitive to secondary impacts is the goal of <u>regional</u> analysis. Its interdisciplinary emphasis has been noted by Meyer (1963). Unlike conventional economics, regional analysis has a geographic focus, be it a watershed, a political unit (e.g., county), or a consumption/export/ import region. This delimitation is quite important, from both practical and theoretical standpoints. The region itself is not necessarily a fixed area but can be redefined according to features of the problem to be addressed and the accessibility of data. The objective is to determine that area which is as homogeneous as possible according to certain boundary criteria (Hochwald 1955; Isard 1972: Ch. 4).

This consideration of an economy in regional terms allows the analyst to work with the concept of interdependence. That is, any economic activity has backward and forward linkage with other sectors (Chenery and Clark 1959: 2-6). The other sectors either supply inputs to the activity in question, or receive that activity's output as an intermediate good or input for futher processing or distribution. This is the so-called multiplier concept, wherein changes in one sector's economic activity ripples forward and backward through the economy.

These economic linkages, relating both priced and unpriced secondary effects (e.g., environmental externalities),have strong implications for the complexion of social activity and, ultimately, social well-being. More specifically, the indirect economic effects of a public sector intervention in the market place influence key social conditions such as residential location, the mix of private and public social services, and changes in short- and long-term access of the population to resources affecting various aspects of social participation.

To operationalize the notions of linkage and multipliers, Paul Eberts (n.d.) has developed social area data files based on a dynamic political economic model of social change. The model attempts to relate aggregate quality of life indicators (e.g., infant mortality, housing quality, etc.) in a region to variations in interregional organizational linkages affecting information and resource flow. According to the Eberts model, variations in extra-local linkages in turn affect key intervening processes of local life, including fluidity (a variable which reflects the volume and flow of political and economic information), income, distributive income equity, migration levels, and differentiation of the community service structure. Eberts applies the concept of multiplier effects (i.e., the cummulative interdependence of a set of economic activities) as a way of expressing and analyzing the extent of differentiation in the community/regional service structure. Ultimately, it appears, quality of life will be expressed as a dynamic function of service differentiation and the other independent variables cited above.

Empirical work on the model is now underway, but clear evaluation and precise specification of the model are not yet possible. The multiplier aspects of the model are consistent with modern economic theory, however. Any exogenous change directed at points within the regional system will induce some multiplier effect (and eventually, perhaps, structural differentiation), depending on the degree of internal systemic linkage. The more inputs produced within the region, or utilized within the region (as intermediate goods or services outputs), the stronger will be the multiplier effect.[4] In any case, the hope is that refinement of Eberts' or similar models will permit association of economic differentiation with key dimensions of social well-being such as relative citizen access to and control over social and economic resources necessary for various aspects of social participation.

These then are some of the prime differences between national aggregate analysis and regional analysis. The former will show only part of the impact from exogenous changes, ignoring other impacted parties and activities. Similarly, for SIA purposes the practice of determining an impact on an "average firm" and generalizing those results over all firms in that specific economic sector in a region is insufficient. Impacts on different size firms need to be ascertained. The input producing and output using sectors directly impacted need attention as well. Once the extent of economic impacts, such as expansion, contraction or relocation, is delineated, the initial efforts in social impact analysis may proceed. Thus, by exploring the interdependencies of the impacted firm(s) and sector(s) in the regional economy, the total direct and secondary effects are detailed, together with a significant portion of those who will be subject to the adjustment stresses of the exogenous change.

The resources to do much of this work (down to the county level) are already well established. Federal agencies such as the Departments of Agriculture and Commerce maintain extensive data files and published reports; other data files and studies exist in many state-level agencies, and in universities. Community economic impact or industrial impact studies have been conducted with varying degrees of sophistication and breadth for a number of years. While the available data can answer many of the questions discussed here, there may be others for which the data base and form of analysis required are still maturing. This does not preclude asking the relevant questions, however.

In the preceding discussion we have attempted to note possible links between policy-related economic changes and social structural changes. It should also be noted that powerful supplementary insights into social structural changes can result from the analysis of property rights changes implicit in program actions and other policy interventions in the private sector.

---

4. Work on the multiplier concept has been advanced from the side of economics by Silvers (1970) and others.

Concluding Observations

In this paper we have tried to stress an approach for expanding traditional cost-benefit analysis using existing economic theory and methodology which at the same time would provide a problem focus for social impact assessment. The need for expanding the traditional analysis has resulted from variance of the applied welfare theory assumptions with reality and the strong potential for unforeseen changes in the formal and informal property rights structure, both effects resulting in unintended and uncounted secondary impacts.

Properly administered CBA satisfies the glaring need in social impact assessment for a culling mechanism to direct sociological investigation to the most intense impacts. To this end, the chain of events ending with social structural disturbance begins with an economic disturbance in a regional setting. The economic disturbance may be a point source such as a water control project or a non-point source such as the usage of chemicals for pest control. Fortunately, this "problem-flagging" application of economic analysis can be implemented using currently available tools.

We proposed that properly conceived regional analysis of economic interdependencies which examines impacts on classes of resources is a constructive approach to the refinement of direct impact CBA. Expansion in scope of this nature will allow social impact assessment to proceed in a more systematic fashion by uncovering and addressing issues requiring sociological analysis. Further, we propose that the branch of economics known as regional analysis is uniquely qualified to fulfill this requirement because of its spatial theoretical orientation and its avowed goal of providing a pragmatic operational methodology for tackling real world problems.

References

Bonnen, James T. (1970) "The Absence of Knowledge of Distributional Impacts: An Obstacle to Effective Public Program Analysis and Decisions," pp. 246-70 in Robert H. Haveman and Julius Margolis (eds.), Public Expenditures and Policy Analysis. Chicago: Markham.

Chenery, Hollis B. and Paul G. Clark (1959) Interindustry Economics. New York: John Wiley.

Clawson, Marion (1975) "A More Comprehensive and Eclectic Approach to Resources and the Environment," pp. 3-10 in Annual Report, Resources for the Future, Inc. Washington, DC: Resources for the Future.

Dales, J. H. (1972) Pollution, Property and Prices. Toronto: University of Toronto Press.

Eberts, Paul R. (n.d.) "Consequences of Changing Social Organization in the Northeast." Unpublished manuscript. Ithaca, NY: Department of Rural Sociology, Cornell University.

Hochwald, Werner (1955) "Conceptual Issues of Regional Income Estimation," in Regional Income, National Bureau of Economic Research Studies in Income and Wealth, Vol. 21. Princeton, NJ: Princeton University Press.

Isard, Walter (1971) Methods of Regional Analysis: An Introduction to Regional Science. Cambridge, MA: M.I.T. Press.

Long, Burl F. (1970) "Concepts and Theoretical Basis for Evaluation of Secondary Impacts," pp. 17-23 in Secondary Impacts of Public Investment in Natural Resources. Miscellaneous Publication No. 117. Washington, DC: Economic Research Service, U.S. Department of Agriculture.

Meyer, J. R. (1963) "Regional Economics: A Survey," American Economic Review, 53, 1 (March), 10-54.

Mishan, E. J. (1972) "The Postwar Literature on Externalities: An Interpretive Essay," Journal of Economic Literature, 9, 1 (March), 1-28.

Pareto, Vilfredo (1935) The Mind and Society. Tr. by Andrew Bongiorno and Arthur Livingston. 4 vols. New York: Harcourt, Brace.

Prest, A. R. and Ralph Turvey (1965) "Cost-Benefit Analysis: A Survey," Economic Journal, 75, 300 (December), 683-735.

Silvers, Arthur L. (1970) "The Structure of Community Income Circulation in an Incidence Multiplier for Development Planning," Journal of Regional Science, 10, 2, 175-189.

Macro and Micro Levels of Analysis in the Social Impact Assessment of a Reservoir Development*

Raghu N. Singh
East Texas State University

The distinction between macro and micro is made in the sociological literature mainly in terms of the size of unit chosen for study. Macro comes from the Greek word udkpo, meaning "large," and micro from ulkpo, meaning "small." Macrosociology looks at the total size, shape, structures and processes involved at large in different dimensions of social experience. At the macrolevel we study "the character of the forest, independently of the trees which compose it" (Ackley 1961). Microsociology, on the other hand, deals with small-scale social phenomena, the "social atoms" of experience. Actually, there is no difference in principle between macrosociology and microsociology--it is simply that macrosociology deals with variables that are highly aggregated. Partly the distinction between the two is a matter of the starting point. While macro-holistic theories such as the Parsonsian model of the social system start with "society in general" and then come to the "units-subsystems of society," the micro-atomistic perspectives start with the "individual-group in particular" and from there draw implications for the total society (Martindale 1960: 501-2; Cohen 1968: 13-15). "Middle-range theories" cut across the distinction between macro and micro sociological problems (Merton 1968: 68).

There is no doubt that the field of social impact assessment (SIA) needs both macro and micro analyses.[1] One should not be allowed to supercede the other, and efforts should be made to build one into the other. In reality, however, that has not been done so far in the SIA literature. The purpose of this paper is to describe the relative merits and demerits of methodological approaches on the macro and micro levels of analysis employed in two different studies assessing the social impacts of a reservoir development in east Texas (Singh 1971; 1975). The major objective is to suggest measures at both levels, especially at the micro level, which might be useful in future social impact studies. Emphasis is placed on micro-level measures because of their great potential utility in revealing aspects of impact which cannot be revealed through macro analysis. Procedures used at the macro and micro levels of the study will be discussed in the following two sections; the final section will present evaluations of both types of procedures.

---

*Research reported herein was conducted under two different projects, "An Environmental Inventory and Survey of the Sulphur River Valley" (Singh 1971) and "Toward a Sociological Interpretation of the Environmental Impact of Watershed Development Projects" (Singh 1975), on which the author worked as co-investigator and principal investigator, respectively. The projects were funded in part by the U.S. Army Corps of Engineers and the U.S. Department of the Interior under the Water Resources Research Act of 1964, as amended. The author expresses his sincere thanks to Kenneth P. Wilkinson and C. P. Wolf for their valuable suggestions toward improving the manuscript.

Macrolevel Study of the Sulphur River Basin

In 1971, the East Texas State University was given a six-month contract by the U.S. Army Corps of Engineers to prepare an "environmental inventory" of the Sulphur River Basin. The inventory of the basin's "environmental conditions" was expected to provide the basic data necessary for preparing an "environmental impact statement" for the proposed Cooper Reservoir Development. The river basin was operationally defined by the Corps of Engineers as consisting of twelve counties (eleven in Texas and one in Arkansas), an area extending from the origin of the Sulphur River in Fannin County, Texas to its confluence with the Red River in Miller County, Arkansas. The basin covers 7,530 square miles and a population of 272,924 (1970 Census). Cooper Dam had been planned for construction at a site almost at the origin of the river. The area closest to the proposed reservoir was expected to benefit most from recreation and water supply while the remaining counties in the basin were expected to gain mainly in terms of flood control.

A multidisciplinary team of social and physical scientists collected data from all twelve counties in the areas of archeology (location of prehistoric sites, artifacts), biology (inventory of algae, mosses, ferns, higher plants, benthic macro-invertebrates, fishes, amphibians, reptiles, insects, birds, mammals), economy (agriculture, industry, wholesale, retail, banking, consumption patterns), geography (climate, hydrology, land use, soil conditions), geology (geomorphology, surface and subsurface stratigraphy, mineral deposits, paleontology), history (cultural growth of the area), recreation (recreational potentials and liabilities of the basin), and sociology (demographic and institutional characteristics, leadership survey).

The sociological analysis in the basin study (Singh 1971) was mainly aimed at an identification of demographic and socioeconomic characteristics of the Sulphur River Basin population and an assessment of attitudes of leaders in communities situated within the boundaries of the basin. Selected reports of the U.S. Bureau of the Census provided descriptions of population characteristics such as rural-urban distribution, occupational distribution, sex ratio, racial composition, distribution of educational levels, income distribution, and housing conditions.

The second part of the sociological analysis examined attitudes of community leaders toward the Cooper Dam. Fifty percent of all incorporated towns (or cities) in the basin's twelve counties were selected randomly. The leaders in each of these communities were selected through a "chain-referral" technique. Using this technique, we entered each community and asked a key position holder (such as mayor, sheriff, or president of local Chamber of Commerce) who the leaders were. We then went to each of those persons named and asked the same question. After compiling a list of names given, those persons were identified as leaders whose names appeared more often than others. In addition to "reputational" leaders, office holders on Soil Conservation and Water Boards were selected from each of these communities. A total of 269 community and water management leaders were interviewed.

A six-page questionnaire, with both fixed-alternative and open-ended questions, was employed in data collection. The data included characteristics of respondents,[2] a vested interest scale,[3] a knowledge of the project scale,[4] participation in local community scale,[5] a scale measuring involvement in water resources development in general,[6] and a scale measuring attitudes toward Cooper Dam.[7] Guttman (1944) scaling procedures were employed in all scale constructions.

The Microlevel Community Study

This study (Singh 1975) was an attempt to identify a set of systematic procedures to assess and evaluate selected social impacts of the Cooper Dam project. The study employed a variety of procedures covering two areas, an action process analysis of the Cooper Dam and an identification of selected aspects of the community field of Cooper (see Table 1). The sequential analysis of an action process and a community structure were instrumental in identifying and assessing selected social impacts of the former on the latter.

TABLE 1. PROCEDURES USED AND IMPACTS IDENTIFIED
IN THE MICROLEVEL COMMUNITY STUDY

	Cooper Dam Action Analysis	Community Survey of Cooper
Procedures Used	Historical review of the action through the use of a guide within framework of five phases. Use of primary and secondary data.	Identification of selected characteristics of the community structure at ecological, cultural and social levels, mainly through a random sample survey of heads of households.
	Delphi Technique	
Impacts Identified	Preparation of preliminary lists of goals of the Cooper Dam project, its impacts on surrounding area, and plausible alternative to it.	Identification of selected impacts on a particular community structure at ecological, cultural, and social levels.
	Ranking each of the project's goals, impacts, and alternatives in terms of relative importance and consensus among judges.	

Action Process

Cooper Reservoir project was viewed as a social process consisting of a temporal sequence of interacting behaviors of individuals and organizations within the framework of five analytical phases of the action process. These were: (1) initiation of the action, (2) organization of sponsorship for the action, (3) goal setting or planning of activities, (4) implementation of plans, and (5) maintenance and evaluation of the action.[8]

A guide consisting of open-ended questions was used to collect the action data from the following sources:

1. Sixteen leaders selected through a snowball technique were personally interviewed using the action guide. Nine of these were voluntary

leaders from local communities close to the dam site; the remaining seven represented influential organizations in the area such as the U.S. Army Corps of Engineers and Soil Conservation District. Most of these actors were reinterviewed when other data were to be collected.

2. A content analysis of a local newspaper in the project area was conducted.

3. Several secondary sources of data provided by the U.S. Army Corps of Engineers were utilized, including pamphlets, work plans, maps, memos, environmental inventories, and other records.

Historical review of Cooper Dam project proved helpful in preparing an initial listing of goals, alternatives and environmental impacts of the project needed in the Delphi approach reported below. Delphi procedures (Gordon and Ament 1969; Dalkey 1969 and others 1972; Clark and Cochran 1972; Crawford 1972) were then used to identify and rank the project's goals, environmental impacts, and alternatives. Three procedural steps were followed:

1. <u>Construction of questionnaire:</u> Sections in the Delphi questionnaire were concerned with the major goals, past and future impacts, and plausible alternatives of the Cooper Dam project. The items under the first and third sections were scaled in terms of a four-level response ranging from "highly important" to "unimportant." The impact statements under the second section were scaled in terms of degree of importance as well as "negative" or "positive" direction of each impact. In addition, each impact statement called for an evaluation by respondents whether the impact had alreadry occurred or was expected to take place in the future. Each section was left open-ended so that respondents could add and react to additional items, if they wished.

2. <u>Selection of respondents:</u> The Delphi approach requires that respondents be carefully selected "experts" in the problem area under study. Two types of "experts" were selected for purposes of this study. First, those who had reputations as being highly influential leaders in the Cooper Dam Project were selected through a "chain-referral" technique. These were generally influential people in each of three communities (Cooper, Sulphur Springs, and Commerce) located adjacent to the project area. Second, a group of professional experts (referred to as "technicians" in the study) from the regional office of the Corps of Engineers was selected, again through a "chain-referral" technique. These were the individuals who had been directly involved in planning and other phases of the Cooper Dam project. In all, thirty-four respondents were selected for the study.

3. <u>Collection and analysis of data:</u> Interviewing the respondents personally constituted the major source of data collection. Most researchers using the Delphi technique have advocated and actually used a mail-out questionnaire approach instead of personal interviews. Interviewing the respondents appeared to be a necessity to use because of the types of respondents involved, especially at the community level. Interviewing the respondents was expected to insure a higher response rate, and the candid reactions and comments elicited during the interviews were considered to be important in evaluating their responses.

Although only thirty-four respondents were involved, the process of interviewing in two rounds took over four months. Interviews conducted during the first round took a greater amount of time compared to those in the second round. The data collected during the second round were restricted to items on which degree of consensus was less than average. Fifty percent of the total items were taken back to each respondent during the second round. Respondents were shown central tendencies (mean, standard deviation, interquartile range) in the previous responses. With this new information, each respondent was asked to reevaluate his former response and change it if he wished. Seven respondents could not be contacted during the second round. The analysis used data from the remaining twenty-seven "experts" who responded to both rounds.

Means and standard deviations were computed for each item on the questionnaire for each of the four groups of respondents (Cooper, Sulphur Springs, Commerce, and Technicians) and for all respondents taken together. The standard deviation on an item represented a degree of consensus among respondents, while the mean response on the scale was an indicator of the degree of an item's importance in relation to other items.

The Community Field
The structural context selected for impact analysis was a community field.[9] Cooper (population about 2,000) located within one mile of the proposed boundaries of the reservoir, was selected for investigation. The components and characteristics of the community field were investigated on three levels of analysis: ecological and demographic, cultural or institutional, and social or interactional. Both secondary and primary sources of data were used. The major primary source of data was a random sample survey of heads of households residing in the community at the time. The sampling technique was a slight modification of area sampling procedures. First, boundaries of the Cooper community were delineated by a group of eight judges, composed of office holders in the community. The community boundaries accordingly extended several miles into countryside beyond the formal city limits of Cooper. Second, the spatial structure of Cooper was divided into six areas/districts on the basis of physical boundaries such as streets and roads. Third, every fourth occupied house was selected and the head of the household was contacted for the interview. In all, 166 interviews, ranging from one to three hours, were conducted. Nine potential respondents could not be interviewed for a variety of reasons.

1. Ecological and demographic characteristics: The spatial patterns of Cooper were examined in terms of land use and land value trends, location of services, and ecological segregation of social groupings (referred to in the literature as "natural areas"). The demographic characteristics of Cooper were identified on the basis of U.S. Bureau of the Census reports and were compared with those of the Sulphur River Basin, the State of Texas, and the U.S. These characteristics included population size, birth and death rates, density of population, population growth trends, emigration and immigration trends, sex ratio, rural-urban ratio, racial composition, age composition, number and sizes of families, selected characteristics of family life, income distribution, recipients of welfare and social security, housing conditions, educational levels, occupational structure, and so forth. The population characteristics were reviewed in historical perspective for the past several decades.

2. Institutional services in Cooper: Selected institutional services in Cooper were investigated in terms of their availability and the residents' satisfaction with them.[10] Services included industry and agriculture, business, health, local government, schools, churches, and recreation (outdoor and indoor). Assessment was also made of the extent to which Cooper residents shopped for selected routine as well as occasional services within the community as compared to shopping elsewhere.

3. Social elements of Cooper: At the social level the community field was studied in terms of individuals (participants and leaders), groups and organizations, and community projects. Assessment was made as to what extent residents participated in local organizations and activities as compared to their involvement in professional and other organizations beyond the community. Each resident interviewed was asked to name the ten most influential leaders of Cooper. In addition, they were asked to rank each leader through paired comparisons in order of their social prestige. Ranking of leaders was standardized with reference to total number of mentions and reputational ranks received by each. Styles and structures of community organizations and projects were analyzed.

Impact of Cooper Dam on Cooper
The impacts of the Cooper Dam action process on Cooper were examined on the same three levels of community analysis, ecological, cultural and social. Two types of impacts were examined: past impacts, assessed in terms of how during its history the action process had already affected the community, and expected future impacts, assessed through survey data.

Impacts at the ecological level included identification of changes in land use, land values, and various demographic characteristics of the community. Changes related to institutional services were identified at the cultural level. At the social level the impacts were divided into two parts, impacts on community structure in terms of leadership dynamics and collective viability,[11] and impacts on aggregates of community residents. For the second category of analysis, the community residents were asked to assess how much the Cooper project had affected them personally in terms of selected criteria.[12]

Discussion
The macro and micro approaches in studies reported above represent two levels of impact analysis, although a few of the data collection and analysis techniques used were identical in both approaches. The difference between them lay mainly in the size of study area, a river basin in the base of macro study. Also, it should be noted, greater amounts of time and financial resources were available to the micro study than to the macro study. Each of the two studies made contributions toward the understanding of the complex phenomena of project impacts, however.

At the micro level, the history of the Cooper Dam action process was reviewed and analyzed systematically in terms of a temporal sequence of activities and phases. This was not done in the basin study, which dealt only superficially with the conceptualization of the action process. Lacking insights into the intricacies of a situation, the basin report emphasized broad indicators of environmental conditions and the impacts of the project on some of those conditions. On the other hand, study of action history at the micro level showed that a sequence of interacting project impacts could be traced in reference to what actually happened--for example, how the community leaders and organizations in Cooper had

developed solidarity during the initial phase of the project and how frictions and
conflicts arose among them during the planning phase. The historical analysis of
the project provided qualitative details of situational contexts and background to
what impacts had taken place and what might be anticipated in the future. Through
the action analysis, not only were we able to identify a number of the project's
impacts, but we could also rank and evaluate each of these in greater detail.
Analysis of impacts at the microlevel was not only more refined but also more inclusive. At this level, the investigation of impacts was relatively more intensive, compared to extensive type of macrolevel study.

The microlevel analysis provided a definite structural context of community where
real impacts and their recipients could be understood and interpreted. That does
not mean that the total basin study made no contribution in impact analysis. On
the contrary, by studying the project in light of a larger area we were able to
relate the Cooper project to other communities and programs in the region. The
assessment of social impacts at the regional level was more difficult than at the
community level, however. Broad indicators of regional impact are of questionable
validity in assessing local impacts. It seems necessary that the regional analysis
of social impacts be supplemented by more intensive community studies.

Footnotes

[1] A need to use microlevel procedures in SIA has been expressed by many writers.
Baur (1973) emphasizes need for intensive impact studies of limited geographical
areas rather than of diffuse populations affected to a lesser degree, and Wilkinson
(1973) calls for detailed case studies of areas affected directly by a project.
Pointing out the inadequacy of aggregate descriptions of impacts of public projects,
Warner (1973: 182) likewise urges the study of specific organizations and community
structures. Stinchcombe (1968) indicates the superiority of micro over macro-
models for causal analysis. Criticism that the boundaries of the potential impact
area in micro level studies are often drawn too tightly (Summers 1973: 187) implies
the equal and opposite need for macrolevel analysis.

[2] Items on personal information of the respondents included their age, number of
years lived in the present community, and socioeconomic status. An index of socioeconomic status was constructed by combining three status variables, viz. educational level, occupational rank, and size of land holding.

[3] The vested interest scale consisted of two parts. The first called for the ways
respondents think they might benefit from the two projects, directly or indirectly,
after these are completed. The second called for estimates of how much would the
projects hurt the personal interests of the respondents.

[4] Knowledge of the project was defined as respondents' self-ranking of their own
familiarity with the project's goals and organization.

[5] Chapin's organizational participation scale was employed for the purpose. In
addition, a "community orientation" scale included the following items:
    a. The people of this community are usually quick to respond when
problems arise requiring action.
    b. This community is well organized for continuing development.

    c. Groups and organizations with different interests work together in this community rather than fighting among themselves.
    d. People here don't care enough about this community to do anything about it.
    e. This community is like a house divided against itself.

[6]In addition to behavioral measures such as position held on a Water Board, the attitudinal scale consisted of the following items:
    a. Man has a real responsibility to manage his water resources as carefully as possible.
    b. How the water resources are managed will be one of the keys to the overall future of this area.
    c. We need not be concerned about water: the laws of nature will take care of it for us.
    d. Water is basic to our local economy.
    e. Water management is seldom as important as it is said to be by people and groups who are trying to promote it.
    f. While we must have it to survive, water is actually more of a problem or threat than a resource.

[7]The scale items were:
    a. The Cooper Reservoir Project is likely to meet with widespread acceptance of people in the Sulphur River Basin.
    b. The economic and other benefits from this project are far greater than its environmental consequences.
    c. Almost everyone in this area will be benefited from the Cooper Reservoir Project.
    d. Only those with property close to the Cooper Reservoir (or Dam) will benefit from this project.
    e. The Cooper Reservoir will create some environmental problems.

[8]For details of the phase model see Wilkinson (1970).

[9]The definition of the community as a social field is treated by Wilkinson (1970a).

[10]At the cultural or institutional level, community has been analyzed in terms of locality relevant functions (Warren 1973); institutionalized units meeting basic human needs (Sanders 1966); the differentiation, elaboration, and scope of interest fields (Wilkinson 1970a); the extent and quality of major services available (Wilkening and others 1973); among others.

[11]See Wilkinson (1973) and Warren (1973). Warner (1973) uses the term "collective interests" to denote the same phenomena. In the present study indicators of viability were people's attitudes toward community, degree of conflict in the community and among community organizations and projects.

[12]A few indicators of impact based on some of these criteria were combined into an Impact on Individual Index. Perceived impacts were scored for each item in the following manner:

A score of 1 was given if the resident was affirmative to the question asking if his residence value had gone up due to the project thus far. The following scores were assigned for resident's estimation of the level of increase in residence value: (a) a score of 1 was assigned if the value increase was below twenty-five percent, (b) a score of 2 for value increase from twenty-six to fifty percent, (c) a score of 3 for an increase from fifty-one to seventy-five percent, and (d) a score of 4 for an increase from seventy-six to one hundred percent. The same scoring procedure was followed for respondent's estimation of changes: (1) in value of residence expected in the future after the dam is built, (2) in present value of farm land owned by residents, (3) future farm value changes expected, (4) changes in other real estate property owned in Cooper, and (5) expected future changes in real estate property.

A score of 1 was assigned if the resident felt that his family's recreational use of the area would increase if the reservoir were built.

A score of 1 was assigned to the resident if he would have to move due to the project.

A score of 2 was assigned if resident felt that the project was of "great personal benefit" to himself, and a score of 1 for "some personal benefit." The same was done in the case of responses regarding personal loss from the project.

On the basis of these scores, individuals were placed on a four-point ordinal scale of (1) high impact, (2) medium impact, (3) low impact, and (4) no impact.

References

Ackley, Gardner (1961) Macroeconomic Theory. Toronto: Macmillan.

Baur, E. Jackson (1973) "Assessing the Social Effects of Public Works Projects." Fort Belvoir, VA: Board of Engineers for Rivers and Harbors, U.S. Army Corps of Engineers.

Clark, L. H. and S. W. Cochran (1972) "Needs for Older American Assessed by Delphi Procedures," Journal of Gerontology 27, 2, 275-278.

Cohen, Percy S. (1968) Modern Social Theory. New York: Basic Books.

Crawford, A. B. (1972) "A Method of Analyzing the Impacts of Alternative Courses of Action on Multiple Evaluation Criteria." Logan: Utah State University.

Dalkey, Norman C. (1969) The Delphi Method: An Experimental Study of Group Opinion. Santa Monica, CA: The Rand Corporation.

Dalkey, Norman C. and others (1972) Studies in Quality of Life: Delphi and Decision Making. Lexington, MA: D. C. Heath.

Gordon, Theodore J. and Robert H. Ament (1969) Forecasts of Some Technological and Scientific Developments and Their Societal Consequences. Report R-6. Middletown, CT: Institute for the Future.

Guttman, Louis (1944) "A Basis for Scaling Qualitative Data," American Sociological Review, 9, 2 (April), 139-50.

Martindale, Don (1960) The Nature and Types of Sociological Theory. Boston: Houghton Mifflin.

Merton, Robert K. (1968) Social Theory and Social Structure, rev. ed. New York: Free Press.

Sanders, Irwin T. (1966) The Community: An Introduction to a Social System. New York: Ronald.

Singh, Raghu N. (1971) "Toward a Sociological Analysis of Sulphur River Basin," pp. 13-49 in Arthur Pullen and others (eds.), An Environmental Inventory and Survey of the Sulphur River Valley. Commerce: East Texas State University.

Singh, Raghu N. (1975) Kona Dam vs. Konatown: A Sociological Interpretation of Selected Impacts of Reservoir Development on a Community Field. Final Completion Report. Commerce: East Texas State University.

Stinchcombe, Arthur L. (1968) Constructing Social Theories. New York: Harcourt Brace and World.

Summers, Gene F. (1973) "Some Comments on Rural Development Models and Concepts," pp. 186-188 in Wade H. Andrews and others (eds.), The Social Well-Being and Quality of Life Dimension in Water Resources Planning and Development. Logan: Institute for Social Science Research on Natural Resources, Utah State University.

Warner, W. Keith (1973) "Some Problems in Measuring of Social Consequences of Large Scale Development Plans," pp. 171-185 in Wade H. Andrews and others (eds.), The Social Well-Being and Quality of Life Dimension in Water Resources Planning and Development. Logan: Institute for Social Science Research on Natural Resources, Utah State University.

Warren, Ronald L. (1973) The Community in America. Chicago: Rand McNally.

Wilkening, E. A. and others (1973) Quality of Life in Kickapoo Valley Communities. Madison: Institute for Environmental Studies, University of Wisconsin.

Wilkinson, Kenneth P. (1970) "Phases and Roles in Community Action," Rural Sociology, 35, 54-68.

Wilkinson, Kenneth P. (1970a)"The Community as a Social Field," Social Forces, 311-322.

Wilkinson, Kenneth P. (1973) "Sociological Implications of Social Well-Being: Frameworks for Evaluation of Water Resources Project," pp. 160-170 in Wade H. Andrews and others (eds.), The Social Well-Being and Quality of Life Dimension in Water Resources Planning and Development. Logan: Institute for Social Science Research on Natural Resources, Utah State University.

Combining Ethnographic and Survey Research

Raymond L. Gold
University of Montana

A recent article by Sam Sieber (1973) pointed out that, although fieldwork (i.e., ethnographic) and survey (i.e., instrument-dependent) methods are essentially "noninterchangeable," "nevertheless, each method can be greatly strengthened by appealing to the unique qualities of the other method." After arousing interest by asserting that the two research methods are basically noninterchangeable, Sieber does not attempt to explain why this is so, but concerns himself with suggesting how each might strengthen the other through being selectively synthesized when designing research, collecting information, and analyzing data. I should like in the present paper to pick up on Sieber's assertion and try to explain why qualitative and quantitative research methods are indeed fundamentally noninterchangeable. I want to attempt this explanation, not only because it is overdue, but because it may help fellow social scientists to realize more fully what they may be getting into if they seek even to selectively combine methods which are so unlike that they actually represent very different ways of conceiving of, studying, teaching about, and otherwise talking about society. If we researchers are to attempt to selectively, and perhaps usefully, synthesize essentially disparate research methods, it certainly behooves us to understand what we are doing and to be aware of the risks of dabbling in what may turn out to be methodological alchemy.

To facilitate comparing and contrasting ethnographic with survey research, I shall use ideal typical depictions of sociologists who subscribe to one or the other of these methods. This usage makes empirical as well as presentational sense because sociologists almost always do research either quantitatively or qualitatively. Advocates of methodological synthesis are rare; rarer still are those who are more than nominal synthesizers.[1] It should be kept in mind that the two ideal types I shall depict are phenotypes, which means that each must be understood as consisting of a given <u>configuration</u> of characteristics and behaviors. It should also be noted that positing two logically opposite ideal types is not to dismiss the possibility that there are empirical types that feel they have a foot firmly planted in each of the two extreme positions. It is my intention to compare the two ideal types in order to show that doing fieldwork as an integral part of studying what goes on between and among human beings leads the ethnographer into conceiving of, teaching, and doing sociology very differently from the researcher who tries to study society without becoming field-involved.

What I mean by being "field-involved" is that the sociologist is observing at

---

1. Many sociologists engage in nominal synthesis which is far short of what Sieber suggests. I do not consider nominal synthesis to be inconsistent with the either-or situation just noted.

first hand the aspects of society he wishes to study and doing so with a view to reflecting on and bracketing the character of mundane experiences. His essential method is to develop relationships, hence, to make society as a means of studying the society as made by his informant. In the process, he necessarily intervenes in the informant's society, using his personal skills as well as the conceptual apparatus of his discipline to generate data. The field observer is part of the data in ways he takes into account and tries to control for when generating, analyzing, and reporting it. Taking part in (and occasionally being a part of) the observed society is his approach to obtaining data.

In contrast, the sociologist who is not field-involved relies upon his subjects' responses to instruments of various sorts and upon secondary sources of data to provide him with answers to questions he raises about society. Those who use this approach rely upon their ability to make inferences from data produced in ways which keep them at least at arm's length from their subjects. In fact, many such students of society question the scientific quality of data obtained under any less controlled conditions, such as through observations or through the face-to-face interaction with informants which personal interviews usually require.

These approaches to studying society are so different that they lead not only to two different ways of conceptualizing society but to two distinctive and essentially incompatible ways of doing, and even talking about, sociology. The two approaches make very different assumptions about virtually all aspects of doing research, for example, about how to sample the people who are to be studied. Statistical sampling is based on the assumption that nothing is known about the population to be studied and that probability sampling must be used to keep the investigation from making too many mistakes in finding and selecting respondents. It has the advantage of providing the researcher with assurance that he can count, compare, examine relationships, and measure research variables with considerable precision. It is not suited to field-involved research, for here the objective is to discover how informants classify or label each other, how they find meaning in activities they care about in life, how they engage in processes in which they individually and collectively define the changes in their situation and the impact of these changes upon their society, their way of life, and themselves. Rather, it is most useful only after the researcher has clearly classified and categorized his data and wishes then to find out how many cases he has in each category of behavior, or what the precise distribution of attitudes of a given sort is among the population under study, or the like. To sample a population with the intention of quickly and inexpensively learning, for example, what the several social groupings of the study area's residents are like from the standpoint of each grouping's members and from those of neighbors, friends, relatives, and community officials who know them, field-involved sampling must be used.

The two principal kinds of field-involved sampling, ordinarily called theoretical and sociological sampling, are "verstehende sociological"[2] in their approach. Both

---

2. (Weber 1947:10; Abel 1948). Early in the present century, Max Weber developed a theoretical and methodological rationale for social research which he called "verstehende sociology." A fair translation of this term is "a sociology of knowing" or "a sociology of meaning." Through developing this research approach, Weber showed sociological fieldworkers how to understand human society through coming to know it as its members do. His approach demonstrated the great value

attempt to sample with a view to depicting the social situation being studied as people in the situation view it. The main difference between the two is that the focused objective of theoretical sampling (Glaser and Strauss 1967: 62-65) is to generate theory, while that of sociological sampling (Gold and others 1974:246-80) is to generate empirically sound descriptions of how the research subjects perceive and experience that which is under study.

Paying particular attention to the act of fitting behavior together, the field-involved sociologist inevitably becomes more concerned with interactional process than with structure. While mindful of the setting or larger situation in which fitting together of behavior occurs, he tends to take the context of interaction into account largely through its meaning for and to the observed interactants. Grounding observations directly and particularly in what goes on between and among those who are making society, and relying heavily upon them to help interpret and explain what is going on in their society, the field-involved sociologist naturally tends to be an ethnographer. The kind of ethnographer he tends to be is uaually of the symbolic interactionist (Blumer 1969) or ethnomethodological (Garfinkel 1967) sort.

The field-involved researcher relies heavily, and teaches his field-involved students to rely heavily, upon informants to help make sense out of what goes on in their society. He is in this respect a verstehende sociologist to be sure, but this does not mean that he is content to depend entirely upon informants for understandings and explanations of their behavior. Rather, his approach to society teaches him again and again that empirically grounded formal theory of human social behavior must be generated and tested in and through society. Such grounding, he concludes, calls for doing fieldwork wherein informants are asked to reality check the observer's formal theories through comparing them with their natural theories or explanations or reasons for perceiving, thinking, feeling, and doing. In this way, the sociologist systematically avoids the intellectual ethnocentrism of those who eschew doing this kind of careful, painstaking, and demanding natural laboratory work.

Indeed, the teacher of field-involved students, following the lead of Robert E. Park and the others who created the famous Chicago School of sociologists, considers the natural laboratory of "the life" to be the primary learning situation for himself and his students, and the classroom a secondary one. In his view,

---

of participating personally, intimately, and meaningfully in the lives of research subjects in order to share their meanings and thereby come to know them as they know themselves. Weber did much to help make fieldwork an indispensable way of refraining from coloring data with one's own views when seeking to study human behavior objectively.

When done in a verstehende sociological manner, sampling entails enlisting the direct and explicit aid of individuals generally regarded by others in the social unit being studied as knowing it well. Those, whom these individuals understand to be good representatives of the particular points of view and types of behavior that the fieldworker is interested in, are contacted and also asked to identify other such representatives. In short order, the informants' natural sociological sampling becomes a basis for the fieldworker's.

learning about human behavior occurs much more intensively and extensively in the natural circumstances of those studied than in the classroom. Symbolic of his conviction that experiential learning situations are much more profitable than contrived or simulated ones is the tendency of the teacher of field-involved students to use the language of the life while in the classroom and to refrain from using classroom language while in the life.

All of this has the effect of so involving the sociologist in society that doing something about its problems seems natural and right. He naturally tends to become action oriented, and evaluation and other applied research appeal to him as meaningful and fruitful accompaniments of basic research. In fact, he continually seeks for ways of combining the best features of so-called basic and applied research, and he does so when both studying and talking about society.

The sociologist who is _not_ field-involved and who does _not_ ordinarily have field-involved students may be briefly contrasted to the foregoing by noting the following:

1. He studies statistical populations, treating them as if they were instances of society, while frequently referring to them as cultures. This referential tendency is particularly appropriate when studying our so-called mass society. Here it is much more likely that people in any statistical population are actually using aspects of culture in common than engaging in social interaction with each other or even knowingly taking each other into account.

2. The sociologist who is not field-involved is inclined to use society and culture as interchangeable terms, with culture well on the way to replacing society as an omnibus concept for referring to both form and content of behavior. As a student of the big picture of what goes on among people in the United States, he concerns himself mainly with surveying structural aspects of culture and cultural aspects of social structure. Inclined to observe social life from a distance, the language he uses in the classroom or in reports is also used when he participates in the life, while language of the life remains there.

3. The teacher who keeps himself and his students at some distance from their subjects almost invariably commits himself entirely to basic research, leaving it to field-involved colleagues to do action-oriented, problem-solving studies which combine basic with applied research. Considering himself a dispassionate observer of society, he is inclined to believe that for him to be field-involved would be to unnecessarily risk being involved in the lives of research subjects. Much more an observer of the human scene than a participant in it, his view of society is that of a person who studies it at a distance.

4. His first, and perhaps only, choice of a learning situation is the classroom, especially the scientific form of classroom called the laboratory.

5. He is highly unlikely to submit his logically deduced formal theories to respondents or to any other noncolleagues for their reactions. Relying almost exclusively on instruments to elicit information, he and his students engage in a questioning process which keeps them so far removed from chal-

lenging interaction with informants that theory may be reality checked only by colleagues who read about it in scholarly and research reports. Indeed, the office- and classroom-bound sociologist feels that people in the life are not in a position to contribute directly to theory building. Instead, he believes that they should be kept at least at arm's length in order not to bias the investigator or otherwise contaminate his data and hence his theories.

In this paper I have attempted to use the method of ideal types to explain why some fundamental issues in sociology, and in the study of human behavior in general, arise and are maintained in actions which function to keep sociologists and their students in or out of the field. My analysis suggests that these actions have contributed not only to the noninterchangeability of fieldwork and survey methods but to the development of two quite distinct ways of conceiving of society, studying it, talking about it, and treating its problems. I have implied that the field-involved sociologist tends to see society as gemeinschaft, whereas the non-field-involved sociologist is inclined to see society as gesellschaft. I have intimated that the basic definitional, ideological, and philosophical differences between the two are so vast as to appear to constitute denominational differences. As noted, however, the denomination-like differences are actually a natural division of labor in which (a) one is a detached, pure researcher who looks at society macroscopically, uses deductive logic and academic jargon to talk and write about it, and validates findings by applying statistical tests and getting colleague reactions to the findings while (b) the other is a heavily participating applied researcher who looks at society microscopically, uses inductive logic and the language of informants to talk and write about it, and validates findings through reality checking them with the people whose narrative accounts of their lives he uses to make up his reports. There is considerable potential for the work of the two to complement and supplement each other despite a lack of methodological, procedural, and conceptual fit. Even though survey and fieldwork are in fact noninterchangeable, so long as each raises fundamental questions about human behavior that only the other is capable of answering both will continue to be needed. Thus, there is no problem in establishing a symbiotic relationship between the two methods because such a relationship already exists. The real problem is in getting the two types of investigators together to work out mutually advantageous procedures for integrating their research designs and dovetailing their study procedures wherever and whenever they can.

Finally, a word concerning implications of the above for strengthening social impact assessments. Keep in mind that public agency officials (e.g., land use planners) who are the principal users of social impact research reports generally criticize the reports for not being (1) useful for agency purposes, (2) written in plain English, (3) sufficiently grounded in the realities of the places studies, (4) readily relatable to research reports on resource variables, and (5) done well enough to stand up in court. In my judgment, the foregoing analysis offers exciting possibilities for so articulating survey with ethnographic research that every one of these (and similar) well-earned criticisms of social impact assessments could be dealt with to the general satisfaction of all concerned. Moreover, since such articulation of research, risky though it may be, would probably be fundamentally much sounder than the either-or types now done, there is every reason to expect that the contributions of social impact assessments to such basic sociological topics as social change would be far greater than they have been.

References

Abel, Theodore (1948) "The Operation Called Verstehen," American Journal of Sociology, 54, 3 (November), 211-18.

Blumer, Herbert (1969) Symbolic Interactionism: Perspective and Method. Englewood Cliffs, NJ: Prentice-Hall.

Garfinkel, Harold (1967) Studies in Ethnomethodology. Englewood Cliffs, NJ: Prentice-Hall.

Glaser, Barney G. and Anselm L. Strauss (1967) The Discovery of Grounded Theory; Strategies for Qualitative Research. Chicago: Aldine.

Gold, Raymond L. and others (1974) A Comparative Case Study of the Impact of Coal Development on the Way of Life of People in the Coal Areas of Eastern Montana and Northeastern Wyoming. Missoula: Institute for Social Science Research, University of Montana, 30 June.

Sieber, Sam D. (1973) "The Integration of Fieldwork and Survey Methods," American Journal of Sociology, 78, 6 (May), 1335-59.

Comprehensive Values and Public Policy*

Ruth P. Mack
Institute of Public Administration

Values in the context of national policy have undergone a dramatic and salutary change. They are no longer identical to growth in Gross National Product or even to change in some of its distributional characteristics; now they include a wide range of other attributes of human well-being. The advent of social indicators is integral to this development. Their chief role, like that of their economic forerunners, is to specify, display, encourage and monitor change. Though many indicators aim at merely describing change, the thrust of this work is strongly normative: the direction of change in an indicator is typically intended to record that more (or less) of some desirable (or undesirable) attribute is being generated. It is in this sense that the extraordinarily vigorous "social indicator movement" underscores the new visions about values in national development.

Yet even social indicators, combined in an ideal index of Gross National Product of Well-Being, would not be much use in showing how well-being should be increased. The information necessary to <u>do something about it--the policy-forming and implementing links--is lacking</u>. Much of the science of economics, particularly post-keynesian economics, addresses a corresponding question in the context of gross national (economic) product. Also, there are economic micro models that correspond to the macro models of national income, capital formation and its components. There are the market and pricing mechanisms to aid in integrating consumption, distribution and production in the context of economic welfare. We are naked of all this conceptual apparatus and understanding (faulty even as it is) in the context of broad societal well-being.

A MICRO MODEL FOR POLICY

If extra-economic aspects of well-being are to be subsumed under public responsibility, and it seems clear that this is the trend of affairs, there is urgent need to construct an adequate mapping of the micro entity--the consumer, the experiencing unit--and its efforts to optimize (in a loose sense) the necessities and satisfactions of life. Such a map provides a micro model for individual total well-being that is relevant to the macro motions of societal total well-being. I shall briefly sketch ingredients of such a model and apply it to the analysis of a public policy problem. I call it an e-model, since its capability is explorative rather than predictive.

My conceptions build upon the work of Gary Becker (1964, 1965) and Kelvin Lancaster (1966, 1971), who picture the utility from consumption as inherent in characteristics

---

*The first section of this essay borrows from a paper read at the 1973 conference of The Institute of Management Sciences and reproduced in Management Sciences: Developing Countries and National Priorities, North-Holland Publishing Company (1976), to whom we are indebted for permission to use the material here.

of goods rather than in the purchased goods themselves. These desirable "characteristics" are generated by consumer "productive activity" which utilize "inputs" of time and personal capital in health and education as well as inputs of purchased goods (or income).[1] This important work, however, defines the utility that consumers try to optimize primarily in economic terms.

A Taxonomy of Human Needs and Wants

For our purposes consumer activity must be viewed as addressed to comprehensive well-being--a notion akin to the value system towards which social indicators grope. How then should comprehensive well-being of the individual unit be described? The list I suggest uses two bases of selection. First, desirables are defined at a level of basic human needs and wants. Among other things, this should serve to keep cultural specifics visible. Second, I have tried to assemble needs into groups that retain contact with classes of things to which people attend and with which government interventions deal. The list follows:[2]

1. Material comfort ranging from absence of pain and freedom from hunger and cold to affluent luxury. This is the category with which economic utility and economic welfare functions are largely concerned.

2. Stability and safety and reasonable continuity between present and future, the absence of threat of violence or of violation to person and personal property.

3. Physical and mental positive health, including enjoyment of physical sense experience, play, motility, vitality and euphoria.

4. Well-being of spirit and mind; enlightenment and exercise of the intellect, aesthetic enjoyment (including the enjoyment of nature), religious experience, reverence and idealism, benevolence and rectitude.

5. Intimacy and family relationships, including affection ranging from liking to loving in a giving-getting interplay.

6. Societal belonging and participation: the perception of self and groups to which one "belongs," equitable participation in societal phenomena including relationships to leadership, sharing of responsibility, trust.

7. Competence and mastery and developing the skills necessary thereto.

8. Self-elevation and influence over people (in the extreme, power).

9. Freedom to choose: the wish to make and carry out one's own decisions about what to do, think, believe and say.

The gratification of each class of wants generates a corresponding quality of utility and the consumer unit endeavors to enhance a utility vector having these

---

1. Other people who have done important work along the same general lines at the National Bureau of Economic Research are Jacob Mincer, Michael Grossman and Robert T. Michael.
2. The taxonomy is quite similar to the one that Harold Lasswell formulated some time ago. For a recent version, see his Preview of Policy Science (1971).

several sorts of utilities as arguments. The endeavor to enhance is optimizing in intent, but it is subject to all of the limitations of perception, information and circumstance (constraints) to which the human being living in a society is heir--call it quasi-optimizing, or simply, "Optimizing." How, then, does the individual or family unit go about it?

Consumption Activity

The consumer unit can be viewed as a mini-firm bent on "optimizing" an expected utility vector.[3] The major functional elements of the process and its setting in society are displayed in Figure 1; they are:

1. <u>Inputs</u>. Purchased goods (including services), goods regarded as free (such as those provided by nature or by governments), own time, and the much neglected item, purposive energy. Inputs consist also of the utilization of own stocks. These include money (a conduit which connects earnings to the input purchased goods), land, consumer durables, personal capital in education (skills, knowledge, capability), in physical and in mental health.[4]

2. <u>Consumer productive activity</u>, which converts inputs into a "commodity" having desirable "characteristics" or into stocks (consumer capital). For example, the commodity, an evening meal, can have the want-gratifying characteristics of: slaking hunger (want category 1), aesthetic pleasure in the quality of the food (4), and the pleasure of family intimacy at dinner (5); it may also build capital in mental health. The "production" of the evening meal may have used the inputs, purchased food, the time and purposive energy devoted to home-produced food and to meal preparation, time at the dinner table, and the use of personal capital in mental health and knowledge to create family intimacy at dinner. Another common productive activity is when time is used at a job, thereby producing in the first instance additions to liquid capital (money), and often also the gratification of the want of societal belonging (6) or competence (7).

3. <u>Evaluative activity</u> plays a double role. On the one hand, it assigns utility to the consumer activity that is in process. On the other hand, it establishes <u>expectations</u> about how the vector of total utility might be optimized by undertaking new activity, given the present situation of the consumer unit and its evaluative structure (tastes), and given the constraints of available resources. This second role suggests which commodities the next bit of consumer activity should produce, and whether for present or future consumption (postponed utility), and consequently what inputs should be engaged.

---

3. Modern management theory is tending to apply an analogous notion to the business firm. Money profits are no longer deemed the be-all and end-all of corporation objectives. See, for example, Baumol (1959: 45-58); Drucker (1954: 63); Cyert and March (1963: Ch. 2).
4. Note that the value of some of these forms of capital is not diminished by use (as for example is an automobile). Capital in skill, for sample, is "utilized" without being "used up"; on the contrary, it is enhanced by utilization. However, the fact that they are not "scarce" in the economic sense should not interfere with the basic structure of the optimizing problem. They are in effect the output of a capital investment having an indefinite useful life.

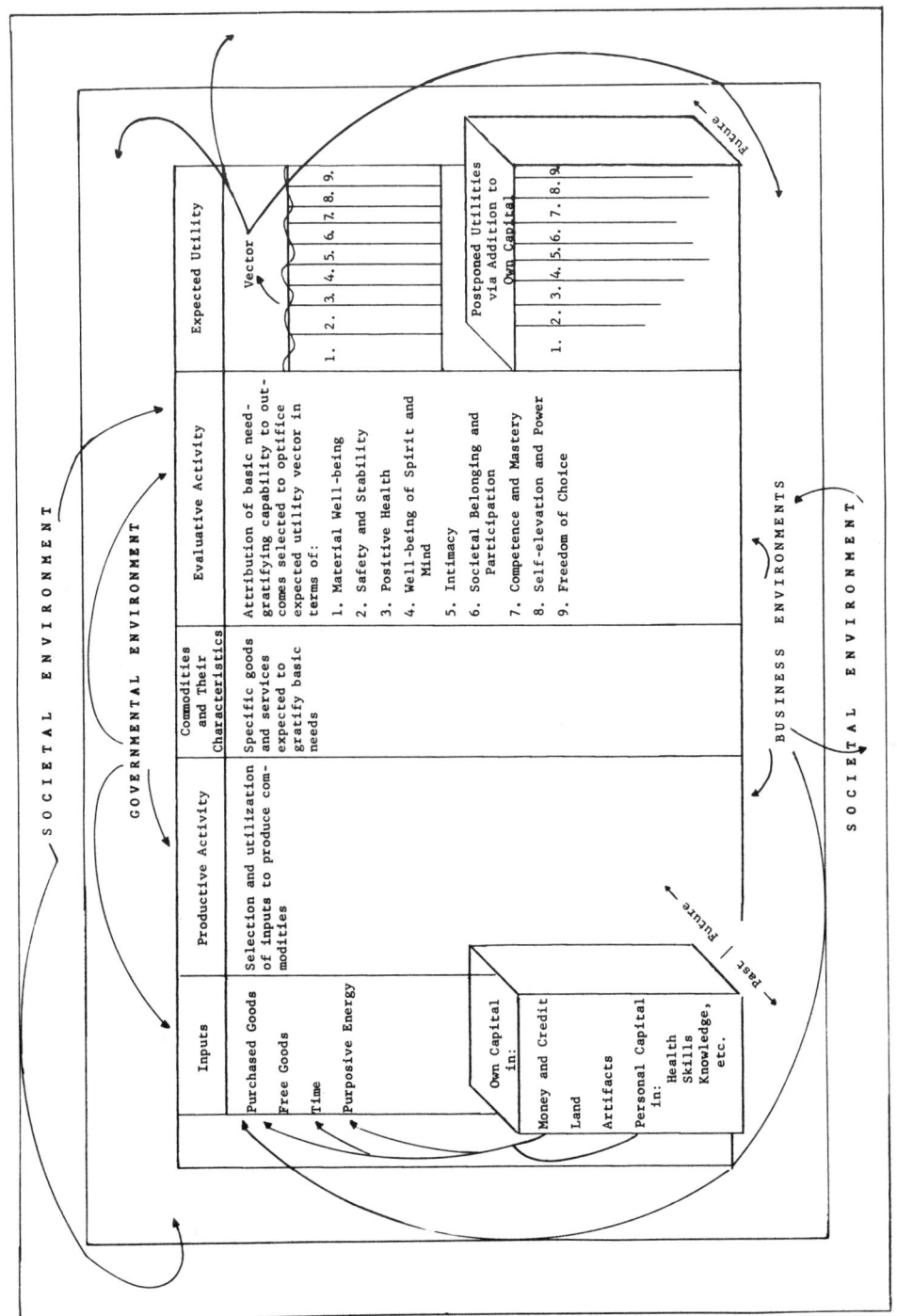

Figure 1. E-MODEL OF THE MINI-FIRM

We can assume that anyone has in some degree virtually all of the nine categories of wants mentioned earlier. It is how they are <u>weighted</u> and <u>combined</u> which is the essence of the evaluative activity. The emphasis on the several categories will differ widely depending on tastes, level of living and cultural values.

Environment of the Consumer Unit

Thus far we have been speaking of the consumer unit as if it existed in a social vacuum. But as the diagram suggests, and as we are all amply aware, the individual consumer is a speck in a large world which influences everything he does or feels. The infinite aspects of that world are represented in the diagram in three groups--business, governments, and society at large (which comprehends everything from a neighbor to a culture). Each environmental sector can enhance (or deteriorate) consumer optimizing activity by affecting its inputs, production functions, or evaluative activity. Likewise, each can be affected by consumer activity, e.g., individuals investment in knowledge can augment the cultural heritage or improve the body politic. A word here on just one of these environments--that of governments.

Policy Objective as Summed Individual Well-Being

The e-model poses the question: How can government intervention increase the sum of consumer utility relative to what it would have been without the intervention? Policy should make this expected difference, viewed over the appropriate time horizon, as large as possible. The question raises a host of matters on which there is a long history of economic argument--interpersonal comparisons and social welfare functions, for example. It also requires explication of the meaning of "as large as possible." This, too, is a long story. Certainly it is <u>expectations</u> of advantage which are relevant, and this means that the framework is probabilistic, not absolute. Certainly also, political as well as task-oriented dimensions of decision processes are pertinent to defining what is possible, and this two-dimensionality (politics and task) can be consolidated by the probabilistic format: political impracticality decreases the likelihood that desirable actions will obtain and thereby decrease the uncertainty-discounted value of the expected outcome.[5] Further, aggregate consumer utility in the long run is often enhanced by policies addressed to the cultural and physical environments--saving forests, promoting mobility, improving administrative capability (building capital in organizations). Governments then can influence consumer well-being by adding to inputs, improving consumption functions, or "improving" (a necessary though subtle notion) consumer evaluative systems or behavior. They can do each via direct action or by influencing the other environments, business or society at large.

Influences do not stop at the first intervention, however. Early influences generate further influences. Implied is an interactive network of linked impacts, potential sequential techniques of intervention, and indeed changing objectives of intervention with somewhat altered capability of enhancing the aggregate utility that is generated. The intricacies of these interactive networks and their cumulative patterns preclude, in the context of broad policy problems, pursuit of the economist's dictum of "optimizing at the margin," however loosely defined.

Instead, a strategy must be formulated which contrives to improve the situation in whatever ways seem most promising, including particularly that of providing a con-

---

5. The point is developed in Mack (1971: Ch. 11).

tinuing, deliberative, active process of jointly designing and effectuating interventions.

E-Model as an Aid in Policy Shaping

This is a large and amorphous order which requires shaping and monitoring devices. The e-model is intended to contribute in a modest fashion to this immodest demand for conceptual structure. It should help in three ways:

1. By providing a point of view and checklist for scanning comprehensively the scope and major characteristics of a problem and defining first the system in terms of which it needs to be dealt with, and second, the strategy whereby objectives can be approached.

2. By affording a systematic method for viewing the particulars of a situation or of interventions in which all significant affected elements, including those in qualitatively dissimilar categories (e.g., serving primarily different categories of needs, or involving what has come to be thought of as economic, social or environmental impacts can be evaluated in parallel. The evaluation may guide choice among alternatives. It may be, and I believe is, most useful in guiding design of alternatives.

3. By providing a framework which is hospitable to scientific information and learning.

I can do no more than suggest how the framework might serve these purposes by presenting three cases where a policy problem is set in e-model terms. The first two deal with problems in developing countries and illustrate the scanning objective which points toward a few policy priorities even prior to efforts to supply quantitative information. The third, which takes the analysis through additional steps, moves much deeper into the deliberative process. A final section discusses some of the more general implications of the analysis and its methodological problems and opportunnities.

TWO CASES OF PRELIMINARY SCANNING

The following two cases list questions to which attention is directed in two policy contexts familiar to developing nations. They deal only with benefits and some opportunity costs. Money costs--the opportunity costs of money spent in other ways--would need separate analysis.

Table 1 concerns the construction of a major new highway. We ask, what groups of individuals are affected, in what way, and when? The question of "when" is answered in terms of two periods of time--during and after construction. Theoretically the final evaluation would balance costs against some sort of sum of benefits to all groups over all years. The benefits to each group would be weighted by the number of people in the group. Since benefits are theoretically stated in terms of a

Table 1

E-MODEL ANALYSIS OF A NEW MAJOR HIGHWAY

Row	Government Action	Incidence: Consumption Phase for C.U. or Environmental Sector ( )[a]	Groups of Individuals Affected		Expected Impact on		
			Type	Size[b]	Desirable (+) / (−) Characteristics[c]	Utility Category Generated (±)[d]	

PERIOD I: HIGHWAY UNDER CONSTRUCTION

Row	Government Action	Incidence	Type	Size	Desirable/Undesirable Characteristics	Utility Category
1	Designation of route	Input: increased value of c.u. capital in land	Landowners along the route	√	Investment in land or Income from sale of land	1 "postponed," 6, 8 1, etc.
2	Spending of construction funds	(Business environment) →	Construction companies and their suppliers			
3		Productive activity: increased productivity of time	Owners and officers of companies	√	Earnings → Increase in money capital	6, 8 1, 2, 6
4		Productive activity: increased productivity of time	Construction workers previously non-farm	√	Earnings → Increase in money capital	6 1, 2, 6
5		Productive activity: increased productivity of time	previously farm	√	Same as row 4 but with sacrifice of family and group belonging	−5, −6
6		(Societal environment)	National image a bit changed			
7		Evaluative activity: early shifts in expectations	People in contact with change	√	Changed weights for utility vectors	

114

PERIOD II: HIGHWAY IN OPERATION

8	No further spending	Continued impacts as per row 1 and rents on capital, row 3		
9	(Business environment) Productive activity deteriorated	Construction workers who do not find new jobs	✓	Earnings	−1
		For those previously on farms and unable or unwilling to return	✓	Home related satisfactions	−1, −7, −5, −6, −2
10	(Business environment) New business due to improved access and multiplier impacts of previous spending			As per rows 3, 4, 5 above	
11	Productive activity: increased productivity of time	Employees getting jobs in new businesses	✓		
12	Productive activity: increased productivity of time	Farmers with new access to supplies and markets	✓	Improved agriculture and Earnings	1, 8
				Increase in money capital	1, 2, 6
13	(Societal environment)	Continued impacts as per rows 6 and 7			

a. Consumption phase refers to the columns of the e-model diagram-- inputs productive activity and evaluative activity of the Consumer Unit. When the governmental intervention's initial incidence is on an environment, the sector is given in parentheses.

b. Check indicates that size of "group" should be estimated. The number of people are a datum bearing on the problem of summation for aggregate wellbeing. See text, page 9.

c. When earning power is increased (via use of time in gainful employment) the earnings, first entered as increased money capital, are immediately available for input to purchase goods. Accordingly category 1 type of utility is enhanced along with other categories associated either with more capital or more consumption.

d. Numbers refer to categories listed in the taxonomy, pages 3 and 4. They are listed in the order of their probable relative importance though many of the attributions are little more than a quick guess, though subject, I have indicated elsewhere, to a great deal of improvement.

surrogate for expected subjective utility, they already reflect distributional impacts.[6] Needless to say, the summations would provide at best only the roughest weighing.

For the period of road construction, the listings speak for themselves. Once the road is in operation the critical question seems to be how much will improved access stimulate business, including that of farmers in the area. Will the new business be large enough to prevent the erstwhile employees or their counterparts, especially those drawn from farm environments, from becoming dispossessed urban drifters? Will it be sufficient to support expectations and stimulate further investment directly and via "income multipliers". The size of multipliers would vary widely depending on such subtle matters as the table lists. In other words, even granting that the road needs to be built, is this the time?[7]

Table 2 deals with a problem in health and family planning. Here a central question appears to be how strongly and rapidly will reduction in births, which reduce populations, be associated with improved infant survival, which increases them. Certainly people's observation of, and response to, infant survival rates may be an important factor bearing on their willingness to limit pregnancies. If so, there will be a delicate matter of timing and magnitude of response upon which the success of the program may depend, as suggested in Row 11. But the analysis points to another aspect of the program. Because it is potentially subject to constant retooling and guidance in the light of unfolding experience, the uncertainties of prediction can be subdued by responsive, purposive design.

My overall reaction to both tables is how deeply interdependent are the many aspects of development--a widened notion of Ragnar Nurkse's "balanced growth." The number of farmers who travel a road to sell and to buy may depend more on the state of their health, and thereby their aspirations, than on the existence of the highway. Conversely, communication systems spread the contagion of disease, of health, of ambition, which leads to family planning. This is why the selection of priorities is really a _strategy_ of staging, timing and devising change within a "system" having comprehensive parameters. The e-model should help to visualize these appropriately wide horizons of relevance in a structured fashion. At least, the boundaries between what can be usefully foretold and what needs to be contrived into being is precipitated into view.

IMPACT OF FLOODS AND FLOOD PLAIN MANAGEMENT

The third case addresses a very different type of problem: what should be done about flood damage prevention in the Connecticut River basin? The work sketched here was based on an investigation done under the aegis of the New England River

---
6. The law of diminishing utility ordains that a given amount of, say, additional food or housing received by a poor man would be expected to generate more utility than the same amount received by a rich man. Also, and significantly, uncertainty discounts are required. See Mack (1971: 3-5, 87-88, 102-111).
7. Many would argue that these questione lie well in the future and their significance would be dwarfed by time discounts. Unfortunately for my own peace of mind, I find the question of appropriate time discounts still largely up in the air.

Basins Commission. The study aimed to formulate desirable policy and move toward
an action phase intended to effectuate the policy.

Desirable policy is described as wise flood plain management. This purpose may be
served by keeping people away from the water, via "nonstructural methods" (zoning,
building regulations, removal, land purchase, etc.) or by keeping floodwater away
from people (via dams and dikes) or by some combination of both. The nonstructural
approach has been emphasized of late in recognition of the fact that the structural
approach grows increasingly self-defeating: development, and thereby damageable
property in flood plains, has increased faster than flooding has been reduced by
the multi-billion dollar expenditure on dams and dikes.

Impacts of a Flood
The novelty of the nonstructural approach makes it important to apply the comprehensive value scheme systematically. Accordingly, we start at the beginning and
endeavor to display the whole range of impacts which policy aims to minimize--
those of the flood episode itself. These must be viewed in the detail required to
construct each line of an e-model exhibit including a final column (not attempted
in Tables 1 and 2) in which the strength of impacts is evaluated.

In theory this last column should concern expected impacts probabilistically set
forth, since it is the chance of specified kinds of losses, not specific sure
losses, which policy aims to reduce. Since before one can tackle the sophisticated
notion of probability distributions it is well to have a firm grasp of the kinds
of impacts that will be distributed, the analysis here goes no farther than an
exploration of one occurrence--the 1955 flood in Westfield, Massachusetts.

The picture is developed in two steps. The first is an "Analytic Narrative"
(Mack 1974) of the flood episode structured to show how many, of what people,
were affected in what way, over what period of time. Impacts are described in
physical terms: during the flood itself--what happened, play by play; and during
the period of reconstruction--what damage was being repaired and at what cost, by
whom, and how. There are qualitative as well as quantitative aspects to such
descriptions, the latter including but not confined to dollar value of damage.

The second step is to incorporate the episode, line by line, in the evaluative
framework of the e-model. A final column undertakes to assay the impact on the
utility vector of affected individuals over a specified period of time. All impacts are expressed in the common denominator, "a utility index point," a procedure
described prior to presenting the table.

E-Model Analysis of the Flood
The narrative description analyzing how the flood and the reconstruction that
followed it affected the well-being of people in the neighborhood must be consolidated into a more formal tabulation of the desirable and undesirable occurrences
and their relative importances. In determining what is desirable, and to what
extent, the reference I use is that of the individual or family unit--the customary
"micro unit" for judging economic well-being. However, since we are interested in
well-being defined more broadly than in terms of goods that have prices (or "shadow
prices"), a common denominator for well-being other than that of a monetary unit
must be contrived.

Table 2

E-MODEL ANALYSIS OF A 20-YEAR PROGRAM FOR INTEGRATED FAMILY PLANNING AND HEALTH CARE*

Row	Government Action	Incidence: Consumption Phase for C, U, or Environmental Sector ( )[a]	Groups of Individuals Affected		Expected Impact on	
			Type[b]	Size	Desirable (±)[c] Characteristics	Utility-Category Generated[d]
		PERIOD 0: PLANNING AND BUILDING CLINICS				
1	Involving local communities in planning and building clinics, etc.	(Societal Environment) → C. U. Evaluative activity	People directly and indirectly involved	✓	Less suspicion of government Sense that the ill can be cured	6, 9 shifted value weights
		PERIOD 1: FIRST 1-5 YEARS OF PROGRAM				
2	Operation of clinics and of other aspects of program	Input: free goods of medical service, education re health and sanitation	Interested people	✓	Improved health and fewer deaths, Knowledge that aid is available	1, 5 6, 9
3		Input: free goods of maternal and infant care and birth control devices	Interested families of child-bearing age	✓	Same as row 2; also, Fewer unwanted births, fewer infant deaths	1, 5, 6, 9 1, 2, 5, 9
4		Productive activity: improved by better health and fewer pregnancies	Some of people in rows 2 and 3	✓	Potential increase in any desirable	1 to 9
5		Input: free good of training and experience	Young doctors and paramedicals	✓	Skill and Earning capacity	7 1

	PERIOD 2: YEARS 6-14		
5 Continued operation of clinics and	Same as in rows 2, 3, 4, 5	Same as rows 2, 3, 4, 5 but wider participation because of gain in acceptability	✓
6 of other aspects			Same as rows 2, 3, 4, 5 but hopefully more impact per unit of program because of more educated response (as per row 2), and for family planning (row 3) observation of higher survival rate of children
7 of			
8 program			
9	Evaluative activity: improved by observation of program results		

PERIOD 3: YEARS 15 AND FOLLOWING AS SURVIVING CHILDREN OF PERIOD 1 BEAR CHILDREN

10 Continued operation of clinics and other aspects of program	Same as above	Increasing demand	Increasing impact
11 Cumulative impact of program	(Societal environment) Unless lower death rates are more than equalled by lower birth rates the increase of population may exceed available new jobs and disappoint rising expectations. If so, there would be	Reversals of the betterment characteristics	Quantitative and qualitative declines in utility
			Same as above but with value system shifted toward interest in quality of life

* Exhibit refers to an integrated family planning, health care and public health program with a strong educational element for the public and for training personnel, as in the Danfa Comprehensive Rural Health and Family Planning Project, Ghana. See "Research Design," School of Public Health, University of California, unpublished paper, July 1972, and "The Danfa/Ghana Comprehensive Rural Health and Family Planning Project — A Community Approach," by F. T. Sai, F. K. Wurapa and E. K. Quartey-Papafio. Reprinted from the Ghana Medical Journal, vol. 11, no. 1, pp. 9-17, March 1972.

† Many of the c. u. utilities generated by the program imply inputs to the societal environment.

a. Consumption phase refers to the columns of the e-model diagram -- inputs productive activity and evaluative activity of the Consumer Unit. When the governmental intervention's initial incidence is on an environment, the sector is given in parentheses.

b. Check indicates that size of "group" should be estimated. The number of people are a datum bearing on the problem of summation for aggregate wellbeing. See text, page 9.

c. When earning power is increased (via use of time in gainful employment) the earnings, first entered as increased money capital, are immediately available for input to purchase goods. Accordingly category 1 type of utility is enhanced along with other categories associated either with more capital or more consumption.

d. Numbers refer to categories listed in the taxonomy, pages 3 and 4. They are listed in the order of their probable relative importance though many of the attributions are little more than a quick guess, though subject, I have indicated elsewhere, to a great deal of improvement.

We have been thinking of well-being in terms of a complex of utilities--net desirables--that a person tried to maximize in some loose sense. It is a vector having arguments, the quality of which differs--intimacy, a feeling of competence, of opulence, of freedom. A common denominator must measure accretions to the satisfaction of these qualitatively different wants or needs along a parallel axis. In addition, it must convert accretions to capital--education, an automobile--to accretions in the flow of desirables expected to accrue from it. How best to perform this alchemy will require much thought and experimentation and indeed it may be found useful to use double standards or different ones for different problems.

As a starter, I propose a "utility index-point," defined as the increase in a person's (or family's) utility vector that is expected to accrue from spending the marginal one percent of annual income. Thus if the families living in the 15 trailers that were swept away by the flood had incomes of $8,000, we would ask them to picture what by way of desirables they might purchase for $80 (including associated values other than material comfort); then, one would ask whether they would have given up these satisfactions, or more, or less, not to have experienced the flood episode. For the utility index scale to be useful the question must seem reasonable; it must be possible to consider it. Moreover, someone other than the person directly concerned should be able, by an extension of his own empathy, to impute to the respondent some reasonable range of answers. Note that answers will necessarily be very approximate. I would expect that a range of five places, from largest to smallest, would often be the best one could hope to locate. Even so they will often differ materially depending on people's life styles. A "hard hat" will answer differently from a "hippie." To slant the analysis toward the routine, I assume for the purpose of this exercise that everyone is a "hard hat."

The figures appear on the right hand side of Table 3 with explanations of how they are derived from the analytic narrative or other sources in the last column and related notes. Gratification of utility along the nine categories is incorporated in the total. However, two subdivisions of the total also appear. Economic gratification (e), heavily involved in material comfort, is shown separately from psychosocial gratification (s), to which the other categories contribute more heavily--gratifications such as the additional pleasure in recreation where environmental quality in a river has been enhanced (category 3); the value of living in a trusted community rather than in a strange one (category 6).

COMPARISONS OF E-MODEL AND CONVENTIONAL ANALYSIS OF FLOOD IMPACTS

The impacts of the Westfield flood as summarized in the e-model gives a picture of relative emphasis of the various kinds and amounts of flood damage which departs in significant ways from the conventional analysis.

A Comprehensive View of Flood Impacts
The summary uses figures generated in the Table and in the "Analytic Narrative" to which the Table refers by line number, e.g. §1.2.3, §1.2.4, etc. (see Mack 1974) and should be thought of as expressing crude orders of magnitude--perhaps little more than a rank order of five as suggested earlier. Though, in the present state of the art, error may be large, the judgment about relative net advantage among policy alternatives will nevertheless often be sufficiently clear to fall within any likely range of error.

First we have seen that impacts other than those commonly thought of as economic--call them psychosocial--are large. They sum to 39 percent of the impacts of the Westfield flood as measured in utility index points. Thus they increased by two-thirds the measured economic damage. Second, the psychosocial elements were a particularly large part of the total damage experienced by townspeople in their capacity as residents of the town, including particularly of the flood plain. They constituted 57 percent of the total damage for these townspeople, more than double the economic damage. Incidentally, only a small part of this total consisted of the calamity of death or serious injury. It consisted rather of deprivations and miseries such as fear, misinformation, confusion, immobility, distaste for foul smells, sights and disrepair during the flood episode itself; thereafter it consisted of loss of sentimentally precious objects, undesirable preemptions of time for clean up, and continued disorder, odors and work of repair.

The impact of floods on townspeople is further highlighted in the e-model frame. For the average flood plain household, economic impacts--the reduction of material well-being associated with floods--has a substantially larger disutility <u>per dollar of damage</u> than is the case for economic damage to large business enterprises or public structures. The differences are a function of several elements in the analysis that attempt to take ability to pay and income distribution into account.

Third, injury to public properties--roads, bridges, water and sewage treatment systems, etc., seems to have been very substantial yet not systematically identified in the descriptions provided through usual channels. My best guess is that it may well have constituted a quarter of the total structural damage reported in dollar terms. Furthermore, damage to some major dam and reservoir structures was presumably not reported even in the total damage figures.[8] To this dollar damage, whatever its total size, should be added the further miseries to townspeople of a psychosocial nature--the hazard and disgust due to damage to sewers and to water lines and to failures in water treatment, and the terror caused by rumors or news of breached dams. Some of these undesirables can continue for many months.

A fourth changed relative emphasis is in the business category. In dollar terms, business damage, including damage to retailers, farmers, manufacturers, railroads, and large industry, summed to 57 percent of the total (residences and public structures constituted the rest). But in terms of a comprehensive value scheme, the injury to the 55 retail enterprises, which included loss of stocks and damage to homes as well as stores, was certainly far more serious, dollar for dollar, than for large plants, in two of which close to 60 percent of the total business loss (33 percent of all loss) took place.

Finally, the flood resulted in a change in public interest in flood control structures. After the flood the Littleville Dam, previously turned down because of its environmental and neighborhood impacts, was endorsed. Clearly the impact of its construction, for good or ill, is more durable than that of other impacts of the flood.

---

8. The Westfield situation is perhaps not unusual. It has been estimated (Holmes 1961) that one-third of the catastrophic flood losses that occurred in the United States between 1903 and 1958 was due to project failure, either through rupture or overtopping or both.

TABLE 3. EVALUATION OF IMPACTS OF 1955 FLOOD AT
PERIOD I: Onset of the Flood to Its Withdrawal

	Groups of Individuals Affected	Persons or C.U.	Days in Per. I	Incidence: Consumption Phase for Consumer Unit (C.U.) or Other Sector	Desirables (+) or Undesirable (−) Produced Type	Category of Utility (±) Generated
I.1	All relevant people living or working in the floodplain, whether or not they experienced particular impacts (for which see lines I.7 ff. below)	10,600[a]	2½	<u>Input</u>: vision of water hazard of unpredictable consequence	Fear, confusion	−2, −6, −9
I.2		6,500[b]	2½	<u>Productive activity</u>: lost time in travel or inability to work	Uncertain and deteriorated outputs	−2, −9
I.3		10,600	4	<u>Input</u>: Undesirable sights and smells	Disgust, fear, inconvenience	−1, −2, −3
I.4		6,100	4	<u>Input</u>: Deprivation re: ample water supply	Inconvenience, etc.	−1,
I.5		2,250		<u>Productive activity</u>: deterioration in conversion of time into money	Less capital and income	−1, −2
I.6	All other people in the town	12,600[a]	2	<u>Input</u>: vision of unpredictable consequences of water hazard to others	Confusion	−2, +8
I.7	People who lost their lives	2[c]	4	Total loss		− All
I.8	Person who suffered heart attack	1	3	<u>Productive activity</u>: curtailed	Constraints on everything	− Any
I.9	People whose dwellings (including trailers) were seriously flooded		4	<u>Input, activity</u>, etc., in limbo	Fear, confusion, worry, loss	−1, −2, −5, −6
	Householders	300[d]				
	Others in dwellings	600				
I.10	In 350, less serious flooded buildings	1,050		<u>Input, activity</u>: deteriorated and preempted	Inconvenience, worry, uncertainty, etc.	−1, −2
I.11	People (exclusive of dealers) whose automobiles were lost or damaged	400	4	<u>Input</u>: loss of transportation service and capital	Loss of property, motility and status	−1, −2, −6
I.12	People whose 40 stores were flooded quite seriously 15 less seriously	80 30	4	<u>Input, activity</u>, etc.: in limbo	Worry and effort to save property	−1, −2, −7
I.13	People with responsibility for 7 industrial plants	15	4	<u>Input, activity</u>, etc.: in limbo	Worry and effort to save property	−1, −2, −7
I.14	Farmers whose fields were flooded	40		<u>Input, activity</u>, etc.: in limbo		
I.15	People with responsibility for hospital and water works					
I.16	Heroes of the storm	15		<u>Productive activity</u>: inspired by others' need	Strength in meeting challenge	+7, +6, +3
I.17	People and groups aiding, managing and befriending	100		<u>Productive activity</u>: inspired by the situation and the needs	Meeting needs of others	+6, +7

WESTFIELD, MASS --- E-MODEL FRAME
AUGUST 18 Through AUGUST 21, 1955

Average Person	Impact over Period on U-Vector in Index Points Total	Type: eco. (e) soc. (s)		
−.1	−1,060	s −1,060	Fear and confusion resulting from hydrological event and reports thereof (including rumors and conflicting information) cause disutility during the first 2 1/2 days which we rate as .1 index point. This means that if the intensity of the feeling were sustained for a year, it would represent about 15 index points over the year.	I.1
−.04	−260	e −200 s − 60	See Analytic Narrative §1.2.3. Chaotic road conditions and inability to make urgent moves for the 2 1/2 day period is rated −.04 index points which at an annual level would be about 6 index points.	I.2
−.02	−212	s −212	See §1.2.4. The disutility of sights, smells and slime is judged as .02 for a 4-day interval -- equivalent to 2 index points over the year.	I.3
−.02	−122	s −122	See §1.2.5. Rated same as 1.2.4 -- line I.3 above.	I.4
−.008	−18	e −18	Fear of loss of jobs due to flooding, see §1.2.6. Assuming people believe any loss to be temporary, we assign 3 day's worth of 1 index point applying to 2,250 people (1/2 the work force of 4,500).[a]	I.5
−.0006	−8	s −8	Likely to cause some mixture of pain and dissonant pleasure (superiority in having chosen to live above floodplain) perhaps small net negative on the average say .1 index point level at height of flooding.	I.6
−1.2	−2.4	e −1 s −1	See §1.2.1. Assuming annual per capita loss of 110 index points (see note c to this table) the allocation for 2 men for 4 days in Period I is −1.2 x 2.	I.7
−.025	−	−	See §1.2.2. Assume loss of 3 index points for 3 days in Period I. Total is negligible.	I.8
−1.5 −.3	−450 −180	e −200 s −250 e − 50 s −130	See §§1.3.1 and 1.3.2. Consider here people whose house or trailers were severely damaged (perhaps 300 dwellings) and people evacuated therefrom. Heads of households might have experienced loss and worry about family escape, etc., during the 4-day episode in the order of 1.5 index point (140 points at the annual level). Other members are assigned .3 points.	I.9
−.1	−105	e −65 s −40	350 dwellings flooded below first floor. We assign −.1 index point disutility during the episode (annual level of 10 points).	I.10
−.05	−20	e −10 s −10	See §1.3.2.	I.11
−.3	−33	e −20 s −13	See §1.3.5. Fear, worry, and frustration in efforts to save stocks,,etc., assumed to have caused loss of utility averaged for the 55 enterprises (110 people) of roughly .3 index points during the 4-day episode (annual level of 27 points), in addition to impact listed, lines I.1 to I.4, above. (Realities of property loss considered re Period II.)	I.12
−.3	−5	e −4 s −1	See §1.3.6. Impact similar to line I.12 above, but there were also substantial payroll costs in efforts to place sandbags, move inventories, etc. However these, though costs to the companies were gains to the community via continued employment, and therefore, we make no effort to record them.	I.13
−.2	−8	e −6 s −2	Same as above, except that farmers were insured and seem to be more aware of floods as a natural phenomenon .˙. traumatic impact of the event may have been less-- say .2 index points.	I.14
			Impacts perhaps not unlike above though, since not implying personal loss, less severe. However, no basis even for a guess.	I.15
+.5	+8	s +8	See §§1.4.3, 1.4.4. Eight people are specifically mentioned in the accounts and we assume there were also others. Mr. Pease and his sons were heroes to others, though he said that the death of the two Puerto Ricans "spoiled it" for them. Strong positive feeling must have resulted for all-- call it .5 index points (annual level of 45) for the 4-day period.	I.16
+1	+10	s +10	See §1.4.5, also individuals who housed neighbors, 1.4.4. Membership in group involved in mitigating crisis and meeting severe needs of others, though wearying, is personally rewarding-- say +.1 index point for the episode. Number of individuals involved is no more than a guess based on the organizations and jobs undertaken.	I.17

PERIOD II: Reconstruction and

	Groups of Individuals Affected	Persons or C.U.	Months in Per. II	Incidence: Consumption Phase for Consumer Unit (C.U.) or Other Sector	Desirables (+) or Undesirables (−) Produced Type	Category of Utility (±) Generated
II.1	People who lost their lives (and their families)	2	96	Total loss		− All
II.2	People who use roads and	1,000	2	Input: deteriorated public service of roads	Inconvenience in travel	−1
II.3	people who repair them	280	2	Input: job opportunity to convert time to more income	Less leisure More income	−3, −4 +1, +7
II.4	People who see and smell wreckage, chiefly people living in western part of the basin	4,000	6	Input: deteriorated town amenities, help in cleanup	Disgust, feeling of disorder, etc. But appreciation of help in cleanup	−1, −3, +5
II.5	Population in the area	23,000	1	Input: deteriorated water supply services	Poor water	−1
II.6	People who repaired damage	100	2	Input: job opportunity to convert time to more income	Less leisure More income	−3, −4 +1, +7
II.7	People who lost jobs in commerce or industry	few				
II.8	People whose dwellings were flooded and undertook repair	661	12	Input: destruction of capital in dwelling Productive activity: time spent on repair, purchases and arrangements	Chaotic living, loss of valued possessions Less leisure Fun in do-it-yourself	−1, −2, −5 −3, −4, −6 +7
II.9	Owners of commercial enterprises	110	5	Input: decreased income on investment in plant and inventories	Less income and prestige	−1, −2, −9
II.10	Owners of industrial companies	40	120	Input: decreased income on capital	Less income	−1
II.11	Owners of farms	32	?	Input: decreased income on investment in land and crops Productive activity: time and energy spent on agricultural and financial repair		
II.12	Owners of the New Haven Railroad	−	−	Input: decrease in income on capital		
II.13	Suppliers of public funds					
II.14	Westfield community	1,000	2	Evaluative activity: Some enhancement of community interests	Feeling of togetherness	+6
II.15	Heroes of the storm	15	12	Evaluative, productive activity: changed by altered self-image	More confidence	+6, +7

Thereafter, AUGUST 22, 1955 On

Impact over Period on U-Vector in Index Points				
Average Person	Total	Type: eco. (e) soc. (s)		
−335[e]	−670	e−360 s−310	Projection of the cutting off of the utilities of life over 8 future years and the grief to others. See note e and §2.2.1.	II.1
−.1	−100	e−50 s−50	Number of times roads are used during the two months when they were in poor shape varies for people in the town from 80 to very few. Say the inconvenience averages .1 index point over the period (annual level of .6).	II.2
+5	+1,400	e+1,400	Assume that of the $710,000 flood damage to highways in the area (see §2.2.3), $200,000 provided net additions to employment at $16 per day. Then about 280 workers could have earned about $700 each in the two month period. Assume $400 is net gain (after allowing for loss in leisure) and represents +5 index points. Impact on people who supply the funds is not estimated, see line II.12, below.	II.3
−.067 +.01	−268 +40	s−200 e−68 s+40	See §2.2.4. Assume the perceived adverse impacts levels off to little or nothing in 3 months as disorder wanes. (Note for first 4 days alone, we assigned −.02 points, line I.3). Index point average .067 for first 4 months (annual level of .2). Also, community help (service and gifts of equipment, e.g., §§2.1.1 and 2.1.2) must have caused appreciation and augmented service of community-- say, +.01 index points for the first half year.	II.4
	−200	e−200	See §2.2.5. Deterioration due to low pressure (particularly in hospital), poor quality, and inadequate reserves. Our estimate of impact is a token amount. It recognizes that work was underway on repair. For impact on people who supply the funds, see line II.12 below.	II.5
+5	+500	e+500	Assuming local people employed by Corps or state will be chiefly as common laborers, and assuming perhaps 100 people might have been used for a total of 2 months, then along lines of reasoning in line II.3 above, we assign +5 index points net impact.	II.6
	not evident		Jobs seem to have been restored rapidly (see §§1.2.6 and 2.2.6), and in so far as gaps remained, they could mesh in and provide qualitative flexibility with new repair jobs as per lines II.3 and II.6 above.	II.7
−10	−6,610	s−2,500 e−4,100	We judge that tax remissions and subsidy (including rebuilding by the Red Cross) cut losses of householders from $1,681,400 to about $1,131,000 on the 633 homes that experienced some flood damage, an average of $1,787 per house.[f] Since they were typically fairly simple houses, assume average family income was about $7,000. Assume further that $500 of the loss would be borne without replacements along with an additional (unassessed) loss of $300 in sentimental values; "do-it-yourself" would repair $400 in damage, leaving about $900 to be borne out of income, savings or borrowing. In index points per household, call accepted loss −2 (mostly re sentimental losses), do-it-yourself work net of satisfaction, −1, and money spent (for some within the year and/or others extended via borrowing) −7.[g]	II.8
−25	−2,750	s−750 e−2,000	The 55 enterprises may have had losses of $344,000 or $6,255 on the average.[h] Suppose a 5-year loan at 4.5 percent interest was negotiated (the rate on short-term business loans was 3.7% in 1955) on declining balances amortized over the period. The five annual payments for interest and amortization would sum to $7,820 and average $1,560 per an. The burden that this represents depends on its relationship to annual income. Assume, without a basis for doing so, that it averages $30,000, thereby giving a figure of 5 index points a year. In so far as insurance was carried, the amount would be smaller and its relation to income, smaller still.	II.9
−70	−2,800	e−2,800	Flood loss was reported as $2,630,000 (see §2.5.1). Assume a 10-year loan is negotiated on which amortization and interest charges average $322,000 a year, which represents perhaps 10% of annual profits (see discussion, §2.5.2). Assume that income from these sources is 70% of each owner's income, thus causing total income to decline 7% or 7 index points each of 10 years. Note that these figures assume that companies do not carry flood insurance, which may not be the case, and that none of the costs are passed on via selling price-- all of which would seem questionable tactics.	II.10
			Damage to 16 farms estimated at $970,000. No way of imputing social impacts due to lack of information on insurance, ecological impact, etc. See §2.6.	II.11
			Losses were reported as $240,000 in Westfield. In view of the dispersion of ownership and the loose relation between earnings and profit distributions, the impact is unassessible.	II.12
			Public financing of expenditure to recoup flood losses was certainly $1 million, and more likely, $2 million, of the total reported loss of $8 million.[i] To this must be added the cost of repair to dams which presumably was not reported. The impact of this financing rests on the final suppliers of funds-- the people who pay taxes and buy government bonds. We have not tried to assess the impact.	II.13
+.25	+250	s+250	Utility generated by the enhanced togetherness would presumably taper off as the crisis recedes. Say it represents for some people, perhaps 1/20 of the town, utility for no more than 6 months, averaging .5 index point at an annual level-- .25 point for half a year.	II.14
+20	+60	s+60	It seems possible that, for example, Pease's view of himself and others' view of him changed in a positive way. To recognize the possibility, which could involve substantial changes in utility, call it 2 index points for 10 years for 3 men.	II.15

Notes to Table 3

a. Sum of residents and workers on the flood plain.
   <u>Residents</u> calculated thus: 1,900 residential properties at 3.2 people per household (average for Westfield as a whole) = 6,100 residents.
   <u>Workers</u> in the 27 factories and 260 commercial enterprises we estimate as perhaps 4,500 people on the basis of several bits and pieces of information--a total population living and working on the plain of 10,600. (Some of the bits were: the population of Westfield was about 23,200 in 1955 and one out of five people worked in manufacturing employing 4,700 people in the town as a whole. On the flood plain, 9 large plants, of the 10 in the town as a whole, employed 75% of the industrial labor on the plain.) Our estimate of industrial labor in the 27 plants is 3,950. This may well be high. We are told in a letter from M. E. McArdle, Chief, Economics Section, NEDCOE, that about 2,200 people were employed in the 19 plants "subject to flooding" in 1971. Since Littleville had been built in the interval, the designation of the flood plain may well have changed, but so could the number of plants and the workers in the plants; there is no ready way to tell. Accordingly, we use our figures, at least they doubtless err on the high side.

b. All workers and 1.3 of residents: 4,500 + 2,000 = 6,500. This implies some double counting (people who both live and work in the area).

c. The utility lost for these two men about 30 years of age was total. Line 1.7 covers the first 4 days only. Total utility is not 100 times that of goods purchased for the last 1% of income. It is based on an <u>average</u> rather than a marginal yield. Say the average yield per 1% of income is about ½ the marginal yield. Thus the total utility lost to the two men is 50 index points (not 100). But some of the money itself will return to the family via insurance payments, and we shall simply subtract the resulting positive utility from the negative impact of 40 index points associated with what money can buy.

Now consider utility flowing from what money does <u>not</u> buy--utilities emphasized in want categories other than category 1, material comfort. Since we are assuming total loss--an average for everything enjoyed rather than marginal increments--these qualitatively different "arguments" of the total utility vector are additive, though their relative importance is strongly conditioned by the individual's value system. We have already said that we assume a "hard hat's" value system. Accordingly, we pick the figure of an additional 70 points, making a total per capita loss per year of 110 points.

d. The number of seriously damaged homes is based on the fact that 500 people were housed and cared for by the Red Cross and perhaps another 100 by other families; this could involve, say, 300 homes. There were 423 dwellings flooded at least to the first floor, and 38 trailers ruined. Thus we are assuming that of these 461 homes, people experienced the need to abandon 300, leaving another 161 in which there was substantial flood damage. In 210 other buildings the water did not get up to the first flood.

e. See note c for basis of the estimate for Period I. How to project the deprivation of death on into the future is perhaps more a philosophical than an economic question, and therefore, any figures are arbitrary. We assume a graduate compensation for loss of earning power of one member of a young family by a gain in that of others; thus, the economic loss is 40 for the first year (as per note c) with subsequent reduction of 5 points a year. Other than economic values drop off faster; thus, the 70 additional utility points drop to 35 the second year and to 10, the next. To this we add 40 in recognition of grief of family and friends (355 in all).

f. **Damage to dwellings and furnishings** was estimated as follows: <u>Dwellings</u>

28 trailers ruined at assumed average value of $2,500............	$ 70,000
423 homes flooded at least to the first floor. Some of these were the 175 buildings "repaired" for the $100,000 reported by the Red Cross. This gives a cost per home of $571.........	100,000
10 houses were "rebuilt" by the Red Cross; assume these cost $3,000 apiece. (The figure may seem low but houses in the flood plain tend to be relatively simple dwellings. We have data on the value of houses built in the flood plain, 1955-1963; there were 37 with an average value of $6,610 when deflated to 1955 prices. There were also 7 houses with an average value of $3,100 in 1955 prices...............	30,000
238 other houses flooded above first floor; assume structural damage averaged $2,500.......................................	595,000
210 other dwellings were flooded less than to the first floor; assume average structural damage of $1,000 in each of these...	210,000
Personal property: Assume that in the 423 buildings flooded at least up to the first floor, personal property deterioration came to $800 apiece.	
Assume that in the buildings in which only basements were flooded, property damage averaged $300...........................	338,400
Total dwellings and furnishings.................................	<u>1,406,400</u>
Other personal property: 550 automobiles damaged at $500 apiece...	275,000
<u>Total dwellings and personal property</u>...........................	<u>$1,681,400</u>

g. The utility assignments assume that individual households experiencing very different amounts and kinds of losses will vary how much they bear, repair themselves, or purchase repair, etc., in accordance with their own problems, preferences and abilities. This internal flexibility would cause the average negative index points to be less than would be appropriate for a homogeneous aggregate. Unhappiness due to disorder until repair is completed perhaps should be explicitly included but was not attempted.

h. **39 commercial properties** had water up to the first floor. We assumed they suffered $8,000 damage apiece to building and stocks net of resale value. Another 16 had water below the first floor. Their average net damage was assumed at $2,000.

i. **Public funds**: Largely federal, supplied to individuals via subsidies and remission of taxes: $550,400. To agencies for repair of water-related structures: at least the reported $415,000 and more probably on the order of $1,500,000. Local funds of $100,000, not counting working time of public employees. Using the $1,500,000 estimate, the total is $2,150,400 of the total reported loss of $8,060,000.

Implications of Evaluation of Flood Episodes for the Design of Flood Management

Couched in qualitative as well as gross quantitative terms, these several shifts in major analytic outlines point to a number of policy implications. First, with regard to cost-effectiveness, a prerequisite of federal financing for flood control works is the showing that expected benefits equal or exceed expected costs. The calculations focus on economic values (though an environmental impact statement is also required). Because damage to a few large plants or shopping centers can be so large, their presence in a flood plain (or the expectation that they will move in) tends to argue for the economic advantage of protection at federal expense. Application of a comprehensive value scheme along e-model lines greatly subdues the tendency for such facts to be impressive. Insofar as large plants are large beneficiaries of protection, justification is required in terms of unique advantage of the flood plain location and in terms of the enterprises' significance to local employment. Neither of these requirements seems to apply in Westfield.

A second policy implication concerns methods of reducing the disutility (comprehensively defined) of the flood itself. At Westfield the impact was worsened, as the analytic narrative describes, by misinformation conveyed by officials and others about what was likely to happen and what to do about it. Clearly the adverse psychosocial as well as economic impacts could have been reduced not merely by real-time weather and river reporting but more particularly by a local command center that kept up constant and reliable communication between trusted town officers and people in need of information, instructions and aid. Thus the analysis endorses the importance of improved weather and river forecasting, which is well-recognized by the governmental agencies concerned, but also the potential usefulness of other interventions such as providing the upkeep necessary to insure existing structures against rupture and accurate and timely flood hazard reporting. The analysis also stresses the value of providing local competence, town by town, for delivery of systematic aid that is calculated to reduce damage, including psychosocial damage, in addition to the usual efforts to reduce suffering that floods occasion.

To determine the worth of such a comprehensive local planning and command center, its "change-impact" can be analyzed in an e-model frame with a specific kind of intervention in mind. Indeed, it can be designed in response to a careful analysis of just which undesirable impacts it should aim to reduce and which desirable ones (such as community solidarity and a confidence in leadership) it should aim to increase. At a very preliminary level, analysis for the Connecticut River suggests that benefits would be many times greater than costs.

A second type of intervention suggested as potentially valuable by the e-model frame of analysis is the relocation of residences in severely threatened flood plain areas such as the 20-year recurrence interval. Relocation has many psychosocial costs and some benefits. Both these and the economic benefits impact differently on different people. Examined in a comprehensive value framework, costs are high for the old people and for those whose way of life is associated with their particular residence and its location; costs are low for renters and, under the Uniform Relocation Act, often for the poor. Some of these difficulties can be considerably reduced by moving houses themselves rather than relocating people in new houses, or by appropriate kinds of management and counseling.

Third, the relative advantages of structural and nonstructural control methods can be probed in some depth by casting the calamity of a flood in the e-model frame, with its emphasis on who benefits and who loses over what period of time. Prospective benefits, in conjunction with existing protection, is illustrated by the building of Littleville Dam in Westfield. Some of the valley property has risen enormously in value following large commercial development. Certainly the land speculators, developers and commercial enterprises have benefited. People of the town may have benefited if the flood plain locations were so uniquely advantageous that the additional employment and tax base could not have occurred in upland locations; we are told this was not the case, however. Costs on the other hand were clearly broadly dispersed in the form of tax dollars to cover construction costs and environmental disamenities that had previously held up approval of the dam. In any event the comprehensive value framework, focused on the micro-implications of the various methods of furthering "wise use of flood plains" provides a check list for examining and designing rational alternatives.

Achieving Cumulative Knowledge

The third service that an analytic framework must serve is to facilitate learning. Two levels at which learning must occur can be touched on here. The first concerns the routine information produced by agencies having the responsibility of reporting on flood damage. In the context of public responsibility for amelioration of damage, distinctions must be made that recognize qualitative differences among kinds of damage to different people for different durations. The data presently produced by the responsible agencies, the Corps of Engineers and the Soil Conservation Service, are inadequate for the purpose. Distinctions are needed not only to apply the particular model I present, but for any responsible description of how floods affect people and communities, and consequently how the problem, and the public responsibility with respect to it, should be conceived and dealt with.

A method for policy analysis must be subject to learning--to cumulating insight, skill and knowledge. Learning requires the selection of relevant information and its application within a framework subject to verification. I purposely use more comprehensive words than "data," "hypothesis," and "test" because it is possible that standard notions of scientific precision will need some accommodation to the low-quantifiability which attention to qualitatively diverse inputs and outputs tend to imply.

Granting then that precision will often need to be sacrificed for relevance, there is a wide variety of methods that have been developed for dealing with qualitative differences and otherwise poorly quantified information. The problem has been confronted in time series via index number construction and social indicators. It has been confronted in studying individual differences at a given time or repetitively by interview and survey techniques. Where imputations must be made there are gaming techniques and the use of expert panels, to mention a few of many possible approaches. Since the point of reference I propose is the individual or family unit, there is a rich data base to be drawn upon.

A relevant value framework is committed to comprehensiveness, and behavior is likely to be an ambiguous and incomplete indication of wants or gratifications. We lack the link between wants and behavior that the expenditure of money for desirables bought at a price has traditionally supplied. This is serious and demands bold conceptions and innovative research methods. Clearly, <u>imputations</u> must be made concerning subjective states and their relationships to observable evidence. A very interesting notion for studying such relationships has been suggested by an eminent economic theoretician, Kenneth arrow (1967). He calls it the method of "extended sympathy." I would guess that it would be exciting to apply it in the context of problems here raised. For policy guidance one would typically wish to study how people conceptualize problems as well as how they felt about what they perceived. This difference is particularly relevant for example in connection with the assumption that people are irrational in their disregard for flood hazard (see Mack 1974: 3-16 to 3-21). The micro model I have sketched has a number of research problems central to its theoretical formulation. Recourse to the household unit's optimizing behavior as a reference for public policy is predicted on the assumption that the individual achieves some kind of rough and ready optimization across qualitatively different values: qualitatively different imputs are combined in productive activity, and qualitatively different utilities are generated in an optimal combination. Thereby the tradeoff surfaces that seem impossible to deal with at an aggregate level are dealt with at the individual level and public policy can safely aim to optimize the sum of individual utility. Is this a correct assumption? Do people apply an optimizing mechanism analogous to desirables purchased for money when they use qualitatively different inputs to achieve qualitatively different utilities?

The question takes a relatively specific form in the "utility index point." This concept assumes that an individual is capable of comparing the desirability of the bundle of utilities which he expects to experience as a result of spending the last one percent of the year's income with that of other bundles of utilities such as those he may receive as the result of taking the time and energy required for leisure enjoyment, or with the misery (in the sense that he would give up the desirables to have avoided the miseries) of four hours of not knowing what happened to his child during the flood. In view of the fact that only very rough comparisons are required it seems reasonable to suppose that skillful survey research techniques could throw some light on matters of these sorts. Indeed, it is possible that study would develop a preferable common denominator, or perhaps several of them applicable to different kinds of policy problems.

Research could also certainly give a sounder basis for dealing with income distribution than that of the uniform percent of annual income. The use of the uniform percent derives from empirical work in economics referred to as the "relative income hypothesis" pioneered by Dorothy Brady and Rose Friedman (1947). But the particulars of the assumption and its application to marginal expenditures at different levels of income needs study. I would assume the relationship must be curvilinear and not in accord with a simple ratio scale. Empirical questions bearing on the theoretical model can be multiplied indefinitely. Clearly years or rather decades will be needed to build the rudiments of a micro model relevant to public interventions addressed to comprehensive well-being.

I believe, however, that long before such knowledge is achieved--indeed almost immediately--the questions that are asked will be improved. Asking who in a community is affected in what way by a problem, or by policy bearing on it, concerns the proper objectives to be sought for the community as a whole in the light of the inevitable conflicting interests and the possibility of compromise among them. Because community objectives have to be built up from the pebbles of individual preference, community objectives can be defined flexibly and with due regard for cultural and situational variables. Statistical fact-finding may be needed, but often merely roughing out the gross matrix of who pays and who benefits reveals, almost intuitively, that certain of the cells are so large and others so slight that insights about selection and design of policy alternatives seem reasonably clear. Analysis of this kind is likewise a type of research that the micro model calls for and is likewise subject to cumulative knowledge and skill.

References

Arrow, Kenneth J. (1967) "Private and Public Values," pp. 3-21 in Sidney Hook (ed.). Human Values and Economic Policy. New York: New York University Press.

Baumol, W. J. (1959) Business Behavior, Value and Growth. New York: Macmillan.

Becker, Gary H. (1964) Human Capital: A Theoretical and Empirical Analysis with Special Reference to Education. New York: National Bureau of Economic Research.

Becker, Gary H. (1965) "A Theory of the Allocation of Time," Economic Journal, 75, 299 (September), 493-517.

Brady, D. S. and R. Friedman (1957) "Savings and Income Distribution," pp. 247-65 in National Bureau of Economic Research (ed.), Studies in Income and Wealth, Vol. 10. New York: National Bureau of Economic Research.

Cyert, R. M. and J. G. March (1963) A Behavioral Theory of the Firm. Englewood Cliffs, NJ: Prentice-Hall.

Drucker, Peter (1954) The Practice of Management. New York: Harper and Brothers.

Holmes, Rolland C. (1961) "Composition and size of flood losses," pp. 7-20 in Gilbert F. White (ed.), Papers on Flood Problems. Research Paper No. 70. Chicago: Department of Geography, University of Chicago.

Lancaster, Kelvin (1966) "New Approach to Consumer Theory," Journal of Political Economy, 74, 2 (April), 132-57.

Lancaster, Kelvin (1971) Consumer Demand: A New Approach. New York: Columbia University Press.

Lasswell, Harold (1971) Preview of Policy Science. New York: American Elsevier.

Mack, Ruth P. (1971) Planning on Uncertainty: Decision Making in Business and Government Administration. New York: John Wiley.

Mack, Ruth P. (1974) Criteria for Evaluation of Social Impacts of Flood Management Alternatives. Phase I Report, Connecticut River Basin Supplemental Flood Management Study. New York: Institute of Public Administration, 15 March.

Sai, F. T., F. K. Wurape and E. K. Guartey-Papafio (1972) "The Danfa/Ghana Comprehensive Rural Health and Family Planning Project--A Community Approach," Ghana Medical Journal, 11, 1 (March), 9-17.

The Social Psychological Level of Analysis in Social Impact Assessment: Individual Well-Being, Psychosocial Climates, and the Environmental Assessment Scale*

Donald H. Deane and Jeryl L. Mumpower
University of Colorado

Introduction
One value position in the field of social impact assessment (SIA) emphasizes concern with the well-being of individual persons. Concern with social and economic systems is derivative rather than primary by this criterion, and characteristics of such systems are relevant to SIA insofar as they either affect or reflect individual well-being, directly or indirectly, in the short or long run.

The value position that emphasizes effects on individuals is reflected both in the governmental documents mandating environmental impact assessment in general and SIA in particular, and in the writings of numerous professionals in SIA and related fields. The Federal interest is exemplified by Senate Document 97 (U.S. Senate 1962: 2), which states: "Well-being of all the people shall be the overriding determinant in considering the best use of water and related land resources." Similarly, the "Principles and Standards" of the Water Resources Council (1973) mandates primary concern with the "quality of life," a concept ultimately traceable to individuals. Among professionals, Wolf (1974: 6) has asserted that social effects should be considered as the primary rather than secondary effects of technological interventions, stating, "...what engineering is about is people and their values; it stands in the relation of providing material means to the satisfaction of human needs." Mack (1974) has developed an SIA method in which impacts (in this case, of water resource development) are defined in terms of personal utilities--satisfaction of the wants and needs, material and intangible, of individuals. Moos (1974) has specified a very similar value orientation--promotion of maximally effective human functioning--as underlying the related field of "social ecology," the multidisciplinary study of the impacts of social physical environments on human beings. The present paper shares with these authors the general premise that individual well-being is properly the matter of basic concern in SIA and related fields.

---

*The instrument development and research reported in this paper was supported in part by U.S. Administration on Aging (HEW-SRS) Research and Development Grant #93-P-75200/8-01, "Alternatives to Institutionalization for the Aged," awarded to the Geriatrics Division of Fort Logan Mental Health Center, Denver. The authors gratefully thank Maxine Long and Nell Swiers for their work in collecting and interpreting the data reported here and for their suggestions regarding administration and revision of the EAS instrument.

Defining the <u>conceptual</u> locus of social impacts in terms of individuals' well-being, quality of life or personal utility leaves open however such crucial <u>methodological</u> questions as: Is an individual the best judge of his own well-being, or is his well-being best assessed through others' "objective" observations of his health, social productivity and so forth? Can researchers or expert informants predict how particular individuals or groups will define their subjective well-being, such that the former can act as proxies for the latter in the assessment process? Can aggregated objective (e.g. census) data about individuals or their environments suffice to indicate or predict those individuals' subjective well-being? The first of these questions is primarily philosophical, while the others are primarily empirical.

Campbell (1976: 118) has addressed both philosophical and empirical issues related to methods of assessing individual well-being. He contrasts "objective" social indicators (those that describe events, behaviors or characteristics of individuals but that do not depend on focal individuals' descriptions of their own lives) with "subjective" social indicators (those based on individuals' personal expression), as follows:

> If we believe that the quality of life lies in the objective circumstances of life, these measures (objective social indicators) will tell us all we need to know; but if we believe...that the quality of life lies in the experience of life, then these are surrogate indicators. They describe the conditions of life that might be assumed to influence life experience, but they do not assess that experience directly. If we are primarily concerned with describing the quality of life experience of the population, we will need measures different from those that are used to describe the objective circumstances in which people live. We will have to develop measures that go directly to the experience itself...the individuals' sense of well-being.[1]

Campbell goes on to discuss results of national sample surveys in which respondents were asked to rate their personal well-being in terms of happiness, satisfaction or the like. Among his conclusions from these results is that adequately reliable assessment of subjective well-being is <u>feasible</u>, as well as desirable, in large-scale social research. Campbell's discussion of empirical issues is taken up again later in this paper.

---

1. Campbell uses the terms "quality of life" and "subjective well-being" synonymously to denote both the subjective experiences of individuals and the individuals' reports of those experiences. Fitzsimmons, Stuart and Wolff (1975: 41) distinguish between "quality of life" and "social well-being," however:
> Quality of Life is an expression of the degree to which <u>individuals and families</u> enjoy their lives in good health, in economic security, and in general peace of mind about the present and future. Social well-being can be evaluated at a higher level of aggregation, i.e., the level of the <u>community and its constituent groups</u>. Social well-being contributes to the quality of life...the future capacity of the community to sustain itself in a character consistent with the desires of its residents and institutions (i.e., the community's social well-being) must be assessed.

The government documents quoted above appear to focus primarily on <u>individual</u> well-being; whether the authors intended the terms "well-being" and "quality of life" to concern social systems characteristics as well is unclear. In the present paper, the terms "well-being," "individual well-being," "subjective well-being" and "quality of life" are used interchangeably to denote individual persons' experiences and reports of those experiences. Any references to social system properties are clearly distinguished.

The preceding discussion shows that SIA must involve work at the <u>psychological</u> level of analysis--the study of individuals' experience and behavior. But the need to predict psychological effects and guide interventions affecting them requires that SIA also continue to work at more macroscopic <u>sociological</u>, <u>economic</u>, and related levels of analysis, since factors at these levels strongly exert psychological effects. The influences of such macroscopic systems on individuals are quite indirect, however, and are mediated by the <u>interfaces</u> between macroscopic and psychological systems. Consequently, if SIA is to predict, assess and influence the psychological effects of environmental interventions, it must study such interfaces as well as, and in relation to, the separate systems they link.

The term "social psychological level of analysis" is used throughout the rest of this paper to denote study of the links between individuals and their socioeconomic environments and the relations between such links and the systems they join. Many distinct foci of attention are possible within this level of analysis. This paper focuses primarily on the individual's subjective perception[2] of his socioeconomic environment--the crucial mediator of his responses to that environment. Relevant responses include overt behavior of various kinds as well as subjective experience of well-being. The paper discusses the following sequence of five topics:

(I) The inadequacy of currently prevailing SIA methods for assessing and predicting individual well-being.

(II) Potential uses in SIA of subjective data at the social psychological level of analysis.

(III) A general approach to assessing the subjectively perceived environment that is systematic, standardized and quantitative. This approach assesses the perceived environment in terms of "psychosocial climate" or "atmosphere."

(IV) The development and use of an instrument, the Environmental Assessment Scale (EAS), which applies the psychosocial climate approach to assess an intervention into a therapeutic milieu for the elderly.

(V) The relevance to and possible uses in SIA of the EAS instrument in particular and the psychosocial climate assessment approach in general.

I. <u>Inadequacy of Prevailing SIA Methods</u>
This section discusses empirical and theoretical bases of the premise that social psychological analysis is necessary for predicting effects of environmental interventions on individuals.

---

2. The terms "perception," "perceived," etc., are used here in a quite broad sense to denote a person's subjective view of and beliefs about a situation. The present usage subsumes cognitive processes often distinguished more precisely as "conceptualization," "judgment," "evaluation," etc. "Perception," as used here, can focus on events which are not present at the time of response as well as events which are.

Much SIA research shares two major characteristics: (1) it focuses on relatively large-scale social and geographical systems and, correspondingly, uses relatively macroscopic levels of analysis; and (2) it relies primarily on "objective," quantitative, aggregated information such as Federal census and other data concerning population, employment, housing, health, crime and so forth. Such data typically are secondary, having been collected for purposes other than the SIA research per se.

Characteristic (1) is understandable in light of the correspondingly large scope of many environmental interventions. Characteristic (2) is understandable in light of the large amount of data which must be collected, the high cost of collecting new data and the need to assess historical trends which began long before initiation of a given SIA effort. There are increasing indications however that both the macroscopic level of analysis and the reliance on objective (particularly secondary) data are inadequate for assessing the well-being of the members of focal systems at any given point in time (before or after implementation of an environmental intervention), let alone for predicting the effects of proposed interventions on future well-being. These indications come from both empirical and theoretical sources representing psychology, sociology and related disciplines.

A. Empirical Basis

The empirical basis for asserting that macroscopic analysis is inadequate for predicting individual well-being can be divided into evidence concerning potential determinants of well-being and indicators of whatever well-being has been attained. Regarding determinants, Campbell (1976) has summarized national survey data showing that various gross characteristics of persons' objective circumstances together account for no more than 17% of the variance in those persons' subjectively-expressed well-being. The objective predictor data concerned persons' stage in the life cycle, urbanicity, age, race, income, occupation, education, religion and sex--variables representative of those which are typically studied in SIA and assumed to be closely related to individual well-being. Regarding indicators, Maddox (1962) found elderly persons' overall subjective well-being (termed "morale" in this case) to be related more closely to their subjective ratings of their own health than to physicians' objective health ratings. This implies that census data on disease rates, doctor visits, etc. cannot be taken as direct indicators of elderly persons' subjective well-being.

Discussing the limited usefulness of objective data on supposed determinants or indicators of subjective well-being, Campbell (1976) predicted that refining measures of situational factors and well-being, measuring additional situational and demographic factors and so forth probably would not significantly improve prediction of well-being from relatively gross objective circumstances. Rather, he hypothesized that significant predictive gains would require much more fine-grained assessment of individuals' psychological predispositions--beliefs, perceptions and values,[3]

---

[3]. Beliefs, perceptions and values are often discussed under the broader concept "attitudes." The "attitude" concept is proving to be too gross to be useful for analytic purposes, however. Distinctly different aspects of "attitudes" are relevant for different purposes; different measures of assumedly the same attitude often fail to covary. At best, use of the attitude concept for analytic purposes is appropriate only after clear specification of factors such as:

(1) The focal object or concept (e.g., dams in general or a particular dam);

as well as more enduring personality traits and patterns of social interaction.

Considerable evidence confirms the usefulness of data on such variables for predicting individuals' subjective well-being and other responses. Jessor and Jessor (1973) and Moos (1974), for example, have presented evidence showing persons' actions to be related more closely to their subjective perceptions of their environments (e.g., families, treatment institutions) than to the more objectively measured characteristics of those environments. Lowenthal and Haven (1968) found personal friendship patterns to be an important mediator of the effects of urban environments and socio-economic status on the incidence of psychiatric disorder.

B. Theoretical Basis

The theoretical basis for asserting that macroscopic analysis is inadequate for predicting individual well-being is congruent with the empirical evidence cited above, and can be presented in terms of three related points.

First, environmental influences on a person's behavior and subjective state are exerted primarily by his immediate physical and social environment rather than by the larger macro-system that includes it but is more remotely related to it (Barker 1968; Boughey 1974; Gump 1968; Jessor and Jessor 1973). Large-scale systems thus form what Gump (1968) has termed the "gross context" of behavior; that is, they affect individuals within them through complex chains of mediation rather than directly.

Second, linkages between macro-systems (e.g., communities), their embedded micro-system components (e.g., work settings, social groups), and ultimately individuals are highly probabilistic rather than deterministic. The probabilism results from the open rather than closed nature of social systems (Indik and Berrien 1968; Katz and Kahn 1966). Consequently, knowledge of macro-system properties is unlikely to suffice for predicting individuals' overt behavior or subjective states. Better prediction, as well as understanding, should be afford by analysis of individuals' more immediate environments.

Footnote 3 continued:

(2) The relevant attitude dimension (i.e., beliefs about the attitude object, evaluation of it, action intention concerning it);

(3) The purpose of assessment (e.g., description of the actor's views at a particular time vs. prediction of his later behavior); and, if the purpose is prediction,

(4) The particular kind of behavior to be predicted; and,

(5) The situation in which that behavior is predicted to occur.

Consequently, the global term "attitude" is not used in this paper except for comparison and contrast between the methods and concepts presented here and those discussed elsewhere in terms of "attitudes." There is a great deal of overlap between the former and the latter.

Third, even analysis of individuals' immediate environments is unlikely to suffice for predicting or explaining their responses if limited to physical observation or to description by an independent, "objective" observer. A longstanding tradition in social science holds that the objective situation (particularly in its social aspects) affects a person only through his perception of it, that the subjectively perceived situation is not isomorphic to the objective one, and that different people are likely to perceive a given objective situation differently. As Zajon (1968: 320) states, "The physical and objective properties of social stimulation and incentives have always been assumed to be less significant for the analysis of social behavior than their subjective counterparts."[4] Consequently, the best prediction of individuals' responses to their environments should come from the social psychological level of analysis; i.e., study of individuals' own perceptions of these environments.

Environmental descriptions by observers such as researchers or expert informants (which are "objective" only in substituting the observers' subjectivity for the subjectivity of the focal individuals) may be useful as surrogate data, but only if the conceptual structures of the descriptions are congruent with the conceptual structures used by the focal individuals, and the observers' use of those structures matches the focal individuals' own use. Researchers are notoriously poor at achieving these conditions, however, particularly when they must rely on assumed cultural similarity between themselves and the focal individuals because direct data on the latters' viewpoints are lacking. Similarly, informants too often fail to represent the viewpoints about which they supposedly are expert.

C. Summary

SIA research typically uses relatively macroscopic levels of analysis and proceeds primarily through secondary analysis of quantitative aggregated data about people and their environments. Empirical evidence and theoretical considerations suggest however that both the macroscopic level of analysis and the reliance on objective, aggregated, secondary data are inadequate for assessment of the well-being of members of the focal populations. Social psychological study of individuals' own perceptions of their environments is likely to yield better prediction of the individuals' subjective well-being and other responses to their environments.

II. Potential Uses of Subjective Data in SIA

Direct assessment of individuals' subjective perceptions of their environment and subjective well-being should be useful in the "social profiling" (pre-intervention baseline measurement), "assessment" during and following intervention, and "evaluation" (judgment of the desirability or undesirability of assessed impacts) phases of SIA as defined by Wolf (1974; 1975). More specifically, collection of such subjective data should be useful in the following interrelated respects.

---

4. The dual premise that persons' experiences of situations comprise the most proximal and therefore strongest determinant of their responses to those situations and that such experiences are not interpersonally equivalent has influenced work in the disciplines of psychology (Lewin 1935, discussed by Deutsch 1968; Murray 1938, discussed by Moos 1974; Brunswik 1952, discussed by Hammond 1966; Jessor and Jessor 1973); organizational behavior (Taguiri and Litwin 1968; Pace 1968; Stern 1970); and sociology (Thomas 1928; Rose 1962; Blumer 1966). Thomas (1928: 572) summarized this premise succinctly in positing his famous "definition of the situation," that "If men define situation as real they are real in their consequences."

A. **Evaluation of Proposed or In-Progress Projects:**
Despite the emphasis by Fitzsimmons, Stuart and Wolff (1975), Mack (1974) and Wolf (1974), that **the values of the affected parties should be the basis for** evaluation (as distinguished from descriptive assessment) of social impacts, most such evaluation apparently is still done by researchers or other project staff. At best, such professionals try to serve as proxies for the affected parties. At worst, the professionals impose their own (or their agencies') values about what is good for the affected parties or for the society in general. Either way, the professionals typically do not know how the affected parties actually would evaluate the situation. Direct assessment of those parties' own views would allow SIA researchers to satisfy more adequately their own professional norms which mandate separation of social description from social evaluation.

B. **Development of Research Methods and Instruments:**
Availability of data on persons' subjective perceptions of their environments and subjective well-being might facilitate the training ("calibration") of observers to predict such subjective responses more accurately. Relatedly, subjective data could serve as criteria in attempts to develop and validate better objective indicators of subjective well-being. Although the data discussed by Campbell (1976) do not inspire optimism about success, neither do they conclusively augur failure. Use of more fine-grained data about objective variables that are more proximal to personal experience, along with development of separate indicators for different subcultures, ethnic groups, age categories, socioeconomic strata, geographical regions, and so forth, might be more fruitful than were earlier approaches. The recognition of social diversity by seeking separate indicators for members of different social groupings may be especially useful in this regard. To the extent that members of different groupings attend to different aspects of their environments and respond differentially to a given aspect, any intragroup consistencies are obscured if data on all groupings are pooled for indicator development.

Success either in calibrating observers or in developing valid objective indicators of subjective well-being could reduce SIA research expenses considerably. Once observers were calibrated or objective indicators developed (and assuming stability in focal individuals' responses to their objectively observable environments), the observers or indicators could then be used in subsequent assessment phases in lieu of repeated direct surveys of the focal individuals. Whether such success is attainable remains an open question at this point, however.

C. **Improvement of Project Performance with Respect to Improving Individual Well-Being:**
Bauer (1967: 43) has noted "a strong tendency for the managers of any system to improve the performance of the system on those variables that are regularly measured." Given this tendency, regular collection of subjective data (or well-validated proxy data) would be likely to lead to improvement in monitoring program effects on subjective well-being. Note however that the observed tendency implies that managers know how to improve effects measurement on a given variable once they are aware that improvement is needed and motivated to seek such improvement. But whether managers generally do know how to significantly improve measurement of project effects on individual well-being, particularly when distributional equity is a major criterion for judging improvement, is highly questionable.

D. **Improvement of Planning of Future Projects:**
Assessment of the ultimate effects of environmental interventions on individuals'

perceptions and well-being would provide the feedback necessary (although not in itself sufficient) for improving the knowledge base for planning and implementation. At the simplest level, such feedback would indicate degrees of success or failure of particular interventions. More fruitful however would be the use of feedback to analyze causal patterns--_why_ and _how_ certain interventions exert certain effects. Such improved causal knowledge would facilitate design of new alternatives as well as choice among available alternatives.

Mack (1974) has discussed an example of the use of feedback about project effects on individuals to improve the planning-relevant knowledge base. This feedback revealed many significantly undesirable social effects that had not been previously recorded, showed significantly differential distribution of social and economic benefits and costs among different parties, and suggested that the overall cost-benefit balance may not have been as favorable as previously thought.

The remainder of this paper concerns methods for realizing the potential benefits of subjective data. The focus is restricted to assessment of the subjectively perceived environment; on assessment of subjective well-being, see Campbell 1976; Andrews and Withey 1976; _Social Indicators Research_ and _Social Indicators Newsletter_; and the general literature on attitude assessment. Attitude assessment efforts concern subjective well-being (satisfaction) per se as well as perception of environments and other factors, often within a single instrument. The three-volume compilation by Robinson and his associates (Robinson, Rusk and Head 1968; Robinson and Shaver 1969; Robinson, Athanasiou and Head 1969) provides the best overview of attitude assessment methods, instruments and findings.

The topic sequence follows the outline presented earlier: a general approach to assessment of the subjectively perceived environment, an instrument representing the general approach and, finally, comments regarding the relevance to and possible uses in SIA of both the general approach and the instrument.

III. Assessment of the Perceived Environment: Psychosocial Climate

"Psychosocial climate" ("atmosphere") has been defined by Taguiri (1968: 25) as ". . . a relatively enduring quality of the total environment that (a) is experienced by the occupants, (b) influences their behavior, and (c) can be described in terms of the values of a particular set of characteristics (or attributes) of the environment." A number of authors have drawn the analogy between the psychosocial climate of an environment and the personality of an individual, noting that both are defined in terms of a relatively global impression inferred by an observer from a much larger number of more discrete events (Brunswik 1952; Hammond 1966; Moos 1976; Murray 1938; Stern 1970; Taguiri 1968). Both a personality and an environment may be seen in terms either of a unitary summary variable or of a profile of more specific dimensions (which may themselves be quite broad).

All approaches to assessing psychosocial climates and related constructs are based on the assumption that the occupants (and/or observers) of a given environment can articulate in some way the environmental characteristics which most strongly affect occupants' various overt and covert responses. This is an empirical question, and there is much evidence (e.g., Sommer 1969) that people cannot articulate _all_ the environmental characteristics which affect them. The relevant question here, however, concerns only the _relative_ usefulness of whatever people _can_ articulate in some way about their environment versus aggregated objective data of the kind discussed earlier for predicting occupants' overt and covert responses. The authors obviously assume the former is better than the latter for this purpose.

Psychosocial climates can be assessed by use of structured survey methods, less structured naturalistic (e.g., ethnological) exploration, or a combination of the two. Only the structured survey approach is explored in this paper. Numerous authors have called for greater use of structured survey methods in order to gain the interrelated benefits of: (1) standardization, thus comparability of results over time, research sites, respondents and researchers; (2) quantification, thus amenability to statistical analysis; and (3) organization of a large mass of data into a more coherent and interpretable form.

In contrast, others have suggested that the limitations of structured assessment with respect to validity and meaningfulness of results outweigh these benefits. No further comparison between structured and less-structured methods is attempted here since the advantages and disadvantages of each are discussed extensively in the social science literature (e.g., Selltiz and others 1964).

The substance of an environment's psychosocial climate is assessed in terms of norm patterns, value orientations, opportunities for or constraints upon action and satisfaction, positive and negative sanctions, formal and informal social relationship, and so forth. Such characteristics are organized into various dimensions, usually 12 or fewer in number. On the basis of both his own research and that of others, Moos (1974) suggested that a wide variety of social environments can be described usefully in terms of three categories of climate dimensions:

1. Relationship: The extent and nature of individuals' involvement with their environment and relations with one another. (Relationship dimensions appear similar across the different types of environments studied.)

2. Personal Development: The basic directions along which personal growth and self-enhancement tend to occur. (Specific Personal Development dimensions depend on the particular goals of different environments.)

3. System Maintenance and System Change: The nature and clarity of authority structures and sanctions, and the relative prevalence of orientations toward stability or change. (System Maintenance/Change dimensions appear similar across the different types of environments studied.)

Environments studied thus far by Moos and others have included total institutions (psychiatric, correctional, military), educational environments (university, junior and senior high school) and naturally-occurring community settings (industrial and other work milieus, social and task-oriented groups, and families). Psychiatric, educational and work settings have received the most attention.

Structured instruments for assessing psychosocial climates are constructed and validated by the standard psychometric methods and criteria relevant to any attitude instrument. In fact, all psychosocial climate measures qualify as attitude measures, and many attitude measures--particularly of occupational attitudes--

qualify as psychosocial climate measures. The different labels seem mainly to reflect differences in researchers' backgrounds rather than in the instruments or their foci. If there is any difference it is mainly in data interpretation. Attitude researchers tend generally to interpret responses as indicating characteristics of respondents; perceived environment researchers seem more inclined to interpret responses as reasonably valid depictions of the environment. Measures of occupational attitudes often concern both job satisfaction per se and perceptions of the work environment dimensions which may affect it (Robinson, Athanasiou and Head 1969). In both psychosocial climate and occupational attitude measures, environmental dimensions commonly are assessed in quite evaluative terms, using item phrasing that either is directly evaluative (like-dislike, good-bad) or is descriptive of general cultural values. (The difference between evaluation and description is a matter of degree, not of kind, and apparently not a useful basis for classifying research instruments.) Although merging description and evaluation of an environment (on a particular dimension or as a whole) eliminates the possibility of studying the relation of the two empirically, it is appropriate when the purpose of investigation is to assess the environment from the occupants' own viewpoint; SIA has the latter purpose much more than the former.

Subjective perceptions of the several dimensions of an environment, even if assessed in primarily descriptive terms, generally are affected by the person's view of the environment as a whole. Nonetheless, researchers have found it worthwhile to maintain distinctions among different dimensions rather than to collapse them into a single index of environmental perception. Dimensions of well-designed instruments appear psychometrically distinct although positively intercorrelated; maximum intercorrelations typically do not exceed .40 (Brigham, Woodmansee and Cook 1976; Moos 1974). More important, Moos (1974) has found different dimensions of the perceived environment to be differentially related to different outcome dimensions. For example, climates most conducive to subjective well-being (satisfaction) seem to differ from climates most conducive to development of interpersonal and productive skill; some level of subjective <u>dis</u>comfort seems to facilitate the latter. Similarly, numerous occupational attitude studies have found little relation between job satisfaction and job performance, although the situational determinants of each remain uncertain (Athanasiou 1969; Vroom 1964).

As expected, these findings show that environments as wholes cannot be predicted or designed to be simply "good" or "bad"; <u>what aspect of the environment</u> is good or bad for <u>what kind of outcome</u> must be specified. Consequently, the authors' Environmental Assessment Scale (EAS), discussed in the following section, distinguishes multiple dimensions of the environment in order to facilitate differential prediction of outcomes.

IV. Development and Use of the Environmental Assessment Scale (EAS)

A. Purpose:

The EAS was developed by the authors to assess the psychosocial climate of a newly established, community-based, therapeutically-oriented boarding home for elderly persons having slight-to-moderate psychiatric disabilities. Such persons do not need psychiatric inpatient care or the physical aspects of nursing home care but cannot cope with totally independent living. The importance of assessing the environment which this program comprised for its participants followed from the program's design as a "therapeutic milieu." The therapeutic milieu concept posits the immediate social environment as a major determinant of one's functioning and subjective well-being (see Cumming and Cumming 1962; Fairweather and others 1969; Gottesman 1969; Gottesman, Coons and Donahue 1966).

Multidimensional assessment of the milieu was necessary because of the need to balance among potentially conflicting therapeutic considerations (e.g., providing social support to participants yet not fostering excessive dependency), and between therapeutic considerations and respect for participants' (residents') right to live as free adults in their own home. The psychosocial climate approach to environmental assessment was selected on the premise that intended social milieu characteristics had to be perceived appropriately by participants in order for those characteristics to exert the effects desired by program planners.

B. *Instrument Design*:

The EAS was designed to assess factors previously found important in studies of community-based psychiatric treatment settings (Moos 1974), nursing homes and other geratric institutions (Lawton 1972; 1973; Lawton and Nahemow 1974; Lieberman 1969; Pincus 1968; Pincus and Wood 1970), and non-institutional, community-based housing for the elderly (Carp 1966; Hamovitch and Peterson 1969; Sherman and others 1968). Ten focal dimensions were defined as follows:

1. <u>Staff Relations with Residents</u>: Degree of warmth, openness and respect in staff members' relations with residents.

2. <u>Encouragement of Independence</u>: Degree to which staff encourage residents to take the most actively independent role possible in their own lives, and to which staff refrain from custodial or dependency-fostering practices.

3. <u>Social Atmosphere</u>: Degree to which the setting constitutes a lively, sociable atmosphere for residents as opposed to a passive, dull or repressive one.

4. <u>Resident-Resident Support</u>: Degree to which cohesive, helpful and supportive relations exist among the residents of the setting.

5. <u>Democratic Orientation</u>: Degree to which the residents can influence policies and practices in the residence, and to which staff treat residents as adults with rights rather than as subordinates or inferiors in a staff-dominated, authoritarian hierarchy.

6. <u>Personal Freedom</u>: Degree of residents' freedom to determine their own daily activities, as contrasted to regimentation of behavior by staff.

7. <u>Norm Clarity</u>: Degree of precision, stability and knowledge by residents of rules, norms and loci of responsibilities.

8. <u>Privacy</u>: Degree to which the environment allows residents to establish and maintain personal domains which are not open to public view and into which staff will not intrude without permission.

9. <u>Integration with the Community</u>: Degree of opportunity for communication with and access to the larger heterogeneous community in which the setting is located.

10. <u>Resources</u>: Degree to which the setting provides opportunities for residents to engage (especially on their own initiative) in a variety of work and leisure activities and, in general, to obtain satisfactions actively or passively.

These dimensions concern the <u>social</u> environment almost exclusively. Physical factors are assessed only with respect to the setting's physical pleasantness and its location relative to the larger community (hence opportunity for interaction with it).

The EAS was constructed as a 50-item scale comprising ten 5-item subscales which correspond to the ten conceptual dimensions. Each item is a declarative statement which potentially describes the living situation. The response format is dichotomous; respondents are asked to state whether each item is "Mostly True" or "Mostly Not True" of the focal setting.

Most items have fairly clear evaluative implications. This was unavoidable since the items were constructed to tap patterns of events, relationships, etc. which are important in people's daily lives and to which both general cultural values and normative therapeutic milieu theory pertain. For example, "A lot of residents here just seem to be passing time,"; "Staff here will never admit when they are wrong"; and "A resident can get enough privacy here" are items from the Social Atmosphere, Democratic Orientation and Privacy subscales, respectively. To control for acquiescence bias, each subscale includes a 3:2 or 2:3 mix between items worded favorably and unfavorably to the focal setting, yielding a 25:25 mix in the instrument as a whole. Social desirability bias, defined as the respondent's efforts to make either himself or the focal environment look good, was dealt with in the interviewing process rather than in instrument construction. The correlation between the EAS and a Housing Satisfaction scale that sought explicitly evaluational responses (in good-bad, like-dislike terms) about various aspects of respondents' dwellings is discussed below under results.

C. <u>Instrument Use</u>:
Seventy-five elderly persons served as EAS respondents during a 20-month period. Of the 75, 23 were members of the "experimental" group living in the geriatric boarding home under evaluation; 52 were "control" group members who were similar to experimental group members in personal characteristics but who lived in other institutional (e.g., State mental hospital) or quasi-institutional (e.g., nursing home, private boarding home) settings. Additionally, 11 staff members of the experimental boarding home program completed the EAS regarding the program. Staff of control settings could not be interviewed, unfortunately.

The EAS was administered to experimental and control group respondents as part of a multi-instrument interview battery designed to assess various aspects of respondents' "quality of life." "Quality of life" was operationalized in terms both of respondents' self-evaluated morale, health and satisfaction with various aspects of their lives (social relations, finances, activities, etc.) and of respondents' self-reported behavior patterns (involving activities, mobility, social interaction, etc.). In addition to the EAS, the full battery contained instruments concerning: Housing Satisfaction, Free-Time and Work Activities, Peer Interaction, Family Interaction, Mobility and Self-Perceived Change (adapted from Lawton 1973), Morale (Lawton 1972), Personal Competence (adapted from Campbell and others 1960), Self-Perceived Health (adapted from various sources), and Self-Perceived Finances (adapted from Thompson and Streib 1958).

D. Results:

Data analysis results are discussed only briefly because research circumstances precluded instrument revision and retesting on the basis of early results and gave insufficient opportunity for validational exploration. The further validational work needed would involve more complete sampling of settings (e.g., a wider range of settings and more respondents in each) and of respondents (e.g., systematically using staff and observers as well as residents), assessment of EAS relations with objective environmental characteristics and assessment of EAS relations with outcome data such as residents' clinically-judged levels of functioning. Because of these constraints psychometric findings regarding reliability and validity, although promising, indicate that considerable revision would be necessary before the EAS were suitable for general use. Clarification of item wordings and of the frame of reference respondents are to use (e.g., ideal vs. realistic) is particularly important. With these major qualifications, the principal methodological and substantive findings were as follows.

1. **Methodological**: Internal characteristics of the subscales and overall scale were assessed in terms of homogeneity ("HR"; Scott 1968) and reliability (Cronbach's "alpha").[5] Not all subscales were found to be homogeneous, reliable, and distinct from one another. Homogeneity, reliability, and distinctness were:

- _Good_ for subscales concerning Staff Relations With Residents, Democratic Orientation, Privacy and Resources;

- _Fair_ for the subscales concerning Social Atmosphere, Personal Freedom and Integration With the Community; and

- _Poor_ for the subscales concerning Encouragement of Independence, Norm Clarity, and Resident-Resident Support.

Reliability of the total scale was high, primarily because of its length, but homogeneity was low (as anticipated) because of the diversity of content it was designed to cover. Note however that because each subscale and therefore the total scale was scored in a "higher is better" direction, items concerning different content areas would be expected to covary somewhat through tapping a general evaluative

---

5. Scott's _Homogeneity ratio_ (HR) reflects the average level of interitem correlation within a scale. It can range from -1.0 to 1.0. The HR, in contrast to the KR-20 or Cronbach's _alpha_ reliability indices, does not vary with the number of items in the scale. A low HR indicates that not all of the items measure a common concept. The maximum HR of 1.0 is possible only when all items are perfectly correlated. Since in practice a compromise is usually sought between diversity and homogeneity among the items in a scale, an intermediate HR is desirable. The statistically optimum HR for dichotomous items is .33. No strictly statistical criterion exists for the lower acceptable limit, but .20 is conventionally used.

set and, insofar as this occurs, the total scale may be interpretable as a measure of perceived <u>overall quality</u> of the social environment.

Discriminative power was assessed by separate one-way analyses of variance (ANOVAs) which used as dependent variables each subscale, the total scale, and all 50 items. Respondents' housing type (setting) was the independent variable in each analysis. Five housing types were distinguished: (1) the focal geriatrics boarding home, (2) other boarding homes, (3) nursing homes, (4) Family Care homes[6] and (5) State mental hospital geriatrics inpatient care. Settings were analyzed by type rather than individually because of the small sample size from most sites, although individual site analysis is desirable when possible because the heterogeneity of sites within each setting type (Kosberg and Tobin 1972; Lieberman 1969) obscures the discriminating power of the instrument. These ANOVAs were approximations of the "known groups" approach to scale validation--approximations because only impressionistic (although convergent) evidence is available about true variation of the sampled living environments on the measured dimensions or on the objective factors most closely related to them.

Only three subscales--Social Atmosphere, Privacy, and Resources--discriminated significantly among housing types; the total scale did not. All individual items that discriminated significantly were in the three discriminating subscales.

Convergent validity was explored in terms of correlations with other scales in the instrument battery. The Housing Satisfaction scale correlated highly with the total EAS (.65) as well as with the EAS' Social Atmosphere (.50), Staff Relations With Residents (.47), Resident-Resident Support (.45) and Privacy (.47) subscales. In a stepwise regression predicting Housing Satisfaction scale scores from EAS subscale scores, these four subscales entered the regression first (in the order listed) and accounted for 43% of the variance. The Morale scale correlated moderately with the total EAS (.28) and with the Privacy (.38), Personal Freedom (.32), and Resident-Resident Support (.28) subscales. It should also be noted that the Morale scale correlated .31 with the Housing Satisfaction scale and .44 with the Free-Time activities scale. These findings are congruent with earlier findings in the geriatrics literature and support the usefulness of both the total EAS and its separate subscales.

2. <u>Substantive</u>: Data analysis revealed several interesting patterns which appear interpretable despite the psychometric limitations discussed above.

First, <u>privacy</u> appears to be very important to elderly (and probably other) residents of congregate living situations. The EAS Privacy subscale was the most closely related to general morale and was strongly related to overall housing satisfac-

---

6. Family Care is a psychiatric treatment modality wherein up to four patients are placed in the home of a specially certified family in the community. Both the patients and the family receive periodic support and supervision from Fort Logan Mental Health Center Staff. Family Care is designed for patients who need a highly structured environment with much socio-emotional support. It is ranked second only to inpatient treatment in therapeutic intensity.

tion as well. These findings support Pincus and Wood's (1970) finding that privacy was the most salient aspect of the perceived environment in nursing homes. When one lives in a congregate setting where privacy is scarce, the value of whatever privacy one can retain apparently is enhanced.

Second, *activities* appear here as elsewhere (Maddox 1963) to be an important correlate, although not necessarily a determinant, of morale and related aspects of well-being. This supports the "Activity Theory" position in gerontology, as contrasted with the "Disengagement Theory" position which holds that the elderly wish to disengage from social relationships and other activity (Kastenbaum 1965; Maddox 1969).

Third, *social relationships* are very important to members of this population. EAS subscales concerning relations with staff and with other residents were the best predictors of overall housing satisfaction and, after privacy, contributed most strongly to prediction of overall morale as well.

Fourth, no significant difference was found between the experimental setting and the control settings (taken collectively) on the total EAS or any EAS subscale. The lack of significant differences was consistent over time during the 20-month research period. This highlights the difficulty of changing objective circumstances (structural or nonstructural) in a way that significantly *improves* those circumstances as perceived by occupants.

Fifth, EAS responses by staff of the focal geriatrics boarding home were consistently more favorable than responses by residents. Differences were particularly marked with respect to Democratic Orientation, Social Atmosphere, and Resources. This discrepancy parallels the consistent finding reported by Moos (1974); it is likely that similar staff-resident discrepancies would have appeared for control settings if their staffs had been interviewed.

V. Conclusions

A. Relevance to SIA

The preceding discussions of the psychosocial climate approach to assessing the subjectively perceived environment and of the EAS instrument representing this approach did not discuss specific applications to SIA because neither has been used in this field. The environments studied thus far in terms of psychosocial climate have been rather small social systems, primarily formal organizations or parts of them, in contrast to the larger scale, less formal systems with which SIA usually is concerned. Additionally, the EAS was developed to assess the effects of an exclusively social intervention, while SIA typically concerns interventions that are at least partly technological (structural). Consequently, some final comments on the more direct relevance of the psychosocial climate approach and the EAS to SIA are in order.

One issue in this regard concerns the nature of the focal intervention and its objectives, in this case the difference between the geriatric boarding home as a social intervention program whose social psychological effects were defined as *primary* and the more technologically-oriented interventions studied in SIA whose social effects are defined as *side* effects. Are research methods and instruments interchangeable between these two settings? The authors believe so because however the forms and major purposes of the interventions may differ, their effects overlap considerably. Whether effects are defined as "primary" or "side" depends on the assessor's purpose, not on the focal system or the effects themselves; granting this, "there are no such things as side effects" (Willems and Campbell 1975: 206). Hence it is appropriate to assess the effects of intendedly social and intendedly technological interventions in terms of a common framework.

A second issue concerns the scope of the intervention and the focal system. Are methods developed for small-scale social systems useful for assessing interventions affecting much larger-scale systems? This divides into two questions: (1) Is research on small-scale systems per se relevant to assessing effects of larger-scale interventions? and (2) Are methods developed for small-scale systems adaptable for application directly to larger-scale systems? These questions are addressed in turn. Both are answered in the affirmative.

Regarding (1), we assume that large-scale systems affect individuals primarily through mediation by the individuals' immediate environments rather than directly. Given this premise, if large-scale interventions have effects relevant to the lives of individuals, these effects will appear in the small-scale systems more proximal to those individuals. Hence research focused on such small-scale systems (e.g., work organizations, schools, hospitals, residential settings) is useful regardless of whether these systems are affected directly by an intervention specifically focused on them or indirectly, through the chain of effects initiated by a more macroscopic physical or social intervention.

Regarding (2), it would seem both appropriate and feasible to extend the psychosocial climate approach to the assessment of larger-scale social systems. Several considerations support this conclusion.

First, this approach has already been used to assess a wide variety of social systems varying in size as well as in many other characteristics. Not all of these involved strictly primary groups, those the respondent confronts face-to-face. Focal systems have included schools, companies, etc. as wholes, large parts of which the respondents could only know indirectly and inferentially. Assessment of communities, political systems, and the like in similar terms would not be a drastic change.

Second, discussions in the SIA literature and elsewhere about changes in communities and larger social systems use concepts which are quite congruent with those already used in psychosocial climate research, concepts such as community cohesion, uncertainty of the future, anomie, powerlessness, stressfulness, dependence, autonomy, opportunity, quality of family and interpersonal relations, and so on. Each of these (overlapping) concepts has a fundamentally psychological component or counterpart--e.g., anomia for anomie, belief in external locus of control for powerlessness, etc. Each can be grouped into one of Moos' (1974) three general categories of climate dimensions (Relationship, Personal Development, System Maintenance/Change). And each, except safety, is reflected to some extent in the ten EAS dimensions. (A Safety dimension should be added in any EAS revision; its omission was an oversight.) Consequently, incorporation of such concepts in measures constructed to assess the psychosocial climates of large-scale systems such as communities would be a natural extension of current work.

A precedent for this exists to some extent in measures of "alienation," "normlessness," "powerlessness," "locus of control," etc. Items such as "Most people really don't care what happens to the next fellow" (Srole 1956) and "The average citizen can have an influence on government decisions" (Neal and Seeman 1964) would fit well into a psychosocial climate assessment instrument. Inclusion of such items in multidimensional psychosocial climate instruments used in wide varieties of settings and circumstances might further help to anchor such social science concepts. For both logical and empirical reasons, however, only such <u>situation-focused</u> items, and not the self-focused (e.g., "What happens to me is my own doing"; Gurin and others 1969) or general ideology (e.g., "Nowadays a persons has to live pretty much for today and let tomorrow take care of itself"; Srole 1956) items that also are included in such scales, should be used in psychosocial climate measures.

The logical reason is to maintain consistency of focus on the <u>situation</u> per se. The empirical reason is the recent evidence indicating plausibly (although in contrast with earlier evidence) that respondents discriminate significantly between situation-focused, general ideological, and self-focused items rather than projecting their personal attitudes equally onto all item types (Gurin and others 1969).

B. <u>Qualifications</u>
This generally optimistic view requires qualification on three counts, however.

First, the psychosocial climate approach is only one of many possible ways of assessing perceived environments. It provides a relatively broad view; finer-grained assessment--e.g., of particular norms, events, and relationships--will often be important but presently must be obtained separately. In principle it would be possible to make a psychosocial climate measure as specific as desired by adding items and scales, but this would limit the range of relevant settings and available respondents, thus reducing comparability.

Second, even if assessment of persons' subjective perceptions of their environments (by the psychosocial climate or other approaches) proves useful for predicting those persons' subjective well-being, the predictions are likely to hold only with situational factors held constant. Prediction of persons' subjective perceptions of well-being in changed circumstance would remain as problematic to SIA researchers as prediction of any other consequences of social change. And asking persons to predict their own perceptions of new situations would be no more fruitful than asking them to predict any other of their responses to situations with which they are unfamiliar.

Third, again assuming that persons' subjective environmental perceptions prove useful to SIA researchers for predicting those persons' subjective well-being, it may or may not be possible to design interventions that are more effective in improving (or avoiding harm to) environments as perceived by those persons. Data about subjective environmental perceptions and well-being might prove useful mainly for indicating what earlier interventions were harmful or useless, and how so. This would suggest (but not prove) what proposed projects should <u>not</u> be carried out--itself no trivial benefit.

In short, all that can be said is that greater attention in SIA to the social psychological level of analysis is highly desirable, and the methodological approaches discussed above appear promising for work at this level of analysis.

The practical utility of these approaches, as of most other SIA methods, remains to be seen.

References

Andrews, F. M. and S. B. Withey (1976) Social Indicators of Well-Being. New York: Plenum.

Athanasiou, R. (1969) "Job Attitudes and Occupational Performance: A Review of Some Important Literature" in J. P. Robinson, R. Athanasiou and K. B. Head (eds.), Measures of Occupational Attitudes and Occupational Characteristics. Ann Arbor: Survey Research Center, Institute for Social Research, University of Michigan.

Barker, R. (1968) Ecological Psychology. Palo Alto, CA: Stanford University Press.

Bauer, R. A. (1967) "Detection and Anticipation of Impact: The Nature of the Task," pp. 1-67 in R. A. Bauer (ed.), Social Indicators. Cambridge, MA: M.I.T. Press.

Blumer, H. (1966) "Sociological Implications of the Thought of George Herbert Mead," American Journal of Sociology, 71, 535-544.

Boughey, A. S. (1974) "Human Ecology," pp. 1-16 in D. Carson (ed.) Man-Environment Themes. Milwaukee, WI: Environmental Design Research Association.

Brigham, J. C., J. J. Woodmansee and S. W. Cook (1976) "Dimensions of Verbal Racial Attitudes: Interracial Marriage and Approaches to Racial Equality," Journal of Social Issues, 32, 2, 9-22.

Brunswik, E. (1952) The Conceptual Framework of Psychology. Chicago: University of Chicago Press.

Campbell, A. (1976) "Subjective Measures of Well-Being," American Psychologist, 31, 2, (February), 117-124.

Campbell, A. and others (1960) The American Voter. New York: John Wiley.

Carp, F. M. (1966) A Future for the Aged. Austin: University of Texas Press.

Cumming, J. and E. Cumming (1962) Ego and Milieu. Chicago: Aldine.

Deutsch, M. (1968) "Field Theory in Social Psychology," in G. Lindzey and E. Aronson (eds.), Handbook of Social Psychology, Vol. 1. Reading, MA: Addison-Wesley.

Fairweather, G. W. and others (1969) Community Life for the Mentally Ill: An Alternative to Institutional Care. Chicago: Aldine.

Fitzsimmons, S. J., L. I. Stuart, and P. C. Wolff (1975) Social Assessment Manual. Cambridge, MA: Abt Associates, July.

Gottesman, L. E. (1969) "Extended Care of the Aged: Psycholosocial Aspects," Journal of Geriatric Psychiatry, 2, 2, (Spring), 220-237.

Gottesman, L. E., D. Coons and D. Donahue (1966) Milieu Therapy and the Long-Term Geriatric Patient. Unpublished manuscript. Ann Arbor: Division of Gerontology, University of Michigan.

Gump, P. V. (1968) "Persons, Settings, and Larger Contexts," in B. P. Indik and F. K. Berrien (eds.) People, Groups, and Organizations. New York: Teachers College Press.

Gurin, P. and others (1969) "Internal-External Control in the Motivational Dynamics of Negro Youth," Journal of Social Issues, 25, 29-53.

Hammond, K. R. (ed.) (1966) The Psychology of Egon Brunswik. New York: Holt, Rinehart and Winston.

Hamovitch, M. B. and J. E. Peterson (1969) "Housing Needs and Satisfactions of the Elderly," The Gerontologist, 9.

Indik, B. P. and F. K. Berrien (eds.) (1968) People, Groups, and Organizations. New York: Teachers College Press.

Jessor R. and S. Jessor (1973) "The Perceived Environment in Behavioral Science: Some Conceptual Issues and Some Illustrative Data," American Behavioral Scientist, 16, 801-828.

Kastenbaum, R. (1965) "Theories of Human Aging: The Search for a Conceptual Framework," Journal of Social Issues, 21, 4.

Katz, D. and R. L. Kahn (1966) The Social Psychology of Organizations. New York: John Wiley.

Kosberg, J. I. and S. S. Tobin (1972) "Variability among Nursing Homes," The Gerontologist, 12, 214-219.

Lawton, M. P. (1972) "The Dimensions of Morale," in D. Kent, R. Kastenbaum and S. Sherwood (eds.) Research Planning and Action for the Elderly. New York: Behavioral Publications.

Lawton, M. P. (1973) "Indices of Well-Being." Philadelphia: Philadelphia Geriatrics Center. mimeo.

Lawton, M. P. and L. Nahemow (1974) "Ecology and the Aging Process," in C. Eisdorfer and M. P. Lawton (eds.) Psychology of Adult Development and Aging. Washington, DC: American Psychological Association.

Lewin, K. (1935) A Dynamic Theory of Personality. New York: McGraw-Hill.

Lieberman, M. A. (1969) "Institutionalization of the Aged: Effects on Behavior," Journal of Gerontology, 24, 330-340.

Lowenthal, M. F. and C. Haven (1968) "Interaction and Adaptation: Intimacy as a Critical Variable," American Sociological Review, 33.

Mack, R. P. (1974) "Criteria for Evaluation of Social Impacts of Flood Management Analysis," pp. 175-95 in C. P. Wolf (ed.) Social Impact Assessment. Milwaukee, WI: Environmental Design Research Association.

Maddox, G. L. (1962) "Some Correlates of Differences in Self-Assessment of Health Status among the Elderly," Journal of Gerontology, 17, 180-185.

Maddox, G. L. (1963) "Activity and Morale: A Longitudinal Study of Selected Elderly Subjects," Social Forces, 42, 195-204.

Maddox, G. L. (1969) "Themes and Issues in Sociological Theories of Human Aging," in Proceedings of the 8th International Congress of Gerontology, Vol. 1. Washington, DC.

Moos, R. (1974) Evaluating Treatment Environments: A Social Ecological Approach. New York: John Wiley.

Murray, H. (1938) Explorations in Personality. New York: Oxford University Press.

Neal, A. and M. Seeman (1964) "Organizations and Powerlessness: A Test of the Mediation Hypothesis," American Sociological Review, 29, 216-225.

Pace, C. R. (1969) College and University Environment Scales. 2nd ed. Princeton, NJ: Educational Testing Service.

Pincus, A. (1968) "The Definition and Measurement of the Institutional Environment in Homes for the Aged," Gerontologist, 8, 3 (Autumn).

Pincus, A. and V. Wood (1970) "Methodological Issues in Measuring the Environment in Institutions for the Aged and Its Impact on Residents," Aging and Human Development, 1.

Robinson, J. P., R. Athanasiou and K. B. Head (1969) Measures of Occupational Attitudes and Occupational Characteristics. Ann Arbor: Institute for Social Research, University of Michigan.

Robinson, J. P., J. G. Rusk and K. B. Head (1968) Measures of Political Attitudes. Ann Arbor: Institute for Social Research, University of Michigan.

Robinson, J. P. and P. R. Shaver (1969) Measures of Social Psychological Attitudes. Ann Arbor: Institute for Social Research, University of Michigan.

Rose, A. M. (1962) Human Behavior and Social Processes: An Interactionist Approach. Boston: Houghton Mifflin.

Scott, W. A. (1968) "Attitude Measurement," in G. Lindzey and E. Aronson (eds.), Handbook of Social Psychology. Reading, MA: Addison-Wesley.

Selltiz, C. M. and others (1964) Research Methods in Social Relations. New York: Holt, Rinehart and Winston.

Sherman, S. R. and others (1968) "Psychological Effects of Retirement Housing," The Gerontologist, 8.

Sommer, R. (1969) Personal Space. Englewood Cliffs, NJ: Prentice-Hall.

Srole, L. (1956) "Social Integration and Certain Corollaries," American Sociological Review, 21, 709-716.

Stern, G. G. (1970) People in Context: Measuring Person-Environment Congruence in Education and Industry. New York: John Wiley.

Taguiri, R. (1968) "The Concept of Organizational Climate," in R. Taguiri and G. H. Litwin (eds.) Organizational Climate: Explorations of a Concept. Cambridge, MA: Harvard University Press.

Taguiri, R. and G. H. Litwin (eds.) (1968) Organizational Climate: Explorations of a Concept. Cambridge, MA: Harvard University Press.

Thompson, W. and J. Streib (1958) "Situational Determinants: Health and Economic Deprivation in Retirement," Journal of Social Issues, 14.

Thomas, W. (1928) The Child in America. New York: Alfred A. Knopf.

U.S. Senate (1962) "Policies, Standards, and Procedures in the Formulation, Evaluation, and Review of Plans for Use and Development of Water and Related Land Resources." Document No. 97. Washington, DC: U.S. Government Printing Office.

Vroom, V. (1964) Work and Motivation. New York: John Wiley.

Water Resources Council (1973) "Water and Related Land Resources: Establishment of Principles and Standards for Planning," Federal Register, 38, 174, (10 September) 24778-24869.

Willems, E. P. and D. E. Campbell (1975) "Behavioral Ecology: A New Approach to Health Status and Health Care," pp. 200-210 in B. Honikman (ed.) Responding to Social Change. Stroudsburg, PA: Dowden, Hutchinson and Ross.

Wolf, C. P. (1974) "Social Impact Assessment: The State of the Art," pp. 1-44 in C. P. Wolf (ed.) Social Impact Assessment. Milwaukee, WI: Environmental Design Research Association.

Wolf, C. P. (1975) "Social Impact Assessment in Cross-Cultural Perspective," Environmental Sociology 6, (April), 18-28.

Zajonc, R. B. (1968) "Cognitive Theories in Social Psychology," in G. Lindzey and E. Aronson (eds.), Handbook of Social Psychology, Vol. 1. Reading, MA: Addison-Wesley.

III Profiling

Profiling is the process of describing the initial conditions of an impact situation. It provides baseline social data of the impact area from which the magnitude and intensity of changes, induced and incidental, can then be estimated. As such, it constitutes a "before" measure of social conditions--before the effects of planned intervention are felt by impacted individuals, organizations, institutions and communities. The profile features on which data are gathered comprise the salient impact categories of later assessment.

The selections in this section[1] employ varied techniques for social profiling. The first, by White, is a case study of two communities potentially affected by a Corps of Engineers dredging project. Using leadership interviews, census data and a local community planning survey, White exemplifies a multi-methods approach to social profiling. The social profile is effectively organized around such community characteristics as interest groups, community cohesion and organization, social problems, occupational structure, growth patterns and demographic trends. His projection of profile data to anticipate post-project conditions through causal modeling illustrates the usefulness of this step.

Savatsky and Freilich advocate the use of leadership surveys as an efficient approach to social profiling. They illustrate this method's potential for SIA by describing four towns and the social change which will possibly result from impending physical changes. Qualitative data on predictive variables such as leadership effectiveness and style are combined with census data in this pilot approach, and assist in their interpretation.

Both White and Savatsky and Freilich compose predominantely qualitative social profiles based largely on informant interviews. The remaining three articles are concerned with quantitative profile data, instructing the reader where and how to obtain computerized data bases, translating census data to geographical areas that differ from census areas, and constructing a social indicator system for comparing the social profiles of cities.

The article by Aidala provides a brief guide to computerized data banks for social profiling. A major problem in their use is the lack of congruence between their

---

1. Profiling is also discussed by Finsterbusch in Section I and by Watkins and Olsen and Merwin in Section II.

154   Profiling

data structure and the data requirements of many SIAs. This problem is addressed by Wallach who describes programs developed by the Center for Census Use Studies for obtaining census data for small study areas which have different boundaries than census enumeration areas.

In the final article of the section, Liu presents social indicator profiles for the 65 largest Standard Metropolitan Statistical Areas (SMSAs) based on 123 measurable quality of life factors. The factors are organized into five quality of life components: economic, political, environmental, health-education, and social. Scores on these components are averaged into an overall score for the 65 SMSAs. Liu also calculates his set of social indicators for all 243 metropolitan areas, thus constituting a data bank of social profile statistics suitably modified. Any SIA centering on his analysis can also serve to guide social profiling of nonmetropolitan areas.

Yaquina Bay: A Case Study in Social Impact Assessment

William T. White
Dames and Moore

Purpose
This paper briefly summarizes the socioeconomic impact portion of an environmental impact statement prepared for a Corps of Engineers dredging project in the Yaquina Bay and Yaquina River, Oregon. The study was conducted in a short time and on a limited budget. Because the Corps of Engineers guidelines require the consideration of impacts both with and without the proposed action, a highly quantitative technique was not chosen. Instead, several scenarios which attempt to project the social and economic profiles of the communities were utilized.

These scenarios were designed to provide relevant information about the project to the public and decision-makers so that they could judge the project fairly. The basic question, then, was "What are the impacts which the community cannot handle?" The answer requires analyzing the social, economic and political institutions of the impact area and identifying the groups who pay the "price" of the project as well as those who stand to benefit.

Study Area
The study area is centered on the Yaquina Bay and Yaquina River in Oregon. There are two municipalities which are likely to be most influenced by the project, Newport with about 5,000 persons and Toledo with about 3,000 persons. Newport, a resort community on the coast of Oregon, has a port and waterfront area which are located on Yaquina Bay. Along the coast runs a north-south highway where commercial development catering to both residents and tourists has occurred. Residential patterns have sprawled somewhat, but there are no physical limitations to further development of housing. Newport is the county seat.

Toledo, on the other hand, is about six miles inland from the coast. Located on the Yaquina River, Toledo is most influenced by the Georgia-Pacific paper mill, which uses the river to barge its products out of Toledo. Its terrain is hilly, and land for housing is limited. In contrast to Newport, Toledo's commercial area shows evidence of decline. There is considerable interaction between Toledo and Newport. Although the paper mill is located in Toledo, many mill workers live in Newport. Furthermore, many of the area's recreational resources are located in Newport and attract young people from Toledo.

Approach
A general approach to the problem of assessing the project impacts is presented in Figure 1. Basically, the social structure may be impacted through one or two paths. The most direct path is the physical impact of a project upon a functioning community. Disruption of the communication channels or physical alteration of a neighborhood are examples of what might result from a project impact. Since the project is not occurring on land, but in a bay and river, the direct physical impact of the project upon the communities was judged to be insignificant. The

FIGURE 1. IMPACT PATHWAYS ON THE SOCIAL STRUCTURE

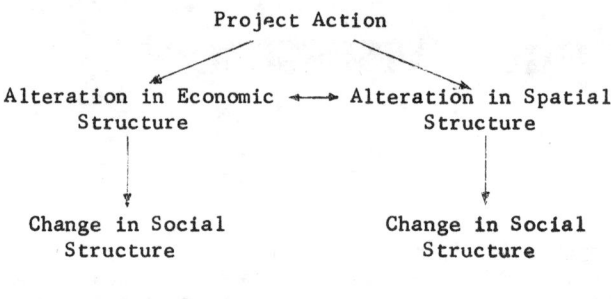

second pathway, and the more likely one in this particular situation, is that dredging of the bay and river will have economic impacts resulting in social impacts. Since economics is only slightly more predictive than sociology, the creation of various scenarios for the impact analysis is an appropriate technique in identifying potential social impacts. For the purpose of this discussion, only one such scenario will be presented.

The next step is to create a working model of both Newport and Toledo. Social variables examined (see Table 1) were chosen to portray the various groups in the communities and how they interact. The groups are then classified into a rough hierarchy in terms of their active participation in local decision-making. This process encompasses "social cohesion" and "desirable community growth" features required by the Corps of Engineers guidelines.

The major data source for collecting the baseline data was a survey of community leaders similar to that discussed by Sanders (1960: 75-77). Data from the community leaders survey were heavily supplemented by demographic data from the U.S. Census of Population. In addition, the results of a local community planning survey were available, and were quite useful in preparing the report.

Baseline Profile

The two municipalities, Newport and Toledo, are quite different in many ways. Newport is a small town characterized by an historic up-and-down growth pattern. Presently it has four main occupational groups, and the stratification system parallels the occupational groupings. These groups are: the commercial fishermen, the merchants along the coastal highway, the lumber mill workers, and local governmental employees. Of these groups the mill workers are most numerous, and least active in local community affairs. Local governmental employees are also a substantial group; however, they have not taken a strong role in local affairs. The last two groups are quite important. The local merchants are very active in local affairs, so much so that some respondents said that the merchants controlled decision-making in Newport. The local commerical fishermen are relatively small in number, but they take an active role in issues affecting the waterfront, an area that once was the focal point of Newport and has been something of a tourist attraction. The fishermen apparently feel that the waterfront is being slighted by local decision-makers in favor of the commercial section along the coastal highway.

TABLE 1. SOCIAL CHARACTERISTICS OF THE STUDY AREA

Characteristic	Newport	Toledo
Power Groups	Merchants Mill workers Commercial fishermen Government employees	Merchants Mill workers
Community Cohesion	Fair: centers around city manager; some dissatisfaction among commercial fishermen	Tenuous: exists in opposition to Newport
Social Problems	Inadequate housing Alcoholism Seasonal employment Counterculture population	Inadequate housing Alcoholism
Occupational Structure	Business Tourism Commercial fishing Government employment Paper mill employment	Business Paper mill employment
Historical Growth Trends	Uneven: between 1950-1960 sustained growth; between 1960-1970 sustained slight decline	Uneven: between 1950-1960 sustained growth; between 1960-1970 sustained slight decline
Migration Trends	Substantial out-migration of young persons aged 20 to 30	Substantial out-migration of young persons aged 20 to 30

Community decision-making takes place by way of two channels. One is through the city manager, who has managed Newport for more than 10 years. A good deal of local governmental policy is left to this official. Lower voter turnouts for mayoral and city council elections indicate general satisfaction with the city manager and his decisions, and interviews support this impression. The city manager appears to draw strong support from the local business community, which dominates the mayoral and city council elections. Apparently, local service clubs are dominated by these same local business leaders; other groups--mill workers, commercial fishermen, etc.--do not seem to be actively involved in the local decision-making process. It is quite possible that a shift in the political structure of Newport could crystallize basic disagreements which may impair the community's ability to handle problems.

Toledo is quite different. It is a declining mill town dominated by the commercial group. Presently, Toledo maintains its identity primarily by opposing Newport. Once the county seat, Toledo maintains a separate port authority, school system and religious organization although combining these could result in a more efficient delivery of services. The need to maintain a separate identity for Toledo is stressed by their local business community.

Newport and Toledo are not without social problems. The major problem mentioned by the majority of respondents is alcoholism. The reasons given for the alcoholism range from unemployment, which is seasonal because of the tourism, lumber and fishing employment, to lack of other activities. The second most common social problem mentioned is broken families--a large percentage of females head families in Newport and Toledo. Another problem, though perceived as such by only a few respondents, is inadequate job opportunities for young persons (aged 20 to 30), which may account for their high rate of out-migration.

Impact Scenario
Figure 2 shows a possible sequence of events which could result in a considerable social impact in the study area. As stated earlier, the social impacts for this study are judged to be the result of alterations in the economic structure of the communities. The economic analysis for the project hypothesized that the project action, channel dredging, would permit tankers to supply liquified natural gas to a regassification facility in Newport. This project in turn would permit the construction of a large ice plant which would greatly increase Newport's attractiveness to commercial fishermen along Oregon's coast. It is possible, then, that the number of commercial fishermen and the amount of fish processing done in Newport would increase.

With increased job opportunities an influx of commercial fishermen might result in population growth of up to 20 percent for Newport and would require more social services for the new residents. It is also possible that the growth would spur a shift in community power structure. Since most of the growth would be associated with the fishing industry, it is reasonable to expect that this group (commercial fishermen and fish processors) would take a more active role in community decision-making. Since most of the growth-inducing activities are associated with fishing and fish processing, it may be expected that the waterfront would become more of a focal point for Newport.

Conclusion
The baseline profile and the impact scenario presented on the next page provide a decision-maker with an idea of potential social impacts associated with the project action. However, the scenario presented is relative to other possible project actions and before it can be applied usefully those for alternative actions must be constructed and compared.

The subjective nature of scenario construction has advantages and disadvantages. One major advantage is cost; a researcher may construct such scenarios relatively inexpensively. The major disadvantage is that the subjective construction of scenarios does not easily lend itself to predicting the magnitude or timing of impacts. Even with this disadvantage a decision-maker may utilize the scenario as a means for balancing potential social impacts with other impacts in areas.

FIGURE 2: IMPACT SCENARIO

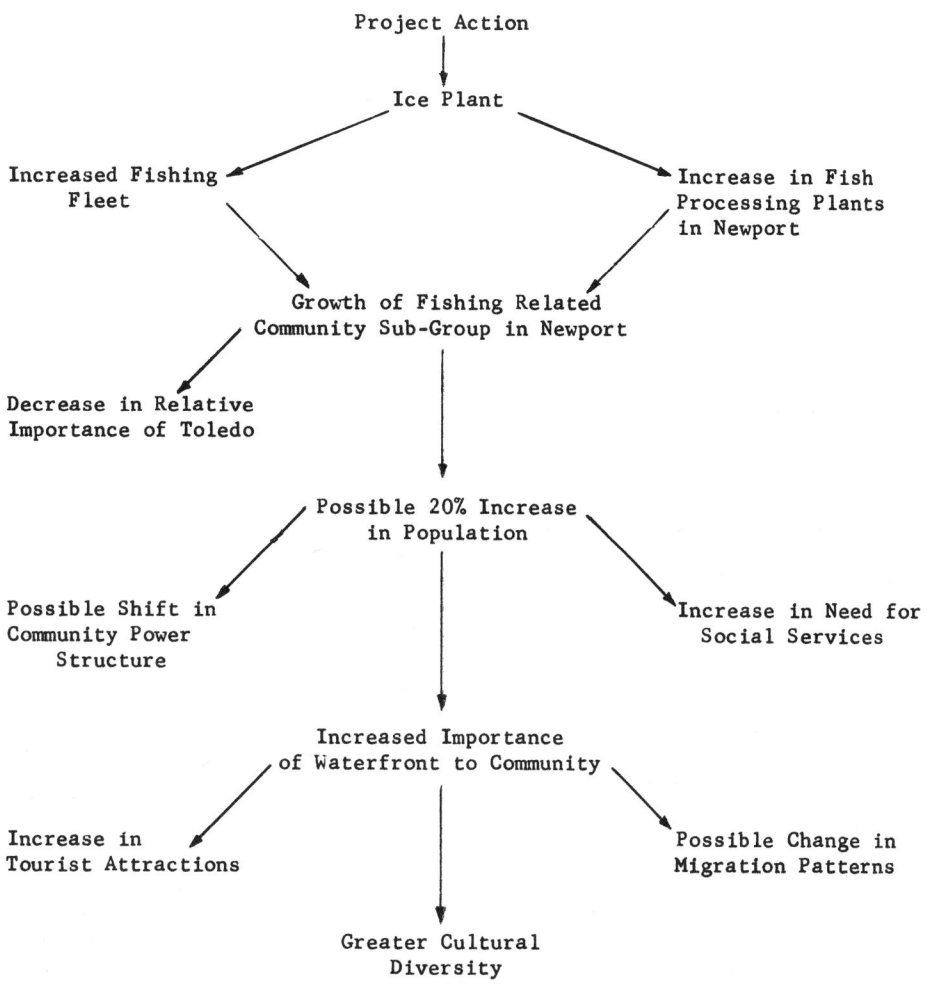

Reference

Sanders, Irwin T. (1960) "The Community Social Profile," American Sociological Review, 25, 1 (February), 75-77.

Leadership Generated Community Social Profiles

Pamela Dee Savatski
Social Assessment Services

Elva Dianne Freilich
Environmental Research & Technology

Leadership informant methodologies are effective techniques for providing the baseline information needed to project probable social effects fostered by a physical change. Of these techniques, Sanders' (1960) "community social profile," used previously for studies of political system interaction, is perhaps the most adaptable proven methodology. It allows for a cost-effective analysis of life styles, social interactions, relative quality of life, direction of perceived social change and aspirations held in common by community members.

In adopting this approach the question naturally arises of the reliability and validity of leaders' responses compared to more broadly-based surveys. The informant technique described by Seidler (1974) is much like the approach used in leadership generated community social profiling. Informants were selected on the basis of the positions they held, having first established their anticipated knowledge and biases. Seidler then elected to use ten informants with "balancing biases" from each category to be examined. Interestingly, he found, "strong reliability was attained only where each sub-group of informants contained five persons. In these cases, one fivesome was almost as good as another."

Seidler admits that some social scientists have had limited success with comparable techniques, but he cites instances such as Campbell's (1955) informant investigation which had a .9 reliability with a large scale sample survey. His concluding thought is that if controlling measures are applied to biases and knowledge inadequacies, internal inaccuracies can be held to a minimum. Similarly, in an unpublished paper entitled "Informed Resources as a Valid Source of Information," Bruce Ergood reports an extremely high correlation between the results of a field program similar to the community social profile and a fairly large randomized cluster survey of residents in Appalachian communities. This finding lends additional support to the belief that knowledgeable respondents give correct information and have an accurate perception of their community. In our own research, we have found marked similarity between the results of a pilot leadership profile and a more intensive survey.

In applying leadership generated community social profile methodology, the first task is to recruit and train an interview team of four or five research assistants, each with some skill in interviewing, some knowledge of how the data will be utilized, and an awareness of the community as a sociological concept and as a social system. This number of researchers tends to provide a built-in cross-check, good group interaction, and prompt data collection. Graduate sociology departments are an excellent source from which to obtain assistants who are trained and available for short time periods.

The members of the research team begin by asking residents within the vicinity of a proposed project for the names of key persons in each of several specified community institutions and areas of interest. From these names, a list of the 25 to 40 most frequently mentioned persons is compiled. It has been found that 20 of these simple contact interviews are usually quite sufficient for this compilation. A greater number quickly reaches a point of diminishing returns.

A standardized though open-ended questionnaire is then used to intensively interview the most frequently named leaders about their perceptions of community interactions, institutions, goals, life styles, and social change. Each leader is asked what he/she likes best about the community and what he/she considers to be its chief problems. This persons is also asked to name eight people whom he/she considers important leaders in the community and to state the reasons for selecting them. Questions are individualized to elicit further commentary. The interviewers, trained in observational methods, are requested to record their impressions and any anecdotes or asides brought up by the informant.

A comparison of the leaders' responses is then made to provide a general feeling of the community. Usually the existence of any major groupings and social divisions which one must further investigate is revealed by this comparison. After completing the interviews, each interviewer develops a description of his/her qualitative perceptions of the community, and these are also compared as a further source of information.

Any apparent discrepancies which run counter to expectation necessitate further interviewing. The interviewed leaders who have shown objectivity may be asked to clarify those differences. Also, when any of the important social divisions which have been identified in the community are not represented, the appropriate spokesperson for each of these groups must also be interviewed. The names of these knowledgeable people have usually been provided by the community leaders. These additional interviews serve to clarify how the social divisions fit into the overall community framework.

The interview material is then superimposed upon a background of census data, newsclippings, reports, and historical information. The research team selects those social traits central to the inquiry and about which there are sufficient data for analysis. From this analysis emerges the "social profile" which highlights, rather than catalogs, the characteristics of a community. A series of such profiles, when analyzed as a single interacting entity, provides regional data. Results are compared and contrasted in order to suggest any social change due to a proposed physical change.

Excerpts from a recent study will help to demonstrate the structure of the data, the potential usage of the "community social profile methodology" and possible theoretical approaches. In this study, Savatsky (1974) compared the social change potentials due to impending physical change in four communities. Social characteristics of the four towns were compared through the leadership generated community social profiles. The social impact assessment data abstracted in this document suggest the following hypotheses:

> The citizens of the towns are in the midst of planning for, or merely accepting, the physical alterations. It is not the physical change itself which most affects each of the four towns, but rather the relative degree of internal resolution which is necessary to adjust to the oncoming change. This is a result of three community dimensions: time in community life cycle; cohesion of social structure; and leadership effectiveness.
>
> The four communities share another physical characteristic. They are each along a major northeastern transportation route in an industrialized area; and though within community distance, none is territorially adjacent to an urban area. They tend to be located in environmentally different areas where relative quality of life is already negatively affected by pollution.
>
> The community change process is a function of the three basic community dimensions mentioned above: (1) <u>Time</u> is of the greatest importance since any force has an effect relative to stage in the community life cycle. (2) <u>Cohesiveness of social structure</u> is basic to the introduction of change into the system. A structure lacking cohesion is easily affected by an external force while effective internal reaction requires stability of social structure. (3) <u>The particular characteristics of change agents</u> and those persons politically working towards desired change are most relevant to the pattern and the effectiveness of this social change in the community.
>
> Four basic patterns of change will be investigated through the four exemplary communities. PA is an example of a community where the old stability is breaking down; a process of population change is in effect and the structural disharmony allows a small internal group, otherwise ineffectual, to make a major decision which may affect the town drastically.
>
> MT is a relatively new community, quite suburban in character; it has a mobile population concerned with quality and style of family life rather than with neighborhood or community interaction. This town is eager to allow a charismatic political leader with multiple self-interests to influence its thinking and behavior. The leader induces neighborhood disruption for the "good of the individuals, economically and environmentally." This is an example of an internal politically structured change.
>
> The third town, PB, may well be devastated by external change as a result of an industrial boundary dispute many years ago. The resulting boundaries have left the town economically deprived. Business has

declined; there is little community interest in the town itself; neighborhoods are decaying; services are becoming poor; buildings are vacant. The governing group in the town is constituted by the last of the successful businessmen. At times, these citizens derive great profit from taking a "let happen what may" attitude towards change. The almost defeatist attitude of the townspeople and leaders creates a field for the negative effects of a highly industrialized external change process.

The last of the four communities, GT, is an economically secure, politically active community where there is stability of leadership but also chance of leadership change through election. The political structure is cohesive and the major function of the town government is planning for a better community. In this case, the physical change is planned for and adjusted to with a minimum of community hardship. Most effects derived from the change appear to be beneficial to the community. Stability is a major characteristic of GT.

Each of the four communities discussed appears to have a totally diverse political orientation. The governmental structure and effectiveness of leadership in each case is the observable force which is the result of time in the historical life cycle of the community and cohesion of its social structure. This political leadership appears to be the intermediary force between the physical change agent and the community.

Each of these communities is adapting (without opposition) to the physical change as a result of the character of the community. This is evidenced within the political structure. Local governmental leadership in each case is establishing the boundaries of community response to physical change.

The profile methodology used in these social impact assessments also provides evidence in the form of population statistics and other background indicators to set the groundwork to draw inductive hypotheses. A demographic investigation is undertaken for this purpose. In these cases, it procured information such as:

GT, originally a farm community with an estimated 1974 population of 5,790, grew rapidly during the 1960s. Population in 1970 (5,638) was 39% higher than it had been in 1960. This rapid growth was almost entirely the result of in-migration by persons of all ages--but especially of those aged 24 to 44 in 1970. This growth and development was due to industrial expansion and the need for employees in the area. New residents have come primarily from other parts of the SMSA, and their arrival seems to have been evenly spread over the entire decade. This latter fact distinguishes the town from the area of which it is a part, where in-migration of those present in 1970 was relatively lighter in the first half of the decade and comparatively heavy after 1965. As in neighboring towns, a significant part of the population (21%) is of foreign stock; persons of Italian parentage constitute the largest single ethnic minority. Only 4% of the population is black and the size of the black population has not changed since 1960.

In terms of income and education, the proportion of adults 25 and older who have completed more than four years of high school is low (9%). However, the proportion of adults who have finished high school is comparatively large (38%), making the median number of school years completed (11.7) almost identical with the county as a whole. Median family income was $10,566 in 1970, up 61% over 1960.

During the period since 1960, the portion of the labor force holding white collar jobs increased in GT rapidly. Increases occurred primarily in professional, technical, and clerical occupational categories. Even so, white collar workers form only 39% of the work force. The predominant segment of the labor force is that composed of skilled and semiskilled blue collar workers: craftsmen, foremen, operative and service workers; together, they comprise 54% of all workers resident in the town.

Superimposed upon these population indicators, field research is accomplished through leadership questionnaires enabling the researchers to explore less quantifiable but highly revealing parameters of the communities. For example:

Education is major conflict area in MT. Children are bused to an adjoining town high school since there are not enough students in MT to justify a high school. The crux of the problem for many MT citizens lies in the question of the quality of education at the high school. With its rising percentage of black students, the high school is reputed by some people to be the seat of unrest and turmoil which has resulted in a lack of social life, double sessions, overcrowding, and shutting down of classes due to riots, violence and fear. It is generally held but not openly stated that blacks are the chief cause of the disruption; hence MT's dissatisfaction with the high school.

For some MT citizens, this controversy has brought into the open the prejudice against blacks. The growing proportion of the black population at the high school is a dilemma for a community that is 100% white and believes that children's values are now acquired primarily in the school rather than in the church or home. Of last year's graduating elementary school class in MT, 50-70% were reported to have gone to private high schools. It is at this point, the education of children, that there is a strong conflict within the values of the town.

Similarly, another educational problem arose when the clergy teaching in the nearby parochial elementary school were sent elsewhere and the school was closed. Community action ensued and the teachers have now been replaced.

MT is caught between a rising educational aspiration and a population too small to support action relevant to aspired needs.

and:

> Of the residents interviewed, most felt that there had been a good deal of community stability until 10 or 15 years ago when an influx of new residents occurred and out-migration of second-generation youths seeking new life styles and occupations began occurring. Evidence of such a change in quality of life in PB is reflected in the deterioration of the central business district and the concomitant need for citizens to travel to regional shopping plazas. The quality of recreational activity has likewise declined in the past several decades, particularly as a result of increased pollution of the local river. The numerous establishments dealing in alcoholic beverages, prostitution, and some limited dispensation of drugs, as well as adult entertainment, shows a lessening of community and family orientation. This change is evidenced by an unofficial growth in crime, observable in the fear of personal safety shown by residents. This change is also seen in the apparent lack of ad hoc interest group organization and the lack of political orientation in the community. As in many communities, there is a very small group of vocal and involved residents who are concerned with community regulation and government.
>
> Medical and dental services in the town are below average. In the past several years both a master plan and a comprehensive health plan have been rejected as has been the hiring of a town manager. PB is a township which is a victim of historical circumstance, damaging politics, and poor administration and planning.
>
> PB has not generally benefited from the economic and industrial development which has been attracted to the county during recent years.
>
> PB's gravest problem is that of damaging politics, politics which not only pervades all areas of life, but which prevents the possibility of progress and development in these areas. For example, it is most interesting to observe that the same individual (a local contractor) in PB is the township's building inspector, the township's zoning officer, and a member of the township's school board and the township council. As one council member expressed, most important decisions are dictated by political considerations. This same individual stated that most of the political leaders refuse to endorse any increase in the tax rate, not because the projects to which added taxes would be applied are unworthy of such attention, but because an increased tax rate would possibly receive the political scorn of the voters. With respect to this same political problem, members of the PB Police Department indicated that politics so pervaded their department that the result has been an unprofessional, untrained police force. These police officers also indicated that this situation has made it impossible for them to maintain order within the community or to provide much security for the citizenry of PB. They even admitted that because of this general situation they were losing the public's respect. These ideas were supported by expressions from townspeople who indicated that citizen safety was not assured, and that the police knew about such crimes as dope peddling and thefts, but did not do anything about them.

It becomes obvious that PB's political climate affects its general administration. Appointments to administrative positions are for the most part politically motivated, with little importance given to competency. The police force situation is only one example. Other probable results of such administration, as indicated by people in PB, are: (1) the existence of 18 saloons, (2) the demise of the central business district, and (3) the lack of any local health facilities.

No one seems to be thinking about how PB might be able to adjust to the future. The political climate seems to so dominate the environment that attention is focused only on the next election. Planning, in its present-day form, is absent.

The comparisons of the evidence gathered in the demographic and document studies form the basis for the qualitative response analysis. In this case, the inductive hypotheses presented earlier were confirmed.

In summary, the community social profile methodology is a highly cost-effective field technique. Following a few weeks of field work by about five research assistants and the amassing of background data, interviews can be effectively analyzed in a week or two by two professionals. Leadership generated profiling has the advantages of: an open-ended subjectivity which is capable of yielding intensive data on many aspects of community life, a broad scope of information for minimal cost and a flexibility to develop hypotheses concerning a proposed change based on intensive personal contact.

References

Campbell, Donald T. (1955) "The Informant in Quantitative Research," American Journal of Sociology, 60, 339-42.

Sanders, Irwin T. (1960) "The Community Social Profile," American Sociological Review, 25, 1 (February), 75-77.

Savatsky, Pamela Dee (1974) "Internal Resolution of External Change: Four Patterns of Community Change." Paper delivered at the Annual Meeting of the Society for the Study of Social Problems, Montreal, PQ, August.

Seidler, John (1974) "On Using Informants: A Technique for Collecting Quantitative Data and Controlling Measurement Error in Organization Analysis," American Sociological Review, 39, 6 (December), 816-31.

Computer-assisted Social Profiling: Some Uses of Computerized Data Banks on Social Impact Assessment

James V. Aidala, Jr.
Harvard University

Those concerned with social impact assessment (SIA) typically face severe information requirements. There is much to be known, and too often there is little time, personnel, or readily available data. What is needed is some system which can quickly and easily locate, scan and select information appropriate to the task at hand. In recent years, computerized data retrieval systems have been developed which can provide such functions. A multitude of such computerized retrieval systems exists; Kruzas (1974) lists over 1000. Space permits only a very brief discussion of the main types of data systems, along with a somewhat more detailed discussion of one exemplary system which can greatly assist the SIA researcher.

TYPES OF DATA SYSTEMS

Some general categories of data generally accessible by computer are: (1) research project abstracts, (2) bibliographic files, (3) "local" data (those collected by local area agencies), and (4) federal government data. Systems can retrieve very specific data of the first two kinds, but the information may be _too_ specific (too narrow) or may be classified under inappropriate categories. The latter two kinds of data entail the problem of different units of aggregation. For example, data can be retrieved according to: census tracts, SMSAs, Bureau of Economic Analysis (BEA) economic regions, BEA water resource regions, the first three digits of zip codes, agricultural producing regions, the ten Federal regions, and many, many more.

Ideal data sources are ones which are national in scope but which can be disaggregated down to locality-sized units. Flexibility of this type makes it possible to "build" localities or regions that closely approximate the impact area. For example, census data can be broken down by counties or tracts and rebuilt in a fashion suitable for the examination of an area such as the cotton counties of north central Texas or urban areas to be affected by highway construction. Research concerned with rural areas would be able to use data mostly on a county level, while urban-related research can utilize the more specific units of SMSA and census tracts. Counties and tracts are probably the most consistently available level of information which can be easily obtained. Problems still persist, however, either because of what is (or is not) measured or because the area or activity to be examined ideally should be depicted on a sub-tract or sub-county level.

There are a number of organizations which offer computerized retrieval of the major social and economic data collected and published by the government. The scope of some of these systems is suggested by a partial list of data bases accessable through the Lawrence Berkeley Laboratories of Berkeley, California (LBL). (Table 1.)

Table 1.

CURRENT DATA BASES AT LBL

DEMOGRAPHY AND SOCIAL SCIENCE	Approx. No. of Records	Approx. No. of Characters
1960 Census of Population	3,100	40 million
1970 Census of Population and Housing - 1st Count	280,000	720 million
1970 Census of Population and Housing - 2nd Count	105,000	1.4 billion
1970 Census of Population - 4th Count	86,000	5.3 billion
1970 Census of Housing (California) - 4th and 6th Count	10,000	770 million
1970 Fifth Count Census	13,000	120 million
1970 Sixth Count Census	140,000	230 million
1970 Public Use Sample	17 million	1.7 billion
County and City Data Book - County Merge, 1952, 1962, 1967	3,100	33.5 million
Current Population Survey, 1968-1973	200,000	44 million
Master Enumeration Districts (Medlist), 1970 Census	390,000	42 million
Census Data - State and County, 1970	3,100	9.6 million
Census Data - Standard Metropolitan Statistical Areas, 1970	243	775 thousand

GEOGRAPHY

Geographic Data Base: State, County, SMSA, and Census Tract boundaries	39,000	

BUSINESS ENTERPRISE

I-O Economic Growth Model - Data Base, 1963, 1970		
Index Items of Industrial Employment		1.75 million
I-O Tables, Mineral Industry, 1958		3.5 million
Location of Manufacturing Plants, 1963, 1967	160,000	40 million
I-O Tables - Interindustry Transactions, Direct and Total Requirements		77 million
OBERS Projections (Series E), 1950-2020	1,200	7 million
Gross Output: National and County level, 1958, 1963		10.78 million

EMPLOYMENT

Employment Security Automated Reporting System (ESARS), from July 1973		100,000 per data set
Employment-Occupation Projections, National, 1970 and 1980		7.1 million
Employment-Occupation Projections: State, State area, SMSA, 1970, 1980		11.26 million

LABOR FORCE, EMPLOYMENT AND EARNINGS

Work Files: GNP by Industry, 1947-1972		6 million
County Business Patterns: National, State and County Summaries	25,000	128 million
Multi-Regional I-O Model Harvard-EDA Data Base, 1947, 1958, 1963		20 million
Income and Earnings, National, 1929-1969	3,100	37 million
Labor Statistics-EDA Eligibility Assistance	1,200	840 thousand
Employment and Earnings, National, States and areas, 1939-1972		10.1 million
Employment by Industry, BEA Sectors, 1963, 1967		80 thousand
Employment by Industry & Occupation, BEA Sectors, 1963, 65, 67, 70, 72		500 thousand

TRANSPORTATION

Transportation of U.S. Trade, 1970	55,000	20 million
Commodity Transportation Survey-Production Areas and States, 1967		15 million
Inter-Regional Commodity Flows & Projections, 1966, 1969		5 million
Inter-Regional Commodity Flow Estimates, 1963		8 million

AGRICULTURE AND HEALTH

U.S. Census of Agriculture, 1949, 1959, 1964, 1969	12,000	84 million
Cause of Death Summary (mortality statistics), 1969-1970	90,000	
Federal Services Maxillofacial Trauma Survey	90,000	

	Approx. No. of Records	Approx. No. of Characters
ENVIRONMENTAL AND NATURAL RESOURCES		
National Geothermal Information Resource (GRID) 1975-1980		
Water Use in Manufacturing, National, 1954, 1958, 1963, 1968		7 million
Water Use in Industry, California by County, 1960, 1970		
Water Waste Permit Application data, San Francisco Bay Delta Area, 1970		2 million
Inland Waterways, Locks & Dams Physical data, Mississippi River, 1974	110,000	
Endangered Species Information System, National, 1972-1973		35 thousand
Energy Transactions: Five Energy Sources, 1963, 1968		40 thousand
Ozone data: Photochemistry in the stratosphere, 1957-present	19,000	1.6 million
PHYSICS		
Particle Properties: Elementary particle research data	20,000	1.6 million
Particle Reactions: Reaction data between elementary particles	250,000	40 million
Isotope Radioactive Decay	40,000	5 million
Isotope Table Scheme Level data	1,000	600 thousand
Annotated Bibliography of Nuclear data, through 1974	10,000	500 thousand
MISCELLANEOUS INVENTORY		
Wiring Configuration data: wiring layouts for engineers	1,000	2.5 million
Cable Connection data: building cable layouts	1,000	2.5 million
Equipment Characteristics: physical electrical and procurement data	1,000	5 million
Inventory: equipment locations and maintenance schedules	1,500	5 million
Building Layout: digitized lab, plumbing and electrical layout for large school	200	100 thousand
Documentation data: engineering drawing, library references & memoranda	1,000	250 thousand
Property Book Inventory, 1973, 1974	1,000	1 million
MANAGEMENT INFORMATION		
Buglist: computer system report data, 1973-1974		100 thousand
Accident Report data: employee accidents at LBL, 1972-1974	1,000	

The U. S. Army Corps of Engineers is a leader in developing these kinds of simple-to-use systems. Their EIAC (Environmental Impact Computer System) computerizes environmental impact assessment procedures, while in the social impact field they have developed SIRAP (System of Information Retrieval and Analysis for Planners), a subset of the data files listed earlier. It includes the Bureau of Economic Analysis OBERS projection series, Census of Population and Housing (first and fourth counts), Census of Agriculture, City and County Data Book Location of Manufacturers Files, and County Business Patterns. These files are available according to the various units commonly found in the published reports (e.g. tract and county for the census data, economic regions and sub-regions for the OBERS files). There are also some short time series data available; for example, one can examine demographic shifts found in the 1960 and 1970 Population Censuses, or agricultural shifts found in the 1964 and 1969 Censuses of Agriculture.

Accessibility of this wealth of retrievable data is greatly facilitated by the development of a simple retrieval program known as Quick Query. Quick Query is a retrieval and report generation program which is a proprietary product of Consolidated Analysis Centers Incorporated (CACI). Absolute beginners in computer programming can learn how to use it in two days or less. All one needs to know is the request format, the code for the area(s) investigated (e.g. county or tract), and the code for the attributes to be retrieved (income, education, etc.). It not only seems easy, but _actually is_ easy to use. Moreover, the output from a request is produced in a form directly publishable, complete with headings and area names.

POSSIBLE LONG-TERM USES

If the researcher is not concerned with SIA for a specific project, but rather is charged with the task of SIA for any number of areas over a period of time, a simple program can be developed to give "standard" baseline profiles of given areas. For example, in the case of agricultural pesticide regulations, the impact of banning or substituting any pesticide will depend on the number of impacted farms, their sales, size, equipment, ownership, and a host of other variables. This "standard" initial profile can also be supplemented by information more specific to the type of project being examined. If the pesticide is used on a certain crop, then other information is needed on that crop: the number of farms growing that commodity, acreage, sales, etc.

This technique has the advantage of comparability with base line information on areas and projects examined in the past. This can be useful since lessons learned from the past projects (i.e. what certain trends of kinds of data "really" mean for SIA) could help to better interpret the base socioeconomic data in terms of their implications for current assessments. Also, once some initial information is known about a given area, the investigation can be more directly tuned to find more specific information. It is after this initial glimpse that examination of bibliographic services, more specific reports, and such can better focus on items of specific concern. It is useful to streamline the search process with this type of preliminary effort, since many of these data banks have millions of entries. Such specificity can be very helpful. For example, a request concerning the effects of noise will return a quite different listing than a request about the effects of noise along with one or two other defining parameters.

Another aspect of many of these data retrieval systems is their ability to produce maps. Graphic displays can give the viewer a picture of the relative levels of concentrations for whatever attributes are being considered. This can be very useful for report writing and for showing what areas are likely to be the most (or least) impacted according to a selected variable (or combinations of variables). Maps can be produced according to a number of units (counties, census tracts, SMSAs), and some systems have the capability of producing not only black-and-white but also color maps.

SOURCES AND COSTS

If such systems as have so far been described appear potentially useful, they can be accessed through LBL or commercial firms such as CACI. Costs of these services vary according to the number of items retrieved and number of areas information is requested for, and also the way the total block of information is stored or retrieved. Some systems require a search of all record files in the process of retrieving data for the user's specific area request. Other systems have more streamlined retrieval routines, which result in much lower costs to the user. This is one of several key items of which one should be aware of when shopping for a computer system.

MODE OF UTILIZATION

There also is a variety of ways in which the data can be delivered. The quickest means of access is via an interactive computer terminal, or a remote batch entry terminal, connected by telephone to the computer facility. If very extensive work with these data files is a possibility, complete summary tapes can also be purchased from commercial firms or the Bureau of the Census. Buying the entire national data set may be unnecessary or too expensive, but buying the tape or the print-out for specific areas might be advisable for researchers who are only going to be concerned with one or a few impact assessments over a long period of time. If one does not have ready access to a computer facility, then some of the services mentioned can be purchased complete.

Reference

Kruzas, Anthony T. (ed.) (1974) Encyclopedia of Information Systems and Services. Ann Arbor, MI: Edwards.

Center for Census Use Studies Small Area Data Technology: Potential Tools for Social Impact Assessment on Urban Areas

Harold C. Wallach
United States Bureau of the Census

General Background on the Center for Census Use Studies

The Center for Census Use Studies (CCUS) is a research, development, and demonstration unit within the U.S. Bureau of the Census. The CCUS staff has developed computer software and statistical methodologies applicable to problems involving small area data and has made these developments available to local users through its educational programs, demonstration projects and publications.

The CCUS was created in September 1966 and was involved in the full scale pretest of the 1970 decennial census procedures conducted in New Haven (1966-1968). Since its inception, the CCUS has conducted extensive research, including the development and demonstration of:

geographic base systems
record matching systems
computer mapping or graphics
special small area data analysis.

One of the key automated products developed by the Census Bureau is the GBF/DIME-System.

Dual Independent Map Encoding

GBF/DIME stands for Geographic Base File/Dual Independent Map Encoding and refers to the computerized files created by the DIME process. This approach combines address information with information sufficient and necessary to describe the urban street network. By considering each street as a series of lines and each intersection as a node, the entire region covered by the file can be viewed as a series of interrelated nodes, lines and enclosed areas. Other features, such as streams or jurisdiction boundaries for example, may also be defined in terms of segments and nodes.

In creating a GBF/DIME-System, each distinctive element represented on a map is examined. At points where streets or other features intersect, end, or curve sharply, a node number is assigned, as seen in the illustration at the top of the next page.

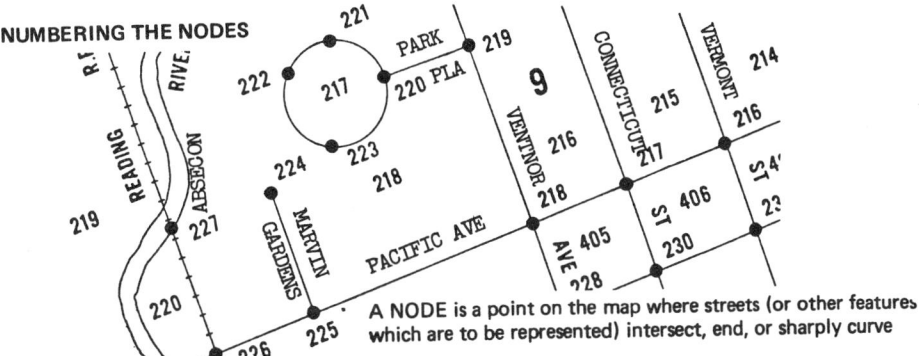

Census Use Study Report No. 15: The Uses of GBF/DIME
U.S. Department of Commerce--Bureau of the Census, June 1974, p. 4

For each segment of a street (i.e., the length between the two nodes) the DIME system contains: the "from" node, the "to" node, the street type (e.g., avenue, drive, way, etc.), the address range on the right-hand side of the street and the address range on the left-hand side. Moreover, each block and census tract is uniquely numbered. The geographic areas (on the left- and right-hand sides of the street segment being defined) are also included for each record in the GBF/DIME-System.

The illustration below shows some of the information contained in the GBF/DIME-System for the 100 block of Atlantic Avenue.

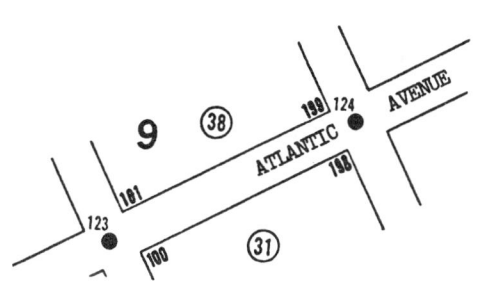

FOR EACH STREET SEGMENT A
DIME RECORD CONTAINS:

From Node	123
To Node	124
Street Name	Atlantic
Street Type	Avenue
Left Addresses	101-199
Right Addresses	100-198
Left Block	38
Left Tract	9
Right Block	31
Right Tract	9

Ibid., p. 5

Dual Independent Map Encoding refers to the creation of the basic file by coding two independent matrices: (a) the nodes as the end of the line segments and, (b) the areas enclosed by the nodes and line segments. The computer constructs these two independent networks--one of line boundaries and one of areas--and matches them.

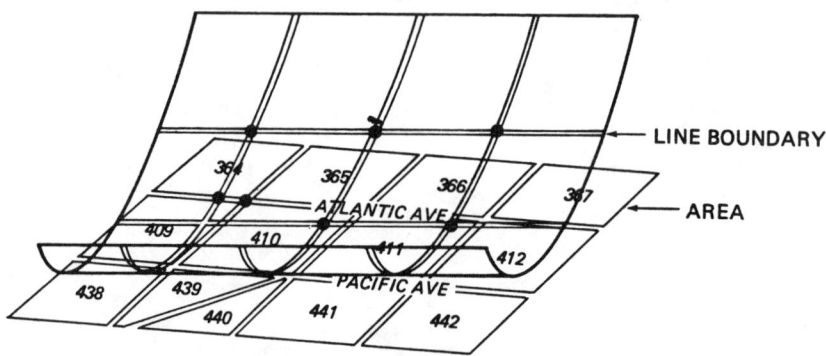

Op. cit., The Uses of GBF/DIME, p. 5

This will ensure that the resultant network is completely represented and all the land is accounted for.

Once a map is digitized, the computer can use this information to plot a complete replica of the source map.

DIME was soon found to have applications for local users. State and local governments and private data users discovered that the GBF/DIME-System could be used for geocoding and integrating their own files and records. Besides, local data could be efficiently related to census data at various geographic levels and information could be easily retrieved by the computer. DIME has been used by local agencies in determining the best location for child day-care centers, restructuring police beats, implementing carpool programs, and designing school bus routes. Numerous applications of DIME technology have also been reported by specialists in transportation, public health, urban and regional planning law enforcement and criminal justice communications, marketing, social welfare, political administration and other fields.

Other major products of the CCUS include ADMATCH and UNIMATCH--automated packages for geocoding and matching data files and GRIDS--a computer graphics package which produces density, shading and value maps.

Computer Graphics
Experimentation with computer techniques for graphically displaying urban data was one of the primary objectives of the Census Use Study. The display of various types of data on maps can be especially useful for understanding the geographic implications of data for an area, whether it be a model city neighborhood, an entire city, or region. For displaying large amounts of data, maps and graphs are

visually clearer and more informative than columns of numbers and are useful not only for planning and analysis, but also for administrative and public information purposes. Systemized routine tasks which provide high resolution and continuous variation are available.

Experience in the Census Use Study demonstrated that computer mapping has several prerequisites:

1. A geographic base file, including street address information and coordinates.
2. Data encoded with addresses which can be matched with the base file.
3. Access to mapping programs and computer equipment.
4. Sufficient staff expertise to carry out the work involved in geographic coding, matching and the computer mapping operations.

The extent to which these necessary inputs are available will determine the success an agency will have in computer mapping.

Examples of computer graphics indicate a geospace plotter map of tracts and blocks in a city (Figure 1); a shaped map of owner occupied housing (Figure 2); and a map reflecting change in population (Figure 3).

These tools, the GBF/DIME-System and computer graphics, have been applied by CCUS and local specialist users in the fields of transportation, public health, urban and regional planning, and public safety, among others. Tested by a staff of experts in the social and behavioral sciences, urban planning, systems analysis, computer programming and statistics, these automated techniques have been recorded in users' manuals and computer programs that are available to local users. This technology is being disseminated by means of this documentation and through technology transfer conferences held in various parts of the country. The CCUS has conducted national week-long workshops and short-session seminars for administrators, planners and technicians. These conferences have considered topics such as the availability of census data for rural planning and such highly technical subjects as a computerized carpooling system. University credit has also been extended to recent workshop participants.

Making highly sophisticated, technical concepts more readily understood to local data users is the objective of the CCUS training and educational activities. In furthering this objective, the CCUS staff has developed curricula, training aids, and a series of fully illustrated publications. These include self-instructional materials, computer assisted exercises and easy-to-read texts. The Center has also produced a technology-made-simple publication series in comic book format.

Potential Application to Social Impact Assessment
The CCUS has been engaged in a wide variety of small area research activities in its nine year history, but some of the subject matter areas which have the most relevance to social impact assessment include:

- a methodology for neighborhood definition
  (see Figure 4)

tools to deal coherently with disparate small
area data and diverse geographic boundaries
(see hypothetical situation shown in Figure 5).

Such tools as the GBF/DIME-System, ADMATCH, UNIMATCH, and GRIDS supply a basis for interrelating data files with inconsistent geographic boundaries (e.g. police precinct data, health district data, planning area data, educational district data and so on) provided basic addresses are available.

One of the programs in the CCUS is the Social/Health Indicators Program. It is this program's efforts which are most akin to social impact assessment. The Indicators Program focuses on studying effects of Federally funded programs at the local level. The points of emphasis of the Indicators Program include:

applications of CCUS small area data technology

monitoring effects over time

focus on rural as well as urban settings (although
the techniques employed in each are different)

reliance on existing census, State, and local data
(as opposed to collecting new data by survey or
other means).

More specifically, the Social/Health Indicators Program was originally designed as a tool for monitoring effects on communities with Office of Economic Opportunity (OEO)-sponsored multi-purpose health centers and health networks. To achieve this objective a system of social/health indicators was developed from a variety of local administrative data files pertaining to such factors as health status, delivery of health services, education, welfare, economics and social pathology. The indicators in the system apply to small areas (census tracts in metropolitan areas, and counties/subcounty areas in rural places) and are obtained in historical series. The major rationale underlying the program is that if a set of highly structured and sensitive indicators could be constructed and made to apply to small areas over time, the local planners and administrators could monitor trends in the level of delivery of health and social services, in the well-being of populations contained in the area, and in other potential problem areas of change.

Potential for use of this technology in social impact assessment is currently being explored. For example, one potential use is examining alternative routes a highway could take to connect two places. The CCUS has also developed a socio-economic basis for characterizing neighborhoods; this, in conjunction with small area geocoding and analysis of trends in local and other data, may serve to provide some substantive inputs to such decisions. The CCUS tools may provide a way to access, organize and analyze local small area data to estimate the effects of national politics on local activities (e.g., energy policy).

Center for Census Use Studies Small Area Data Technology 177

FIGURE 1: **Geospace Plotter Outline Map Identifying Tract and Block Areas**

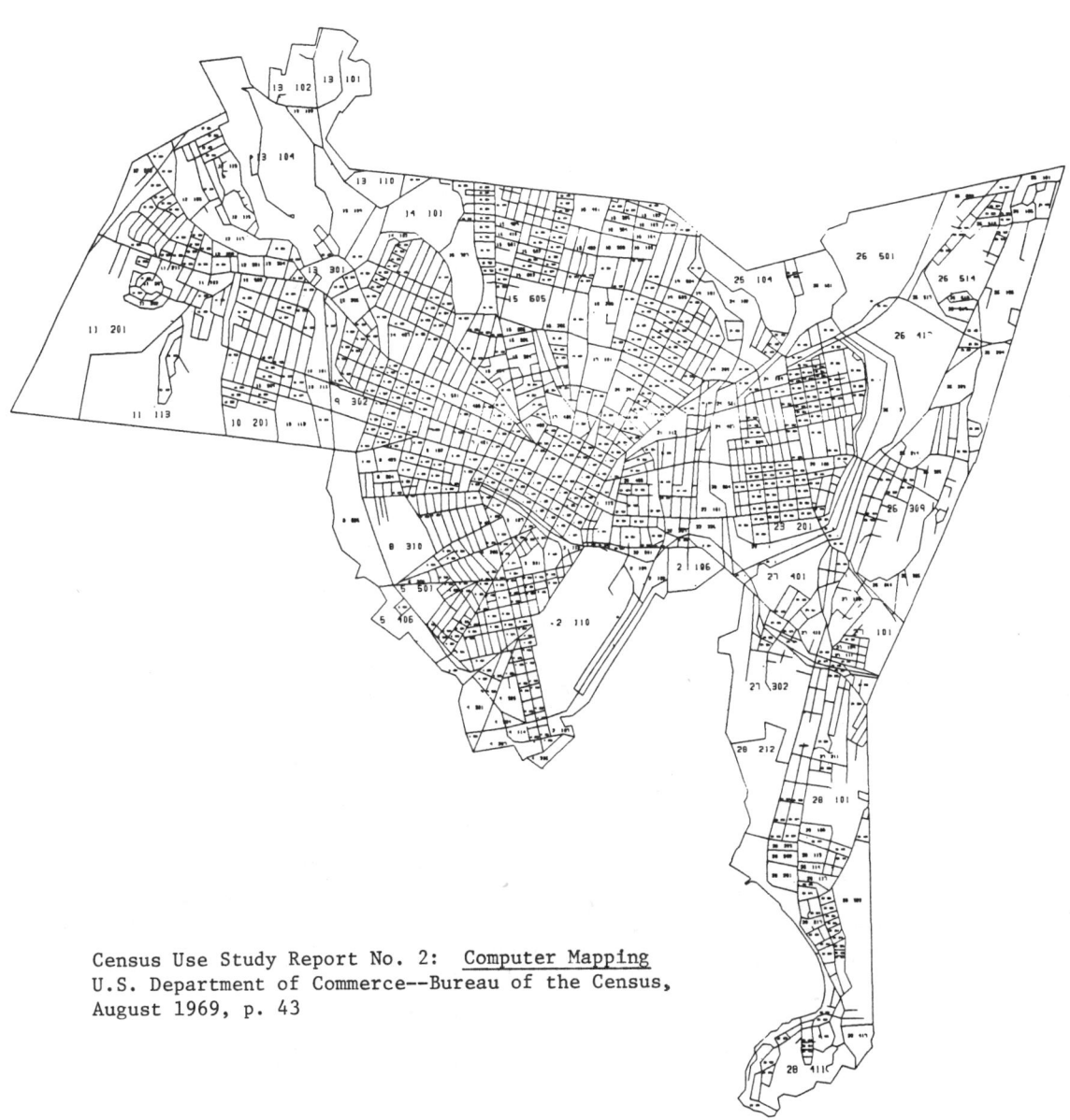

Census Use Study Report No. 2: Computer Mapping
U.S. Department of Commerce--Bureau of the Census,
August 1969, p. 43

FIGURE 2: Geospace Plotter Shading Map Identifying Block Area Levels
Percent of Owner Occupied Housing

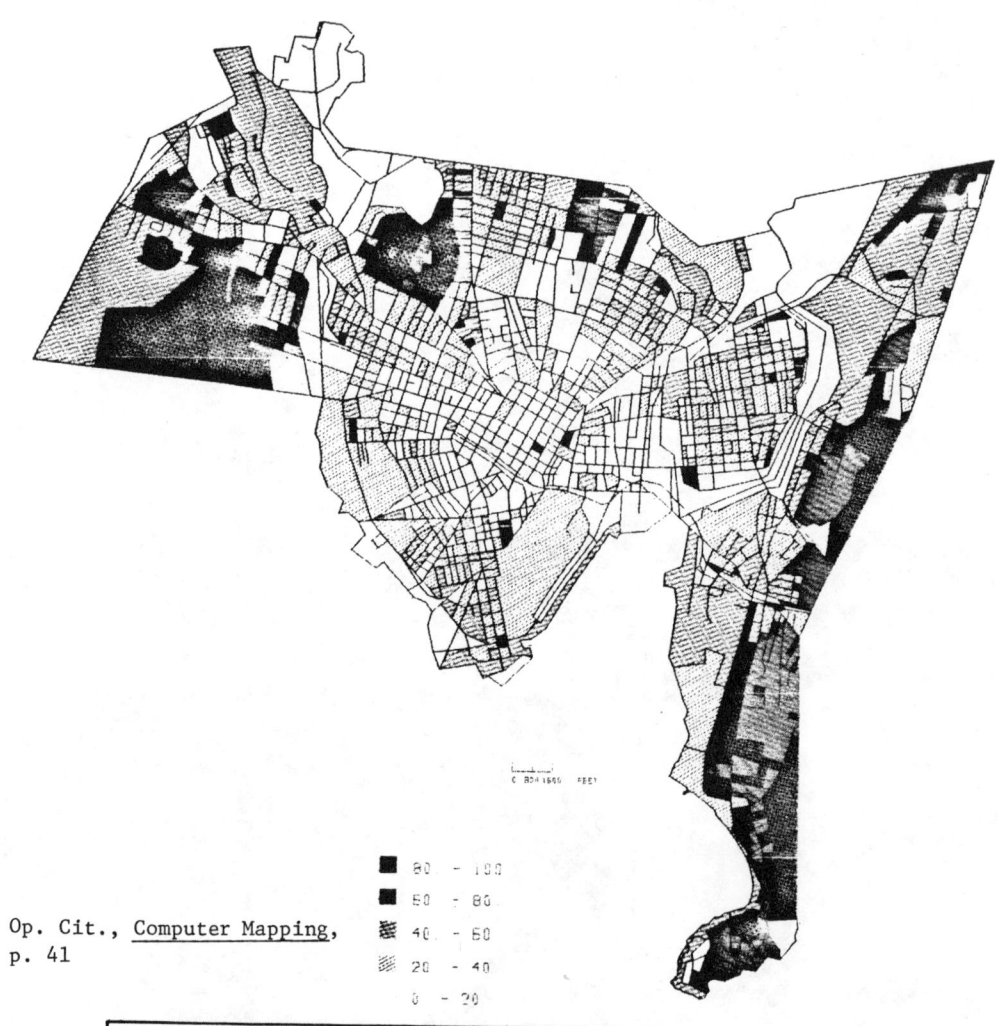

Op. Cit., Computer Mapping, p. 41

■ 80 - 100
■ 60 - 80
▩ 40 - 60
▨ 20 - 40
░ 0 - 20

The Geospace Plotter is the most recent development in computer hardware. A lens project an image from a CRT onto photographic film or photosensitive papter attatched to a rotating drum.

Center for Census Use Studies Small Area Data Technology 179

FIGURE 3: Example of GRIDS Shaded Map

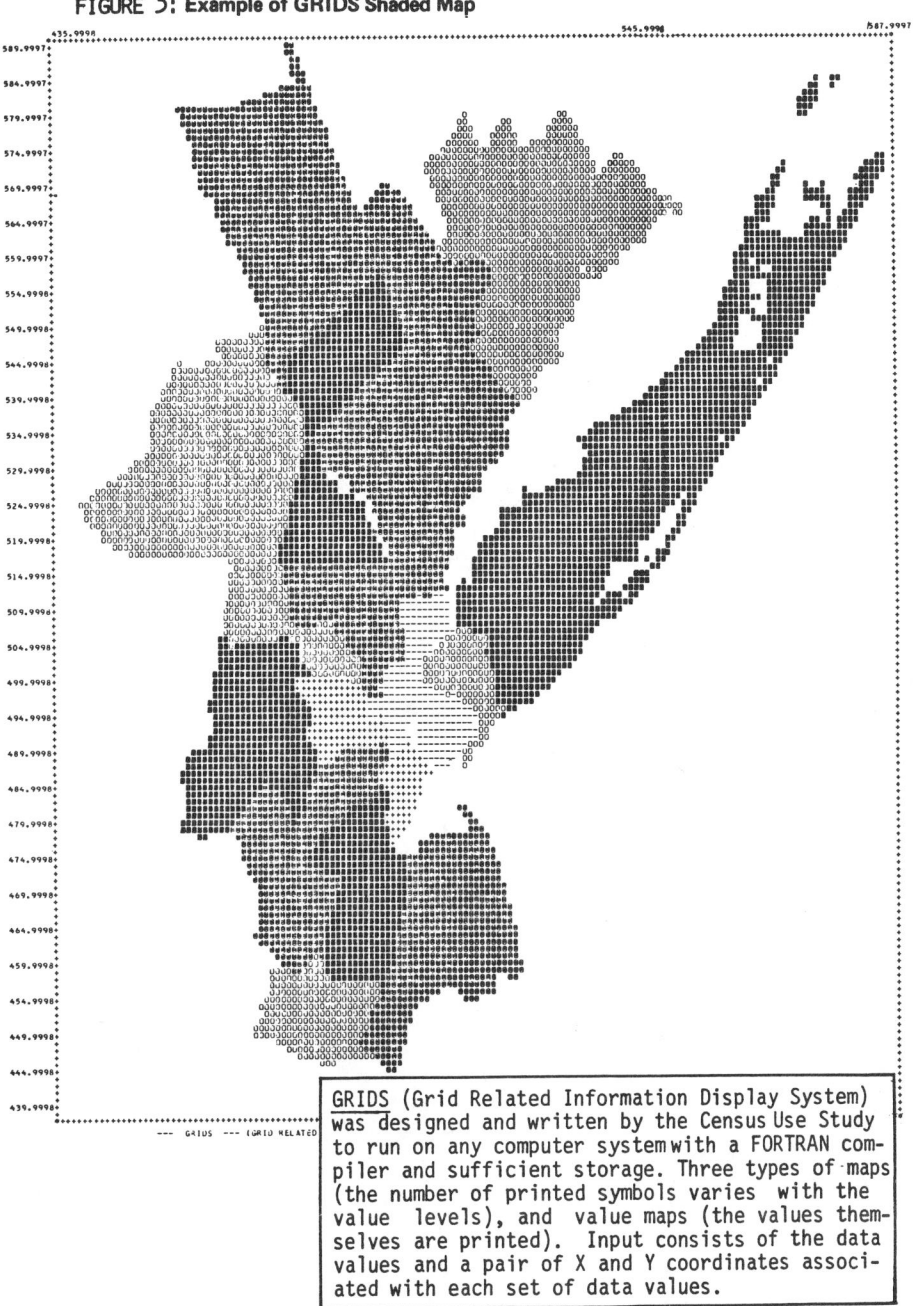

GRIDS (Grid Related Information Display System) was designed and written by the Census Use Study to run on any computer system with a FORTRAN compiler and sufficient storage. Three types of maps (the number of printed symbols varies with the value levels), and value maps (the values themselves are printed). Input consists of the data values and a pair of X and Y coordinates associated with each set of data values.

Census Use Study: Grids: A Computer Mapping System by Matt Jaro,
U. S. Department of Commerce--Bureau of the Census, April 1972, p. ix

FIGURE 4: **Neighborhoods Delineated by Five SES Dimensions**

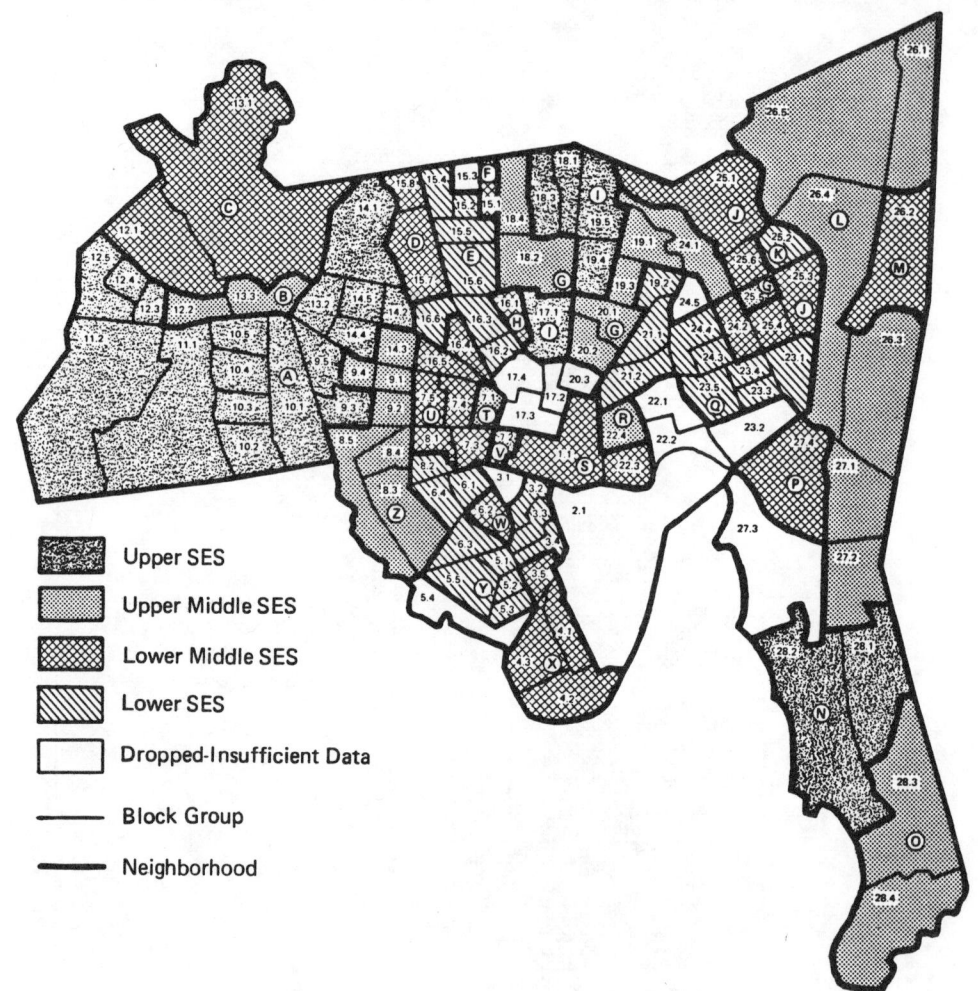

City of NEW HAVEN
Census Block Groupings 1967

Note: Digits refer to track and block group designations (ie 10.3 = tract 10 block group 3).

Census Use Study Report No. 12: Health Information System-II
U.S. Department of Commerce--Bureau of the Census, March 1971, p. 55

FIGURE 5: COUNTY HEALTH DISTRICT MAP

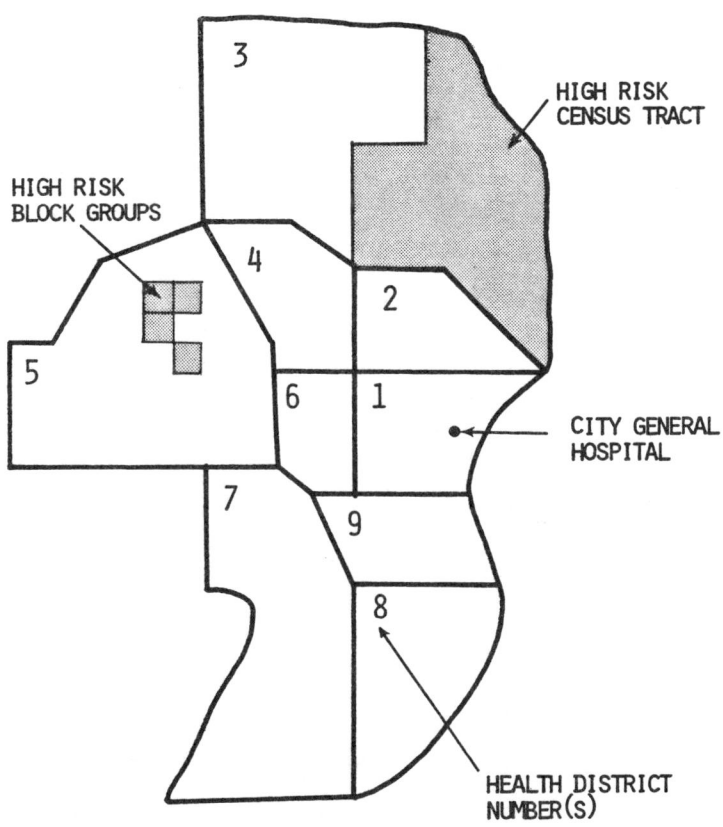

Adaptation of map on p. 185 of Guide to Data for Health Planners
HEW Document No. HRA 76-14502, April 1976

A Quality of Life Production Model for Project Impact Assessment

Ben-chieh Liu
Midwest Research Institute

I. Introduction

This paper develops a quality of life production model which attempts not only to integrate the economic, social, political, and environmental considerations but also to synthesize some controversial issues regarding efficiency and equity. In the form of social indicators, the methodology underlying the model resembles the conventional estimation of a Cobb-Douglas production function employed by economists. However, instead of measuring only the efficiency impacts by the dollar changes in benefits and costs, or in the volume of output and input, the model produces quality of life indexes by which various efficiency and equity impacts are identified, measured, and weighted. By these resultant indexes a project can be better evaluated.

In order to promote the general welfare, there is an urgent need for a mechanism which can distinguish better from worse. "For many of the important topics on which social critics blithely pass judgment, and on which policies are made," said Bauer (1966), "there are not yardsticks by which to know if things are getting better or worse." As it now stands, the United States has no comprehensive set of social statistics that reflect our changes in values and measure social progress or retrogression. However, as Fox (1974) states and demonstrates, "In the present state of the field, many useful insights can be obtained by applying simple models to existing data." It is hoped that the present model may represent one step toward the social need in general and the methodological advancement in impact assessment in particular.

II. The Quality of Life Model

Although it is generally understood that the need for quality of life or other social indicators is urgent for purposes of social accounting and assessment of national goal setting and priority ranking, program development and project planning and performance evaluation, there is no consensus as to what the quality of life is all about, how the quality of life or other social indicators should be defined, and for whom and in what manner they should be constructed. This failure to reach a consensus can be substantially attributed to the absence of a commonly accepted social welfare function.

Despite much recent interest and attention the need persists for a systematic, interrelated approach by which social indicators can be constructed and analyzed. The model suggested in the following paragraphs is taken from the one developed earlier by the author (Liu 1974; 1975) and is termed the quality of life production model.

Given that the quality of life (QOL) indicators represented by a set of statistics on economic, political, environmental, health and education, and social conditions may offer clues to human attitudes and behavior and social performance over time, the quality of life that each individual attempts to maximize may be expressed as an output function with two factor inputs as arguments--the physical and the psychological--a portion of which he owns and shares with other people in the community at any given time. The physical input consists of quantifiable goods, services, material wealth, etc., while the psychological input includes all subjective, spiritual, sociological, and anthropological factors such as community belongingness, esteem, self actualization, love, affection, etc., which are ordinarily nonquantifiable. Although the production function expressing the relationship between output and input factors of quality of life is known to be enormously complex--there are as many such factors as there are people--an aggregate homogeneous production function may be assumed for the community as a whole.

The model proposed here is similar to the conventional production models employed to study the behavior of firms. The two axes, instead of being labeled as capital and labor per unit of time are, respectively, the ordinal measures of the psychological inputs and the cardinal measures of the physical inputs. The iso-quant curves are hereby replaced by the iso-quality of life curves, and the budget lines are substituted by the individual's capability curves which, in this case, would likely be concave to the origin. The optimal level of quality of life is produced only by combining both the physical and psychological inputs in such a form as to locate the tangency point between the iso-quality and the capability constraint curves. Therefore, the quality of life that each individual perceives is assumed to be directly dependent on his capability constraints to exchange and to acquire, while the major concern for a society is how to improve an individual's capability by shifting the constraint curve outward to the right.

The theoretical quality of life model described above can be used to produce a considerable volume of useful information for impact assessment regarding both efficiency and equity. For any public investments or other projects, the resultant change in the quality of life production quantitatively measured by the model with and without the project is defined as the net project impact. The net impact can be multidimensional and decomposed into five components of common concerns--economic, political, environmental, health and education, and social. The model itself has a built-in adjusting mechanism between conflicting concerns such as economic growth and environmental degradation. For practical purposes the model would take the following form:

$$QOL_0 = A_0 \left[EC_0^a \ PW_0^b \ EN_0^c \ HE_0^d \ SO_0^\gamma \right] e^{\mu_0}$$

$$QOL_1 = A_1 \left[EC_1^a \ PW_1^b \ EN_1^c \ HE_1^d \ SO_1^\gamma \right] e^{\mu_1}$$

where EC, PW, EN, HE and SO are respectively the indexes for the five QOL components--economic, political and welfare, environment, health and education, and social.

a, b, c, d, γ are, respectively, the weights of each component and jointly they should add to 1.0, i.e., $(a + b + c + d + \gamma) = 1.0$.

e^μ is the stochastic disturbance term which is independently distributed with zero mean and constant variances.

The subscripts 0 and 1 refer to two specific points in the planning time horizon, e.g. with and without the project; and A is a shift parameter, reflecting the general community status and special characteristics.

The shift in the preferences and value concept of the affected population with respect to the five QOL components are reflected in the model by the changes in the values of the parameters or weights, a, b, c, d and γ. If these five parameters associated with each of the five QOL components are not affected by the implementation of the project, or, equivalently, the preference system of the affected population is kept intact, these two equations can be employed to quantitatively assess the project impacts for each relevant QOL component area as well as for overall QOL solely by comparing the changes in the index values, with and without the project. However, should a project alter not only the index values of the five QOL components but also the weighting preferences of the affected population, it is then necessary to know both the values for the variable component index and the parameter weights.

It is so far fairly clear that the model is characterized by the following important aspects with regard to impact assessment.

1. The model takes into account the interdependent relationship among the common concerns in the economic, political, environmental, health and education, and social arenas. Thus, the beneficial and adverse effects can be jointly measured and evaluated for conflicting results or byproducts such as economic development and ecological damages.

2. The model is flexible in that not only the QOL component index values will change depending on the objective, physically measured conditions, but also the weights represented by the parameters can vary in order to reflect the subjective value differences among the five components for the entire population affected by the project over time.

3. The efficiency criterion is incorporated in the index computation, while the equity consideration or value judgment may be collectively reflected in the parameters for the affected community as a whole. For example, a project may lead to significant economic growth by which the index of EC increases substanially while the index for the environmental component EN decreases moderately. By this model, the project may still be rejected if the affected community determines that the weight for the EN should be raised and that for the EC be lowered. Consequently, QOL_1 (with the project) is less than QOL_0 (without the project), holding everything else constant.

III. Application of the Model and Empirical Results

Utilizing the quantifiable physical statistics for the 65 largest Standard Metropolitan Statistical Areas (SMSAs) in the country with population greater than 500,000 in 1970, objective QOL indexes were computed using 123 measurable factors relating to the five QOL components. The factor structure of the components and the index organization are presented in the five panels in the Appendix, and the values of the QOL indexes by component are shown in Table 1. The indexes were developed as follows:

1. The data for 1970 were collected for the 65 largest SMSAs and standardized "Z" values were computed for all factors.

2. On the basis of the percentile distribution of the "Z" values, SMSAs were divided into five groups and assigned points 5, 4, 3, 2, or 1, respectively, for outstanding, (A); excellent, (B); good, (C); adequate, (D); and substandard, (E). Factors within the same subcategory were then weighted equally to obtain a subcomponent score.

3. Finally, the average of the subcomponent scores was taken to show the component index for each SMSA, which was subsequently rated by the indexes in comparison with other SMSAs.

In order to derive the overall QOL indexes, the weight for each of the five QOL components can be obtained by the delphi approach or panel discussion among the concerned or affected citizens in the community in which the project is to be undertaken. In this metropolitan QOL study, however, an equal-weight scheme was adopted for the sake of simplicity, and the overall QOL index in Table 1 was the average of the five component indexes.

To generate some useful information, such as the average weighting scheme for the five components across the 65 metropolitan areas, the least-squares technique could be employed to estimate the parameters a, b, c, d, and γ after the indexes were first transformed into logarithm values; i.e., transforming the model from

$$QOL_0 = A_0 \left[EC_0^a \, PW_0^b \, EN_0^c \, HE_0^d \, SO_0^\gamma \right] e^{\mu_0}$$

into

$$\text{Log } QOL_0 = a \text{ Log } EC_0 + b \text{ Log} PW_0 + c \text{ Log} EN_0 + d \text{ Log} HE_0 + \gamma \text{ Log} SO_0 + V_0$$

where V_0 is equal to $(\text{Log } A_0 + U_0)$.

With the component index inputs from Table 1 and the unscaled overall QOL indexes, the average metropolitan weighting scheme from the example is shown as follows:

$$\log QOL = 0.13 \log ET_0 + 0.15 \log PW_0 + 0.06 \log EN_0 + 0.10 \log HE_0 + 0.15 \log SO_0$$
$$(0.02) \quad\quad (0.02) \quad\quad (0.01) \quad\quad (0.02) \quad\quad (0.05)$$
$$+ 0.79$$

$$R_2 = 0.91$$

or

$$QOL = 0.79 \, EC_0^{0.13} PW_0^{0.15} EN_0^{0.06} HE_0^{0.10} SO_0^{0.15}$$

or $\quad QOL = 0.79\ EC_0^{0.22}\ PW_0^{0.25}\ EN_0^{0.10}\ HE_0^{0.18}\ SO_0^{0.25}$

Figures in the parentheses in the equation are standard errors of the estimated weights. Based on these cross-metropolitan indexes, it is found that social and political considerations carry the most weight, followed by economic concerns. Environmental factors are estimated to have the lowest weight among the five as far as the computed indexes are concerned.

The equation has the property that the estimated weights are summed to 1.0. The average weights so estimated may be substituted for the actual parameters in impact assessment in the absence of an empirical survey of concerned citizenry in the community or an equity consideration scheme determined by the decision-makers. Holding the parameters estimated in the equation constant, the economic, political, environmental, health and education, and social impacts of any project can be technically assessed and presented in such a numerical form. Comparisons between the conditions with and without the project can be made either by comparing each QOL component individually or by the overall QOL indexes. In short, the model suggests that only two sets of QOL indexes be constructed and two weighting schemes be estimated for impact assessment: one for "with" and another for "without" the project. If the average or the constant, equal weighting scheme is adopted, only the two sets of QOL indexes are required.

IV. Concluding Remarks

This paper suggests that for project impact assessment, it is probably more informative and accurate to employ a quality of life production model in which various economic, political, environmental and social concerns are interrelated inputs, and some efficiency as well as equity considerations are incorporated. With the model, indexes based on objective measures from physical changes can be quantitatively constructed for the QOL components with and without the project. The difference in the component indexes can be used to reflect the project impact on various grounds so that the alternatives can be differentiated, priorities set, and decisions made. The weighting scheme attached to the QOL component indexes serves as a built-in adjuster such that the subjective value judgments or equity criteria can be included in the model for decision-making, and projects may not necessarily be approved or rejected simply on the judgments of physical changes in material well-being alone.

Although it is generally not sound to use one indicator, theoretically speaking the model can produce information about the changes in overall quality of life with and without the project, provided that such a single overall QOL indicator is considered desirable. As long as no changes are detected in the value system or time preferences among the affected population, the parameters for the QOL components in the model can be assumed unchanged, and the indexes themselves alone might serve the impact assessment well. The proposed methodology, although requiring further modification, is considered a step forward in the areas of social indicator development and project impact assessment.

References

Bauer, Raymond and others (1966) Social Indicators. Cambridge, MA: M.I.T. Press.

Fox, Karl A. (1974) Social Indicators and Social Theory. New York: John Wiley.

Liu, Ben-chieh (1974) "Quality of Life: Concept, Measure and Results," American Journal of Economics and Sociology, 34, 1 (January), 1-14.

Liu, Ben-chieh (1975) Quality of Life Indicators in U.S. Metropolitan Areas, 1970. Washington, D. C.: U.S. Government Printing Office.

APPENDIX

PANEL 1. FACTORS IN ECONOMIC COMPONENT

Factor Effect	Factors
	I. Individual Economic Well-Being
+	A. Personal income per capita ($)
	B. Wealth
+	1. Savings per capita ($)
+	2. Ratio of total property income to total personal income
+	3. Percent of owner-occupied housing units
+	4. Percent of households with one or more automobiles
+	5. Median value, owner-occupied, single family housing units ($1,000)
	II. Community Economic Health
+	A. Percent of families with income poverty level
−	B. Degree of economic concentration, absolute value
	C. Productivity
+	1. Value added per worker in manufacturing ($1,000)
+	2. Value of construction per worker ($1,000)
+	3. Sales per employee in retail trade ($1,000)
+	4. Sales per employee in wholesale trade ($1,000)
+	5. Sales per employee in selected services ($1,000)
+	D. Total bank deposits per capita ($)
	E. Income inequality index
−	1. Central city and suburban income distribution
	2. Percent of families with incomes below poverty level or greater than $15,000
−	F. Unemployment rate
+	G. Number of full-time Chamber of Commerce employees per 100,000 population

A Quality of Life Production Model for Project Impact Assessment

PANEL 2. FACTORS IN POLITICAL COMPONENT

Factor Effect	Factors
	I. Individual Activities
	A. Informed citizenry
+	1. Local Sunday newspaper circulation per 1,000 population
+	2. Percent of occupied housing units with TV available
+	3. Local radio stations per 1,000 population
+	B. Political activity participation--ratio of Presidential vote cast to voting age population
	II. Local Government Factors
	A. Professionalism
+	1. Average monthly earnings of full-time teachers ($)
+	2. Average monthly earnings of other full-time employees ($)
+	3. Entrance salary of patrolmen ($)
+	4. Entrance salary of firemen ($)
+	5. Total municipal employment per 1,000 population
+	6. Police protection employment per 1,000 population
+	7. Fire protection employment per 1,000 population
+	8. Insured unemployment rates under state, federal, and ex-servicemen's programs
	B. Performance
−	1. Violent crime rate Per 100,000 population
−	2. Property crime rate per 100,000 population
+	3. Local government revenue per capita
+	4. Percent of revenue from Federal Government
+	5. Community health index
+	6. Community education index
	C. Welfare assistance
+	1. Per capita local government expenditures on public welfare ($)
+	2. Average monthly retiree benefits ($)
+	3. Average monthly payments to families with dependent children ($)

PANEL 3. FACTORS IN ENVIRONMENTAL COMPONENT

Factor Effect	Factors
	I. Individual and Institutional Environment
	A. Air pollution index
−	1. Mean level for total suspended particulates ($\mu g/m^3$)
−	2. Mean level for sulfur dioxide ($\mu g/m^3$)
	B. Visual pollution
−	1. Mean annual inversion frequency
−	2. Percent of housing units dilapidated
+	3. Acres of parks and recreational areas per 1,000 population
	C. Noise
−	1. Population density in the central city of the SMSA, persons per square mile
−	2. Motor vehicle registrations per 1,000 population
−	3. Motorcycle registrations per 1,000 population
−	D. Tons of solid waste generated by manufacturing per million dollars value added
−	E. Water pollution index
	II. Natural Environment
	A. Climatological data
−	1. Mean annual inversion frequency
+	2. Possible annual sunshine days
−	3. Number of days with thunderstorms occurring
−	4. Number of days with temperature of 90° and above
−	5. Number of days with temperature of 32° and below
	B. Recreation areas and facilities
+	1. Acres of parks and recreational areas per 1,000 population
+	2. Miles of trails per 100,000 population

PANEL 4. FACTORS IN HEALTH AND EDUCATION COMPONENT

Factor Effect	Factors
	I. Individual Conditions
	A. Health
−	1. Infant mortality rate per 1,000 live births
−	2. Death rate per 1,000 population
	B. Education
+	1. Median school years completed by persons 25 years and over
+	2. Percent of persons 25 years and over, who completed 4 years of high school or more
−	3. Percent of males ages 16 to 21 who are not high school graduates
+	4. Percent of population ages 3 to 34 enrolled in schools
	II. Community Conditions
	A. Medical care availability and accessibility
+	1. Number of dentists per 100,000 population
+	2. Number of hospital beds per 100,000 population
+	3. Hospital occupancy rates
+	4. Number of physicians per 100,000 population
+	5. Per capita local government expenditures on health
	B. Educational attainment
+	1. Per capita local government expenditures on education
+	2. Percent of persons 25 years old and over who completed 4 years of college or more

PANEL 5. FACTORS IN SOCIAL COMPONENT

Factor Effect	Factors
	I. Individual Development
	A. Existing opportunity for self-support
+	1. Labor force participation rate
+	2. Percent of labor force employed
+	3. Mean income per family member ($)
+	4. Percent of children under 18 years living with both parents
−	5. Percent of married couples without own household
+	6. Individual education index
	B. Promoting maximum development of individual capabilities
+	1. Per capita local government expenditures on education ($)
+	2. Percent of persons 25 years old and over who completed 4 years of high school or more
	3. Persons ages 16 to 64 with less than 15 years of school but with vocational training
+	a. Percent of males
+	b. Percent of females
+	4. Individual health index
	C. Widening opportunity for individual choice
	1. Mobility
+	a. Motor vehicle registrations per 1,000 population
+	b. Motorcycle registrations per 1,000 population
+	c. Percent of households with one or more automobiles
	2. Information
+	a. Local Sunday newspaper circulation per 1,000 population
+	b. Percent of occupied housing units with TV available
+	c. Local radio stations per 1,000 population

A Quality of Life Production Model for Project Impact Assessment

PANEL 5. FACTORS IN SOCIAL COMPONENT (Continued)

Factor Effect	Factors
	3. Spatial extension
−	a. Population density in SMSA, persons per square mile
−	b. Percent of population under 5 and 65+ living in central city
+	4. Individual equality index
+	5. Individual and institutional environment index

II. Individual Equality

  A. Race

Factor Effect	Factors
+	1. Ratio of Negro to total persons median family income adjusted for education
+	2. Ratio of Negro to total persons in professional employment adjusted for education
−	3. Ratio of Negro males to total males unemployment rate adjusted for education, absolute value
−	4. Ratio of Negro females to total females unemployment rate adjusted for education, absolute value

  B. Sex

Factor Effect	Factors
−	1. Ratio of male to female unemployment rate adjusted for education, absolute value
−	2. Ratio of male to female professional employment adjusted for education, absolute value

  C. Spatial

Factor Effect	Factors
−	1. Percent working outside county of residence
−	2. Income inequality index--central city and suburban income distribution, absolute value
−	3. Housing segregation index, absolute value

PANEL 5. FACTORS IN SOCIAL COMPONENT (Continued)

Factor Effect		Factors
	III.	Community Living Conditions
		A. General conditions
+		1. Percent of families with income above poverty level
+		2. Percent of occupied housing units with plumbing facilities
−		3. Percent of occupied housing units with 1.01 or more persons per room
+		4. Percent of occupied housing units with a telephone available
+		5. Percent of workers who use public transportation to work
−		6. Total crime rate per 100,000 population
−		7. Cost of living index
		B. Facilities
		1. Recreational facilities
+		a. Number of swimming pools per 100,000 population
+		b. Number of camping sites per 100,000 population
+		c. Number of tennis courts per 100,000 population
+		d. Miles of trails per 100,000 population
+		2. Number of banks and savings and loan associations per 1,000 population
+		3. Number of retail trade establishments per 1,000 population
+		4. Number of selected service establishments per 1,000 population
+		5. Number of hospital beds per 100,000 population
+		6. Volumes of books in the main public library per 1,000 population

PANEL 5. FACTORS IN SOCIAL COMPONENT (Concluded)

Factor Effect	Factors
	III. C. Other social conditions
−	1. Death rate per 1,000 population
−	2. Birth rate per 1,000 population
+	3. Sports events in the metropolitan area
	4. Cultural events in the metropolitan area
+	a. Dance, drama, and music events
+	b. Cultural institutions
+	c. Fairs and festivals held
+	5. Community health and education index
+	6. Natural environment index

TABLE 1

QUALITY OF LIFE INDEXES AND RATINGS IN LARGE SMSA'S

SMSA	Economic Value	Rating	Political Value	Rating	Environmental Value	Rating	Health and Education Value	Rating	Social Value	Rating
1. Akron, Ohio	1.8786	C	2.6319	C	-0.9667	C	1.1250	C	0.1835	E
2. Albany-Schenectady-Troy, N.Y.	1.3286	D	3.7431	A	-1.2917	D	1.8625	B	0.5836	B
3. Allentown-Bethlehem-Easton, Pa.-N.J.	1.4286	D	2.4792	C	-0.6167	A	0.3875	D	0.2173	D
4. Anaheim-Santa Ana-Garden Grove, Ca.	2.1786	B	8.0486	B	-1.0500	C	2.0125	A	0.4762	C
5. Atlanta, Ga.	2.4714	A	1.8750	E	-1.2833	D	0.8375	D	0.2806	D
6. Baltimore, Md.	1.3429	D	2.5278	C	-1.2667	D	0.3625	D	0.1392	E
7. Birmingham, Ala.	1.0500	E	1.6944	E	-1.4250	E	-0.0250	E	0.0931	E
8. Boston, Mass.	1.1786	E	3.3889	A	-1.2500	D	2.0125	A	0.6036	B
9. Buffalo, N.Y.	1.8357	C	3.8819	A	-1.2000	D	1.4250	B	0.7019	B
10. Chicago, Ill.	2.3643	A	2.9653	B	-1.8167	E	0.6625	D	0.3056	D
11. Cincinnati, Ohio-Ky.-Ind.	2.3429	A	2.8403	B	-1.0333	C	0.6250	D	0.0711	E
12. Cleveland, Ohio	2.5143	A	2.7847	C	-1.4250	E	1.0875	C	0.5837	B
13. Columbus, Ohio	1.7857	C	3.0208	B	-1.0917	C	1.4875	B	0.7621	B
14. Dallas, Texas	2.7571	A	1.4653	E	-0.9083	B	0.7625	D	0.4585	C
15. Dayton, Ohio	2.1214	B	2.5625	C	-1.3167	D	1.0625	C	0.3421	D
16. Denver, Colo.	1.8357	C	3.0903	B	-0.9917	C	2.5000	A	0.9604	A
17. Detroit, Mich.	1.8929	B	3.2222	B	-1.7250	E	0.9625	C	-0.0248	E
18. Fort Lauderdale-Hollywood, Fla.	2.3143	A	2.1319	D	-1.0833	C	0.2000	E	0.5823	B
19. Fort Worth, Texas	2.4786	A	1.7986	E	-0.8583	B	0.3500	D	0.4372	C
20. Gary-Hammond-East Chicago, Ind.	1.3929	D	2.2778	D	-1.1750	D	0.7000	D	0.2106	D

TABLE 1 (Continued)

SMSA	Economic Value	Economic Rating	Political Value	Political Rating	Environmental Value	Environmental Rating	Health and Education Value	Health and Education Rating	Social Value	Social Rating
21. Grand Rapids, Mich.	2.2643	B	3.6319	A	-1.0333	C	1.5375	B	0.5527	C
22. Greensboro-Winston-Salem-High Point, N.C.	1.1571	E	1.8333	E	-1.3000	D	0.1000	E	0.2337	D
23. Hartford, Conn.	2.0357	B	3.6181	A	-1.1250	C	2.2750	A	0.5981	B
24. Honolulu, Hawaii	1.1357	E	2.1458	D	-0.4583	A	1.5375	B	0.4496	C
25. Houston, Texas	2.7000	A	1.9167	E	-1.0000	C	1.0875	C	0.5573	C
26. Indianapolis, Ind.	2.5143	A	2.4236	D	-1.5250	E	0.6500	D	0.4303	C
27. Jacksonville, Fla.	0.8929	E	1.7569	E	-1.2500	D	0.1125	E	0.3169	D
28. Jersey City, N.J.	0.5857	E	2.1250	D	-1.0167	C	-0.5250	E	-0.1694	E
29. Kansas City, Mo.-Ks.	1.6857	C	2.0486	D	-1.1250	C	1.1125	C	0.8089	A
30. Los Angeles-Long Beach, Ca.	2.0500	B	2.5278	C	-1.0583	C	1.7375	B	0.8315	A
31. Louisville, Ky.-Ind.	1.9071	B	2.3403	D	-1.4167	E	0.3125	E	0.2603	D
32. Memphis, Tenn.-Ark.	0.9429	E	1.8264	E	-1.2083	D	0.6125	D	0.1198	E
33. Miami, Fla.	1.2857	D	1.9097	E	-0.4167	A	0.6000	D	0.7634	B
34. Milwaukee, Wis.	2.1786	B	3.2708	A	-1.0417	C	1.7000	B	0.8453	A
35. Minneapolis-St. Paul, Minn.	1.9357	B	3.4722	A	-0.9000	B	2.2375	A	0.8329	A
36. Nashville-Davidson, Tenn.	1.7286	C	2.0833	D	-1.0833	C	0.6375	D	0.7218	B
37. New Orleans, La.	0.7857	E	1.5625	E	-1.2667	D	0.4250	D	0.1783	E
38. New York, N.Y.	1.9500	B	2.2014	D	-1.3333	D	1.2125	C	0.5179	C
39. Newark, N.J.	1.2571	D	2.9931	B	-1.2000	D	1.2625	C	0.1000	E
40. Norfolk-Portsmouth, Va.	0.8500	E	1.9306	E	-0.8667	B	0.0625	E	0.2507	D
41. Oklahoma City, Okla.	2.1143	B	2.8056	B	-0.8250	B	1.3750	B	0.8852	A
42. Omaha, Nebraska-Iowa	2.2786	B	2.5833	C	-1.3083	D	1.7500	B	0.9966	A
43. Paterson-Clifton-Passaic, N.J.	1.9357	B	1.8542	E	-1.0000	C	1.4625	B	0.1371	E

TABLE 1 (Continued)

SMSA	Economic Value	Rating	Political Value	Rating	Environmental Value	Rating	Health and Education Value	Rating	Social Value	Rating
44. Philadelphia, Pa.-N.J.	0.9500	E	2.4306	D	-1.0250	C	0.3000	E	0.2234	D
45. Phoenix, Ariz.	1.2786	D	1.9097	E	-0.5917	A	1.6000	B	0.7246	B
46. Pittsburgh, Pa.	1.5929	C	3.1181	B	-1.8667	E	0.7875	D	0.3510	D
47. Portland, Oreg.-Wash.	2.6786	A	3.5486	A	-0.6500	A	2.1375	A	1.0273	A
48. Providence-Pawtucket-Warwick, R.I.-Mass.	1.0786	E	3.0347	B	-0.7667	B	-0.1750	E	0.1606	E
49. Richmond, Va.	2.3357	A	2.4722	C	-1.1333	D	0.4500	D	0.1123	E
50. Rochester, N.Y.	2.3214	A	3.6667	A	-0.7000	B	2.0000	A	0.2196	D
51. Sacramento, Ca.	1.5929	C	3.6181	A	-0.2000	A	2.1875	A	0.9576	A
52. St. Louis, Mo.-Ill.	2.0357	B	2.5833	C	-1.5833	E	0.5625	D	0.1583	E
53. Salt Lake City, Utah	1.3714	D	3.3542	A	-1.0250	C	2.5625	A	0.5728	B
54. San Antonio, Texas	0.7857	E	1.3403	E	-0.8333	B	0.2875	E	0.2463	D
55. San Bernadino-Riverside-Ontario, Ca.	1.2000	D	2.6944	C	-0.4750	A	1.3625	B	0.6042	B
56. San Diego, Ca.	1.8786	C	3.1111	B	-0.5333	A	1.8125	B	0.9020	A
57. San Francisco-Oakland, Ca.	1.8357	C	2.9444	B	-0.7000	B	2.3750	A	0.8189	A
58. San Jose, Ca.	1.7500	C	2.9167	B	-0.5333	A	2.7250	A	0.7364	B
59. Seattle-Everett, Wa.	2.1071	B	3.0347	B	-0.2667	A	2.2625	A	1.0144	A
60. Springfield-Chicopee-Holyoke, Mass.-Conn.	1.1357	E	2.6667	C	-0.6167	A	0.7000	D	0.4634	C
61. Syracuse, N.Y.	1.2071	D	3.6458	A	-1.1500	D	1.8500	B	0.6157	B
62. Tampa-St. Petersburg, Fla.	1.6214	C	1.9514	E	-1.0583	C	0.0000	E	0.5526	C
63. Toledo, Ohio-Mich.	2.1714	B	3.0278	B	-1.1833	D	0.9375	C	0.5617	C
64. Washington, D.C.-Md.-Va.	1.8571	C	2.3403	D	-0.8333	B	2.1000	A	0.6848	B

TABLE 1 (Concluded)

SMSA	Economic Value	Rating	Political Value	Rating	Environmental Value	Rating	Health and Education Value	Rating	Social Value	Rating
65. Youngstown-Warren, Ohio	1.5857	D	2.7222	C	-0.9667	C	0.6375	D	0.3634	D
Mean ($\bar{x}$) =	1.7390		2.6219		-1.0342		1.1252		0.4809	
Standard Deviation (s) =	0.5475		0.6466		0.3452		0.7868		0.2928	

A = Outstanding ($\geq \bar{x} + s$)
B = Excellent ($\bar{x} + .28s \leq B < \bar{x} + s$)
C = Good ($\bar{x} - .28s < C < \bar{x} + .28s$)
D = Adequate ($\bar{x} - s \leq D \leq \bar{x} - .28s$)
E = Substandard ($\leq \bar{x} - s$)

IV Projecting

Social impact assessments require a broad range of analytical operations and the use of a wide variety of research tools and techniques. One of the most difficult analytical operations required by SIAs is that of projecting future impact situations. It is a necessary step since policy decisions must weigh a future state of affairs "with and without" the consequences of a proposed action. Moreover, part of the predictive problem is that the evaluative criteria by which present actions are judged in the future may--most likely, will--themselves have changed. Presently a large number of techniques for projecting alternative futures are being introduced to meet these demands. In this section the state of the art of projection techniques is described and illustrated. The array of techniques indicates both impressive achievement and monumental challenges.

The first article, by Miller, surveys the range of available methods for estimating societal futures and develops a "Metagrid" framework to map comprehensively the variety and complexity of potential futures. He persuasively argues for a view of SIA as "applied futuristics".

Many futures studies utilize scenarios. The article by Vlachos demonstrates their utility for visualizing the range of plausible alternative futures. In spite of the fact that the likelihood of occurrence of various scenarios is unassertainable, Vlachos argues that they can be helpful to policy makers in alerting them to undesirable possibilities and in conveying an understanding of likely combinations of consequences of policies.

While scenario writing tends to encompass "whole futures" in its projections, more specific features of the future are probed by DeLuca's and Byrne and Sucov's use of correlation techniques.

DeLuca employs correlation techniques to predict the capacity of communities to respond constructively to their environmental problems. Based on a social structural framework, he tests 142 hypotheses, of which 82 are supported by his data. His technique can be generalized to predictive efforts for other types of community concerns. DeLuca's focus on community capacity for dealing with problems is particularly useful for policy making purposes.

Byrne and Sucov are specifically interested in predicting community acceptance of power plant siting decisions. They develop a predictive instrument profiling correlations of 23 economic, ecological, sociopolitical and demographic descriptors of eleven communities having experience with power plant siting. Their approach can also be generalized to predicting community acceptance of other kinds of installations or developments.

The final article, by Ben-Dak, explores the potential of simulation and gaming in projecting social impacts and responses. While these techniques are seldom used in SIAs, requiring uncommon skill and experience and substantial investments of time and effort, they hold unique promise for purposes of projection. Although containing assumptions of uncertain probabilities, and producing results that may not be transferable to the real world, simulation and gaming are useful when more reliable methods are not readily available. Their combined use can yield the greatest analytic power.

Methods for Estimating Societal Futures*

David C. Miller
DCM Associates

Social Impact Assessment seeks to anticipate and appraise potential results (expected and desired impacts) and consequences (unexpected or undesired impacts) on each typical significant party and stock of resources affected by the proposed societal occurrence under study. In this assessment questions typically arise as to: Who are the important parties engaged or affected? What are the important resources? Which are the significant occurrences? What crucial outcomes can be realized? What substantial impacts (results and consequences) may be experienced by the parties? What alterations in the outlooks and purposes of each of the parties might be anticipated? The objective of this discussion is to survey the field of social forecasting and appraise the usefulness of its tools for addressing such questions.

TYPES OF SOCIETAL FUTURES

Estimates of societal futures may be usefully subdivided into four types: predictions, projections, conjectures, and forecasts. Each of these types of futures estimates is briefly characterized below.

1. Prediction

As used here, the prediction is the simplest but least useful kind of futures estimate. A prediction is a blithe assertion that X will exist or occur hereafter. It does not specify the causality modes invoked; probabilities of occurrence or non-occurrence are estimates; and often no date is cited by which the prediction is to be realized.

2. Projection

A projection (or extrapolation) is a more or less straightforward extension of past and present trends into the future on the basis of some stated assumption, most often the assumption that the future will resemble the present. In and of itself,

---

*This chapter draws extensively on the Handbook of Forecasting Techniques developed for the U.S. Army Engineer Institute for Water Resources by Stanford Research Institute's Center for the Study of Social Policy (Mitchell and others 1975), to which the author was a consultant.

the projection makes no claims to foresee what will happen, contenting itself with merely indicated what would happen if its stated assumptions should happen to be realized. Projections as such also ignore cause-effect explanations, treating their subject as a black box which is behaving in a certain way, for whatever reasons. Population projections are a familiar example.

3. Conjecture

A conjecture is an "if...then" proposition in which the if is stated at the outset while the then is inferred and examined on the basis of implications inherent in the if. This is of course the approach taken in making a projection, but other forms of conjecture go on to identify and analyze the important causality modes involved. On the other hand, the conjecture may pay no attention to timing and scheduling of potential future situations and events. Under the term "contingency analysis," a conjecture may examine sequential cause-effect relationships without ever setting these in a particular time frame. Generally speaking also, the conjecture does (or is amenable to) examine a more numerous and varied range of possibilities than the typical projection. A conjecture may (but need not) appraise the probabilities of the actual occurrence of potential future situations and events.

4. Forecast

As prediction is the simplest but least useful form of futures estimate, so the forecast is the most difficult and most useful form. The forecast delimits its topic with the greatest possible precision, explores a range of potential futures outcomes in the least ambiguous terms possible, specifies and analyzes the salient cause-effect relationships in the greatest feasible detail, fixes potential scheduling of future situations and events as closely as possible and details the estimated probabilities of every potential future with the greatest attainable precision. Judged by these stern criteria many futures estimates submitted as forecasts are in fact something less--predictions, projections, or conjectures.

POTENTIAL, NON-PRESCRIPTIVE AND PRESCRIPTIVE FUTURES

Overlaying and intertwined with all four kinds of futures estimates mentioned above are three concepts of great importance in futures studies. They are potential futures, non-prescriptive and prescriptive futures.

"Potential futures" (or "alternative futures") refers to the fact that a possible occurrence is never certain until it has happened. What might happen must always exceed what eventually does happen--possibilities outnumber actualities. Faced with this problem, and his own finite resources, the futurist must invoke some principle of selection. One selective principle regularly employed is to distinguish between non-prescriptive (or exploratory) potential futures and prescriptive (or normative) potential futures.

Loosely speaking, non-prescriptive potential futures can be thought of as those stemming from the operation of physical-historical causality--those which might plausibly evolve from present situations if no person or group actively intervened to influence the course of events. These potential futures might also be called the "if present trends persist" futures. Prescriptive futures, in contrast, are those potential futures which appeal to the investigator's aspirations or apprehensions.

As mentioned earlier, any futures study or social impact assessment invariably implies many more potential futures than the investigator can handle. The internal structure and dynamics of each potential future is apt to be complex, and the many significant interrelations between pairs and among subsets of potential futures is certain to be even more complex. As a practical matter, some workable organizing scheme is essential to managing these complexities. What is required is a framework which can acknowledge and respect complexity while dealing with its topic comprehensively and yet keeping the study manageable. Devising, developing, and using such a framework is a major challenge to futures researchers and social impact assessors alike.

METHODS FOR SOCIETAL FUTURES ESTIMATION

A great many varied methods have been or plausibly might be employed in developing estimates about potential future states of society. None has been shown to be very powerful, however; most yield projections and conjectures when applied in societal estimates rather than true forecasts.

To suggest the range and variety of these methods, Table 1 arrays a preliminary listing of 73 derived by the Stanford Research Institute team (Mitchell and others 1975; see also Duncan (1969) and Spilerman (1975) for state-of-the-art reviews of social forecasting). From this a short list of 12 main techniques was distilled and grouped into three broad categories (Table 2):

TABLE 2. MAIN TECHNIQUES OF SOCIAL FORECASTING

I. Techniques Using Time Series and Projections

1. Trend extrapolation
2. Pattern identification
3. Probabilistic forecasting

II. Techniques Based on Models and Simulations

4. Dynamic models
5. Cross-impact analysis
6. KSIM
7. Input/out analysis
8. Policy capture

III. Qualitative and Holistic Techniques

9. Scenarios and related methods
10. Expert-opinion methods
11. Alternative futures
12. Values forecasting

TABLE 1. CANDIDATE FORECASTING TECHNIQUES

1. Cost-benefit Analysis
2. Statistical Models (Bayesian)
3. Marginal Analysis
4. KSIM
5. Mission Flow Diagrams
6. Parameter Analysis
7. Cross-Impact Matrix
8. Input-Output Analysis
9. World Oil Price Simulation
10. Breakthroughs
11. Precursor Events
12. Econometric Forecasting
13. Dynamic Models
14. Structural Models
15. Decision Analysis
16. Morphological Modelling
17. Decision Matrices
18. Relevance Trees
19. Theoretical Limits and Barriers
20. Analysis of Industrial Behavior
21. Technological Audit
22. Social Trend Analysis
23. Scenario Writing
24. Canonical Trend Variation
25. Surprise-free Projections
26. Social Indicators
27. Leading Indicators (Economic)
28. Change Signals Monitoring
29. Critical Factors Analysis
30. Estimates of Preferences
31. Subjective Estimates of Probability
32. Prediction of Changeover Points
33. Amplitude-adjusted Index
34. Diffusion Index
35. Authority or "Genius" Forecasting
36. Surveys of Intentions or Attitudes
37. Surveys of Activities or Units
38. Panels
39. Delphi
40. Psychographics or Life Style
41. Activities, Interest, Opinions
42. Life Ways
43. Historical Analogy
44. Alternative Futures (FAR)
45. Divergence Mapping
46. Introspective Forecasting
47. Utopias/Dystopias
48. Modes and Mechanisms of Change
49. Study of Forces of Change
50. Macrohistorical Cycle
51. Cross-cultural comparisons
52. Synectics
53. Brainstorming
54. Bionics
55. Science Fiction as Forecasts
56. Exponential Smoothing
57. Simple Regression
58. Moving Averages
59. Multiple Regression
60. Envelope Curves
61. Growth Curves
62. Link-relative Prediction
63. Box-Jenkins
64. Cycle Analysis
65. Systems Analysis
66. Risk Analysis Simulation
67. Contextual Mapping
68. SRI Gulf Energy Models
69. Games
70. Policy Capture
71. Probabilistic Forecasting
72. Normex Forecasting
73. Substitution Forecasting

Following are some general comments on and typical examples in the major categories.

Methods Using Time Series and Projections

This category includes all methods for trend extrapolation, data-based pattern identification, and probabilistic estimation. These methods manipulate historical time-series data statistically in order to arrive at expectable future values for one or more variables. Statistical measures of confidence in the expected values may also be generated.

An example in this category is the method developed by G.E.P. Box and G.M. Jenkins (1970). The Box-Jenkins method is useful in cases where it is suspected that time series data conceals significant latent patterns. Such cases are often encountered by market researchers, demographers, and others in the behavioral and social sciences. To employ the Box-Jenkins method, one must first postulate a general class of patterns which it is suspected may be demonstrable within the data file. Within this general class, one then selects (by hunch or at random) a particular member of the class with which to test the file by mapping the data into a set of parameters such that the average variance about the parameters is purely random.

Should this occur on the first trial, one has verified that the particular pattern tested for is in fact demonstrable from the data. Most often, no fit or a partial fit is obtained. When a partial fit results, one is able from the nature and extent of fit to make an informed guess about the actual pattern, and to repeat the operation based on this new estimate. Thus one proceeds until a complete fit is obtained, or it appears that no fit can be found. When no fit is found, one may substitute another general class of patterns and begin anew, or turn to other methods. Investigators who wish to apply time-series and projective methods to social impact assessment studies may find the Box-Jenkins method useful.

Methods Based on Models and Simulations

Static models in which each component is fixed in one single relationship with all the others are of limited use in developing potential futures estimates. That is why dynamic models are usually employed in which each component can move through a range of values and relationships relative to the other components. Such dynamic models can simulate actual or hypothetical realities, past, present, or future. If we set a model initially at values and in relationships judged to represent the current situation, subsequent manipulations of the model can be taken as representing potential futures. In turn, projections, conjectures, and even forecasts can be prepared based on analytic insights arrived at by exercising and observing the model.

Whereas extrapolative methods tend to focus on one or a few variables, dynamic models typically incorporate numerous variables. Which variables are included and the range of permissible values assigned to each may be determined by using extrapolative methods. However dynamic models also invite and facilitate investigation of complex interaction among variables simulating past or future history as the series of iterations progresses. This is accomplished by establishing appropriate feedback loops in which the output of one iteration becomes the input of the next. A familiar example might be a population growth model, where the simulated birth and death rates in one interval become boundary variables constraining the range of values for population size in subsequent intervals.

Qualitative and Holistic Methods

In one form or another, qualitative-holistic potential societal futures estimation methods amount in the end to systematic storytelling. The investigator usually begins with an intuitive sense about the general sort of potential future society he wishes to examine. Often, the first step is to come up with a descriptive name for what one has in mind: "transformational," "achieving," "good times," "imperialist" or "technocratic," to mention a few which have actually been used. Having generally if vaguely in mind the sort of society one wishes to consider, the next step is to decide what societal issues are central for purposes of the present study. To this end, a taxonomic list of societal issues can be generated and used to make the selection. In an unpublished proprietary framework developed for the Weyerhaeuser Company, of which I was co-developer, major topics were listed under such headings as Social, Technological, Political, and Economic. Under each particular topic, two or more alternative courses of evolution were provided, while others could be added as desired. By selecting one alternative for each topic consistent with the general sort of society one had in mind, it was possible to generate a brief outline for each of a series of different potential futures. This outline could then be elaborated into a fullblown narrative, complete with supportive trend data and information from a variety of sources. After (in practical fact, coincidentally with) a characterization of a potential future has been roughed out and seems coherent and plausible but not yet finished, the investigator should ask: But through what plausible sequence of situations and events over the months or years ahead might society evolve from its present state into the state our scenario describes?

In every qualitative-holistic conjecture about potential futures, regularly there emerge turning points beyond which the future could with equal plausibility evolve in two or more different directions. In terms of a baseline or "surprise-free" future, Kahn and Weiner (1967) characterize each of these several different possibilities as "canonical variations" around the dominant theme.

Yet another qualitative-holistic approach is to examine the modes and mechanisms of change pertinent to a given study topic. This approach amounts to selecting some particular profile of physical-historical causality and combining it in some fashion with a given profile of purposive-futuristic causality. Given the study topic appropriately described and characterized and some particular specification of causality, it is feasible systematically to identify, describe, and explore a range of significant potential future situations and events. Looking backward rather than forward, this is in fact more or less the approach taken by historians. The technique brings with it all the advantages accruing to explicitness, comprehensivity, coherence, consistency, and logic. On the other hand--noting that historians of various stripes dispute what happened in the past as vigorously as futurists dispute what may happen in the future--the technique also has intrinsic disadvantages, brilliantly exposed, analyzed and documented by David Hackett Fischer in <u>Historians' Fallacies</u> (1970).

Concluding this discussion of qualitative and holistic methods, I will briefly describe Divergence Mapping, an intensive client-participatory method of which I am co-developer. Divergence Mapping (hereafter, D.M.) is so named because it assumes that the range of potential societal futures must broaden or diverge as one moves away from the present towards the more-distant future. The method was designed on the basis of experience in the corporate sector. In that environment, corporate planners and top managers regularly must make decisions whose costs and import are awesome, in an environment of enormous ignorance and uncertainty. D.M. assumes that decision-makers in such a climate dare not and will not respond to environmental signals they do not comprehend, and that they cannot comprehend images of potential futures which they themselves had no active part in designing. D.M. enables policy and decision makers to explore, quickly if cursorily, a range of 22 potential futures treating issues which they themselves have previously identified as most important for their organizations. Beyond this preliminary examination, any subset of individual or combined potential futures judged to be of particular importance can be elaborated and studied in whatever depth seems justified.

The identification of and agreement upon a small set of crucial issues for the organization or group of participants is the first step in D.M. Usually, these issues are selected within an agreed-upon time horizon--say, 15-30 years. Incorporating these issues, futurists experienced in scenario development prepare a set of 22 500-750 word mini-scenarios called Frames, depicting a variety of contrastive potential futures in each of which one or more of the issues is dealt with. This set of 22 Frames is distributed to participant users, revised if necessary on the basis of their critiques, and redistributed to become the primary working papers for a D.M. Workshop.

The D.M. Workshop begins with participants identifying and agreeing on those situations, events, and trends in the present which they deem most important in relation to the critical issues previously identified. This working characterization of the present thereafter is used as the reference standard against which the 22 Frames are contrasted and positioned on the D.M. Map Form.

The D.M. Map Form consists of a fan-shaped array of 22 blank cells, with room in each cell to record the number of one Frame. At the apex of the fan a separate cell represents the present. Along one side of the fan is a Sooner-Later line. The fan proper consists of four layers or tiers of cells fanning out from the present, with four, five, six, and seven cells in the first, second, third, and fourth tiers respectively. The Sooner end of the Sooner-Later line is opposite the first tier, while the Later end is opposite the fourth tier.

In the D.M. exercise, any Frame may be assigned by number to any unoccupied cell in any tier on the Map. Assignments are made on the presumption that those Frames judged to be most like the present are potential futures which could be realized sooner and so should be assigned to the first tier. Correspondingly, those Frames which the group judges to be least like the present as characterized by the group are held to be those which could be realized only Later, and so should be assigned to the fourth tier. (No significant distinction is made among Frames within a given tier, insofar as timing is concerned.) Typically, the group first makes assignment of four Frames to the fourth (latest) tier, and finally assigns the remaining eleven Frames to the second and third tiers. All assignments are made on the basis of whole-group consensus, preceded by trial assignments in two or more subgroups.

Once a group has completed its D.M. Map Form, it is required to develop three alternative future histories, again working first in subgroups and then as a committee of the whole. Usually, the group is asked to outline a future history which represents the most optimistic potential future for the organization, a second which outlines the most pessimistic future history, and a third which represents the most likely potential future. Each future history consists of at least one cell in each of the four tiers, with each cell assigned the earliest possible date by which it might be realized. Satisfactory explanations of how the situation described in each cell might plausibly evolve into the situation described in the next cell are also required. Again, however, the only judgment criteria required is that of group consensus. The ground rules permit more than one Frame in a tier to be used in a single future history if the group wishes; by the same token, a given Frame may be and often is incorporated in more than one future history. Connecting links drawn in three colors on the D.M. Form records the future histories selected by the group.

After future histories have been developed, the group finally turns once more to the critical issues identified by the participants before the Frames were drafted. Through informal discussion or by using any of several more structured techniques, the group is asked to review the issues it had selected. Should certain issues be deleted? Should new ones be added? Should issues be modified? How critical might each of the issues be in each of the three future histories, and how might each be characteristically presented and dealt with? Which issues seem to remain critical in all future histories, and which vary in importance from one to another? In conclusion, the group recommends which Frames and future histories, if any, should be elaborated and refined and also indicates what new Frames and future histories, if any, should be developed subsequently.

D.M. has been used with good results by a number of corporate senior planning staffs and top managers, and by local school boards, college classes, and academic administrators. The method is flexible and can be expanded or contracted, simplified or elaborated upon according to available time, interests, needs, and resources.

CONCLUSION

In this chapter, I have briefly discussed different types of potential futures estimates (predictions, projections, conjectures, and forecasts) and conceptions of the future (potential, non-prescriptive and prescriptive). I have presented an array of methods for societal futures estimation and described and commented on three broad classes of them: methods based on time series and projections, methods based on models and simulations, and methods using qualitative and holistic techniques. If my emphasis has fallen heaviest on the last of these, it is because they may appear less familiar and convincing. My experience has been that they possess considerable utility for futures research and potential for application in social impact assessment.

REFERENCES

Box, G. E. P. and G. M. Jenkins (1970) "Time Series Analysis: Forecasting and Control." San Francisco: Holden Day.

Duncan, Otis Dudley (1969) "Social Forecasting: The State of the Art," The Public Interest, 17 (Fall), 88-118.

Fischer, David Hackett (1970) "Historian's Fallacies." New York: Harper and Row.

Kahn, Herman and A. J. Wiener (1967) "The Year 2000: A Framework for Speculation on the Next Thirty-Three Years." New York: Macmillan.

Mitchell, Arnold and others (1975) "Handbook of Forecasting Techniques." IWR Contract Report 75-7. Fort Belvoir, VA: U. S. Army Engineer Institute for Water Resources, December.

Spilerman, Seymour (1975) "Forecasting Social Events," pp. 381-401 in Kenneth C. Land and Seymour Spilerman (eds.), Social Indicator Models. New York: Russell Sage Foundation.

The Use of Scenarios for Social Impact Assessment

Evan Vlachos
Colorado State University

I. Introduction

Social forecasting involves analysis of probable social consequences of current trends and events, projections of future technological and social developments, and understanding of the "images of the future"--the anticipations, fears, hopes and goals that motivate present action toward the creation of desired future states. Scenario writing is a technique of futures research that blends these facets into narrative descriptions of potential courses of development. It attempts to sketch a logical sequence of events in order to show how, under present conditions and assumptions, a future state or set of alternative states might evolve. A scenario then is a synoptic view of developments that appear relevant to a particular situation or setting; it is an imaginative narrative of possible alternative futures based upon assumptions and analyses regarding trends and events. By examining a number of alternative scenarios one can seek to identify significant future consequences that may affect current decisions to proceed or not with a given public project. Scenario writing thus includes:

1. A statement of assumptions about future developments on a wide spectrum of technical, economic, social, political, and ecological conditions;

2. Elaboration of constraints in implementing a variety of actions that may alter the sequence of events and contribute to desired future environments;

3. Speculation on alternative futures and alternative possible outcomes as a result of projected trends and normative positions;

4. Consideration of the dynamics of interacting forces and of the effects that a particular event may have on another; and

5. Retrospective analysis of alternative possible outcomes of certain real past and present events.

In scenario writing we are dealing with "sufficient" (what might happen) and not "necessary" (what must happen) futures (Sage and Chobot 1974: 169). Whatever form they may take, scenarios remain a product of the imagination--conjectures about potential futures rather than exact predictions of what will actually occur. Indeed, the generation of __alternative__ futures is a conscious aim of this approach. Despite the lack of exact predictive power, scenarios can be useful for disciplining the imagination and for making some broad inferences about an uncertain or unknown future.

There are obvious methodological difficultires in social forecasting as well. One is the rapidity and fluidity of change itself, challenging the assumption that the future will be a linear extrapolation from the past. This uncertainty over the course of future developments points to a fundamental problem of knowledge, that "However good our futures research may be, we shall never be able to escape from the ultimate dilemma that all our knowledge is about the past, and all our decisions are about the future" (Ian Wilson, quoted in Zentner 1975: 23). Other writers (e.g., Ayres 1969; Hoos 1974) have noted such pitfalls as unreliability of data, the temptations of affective thinking, the fatal attraction of ideology, narrow views of the system under examination, forcing soft facts into preconceived patterns, intrinsic uncertainties and historical accidents, premature quanitification, elaborate paradigms supported by inconclusive evidence, and definitional pedantry.

II. Types of Futures and Alternative Scenarios

There are essentially two basic directions from which one can approach the study of the future and impact forecasting in particular (Arnstein and Christakis 1975: Ch. 16). One may be described as the _exploratory_ or _extrapolative approach_. Through an historical, predictive model we ask ourselves what trend or event forecast can be made with regard to existing social, political, economic, and technological situations that may lead to future states. The second direction may be broadly labeled as _normative_ or _teleological_, and involves essentially preferred futures and a delineation of desired goals and objectives about our future and about alternative worlds that we want to achieve through a conscious process of social change. In exploratory forecasting one moves from the present (with knowledge of the past) towards the future, while normative forecasting implies a "backward" movement from idealized or desired future states to the present. In exploratory forecasting we emphasize trajectories; in normative, means to achieve desired states

Following on this distinction are three conceptions of futures that can be used to establish scenario parameters:

1. _Potential_ futures, based on varying degrees of likelihood:

    a. _Probable_ futures--the reasonably expected events resulting from well-defined past trends and relatively clearly understood present conditions.
    b. _Possible_ futures--likely potential developments, but with a higher degree of uncertainty than the probable; they refer to the types of trends or events which make more or less credible certain developments affecting the range of alternatives envisaged.
    c. _Plausible_ futures--conceivable alternatives within more remotely imaginable developments. Although highly unlikely and full of speculative assumptions, plausible futures are still supposable or assumable.

2. _Preferable_ futures raise the question as to where do we _desire_ to go from here. In this perception of the future we emphasize goals or objectives that we would like to attain or should pursue in a consciously planned society. Such conceptions of the future reflect normative or teleological concerns.

3. **Practicable** futures involve an ultimate synthesis of where we expect and desire to go from here--the synergistic question of what are the most probable paths that we could take, given both possible trends and events and at the same time, goals and objectives that we would like to achieve.

These varying conceptions of the future are embodied in four generic types of scenarios:[1]

1. **Extrapolative scenarios** which involve a delineation of **probable** developments and a sequence of events that are most likely to occur, or consequences **reasonably** expected. This type of scenario can be also described as one of "surprise-free" projections. In this case, components of the scenario are usually assigned some index score of probability of occurrence.

2. **Normative scenarios** that may provide guidance for present actions in order to achieve desired future states. This type of scenario may be described as teleological since it implies a movement from the future to the present rather than the other way around.

3. **Speculative scenarios** refer to those "future histories" that may be primarily involved in trying to contain the unanticipated or the unforeseen. They revolve around **plausible** or conceivable futures, and embody highly imaginative anticipations of significantly different alternatives, the so-called "canonical variations" of Kahn and Wiener (1967).

4. **Dialectic scenarios** derive from the philosophical formulations of thesis and antithesis; one may make a given forecast and then propose an extreme opposite or counter-forecast. Both extreme alternative futures are then subject to critical argument. In doing so, one simply tries to combine "surprise-free" projections and "canonical variations" and to subject to criticism a series of assumptions and alternative visions concerning future states.

The above typologies (in many respects overlapping) indicate essentially an increasing shift from the purely probabilistic and extrepolative mode of thinking to the more intuitive, speculative and far-reaching efforts in trying to handle strategic uncertainty.

III. The Design of Scenarios

The proper criterion for evaluating the usefulness of scenarios is not so much whether any prediction or assessment is "correct" as whether the prediction is based on some systematic way of exposing logical sequences of events leading to a firmer basis for "rational" decision-making. Therefore, there is no one "right" scenario. There are certain necessary ingredients in scenario design, however. Zentner (1975:25) lists them as credibility, utility and intelligibility.

---

1. The discussion here relies heavily on an earlier work on the topic (Vlachos 1974). Landford (1972) distinguishes three main types of scenarios by the technique used in their construction: consensus, "iteration-through-synopsis" and **cross-impact.**

Similarly, Lanford (1972: 29) offers four prescriptions to increase a scenario's plausibility:

1. Within its area the scenario should be reasonably complete, i.e., it should provide a decision on occurrence or non-occurrence of most of the major potential developments relevant to that domain.

2. A plausible scenario should also be as probable or possible as other equally complete scenarios based on the same set of circumstances.

3. A way of reinforcing scenarios is to take into account <u>a priori</u> probabilities so that the frequency distribution of occurrence and nonoccurrence among component developments of a scenario should approximately reflect those <u>a priori</u> probabilities.

4. The scenario should be reasonably internally consistent; it should not articulate the simultaneous occurrence of developments which by virtue of their cross-impact relationship have little chance of both being realized.

We can now delineate the basic principles involved in the construction of scenarios (see also Abt, Foster and Rea 1973; Gerardin 1973). The following general tasks seem necessary to formulate alternative futures for any of the types of scenarios cited above:

1. Identification of potential users and uses of scenarios.

2. Statement of assumptions, or "visions" about the world around us and about the future.

3. Problem definition and structure, including identification of factors which affect development, elaboration of "themes" and selection of critical issues.

4. Selection of time horizon suitable to the specific problem requirements.

5. Collection and compilation of relevant data for an information base to be used in developing the scenarios.

It is futile to develop scenarios without careful consideration of potential users and uses of the projected output. The level of sophistication and the depth of critical analysis will vary according to the audience and their eventual use of alternative scenarios in evolving any proposed plan.

Numerous assumptions underlie scenarios of the future. Some generalized conceptions of man, nature, society, technology, and their interrelationships must be selected along with the basic forecasting method. Such assumptions include faith in surprise-free techniques; basic commitment to the ability to foretell the future; the notion that subjective judgment is a practical and useful way to select potential futures; and the belief that systematic exploration of subjectively elaborated futures can aid in their clarification.

A particular difficulty arising at this point involves uncertainties in long-range, future-oriented planning. These broader categories of planning uncertainty include uncertainties in knowledge of the external planning environment; uncertainties as to future intentions of other decision-makers in related fields of choice; uncertainties as to appropriate value judgments; and, finally, the all-encompassing idea of strategic uncertainty caused by broader institutional and social changes, either because certain facts of life have been changed by unforeseen events or because the sociocultural context has been changed. Strategic uncertainty refers to such elusive phenomena as social changes and major shifts in the social culture (e.g., values) as well as economic and political transformations; institutional changes and significant alterations in organizational structures; environmental changes, including new knowledge of the ecosystem and long-range consequences from seral disturbances; and technological changes and the consequences for collective life from their application.

Another central task in scenario writing concerns the requirement for a definition and structuring of the problem. This can be accomplished through some typical synopsis of the situation under consideration, including ambient conditions or constraints of the system; resource base capabilities; planning problems and proposed parameters of programming; problems of priorities and definitions of the hierarchy' of objectives; reconnaissance of institutional and technical capabilities and limitations; and larger sociopolitical considerations in anticipated developments. In this context it is important to consider in some systematic fashion key technical, economic, social, political, and ecological variables or groups of factors which affect trends and events. In searching for appropriate "variables" or groups of factors in the affected environments, one should distinguish between:

1. Relatively stable variables or factors with a high degree of built-in stability which for short-run periods can be treated almost as constant (e.g., climate, topography, language, etc.).

2. Changing variables or factors either linear or exponential (e.g., population, education, capital resources, etc.).

3. Incalculable variables or factors which may be wholly fortuitous and unpredictable, and complex conditions involving unknown or unanalyzed mechanisms (Natural calamities, political upheavals, technological breakthroughs, historical accidents, etc.).

The quest for key variables does not differ from other types of methodological design. The difficulty, however, lies in the fact that one must consider a variety of variables that may not be crucial in the present but which may be of significance in future environments. It is also during this stage that basic "themes," critical issues and relevant topics are selected around which consistent sets of scenarios can be developed, and potential operating plans and major decision points can be identified.

Time horizon will vary from project to project, but it is interesting to notice that generally the longer the span of a forecast the more extreme its optimistic

or pessimistic character (predominantly the latter). Short-term projections can
carry more forcefully the wishful commitment to solve pressing problems and, thus,
make "feasible" scenarios more acceptable to planners and users. Long-term forecasting (say beyond 10 years) rests on more imaginative thrusts, has to incorporate
a variety of exogenous factors, and is under the perennial cloud of the "unexpected."

The final general task is the collection of relevant data and the establishment of
an information basis. In addition to uncovering information that leads to a better
understanding of probable and possible consequences from any alteration in the
environment, it is desirable to generate some quantative data, e.g., computer
scenarios which require the assignment of index numbers within certain internal
range limitations.

Another way of viewing the proposed tasks relating to the design of scenarios is
to graphically summarize a typical sequence of steps in their generation (Figure 1).

IV. Examples of Scenario Writing in Applied Research
     An increasing variety of studies incorporate scenarios as part of their
reasoning process to account for either the effects of certain projects or for
forecasting future environments within which long-range consequences may occur.
For example, the Federal Energy Administration's Project Independence report (1974)
employs a set of alternative energy scenarios. The Corps of Engineers' Omaha-
Council Bluffs Urban Study (Omaha District 1975) postulates a set of alternative
land use scenarios. The U.S. Environmental Protection Agency's Office of Pesticide
Programs arrays a set of alternative scenarios relevant to past management policies
(Elgin, MacMichael and Schwartz 1975). In our own work (Burke and Vlachos 1974;
Brown and Vlachos 1975) we have used scenarios in a variety of situations, including
the social impact assessment of public projects. The following are sample scenarios
relating to public policies in the arid West, presented in abbreviated form to illustrate the use of scenarios in typical situations involving natural resources
commitments.

A. Assumptions
    To initiate future histories and the assessment of long-range effects from
interrelated developments in the area, we need to establish a tentative list of
the general assumptions that direct our thinking on the range of probable or plausible developments associated with the project. These can be summarized in four
propositions:

   1. In varying degrees, all proposed activities redistribute welfare from
      group to group, time to time, and place to place.

   2. In any alteration of surrounding environments, social conflict
      among advantaged and disadvantaged groups is generally present.

   3. Certain areas of the nation are of critical national concern and
      their alteration would mean irrevocable loss of resources unique
      to the particular region.

   4. Industrialization and urbanization alter irrevocably the relatively
      isolated and pristine character of the surrounding environment.

FIGURE 1. STEPS IN SCENARIO GENERATION

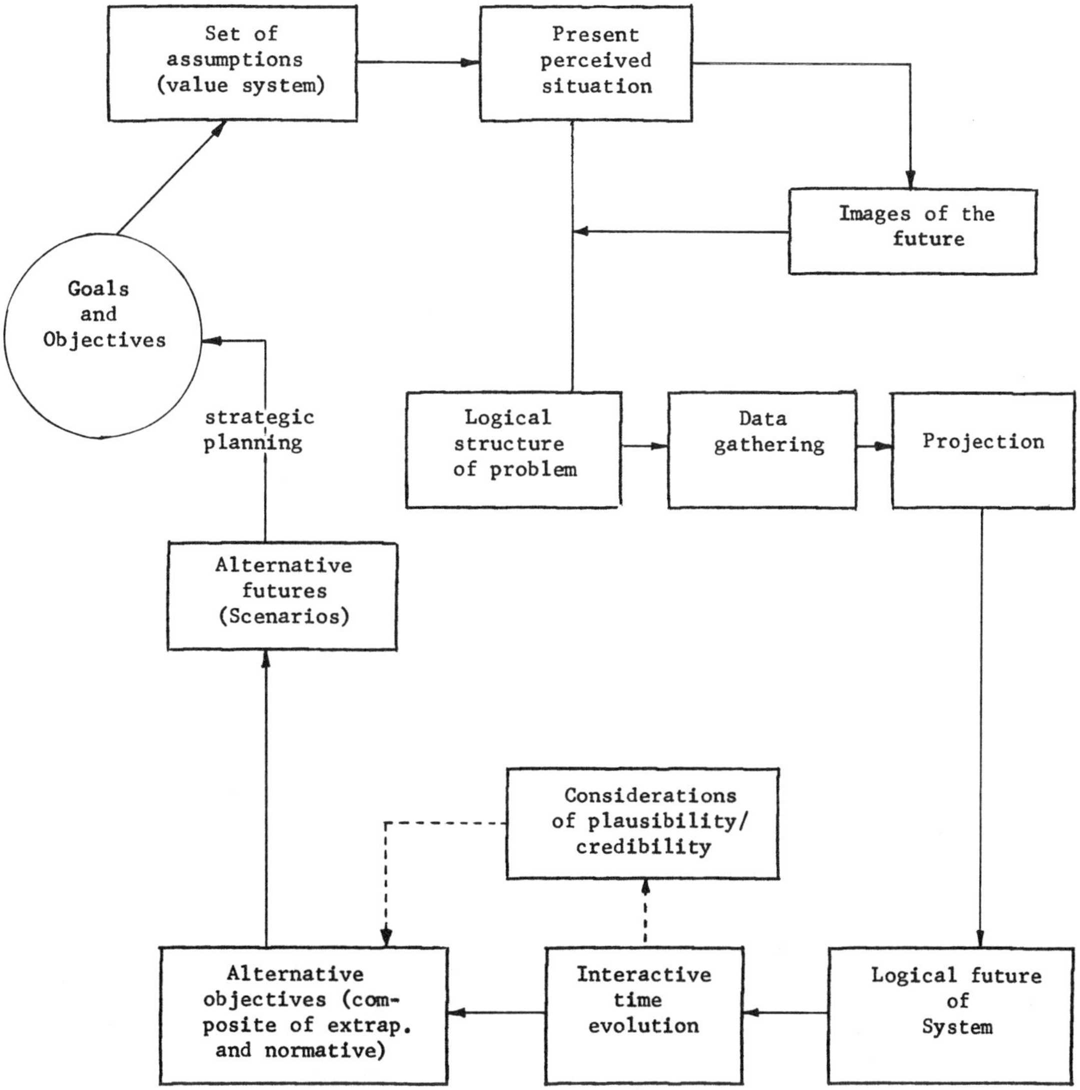

B. Probable Developments
   1. <u>Population and general activities</u>

      - Dramatic population growth and population mobility will be taking place in the coming years, as well as strong urbanization.

      - It is expected that there will be increased leisure and recreation demands on a national scale that will impinge on the opportunities and attractiveness of the region.

      - There is high potential for increased commercialization in the area.

      - Increased emphasis will be placed on agriculture as a result of growing demands for food. Tourism and industry may also create the option of abandoning farming in the area, however.

      - A result of energy developments, industrial expansion will affect population and services.

   2. <u>Natural resources, especially water, in the West</u>

      - Increased discussion will occur as to the role of natural resources, due to the ineffectiveness of existing resource plans on a regional scale.

      - Demand for and abuse of water resources may occur as a result of increasing affluence.

      - Another probable event is the diversion of western rivers and streams for municipal, industrial, and agricultural uses, thus destroying a number of fishing grounds and scenic beauty.

      - Probable is also groundwater salinization in heavily irrigated arid and semi-arid basins.

      - Increased concentrations of chemical pollutants in natural waterways will accentuate water related problems.

   3. <u>Value environment</u>

      - Continuous discussion and debate will occur in the coming years between western problems vs. national interests.

      - Continued ecological awareness and public involvement will be part of the national and regional scene of the future.

      - There will be increased preoccupation with reduction of access to natural areas so that the environment can remain in more or less a primitive form, thus guaranteeing its enjoyment by future generations.

- Occasional conflicts will continue to exist between environmental and developmental interests.

- As a result of legislation and of the emerging environmental ethos, emphasis will be placed on comprehensive planning requirements and cogent land use policies both locally and nationally.

- Public confidence in governmental officials and technical specialists and the information they provide regarding planning and managing of natural resources will continue at least at the same level.

C. Themes - Scenarios

From a variety of sources, commitments and demands, three broad policy options seem to emerge: (1) accelerated growth, (2) moderate growth and (3) limited growth.

Scenario of Accelerated Growth

After a short period of depression the nation has now entered an era of optimism and expansion. The debate about national versus western benefits has been resolved by placing the larger interests of the nation above and beyond regional policies. Industrial expansion becomes the order of the day, accentuated by demands for meeting national food and fiber needs. Emphasis on agricultural expansion results from a national policy of increased agricultural exports to offset continuous drought in Asia.

Technological breakthroughs in the mining industry have created a new rush to the West, and many undiscovered areas of the region are also sought after by "urban refugees" from the East and from California. The movement of population is further encouraged by Federal policies and actions directed towards the distribution of growth and the need for what is called a "new frontier." A policy to colonize the area is part of this national population dispersion policy aimed at reducing eastern population pressures.

Major international complications following the Mideast conflict of 1978 makes imperative maximum development of reliable energy sources in the West through large investments in natural resources related industries. NEPA has been watered down by Congress through a revocation of provisions requiring environmental impact statement preparation. The catastrophic events of previous years, the bitter taste left after the mild depression of the middle seventies, and a spirit of expansion (brought about also by a return to higher birth rates) underscore the ideological commitment to maximum economic growth policies. Expanding industries and population in the West are creating new forms of employment and increased personal income, which contribute to increased demands for leisure and recreation and a search for relatively unexplored parts of the nation.

Industry is booming as a result of guaranteed prices, low interest loans, accelerated depreciation, investment tax credit, and a series of other specific subsidies which contribute to an air of well-being and rapid growth. Such investments are also contributing to the atmosphere of a new "gold rush" to the West, where a deliberate choice is made to develop economically while retaining some areas in relatively pristine conditions. Under these conditions, the Federal government labels part of the West an "Accelerated Development Area" and officially washes its hands of all social and environmental consequences from the decision to go full speed ahead.

At the same time, development interests have filed suit challenging growth limitations as an unconstitutional abridgement of private property rights. Community growth regulations are declared unconstitutional by the courts. The booming atmosphere of the region is also helped by long-distance water diversions that replenish reservoirs depleted by the earlier drought and the high demands of the power plants. The water is used for maximum economic growth through additional reservoir storages, with irrigation water being effectively transferred to urban and industrial uses.

The manifestations of this economic dynamism of the region are not hard to detect. The retirement and tourist potential of the area are further exploited, triggering an increase in the in-migration of older persons. A new town for retired persons, Eliopolis, is advertised nationally as the answer to the smog-ridden communities of Arizona. The employment multipliers reflect a more optimistic economic attitude with respect to the future development of the area. There is now an increased ability to finance public services through increased tax revenue as well as new options for further development in the area. New school systems, hospitals, sanitation facilities and other services are now becoming available in greater numbers.

Such conditions incorporate many of the feared characteristics of boom development. The strains from such explosive growth can already be seen in a number of communities all over the West. In cases like these, there is always a lag between the ever-expanding needs of communities and the development of a viable tax base. The almost predatory character of growth and expansion is not conducive to comprehensive long-range planning or concerted policy action. In this type of growth the "boom town" characteristics and helter-skelter developments create the potential for large scale social breakdowns.

Such rapid developments impinge also upon the environment that once was thought to be the very basis of attraction. Open space begins disappearing and smog becomes a frequent occurrence. While many residents, particularly in areas least visited by tourists, have eagerly adopted developments that brought jobs for them and their children and a boost to their business, they have also started complaining about the more frequent incidences of smaze that obscure what used to be the West's limitless vistas. The effects on wildlife are also dramatic. Expanding urbanization, masses of tourists, new transportation networks, and industrial noise decimate the wildlife populations.

Under such circumstances the ramifications on both the social structure and the cultural life of all surrounding communities are severe and long lasting. The alteration in land use, extreme commercialization, rapid industrialization and urbanization promote not only removal of crop production areas but also encourage land speculation that results in soaring prices and lands passing into corporate hands. As tourism increases traffic jams also result from increased commuting over a more complex network of roads. A highly mobile, heterogenous young population brings about inevitable cleavages with old-timers, thus increasing bitterness on local issues and in the long run contributing to a significant loss of the earlier tranquil way of life. Despite the economic growth, there is a pervasive mood of pessimism and a prevailing sentiment against exploitative developments that for many people create a disparity and a drifting away from a natural environment and from the "western way" of life. Some even say that the West has been rewon by a new invasion of people who stand apart from the cherished values of a quiet, shared, more leisurely community lifestyle.

"Boom towns" make also their appearance. Helter-skelter developments dot the countryside. Housing becomes impossible to find, with a large portion of the population living in trailers. Despite the need for laborers, job turnover and absenteeism are high as a result of social problems in the community. Increased suicide attempts, higher divorce rates, crime and drunkenness become for many the obvious trademarks of the new communities.

Scenario of Limited Growth

Trends of limited growth continue more or less the same, even reaching the level of zero development. The emphasis is on comprehensive environmental planning requirements, strict enforcement of environmental guidelines, accentuation of quality of life dimensions, continuous environmental awareness and involvement, no industrial expansion and maintenance of the traditional atmosphere of remoteness in the area.

On both a national and regional scale, population growth has stabilized; there is no pressure from rapidly expanding or migrating populations. Energy demands have eased since the instituting of strong energy conservation measures. Technological breakthroughs and alternative means of energy provide welcome relief from continued energy demands. The "steady state" economy is widely discussed and governmental efforts support frugality and non-energy intensive lifestyles.

The backlash from large-scale interference with "nature" has become apparent all over the nation and growth is discouraged, especially in the West where the environment has been officially declared as "fragile." Agricultural production remains about constant with little interest in developing additional land because of low prices and high cost. At the same time, the industrial sector actually decreases due to lack of product demand and reduced local growth. Heavy industry is not only finding it unattractive to establish its presence in the West but is actively discouraged from locating in the rural hinterland through a variety of legal and social measures.

Continuous gas rationings and scarcity, as well as limited income, have curtailed individual travel. At the same time, technological breakthroughs have made conventional transportation obsolete, with new methods of mass transportation becoming quite prominent. An important change in the citizenry's attitude concerning the traditional "love affair" with private automobiles has taken place to dampen the demand for more highway networks. Indiscriminate private car use is legally prohibited.

Local resistance against "outsiders" is accentuated by the commitment to devote urban land to "green belts" and open spaces and to preserve the unpopulated areas through strict controls. There is an intentional reduction in access to wild and scenic rivers for fishing and solitary experience.

The new value system that encourages growth relative to carrying capacity is contributing towards a willingness of individuals to sacrifice amenities, to work towards a common goal, to emphasize quality of life, to reassess human needs, and to publicly debate the ultimate concern of human survival.

As a result of this debate, there is a transformation towards a highly planned society, including passage of stricter Federal environmental quality legislation and of constitutional amendments promoting comprehensive land use policies and controls. Areas previously unregulated adopt growth limitations in adjacent areas. The increased taxation of what were considered in the seventies as "free goods," coupled with heightened air and water quality standards, tends to preclude any notion of industrial development, including construction of new electric generating facilities. Initial environmental damages from the construction of a few highways and tourist facilities have been absorbed by the sparseness of the region, which still remains a major aesthetic magnet for a limited but continuous tourist influx. Hunting still remains a major activity, and by 1990 conservation measures have secured the return of an increasing number of species.

Despite the fact that the region maintains its pristine character, the economy is susceptible to wide oscillations. With declining services and facilities, local authorities can offer few inducements to retain their younger people. An air of pessimism prevails among many citizens who have come to believe that unless some major development takes place there is no hopeful future for the region. The major objective of maintaining environmental quality imposes costs on community economic and social life and intensifies the perennial dilemmas of combining growth with stability and integration with diversity.

V. Summary

It has been said that the value of a scenario rests not so much on the capability to predict the future but that it should be measured by the degree of influence it can have on decisions taken today. Scenario writing, then, is not only a potentially useful forecasting technique. It may also become a "self-fulfilling prophecy," a paradigm of reality, a version of the future to be avoided, or an end to aspire to. As constructs of the imagination, scenarios throw the real world into a new perspective and challenge our tacit assumptions. Thus, images of the future incorporated in scenarios can be viewed as means for negotiating present obstacles, either in achieving a better future or in averting potential catastrophies.

References

Abt, Clark C., R. N. Foster and R. H. Rea (1973) "A Scenario Generating Methodology," pp. 191-214 in James R. Bright and Milton E. F. Schoenman (eds.), A Guide to Practical Technological Forecasting. Englewood Cliffs, NJ: Prentice-Hall.

Arnstein, S. R. and A. N. Christakis (1975) Perspectives on Technology Assessment. Jerusalem, Israel: Science and Technology Publishers.

Ayres, Robert U. (1969) Technological Forecasting and Long-Range Planning. New York: McGraw-Hill.

Brown, Perry and Evan Vlachos (1974) "Probable Social Impacts from Planning Alternatives at the Glen Canyon National Recreation Area." Denver, CO: National Park Service, August (draft report).

Burke, Hubert D. and Evan Vlachos (1975) Regional Oil Shale Study: Environmental Inventory, Analysis and Impact Study. Boulder, CO: Thorne Ecological Institute.

Elgin, Duane S., David C. MacMichael and Peter Schwartz (1975) Alternative Futures for Environmental Policy Planning: 1975-2000. Washington, DC: Office of Presticide Programs, U.S. Environmental Protection Agency, October.

Federal Energy Administration (1974) Project Independence Report. Washington, DC: U. S. Government Printing Office, November.

Gerardin, Lucien (1973) "Study of Alternative Futures: A Scenario Writing Method," pp. 276-88 in James R. Bright and Milton E. F. Schoeman (eds.), A Guide to Practical Technological Forecasting. Englewood Cliffs, NJ: Prentice-Hall.

Hoos, Ida R. (1974) "Criteria for 'Good' Futures Research," Technological Forecasting and Social Change, 6, 2, 113-32.

Kahn, Herman and A. J. Wiener (1967) The Year 2000: A Framework for Speculation on the Next Thirty-Three Years. New York: Macmillan.

Lanford, H. W. (1972) Technological Forecasting Methodologies: A Synthesis. New York: American Management Association.

Omaha District (1975) Water and Related Land Resources Management Study: Vol. III. Plan Formulation Appendix. Annex A - Alternative Futures. Omaha, NB: Omaha District, Corp of Engineers, June.

Sage, Daniel D. and Richard B. Chobot (1975) "The Scenario as an Approach to Studying the Future," pp. 161-78 in Stephen B. Hencley and James R. Yates (eds.), Futurism in Education: Methodologies. Berkeley, CA: McCutchin.

Vlachos, Evan (1974) "Scenario Writing for Natural Resources Research: Applications of Futurism." Paper presented at the Annual Meeting of the Rural Sociological Society, Montreal, P.Q., August.

Zentner, Rene D. (1975) "Scenarios in Forecasting," Chemical and Engineering News, 53, 40 (6 October), 22-34.

Community Structure, Resources, and the Capacity to Respond to Environmental Problems: New Concepts for Social Impact Assessment*

Donald R. DeLuca
Yale University

It is readily apparent that significant differences exist among communities with regard to their abilities to initiate environmental protection programs and put them into effect. Given equal levels of water quality problems and holding state and federal policies constant, some communities will successfully apply for and institute a sewage disposal facility, for example, while others are unable to adequately define their problem or mobilize their resources to undertake corrective action. Likewise, some communities are able to adequately control "sprawl-type" growth and development, whereas others fail to respond to such land misuse even though it is within their jurisdiction to do so. This research is concerned with why such differences exist. Specifically, it will identify some aspects of community social, demographic, economic, and political structures which have important effects on the level of community response to environmental problems of water pollution and land use.

The Basic Exploratory Model
Figure 1 displays the basic exploratory model--the concepts and their hypothesized causal relationships. Some of the propositions are derived from a careful review of the literature while others are heuristic in character. From this exploration it is hoped that a more coherent picture of the community as a social system of interacting elements will emerge. The ultimate goal is to develop a theory of public policy which articulates a community's capacity to respond to environmental problems. The proximate goal is to develop a causal model that will explain variation in environmentally related public policies.

Propositions I and II in Figure 1 are derived from the environmental problems literature. Myriad causes and cures of environmental degradation have been suggested, by Ehrlich (1971), Hardin (1969; 1970), Commoner (1971), England and Bluestone (1971), Salgo (1973), White (1967), Moncrief (1972), Meadows and others (1972) and Heilbroner (1974). The first two propositions discriminate two sets of community level social characteristics expected to predict higher levels of environmental deterioration:

---

* This paper reports on one aspect of a research project supported by a grant from the Rockefeller Foundation. Other members of the research team whose contributions are gratefully recognized and appreciated are Harold R. Capener, Joe D. Francis, Bruce Brower, Oscar Larson, and Kenneth Pigg. Special acknowledgment is given to Ralph Richardson and Gary Toenniessen of the Rockefeller Foundation and to C. David Loeks, Chadbourn Gilpatrick and Leonard Dworsky of the Hudson Basin Project for their support of this research.

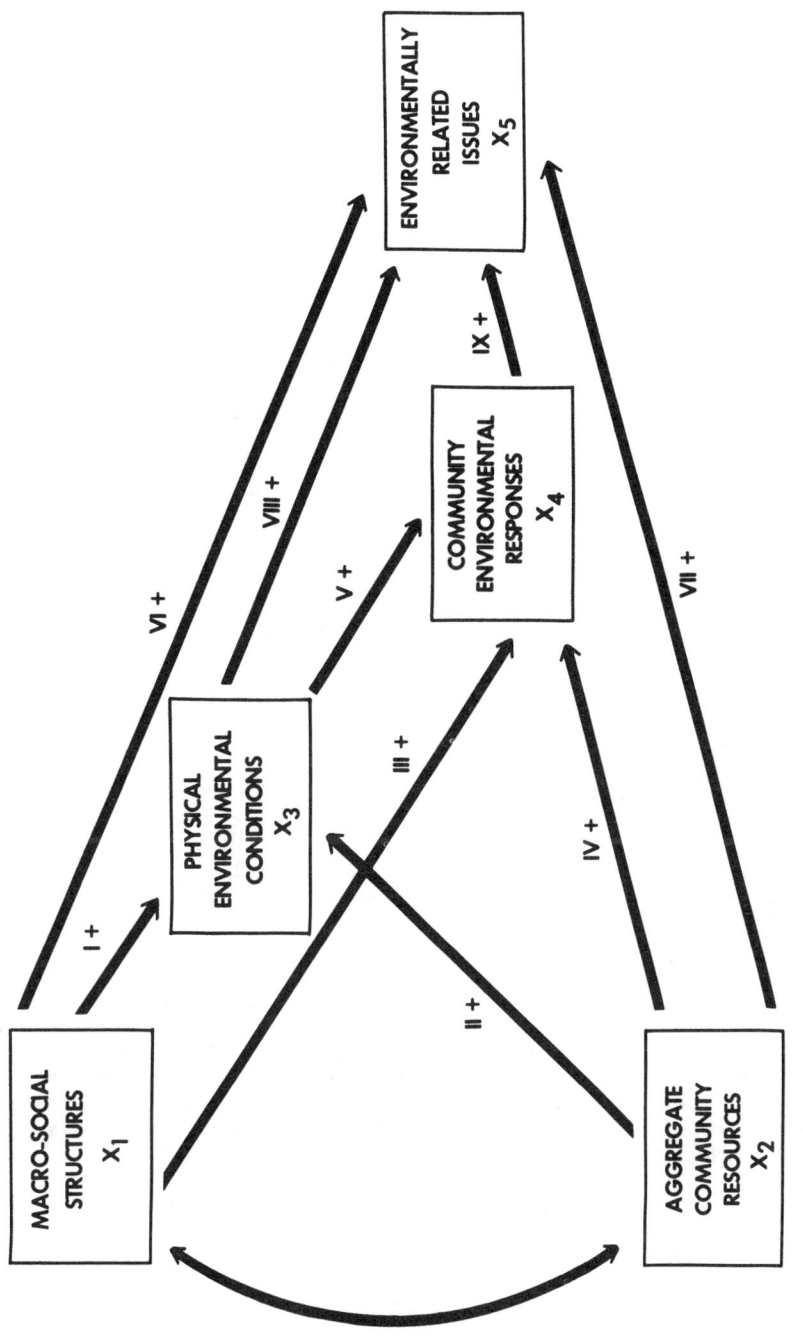

Figure 1. Schematic Representation of the Basic Exploratory Model

225

Proposition I: More complex forms of community social structure will be positively related to higher levels of environmental degradation.

Proposition II: Higher levels of aggregate community resources will be positively related to higher levels of environmental degradation.

The next three propositions follow in the growing tradition of community research literature which focuses upon the policy consequences of different configurations of social structure in local communities. Community structures are designated as independent variables explaining variations in community policies. A great deal of this literature is comparative in nature, using reasonably large samples of communities and multivariate analysis techniques. Community response, variously characterized as community decision-making, community innovation, community decision outcomes, and policy outputs, has been studied in a variety of issue areas: urban renewal (Aiken and Alford 1970; Duggar, 1961; Hawley 1963; Clark 1971), fluoridation (Crain, Katz and Rosenthal 1969), poverty (Aiken and Alford 1968), public housing (Aiken and Alford 1970a), and public welfare (Paulson, Butler and Pope 1969), to name a few. The present research predicts three conditions will be positively related to community response to environmental problems:

Proposition III: More complex forms of community social structure will be positively related to community environmental responses.

Proposition IV: Higher levels of aggregate community resources will be positively related to higher levels of community environmental responses.

Proposition V: Higher levels of environmental degradation will be positively related to community environmental responses.

Empirical research using community as the unit of analysis that lends support for these relationships includes: Clavel (1969), Kluess and Clavel (1969), Eberts (1972), and Turk (1971).

The final set of propositions deals with environmentally related social issues. Taking the lead from Crenson (1971), a distinction is made between environmental "problems" and environmentally related "issues." Whereas an environmental problem is defined as a physical environmental insult or stress situation, environmentally related social issues are defined as those matters related to the physical environment that have produced public discussion and/or debate. The intensity of environmentally related social issues is hypothesized to be predicted by the previously considered variables in the model:

Proposition VI: More complex forms of community social structure will be positively related to the intensity of environmentally related social issues.

Proposition VII: Higher levels of aggregate community resources will be positively related to the intensity of environmentally related social issues.

Proposition VIII: Higher levels of environmental degradation will be positively related to the intensity of environmentally related social issues.

Proposition IX: Higher levels of community response to environmental problems will be positively related to the intensity of environmentally related social issues.

Research Design

The theoretical argument developed above has been made explicit in the statement of hypotheses which can be subjected to a series of empirical tests. Specifically, it is possible to determine (1) the nature of the bivariate relationship among all of the subdimensions of the five concepts in the exploratory model, (2) the partial contribution that each independent variable makes towards explaining the variance in each of the dependent variables, (3) the direction and strength of the "causal paths" specified in the model, and (4) the direct and indirect effect of the independent variables on the dependent variables in the model. Operational indices of the independent and dependent variables have been constructed to perform these tests.

The research setting in which hypotheses testing was conducted is the upstate New York portion of the Hudson River region, an area containing nearly three million residents located in 279 Minor Civil Divisions. The units of analysis are a sample of 132 communities, consisting of 25 cities and 107 suburban and rural towns.

Much of the data used to construct indices for variables in the model were collected from secondary sources, although additional data were gathered in the field by a macrosurvey using key informants (see Francis and DeLuca 1975). Space does not allow a full treatment of the operationalization of variables; Table 1 summarizes the indicators used as measures of the concepts in the exploratory model. For details of the operational definitions see DeLuca (1976).

Preliminary Results

The empirical findings reported below are preliminary and exploratory. The analysis will focus on one aspect of the research design: the nature of the bivariate relationship among all of the indicators of the five concepts in the model. Much is left out, or left partially developed in the analysis which follows. Nevertheless, if various hypotheses suggested by the model are supported, this will provide some encouragement that the indicators are appropriate and that its further implications are worth continued exploration.

Hypotheses Testing

The hypotheses are tested by measuring the linear bivariate relationships between the indicators. The coefficients are Pearson's product-moment correlations. Statistical significance is evaluated by examining a one-tailed test derived from Student's t, with N-2 degrees of freedom. Table 2 displays the zero-order correlation matrix for all the indicators of the subdimensions of the five concepts in the model and the hypothesized relationships associated with each of the nine exploratory propositions. Where there are multiple indicators of a concept, the correla-

Table 1. Operational Measures of the Concepts in the Exploratory Model

Category	Abbreviation	Variable
Macro-Social Structures	DIFFER	Guttman scale of commercial differentiation
	ORGFLU	Organizational fluidity index (interest areas)
	POLCOM	Political party competition index
Aggregate Community Resources	MEDINC	Median family income
	MEDEDUC	Median education
	POP	Population size
	DENSITY	Population density
	PCHANGE	Population change
	PCREVENU	Per capita total revenues
Physical Environmental Conditions	LANDINT	Intensity of land-use index
	MULTIUSE	Multiplicity land-use (conflict) index
	WPOLUCOM	Quantity of water pollution all sources
	WPOLUIND	Quantity of water pollution industry
	WPOLUMUN	Quantity of water pollution municipality
	COMMWWQS	Community waste water quality scale
	INDWWQS	Industrial waste water quality scale
	MUNWWQS	Municipal waste water quality scale
Community Response	LANDRESP	Community response to land-use index
	ABATSTUS	Water pollution abatement status scale
	WATREXP	Expenditures for water/sewage
Local Social Issues	LANDISSU	Intensity of land-use issues index
	WATRISSU	Intensity of water issues index

Table 2. Zero-Order Correlation Coefficients Between Indicators of the Concepts in the Exploratory Model.

INDICATORS	DIFFER	ORGFLU	POLCOM	MEDINC	MEDEDUC	POP	DENSITY	PCHANGE	PCREVENU	LANDINT	MULTIUSE	WPOLUCOM	WPOLUIND	WPOLUMUN	COMMWQS	INDWQS	MUNWQS	LANDRESP	ABATSTUS	WATREXP	LANDISSU	WATRISSU
DIFFER	1.000																					
ORGFLU	.854	1.000																				
POLCOM	.538	.546	1.000																			
MEDINC	.318	.373	.273	1.000																		
MEDEDUC	.187	.226	.065	.673	1.000																	
POP	.805	.804	.575	.584	.348	1.000																
DENSITY	.780	.766	.567	.451	.159	.880	1.000															
PCHANGE	-.193	-.190	-.070	.372	.317	.062	-.152	1.000														
PCREVENU	.159	.133	.088	-.188	-.202	-.036	.018	-.361	1.000													
LANDINT	.677	.678	.480	.273	.031	.720	.876	-.322	.231	1.000												
MULTIUSE	.426	.420	.399	.258	.070	.506	.689	-.188	.061	.588	1.000											
WPOLUCOM	.660	.620	.443	.284	.134	.696	.649	-.123	-.009	.565	.318	1.000										
WPOLUIND	.365	.324	.210	.126	.034	.397	.412	-.178	.114	.398	.170	.671	1.000									
WPOLUMUN	.653	.610	.465	.314	.202	.687	.587	-.054	-.028	.516	.259	.916	.436	1.000								
COMMWQS	.529	.504	.402	.305	.187	.579	.522	-.030	-.152	.373	.289	.911	.513	.835	1.000							
INDWQS	.328	.311	.188	.169	.057	.366	.379	-.133	-.096	.324	.186	.637	.945	.403	.544	1.000						
MUNWQS	.519	.494	.418	.317	.239	.575	.479	-.015	-.162	.363	.224	.858	.379	.928	.914	.370	1.000					
LANDRESP	.533	.526	.346	.505	.424	.637	.508	.253	-.222	.315	.265	.458	.254	.449	.430	.265	.419	1.000				
ABATSTUS	-.282	-.327	-.207	-.163	-.092	-.350	-.338	-.004	-.124	-.205	-.153	-.506	-.290	-.447	-.538	-.285	-.515	-.281	1.000			
WATREXP	.673	.719	.439	.376	.170	.749	.721	-.164	.267	.676	.485	.599	.358	.554	.506	.354	.457	.431	-.315	1.000		
LANDISSU	.026	.009	.069	.154	.103	-.028	-.076	.198	.073	-.105	-.070	.005	.094	-.042	.014	.085	-.031	.027	-.053	.027	1.000	
WATRISSU	.065	.081	.044	.145	.239	.159	.071	.221	-.118	-.015	.021	.132	.094	.099	.184	.122	.154	.122	-.172	.097	.098	1.000

N = 132
Significance at p ≤ 0.01 where r > 0.214.

tions are substantial (but not sufficiently high to be considered redundant) with some noticeable exceptions.

Proposition I predicted a positive relationship between complex forms of social structure and environmental degradation. The correlations exhibited in Table 2 suggest strong support for the hypotheses derived from this proposition. Commercial differentiation (DIFFER) and organizational fludity (ORGFLU) have particularly high correlations with the intensity of land use (LANDINT) and the total community contribution to water pollution (WPOLUCOM and COMMWWQS). Political party competition (POLCOM) is positively correlated with the indicators of physical environmental conditions at moderate levels, except for the measures of community contribution to water pollution from industrial sources (WPOLUIND and INDWWQS) which are barely significant ($p < 0.05$).

Proposition II, derived from the environmental problems literature, postulated a positive relationship between aggregate community resources and environmental degradation. The correlations for the hypotheses of this proposition show mixed results. In contrast to Howard's (1969) theory, community socioeconomic levels (MEDINC and MEDEDUC) indexing the affluence factor are not highly related to environmental degradation. Although median income (MEDINC) shows significant correlations with land-use intensity (LANDINT), land-use multiplicity (i.e., conflict) (MULTIUSE), and community contribution to water pollution, these are not very substantial. Median education (MEDEDUC) is not significantly related to environmental decay in communities. The two population resource indicators, population size (POP), and persons per square mile (DENSITY), are very highly correlated with the environmental degradation variables. The negative correlation with population change 1960 to 1970 (PCHANGE) is a surprise that demands further study. The measure of economic resources (PCREVENU) was not significantly related to the indicators of physical environmental conditions except for land intensity, which exhibited a low correlation in the predicted direction.

Proposition III postulates that there will be a positive relationship between the complexity of community structure and community response to environmental problems. The correlations suggest strong support for the hypotheses related to this proposition, except for the negative correlation with abatement status (ABATSTUS). This measure has been determined to be an invalid indicator of the concept (see DeLuca 1976). This confirms findings reported in other community studies in different problem areas (Aiken and Alford 1970; 1970a), but disputes studies that found a concentration of power positively related to community outputs (Hawley 1963; Crain, Katz and Rosenthal 1969).

Proposition IV predicted a positive relationship between aggregate community resources and community environmental response. The moderately high positive correlations between these aggregate resources and community response to land use (LANDRESP) and total expenditures for water/sewage adds further evidence to the findings reported by Crain and Rosenthal (1967), Clark (1968 and 1971), Foley (1974) and Smith (1973). Again, the inverse relationship of the aggregate resources indicators with abatement status suggests that the revisionist interpretation of that indicator is correct; that is, abatement status is not a valid indicator of community response to water pollution. The negative correlation between per capita total revenues (PCREVENU) and community response to land use (LANDRESP) was not expected and will need to be examined more thoroughly.

Proposition V stated an expected positive relationship between levels of environmental degradation and community response. All of the correlations related to this proposition are significant, although not particularly impressive. Once again abatement status (ABATSTUS) is reversed. The relationship between environmental conditions and community response discovered here will be used in later analysis as a control on the relationship between macrosocial structures and aggregate community resources with community response.

Propositions VI, VII, VIII, and IX postulated a positive relationship between various independent variables and the intensity of environmentally related social issues (LANDISSU and WATRISSU). The correlations exhibited in Table 2 suggest a disappointing rejection of the hypotheses associated with these propositions. The potential explanations given above concerning the measurement problem with the issue variables (LANDISSU and WATRISSU) seem reasonable; however, much further systematic analysis will be required concerning these hypotheses. At the moment, no support can be given to the expected pattern that was originally adapted from the work of Crenson (1971).

Analysis Summary

A total of 142 bivariate relationships were examined, representing the subcomponent hypotheses of nine exploratory propositions. The following summarizes this analysis:

```
I. Total Hypotheses Tested . . . . . . . . . . 142
   A. Hypotheses Supported . . . . . . . . . . . .  82
      1. Significance p < 0.01 . . . . . . . . . . . .  71
      2. Significance p < 0.05 . . . . . . . . . . . .  11
   B. Hypotheses Rejected . . . . . . . . . . . .  60
      1. Resulting from ABATSTUS not
         being a valid measure . . . . . . . . . . . .  16
      2. Resulting from hypotheses in-
         volving the intensity of social
         issues (LANDISSU and WATRISSU). . . . . . . .  22
      3. Other rejected . . . . . . . . . . . . . . . .  22
         a. Resulting from hypotheses
            involving PCHANGE or PCREVENU . . . . . . .  16
         b. Random . . . . . . . . . . . . . . . . . . .  6
```

Although several methodological and theoretical disappointments were encountered, this preliminary investigation warrents more sophisticated multivariate analysis.

Discussion

The purpose of this paper is to provide a very brief summary outline of both the theoretical orientation and some preliminary results of a basic research project studying the relationship between community social systems and the physical environment. Hence the present research was not intended to be a site-specific or insult-specific social impact assessment of the Hudson River region. On the other hand, social impact assessment has been broadly defined as "an exercise in social prediction" (Wolf 1974: 85) and would benefit by including a framework for understanding (and predicting) the conditions under which policies impact communities. The two sets of conditions specified in the exploratory model--community structure and aggregate resources--provide the foundation from which communities gain a capacity to respond to their problems. By examining the conditions leading to, and the effects of, community response to <u>routine</u> environmental problems, insights may be gained that can be applied to more specific insults requiring social impact assessments. At any rate, these variables--community structure, aggregate resources, and community response--could be used in SIAs as independent variables in trying to predict the differential effect they have on how policies will impact communities.

The point is that a public program administered equally over all jurisdictions will not have equal results. The capacity of communities to respond to a state, federal, or even county program differ, so the results of the same program features and procedures used in each will vary greatly. A recent task force report on "Land Use/Natural Resource Management" (Friday 1974: 156) summarizes this point succinctly:

> Program features and procedures, particularly technical assistance and political resources, may have to be more closely tailored to the capacity of the target communities if satisfactory results are to be achieved. Public administration philosophies of equal treatment, of uniform application of the law, of due process, or equal protection, may need to be reexamined not only from the standpoint of varying physical resource settings. Varying community capacity also must be understood and dealt with.

Likewise, the capacity of communities to respond to specific environmental insults differs. The policy implications of determining factors causally related to higher levels of environmental deterioration seem obvious. If a social impact assessment can identify particular social, demographic, economic and political structures which can be empirically demonstrated to be related to environmental decay, then policies could be suggested to manipulate these structures into less impacting forms. In that way, the SIA would become a part of the planning process itself, gaining legitimation by providing input at all stages of policy development: initial policy formulation, agency and budget allocation, program development, project implementation, and evaluation.

References

Aiken, Michael and Robert Alford (1968) "Community Structure and Mobilization: The Case of the War on Poverty." Ann Arbor: Institute for Research on Poverty, University of Michigan.

Aiken, Michael and Robert Alford (1970) "Community Structure and Innovation: The Case of Urban Renewal," American Sociological Review 35 (August), 650-655.

Aiken, Michael and Robert Alford (1970a) "Community Structure and Innovation: The Case of Public Housing," American Political Science Review, 64, 3 (September), 843-864.

Clark, Terry N. (ed.) (1968) Community Structure and Decision Making. San Francisco: Chandler.

Clark, Terry N. (1971) "Community Structure, Decision-Making, Budget Expenditures, and Renewal in 51 American Communities," American Sociological Review 33, 4 (August), 576-593.

Clavel, Pierre (1969) "Correlates of Community Response: Findings from New York State Counties." Unpublished manuscript. Ithaca, NY: Department of Rural Sociology, Cornell University.

Commoner, Barry (1971) The Closing Circle. New York: Alfred A. Knopf.

Crain, Robert L. and Donald B. Rosenthal (1967) "Community Status as a Dimension of Local Decision-Making," American Sociological Review 32, 6 (December), 970-984.

Crain, Robert L., Elihu Katz and Donald B. Rosenthal (1969) The Politics of Community Conflict. Indianapolis, IN: Bobbs-Merrill.

Crenson, Matthew A. (1971) The Unpolitics of Air Pollution. Baltimore: John Hopkins Press.

DeLuca, Donald R. (1976) Community Response to Environmental Problems and Related Social Issues. Unpublished doctoral dissertation. Ithaca, NY: Cornell University.

Duggar, George (1961) "The Relationship of Local Government Structures to Urban Renewal," Law and Contemporary Problems, 26 (Winter), 49-69.

Eberts, Paul R. (1972) An Exposition of NE-47: Consequences of Changing Social Organization of the Northeast. Unpublished manuscript. Ithaca, NY: Cornell University, Department of Rural Sociology.

Ehrlich, Paul R. (1971) The Population Bomb. 2nd ed. New York: Ballantine.

England, Richard and Barry Bluestone (1971) "Ecology and Class Conflict," Review of Radical Political Economics 3, 31-55.

Foley, John William (1974) "The Structural Determinants of Public Policies: A MultiVariate Analysis of 300 American Communities." Unpublished doctoral dissertation. Ithaca, NY: Cornell University.

Francis, Joe D. and Donald R. DeLuca (1975) "The Reliability of Key Informants in Providing Information About Social Structure." Paper presented at the annual meeting of the Rural Sociological Society, San Francisco, CA, August.

Friday, Richard E. (ed.) (1974) Report of the Land Use/Natural Resource Management Task Group. Unpublished report to the Hudson Basin Project. New York: Rockefeller Foundation.

Hardin, Garrett (ed.) (1969) Population, Evolution and Birth Control. 2nd ed. San Francisco: W. H. Freeman.

Hardin, Garrett (1970) Birth Control. New York: Pegasus.

Hawley, Amos H. (1963) "Community Power and Urban Renewal Success," American Journal of Sociology, 68, 4 (January, 422-431).

Heilbroner, Robert (1974) An Inquiry into the Human Prospect. New York: W. W. Norton.

Howard, Walter E. (1969) "The Population Crisis is Here Now," Bioscience 19, 779-784.

Kluess, Pluma and Pierre Clavel (1969) "An Operational Index of System Response Capacity." Unpublished manuscript. Ithaca, NY: Department of Rural Sociology, Cornell University.

Meadows, Donella and others (1972) The Limits to Growth. New York: Potomac Associates.

Micklin, Michael (ed.) (1973) Population Environment, and Social Organization: Current Issues in Human Ecology. Hinsdale, IL: Dryden Press.

Moncrief, Lewis (1972) "The Cultural Basis of Our Environmental Crisis," pp. 284-294 in Robert Dorfman and Nancy Dorfman (eds.) Economics of the Environment. New York: W. W. Norton.

Paulson, Wayne, Edgar W. Butler and Hallowell Pope (1969) "Community Power and Public Welfare," American Journal of Economics and Sociology, 28, 1 (January), 17-27.

Salgo, Harvey (1973) "The Obsolescence of Growth: Capitalism and the Environmental Crisis," Review of Radical Political Economics, 5, 26-45.

Smith, Richard Allen (1973) "Community Structure and Innovation: A Study of the Effects of Social Structure on Program Adoption and Implementation." Unpublished doctoral dissertation. Ithaca, NY: Cornell University.

Turk, Herman (1971) "The Occurrence of New Inter-Organizational Events in Urban Communities: An Application of Nominal Theory and Specification to Social Systems Analysis." Paper presented at the annual meeting of the American Sociological Association, Denver, CO, August.

White, Lynn (1967) "The Historical Roots of Our Environmental Crisis," Science, 155 (10 March), 1203-7.

Wolf, C. P. (ed.) (1974) Social Impact Assessment. Milwaukee, WI: Environmental Design Research Association.

Correlational Tools for Predicting Community Acceptance of Nuclear Power Plant Sites

J. F. Byrne and E. W. Sucov
Westinghouse Research Laboratories

I. INTRODUCTION

This paper describes an application of Q Factor analysis and multiple regression analysis to the problem of evaluating candidate facility sites for their potential acceptance by the relevant nearby community. The stimulus for this research arises out of the difficulties faced by utilities when, after having completed their studies and their selection of a preferred site, community opposition for which the utilities were not prepared surfaced. The intent of this research, then is to assist utilities, or other agencies concerned with siting of facilities, in choosing locations that will be least likely to generate legal opposition. This approach is consistent with requirements of NEPA to evaluate the social impact of a proposed facility.

Citizen attitudes are not directly assessed in this study. Our strategy has been to examine the characteristics of communities where controversies over siting of nuclear power plants have taken place. Community descriptors are examined by correlational techniques to identify those that are highly related to the degree of difficulty encountered in the obtaining of permits. The degree of difficulty encountered by the utilities is used as an indirect measure of community attitude. Site selection outcome profiles and a regression equation based on the selected community characteristics are produced by this strategy for use in "predicting" outcomes of future site permit applications.

There are three stages in the site selection process:

1. Rough evaluation of possible sites and elimination of clearly undesirable ones.
2. Closer inspection of remaining candidates to eliminate all but about 2 or 3.
3. Detailed analysis of the finalists to select the one that best satisfies the broad range of objective and subjective criteria.

Prudent handling of resources requires that the amount of effort spent per site be very low in stage 1 and be quite high in stage 3. Thus, the geologists in stage 1 may refer to maps and public documents, in stage 2 may do field visits, and in stage 3 may require test borings. Similarly, the social scientist in stage 1 might

---

* This work was sponsored by the Westinghouse Environmental Systems Department and was presented to the EDRA 6 meeting by John E. Singley, Westinghouse Environmental Systems Department, P.O. Box 1899, Pittsburgh, PA 15230.

use census data, in stage 2 might study local newspapers, and in stage 3 might observe the social dynamics of the community at close hand. The tool to be described was developed under the constraint that it was to be used by planners early in the site selection process, that is, in stage 1. Thus, its data are easily available from public documents; the tool provides a way to read significance into those data. A computer program to complete the level 1 analysis is on file at the Westinghouse Research Laboratories.

The Controversial Sites

Eleven nuclear power plants were selected to cover a range of the following four outcomes of the permit application process: Outcome 1, No Trouble; Outcome 2, Negotiation; Outcome 3, Lawsuit; Outcome 4, Cancelled. Table 1 presents the names, locations and outcomes associated with each of the eleven plants.

TABLE 1. LISTING OF NUCLEAR POWER PLANTS AND OUTCOMES

Nuclear Power Plant	Outcome
1. Connecticut Yankee (Middlesex, Connecticut)	No Trouble (1)
2. Millstone (N. London, Connecticut)	No Trouble (1)
3. Zion-1 (Zion Lake Co., Illinois)	Negotiation (2)
4. Indian Point-2 (Westchester County, NY)	Negotiation (2)
5. Quad Cities (Rock Island Co., Illinois)	Negotiation (2)
6. Palisades (Van Buren Co., Michigan)	Negotiation (2)
7. Monticello (Wright Co., Minnesota)	Lawsuit (3)
8. Turkey Point (Dade Co., Florida)	Lawsuit (3)
9. Bell Station-Cayuga-1 (Tomkins Co., New York)	Permits Not Obtained. Project Cancelled (4)
10. Ravenwood (New York City, New York)	Cancelled (4)
11. Bodega Bay Atomic Park (Sonoma Co., California)	Cancelled (4)

II. THE COMMUNITY DESCRIPTORS

After pilot analysis of literature surrounding recent controversies, 23 variables were chosen to reflect those forces that seemed important in causing a community to react the way it did to the prospect of a nuclear plant. Sources for the data were: AEC Docket files, Preliminary and Final Safety Analysis Reports (PSAR and FSAR), environmental impact statements, trade journals such as Nuclear Industry and Nuclear News, national newspapers and new magazines, local newspapers, and

U. S. Census information. Table 2 presents the type and description of the 23 variables analyzed in this study.

TABLE 2. POTENTIAL PREDICTOR VARIABLES

A. Ecological-Economic Descriptors:

1. Amount of land to be condemned.

2. Number of people to be displaced.

3. Area of fish, game or wildlife habitat affected by the plant.

4. Size of the plant.

5. Population density.

6. Area of the plant site.

7. Land uses: recreation or agricultural.

8. Thermal pollution.

9. Danger to aquatic life.

10. Noise pollution.

11. Radioactive pollution.

B. Socio-Political Descriptors:

12. Number of citizen groups in the county.

13. Number of conservationist-environmentalist leaders residing in the county.

14. Distance of the site from a prominent academic institution.

15. Magnitude of population influx in the county.

16. Proportions of families in the county below the poverty level, unemployed, and earning over $15,000.

17. Proportion of professionals in the affected population.

18. Proportion of married women in working force.

19. Educational level in the county.

20. Number of landowners of site area.

21. Distance of proposed site from population centers (of size 5,000; 50,000; 500,000).

22. Percent urban in county.

23. Percent of workers in manufacturing in county.

III. THE METHODOLOGY

Four steps were taken in order to identify those variables that were most strongly correlated to the various outcomes. The first step utilized Q Factor analysis and discriminant analysis to eliminate variables that tended to have similar values for different outcomes and to keep variables whose values correlated well with the four different outcomes. The second step involved constructing a profile for each outcome by averaging scores for each kept variable for sites within each outcome category. The third step constructed a regression equation out of the subset of variables selected in step 1 and calculated the coefficients that would permit prediction of outcome 1, 2 and 3. That is, the regression equation should generate a number (predict an outcome) from one to three when values for the variables from the candidate sites are substituted into the equation. The fourth step was to add a weighted predicted Y from step 3 to the profile variable list. In effect, this weights the influence of the most linearly related variables in the profile. Candidate sites can then be evaluated by two estimation procedures, correlation of their profile with outcome profiles and substituting their profile values into a regression equation to "predict" outcome 1, 2 or 3. In the event that the regression prediction and the best profile match do not agree, the authors recommend averaging the two predictions.

Variables Selected in Step 1
The variables selected in step 1 are presented in Table 3.

TABLE 3. SELECTED DESCRIPTOR VARIABLES

	Descriptor Category	Descriptor Name
1.	Ecological-economic	Recreational land use
2.	Ecological-economic	Agricultural land use
3.	Ecological-economic	Degree of thermal pollution
4.	Socio-political	Number of citizen groups in the county
5.	Socio-political	Number of conservationist environmentalist leaders living in the county
6.	Socio-political	Proportion of families in county below poverty level

7. Socio-political   Proportion of families earning
                              over $15,000

8. Socio-political   Proportion of professionals in
                              the affected area

Table 4 presents the average values of each site descriptor for sites within outcome types. Values down the columns represent outcome profiles, i.e., the average values for sites having that outcome.

TABLE 4. PROFILE VALUES FOR EACH OF THE 4 TYPES OF OUTCOMES

Descriptor	Type of Outcome			
	1	2	3	4
1. Recreational land use (1=yes, 0=no)	0.5	0.8	1.0	0.3
2. Agricultural land use (1=yes, 0=no)	1.0	0.8	1.0	0.3
3. Degree of thermal pollution	1.5	2.3	2.5	2.3
4. Number of citizen groups in county	2.5	4.8	6.5	6.0
5. Number of conservationist environmental leaders in county	1.0	2.5	5.0	3.0
6. Proportion of families in poverty	6.8	7.2	10.9	8.4
7. Proportion of families earning over $15,000	23.3	29.9	17.4	20.1
8. Proportion of professionals living in the area	22.6	15.4	11.4	20.0
9. Dummy variable in profile	1.0	10.0	15.0	20.0

Descriptors 1, 3, 4, 5, 6 and 8 appear to be linearly correlated to outcomes 1, 2 and 3, but not to outcome 4; they are underlined in Table 4.

The Factor Loading Matrix That Supports the Selected Variables

Another way of examining the predictive power of the variables presented in Table 3 is to determine whether Q Factor analysis of these variables will match the original site data to the known outcomes. This can be judged by reviewing the Q Factor analysis intercorrelation matrix of site profiles. Knowledge of the site outcome was included in the site profile data to "anchor" the matrix. An eigenvalue of 1.00 was used to limit the number of factors and varimax rotation was used to produce the final factor loading matrix. Similar site controversy outcomes and their correlational factor loadings are presented in Table 5. The correlational loadings which appear to have identified a factor (outcome type) are bracketed. It can be seen that factor I identified site outcome 1; factor II identified site outcomes 2 and 3; and factor III identified site outcome 4.

TABLE 5. FACTOR STRUCTURE OF SITE PROFILES BASED ON SELECTED DESCRIPTOR VARIABLES

Site	\multicolumn{3}{c}{Factors and Loadings}		Outcome
	I	II	III	
Connecticut Yankee	.87	.27	.13	1
Millstone	.90	-.01	.02	1
Zion-1	.27	.85	.00	2
Indian Point	.10	.61	-.49	2
Quad Cities	-.02	.24	.68	2
Palisades	.00	-.90	.07	2
Monticello	-.49	-.57	.06	3
Turkey Point	.28	-.73	.13	3
Cayuga Lake	-.32	.31	-.66	4
Ravenwood	-.58	.16	-.68	4
Bodega Bay	-.73	.05	-.28	4

One exception that is evident in this analysis is that the site named Palisades appeared more like the sites in the outcome 3 group than like the members of its own group. Although the factor structure reported in Table 5 does not perfectly separate the different types of site outcomes, basic differences are suggested. This appears to be the best correlational summary of the history in the data that is possible.

The Multiple Regression Equation

After evaluating possible descriptor combinations one regression model was found to be the best predictive combination of descriptors 1, 3, 4, 5, 6 and 8. This model uses descriptors 3, 4 and 6 to predict site outcomes 1, 2 and 3 and is expressed by the equation:

$$Y = a_0 U + a_1 X_2 + a_2 X_2 + a_3 X_3 + E$$

Where Y = site outcomes 1, 2 and 3

U = regression unit vector

X_1 = degree of thermal pollution

X_2 = number of citizen groups in the county

X_3 = proportion of families in poverty in county

E = error associated with predictive equation

and where a_0, a_1, a_2, a_3 are partial regression coefficients.

The dependent variable in the multiple regression equation leaves out site outcome 4. Ordinarily it is best to have a lower R^2, but use the complete ordinal outcome variable. In this application it seemed appropriate to omit outcome 4 from the dependent variable because the regression model does not represent all the relevant variables which must be reviewed in stage 3 of the site selection process to judge if outcome 4 will occur. It seemed best to leave outcome 4 to stage 3 of the selection process and the profile correlation and obtain the highest R^2 for the model over outcomes 1, 2 and 3. The regression model, therefore, predicts outcomes 1, 2 or 3 with the reservation that other factors may be operating to change this prediction into a 4 (cancelled).

The obtained values for the partial regression coefficients in the additive model are:

a_0 = -.99341

a_1 = .73887

a_2 = .16728

a_3 = .09636

These coefficients accounted for 90% of the variation in the dependent variable. The model was significant at the .007 level.

Comparison of Profile and Regression Methods
The profiles developed in Table 4 plus the dummy variable were correlated with profiles for each of the eleven sites which included their expected Y value. Results are shown in Table 6. As would be expected, the degree of correlation between site profiles and outcome profiles was quite high; correlation coefficients ran for the most part between .80 and 1.00. The expected Y value was weighted by 5 to minimize the product moment correlation between outcome profiles.

One discrepancy is apparent, however; Indian Point's profile is clearly more similar to outcome 1 than to its actual outcome 2, but the regression model's prediction is closest to the actual outcome. Values for the site outcome, Y, in the regression equation were calculated for each of the eleven sites with the results shown in the second column. The match between the calculated outcomes and actual outcomes 1, 2 and 3 is quite good; the match to outcome 4 is unclear. This observation further

Table 6. Site Selection Analysis

Site Name	Regression Analysis Expected Value of Y	Profile Analysis: Correlation of Site Profile with Outcome Profile Number			
		1	2	3	4
Outcome 1	1.19	1.00*	.12	.02	.00
Connecticut Yankee	1.12	.98*	.09	.03	.00
Millstone	1.26	.96*	.16	.01	.01
Outcome 2	2.19	.12	1.00*	.75	.86
Quad Cities	2.17	.07	.98*	.83	.93
Indian Point	1.59	.79	.30	.00	.04
Zion-1	2.06	.33	.89*	.43	.57
Palisades	1.83	.23	.82*	.49	.62
Outcome 3	2.99	.02	.75	1.00*	.97
Monticello	3.20	.03	.72	1.00*	.96
Turkey Point	2.78	.01	.80	1.00*	.98
Outcome 4	2.52	.00	.86	.97	1.00
Ravenwood	2.47	.01	.92	.93	.98
Bodega Bay	2.56	.01	.75	.99	.98
Cayuga Lake	2.60	.00	.86	.96	1.00

*Indicates agreement between the regression model's predicted outcome and the best profile match. For the first three outcomes, there are 10 cases of agreement between the two estimating procedures.

---

underlines the authors' assumption that outcome 4 is a matter for broad consideration at stage 3 of the selection process. Taken at face value, however, it would appear that when predictions for a site are low for outcome 1, but high for outcome 2, 3 and 4, outcome 4 is most likely to occur. In the context of this exercise, outcome 4 is a disjunctive concept.

In the event that the Y outcome value predicted by the regression model does not agree with the best profile match, the authors recommend that the discrepant predictions be averaged together, unless the outcome 4 pattern is present, and the average of the two predictions be used as the stage 1 prediction. In the event of a tie, assume that the less optimistic outcome is most likely. This seems consistent with the underlying purpose of providing a means of simplifying complexities by surfacing and summarizing the strongest correlations between community characteristics and site application outcomes.

IV. PREDICTIVE POWER OF THE TOOLS

Data were collected for six nuclear sites that were pending at the time this analysis was conducted. A test of the predictive tools was made by obtaining an expected Y outcome prediction for each pending site and correlating the pending site profile plus the weighted expected Y outcome value with each outcome profile. Table 7 presents the results of each test and compares their predictions for each site.

Discussion

The profile descriptors enable the user to identify the closest match between a potential site and a past site outcome while the additive regression model estimates the outcome of a potential site if only the most linear variables are considered. The agreement between profile and regression predictions for these seven cases is not as high as in the historical analysis. Increasing the data base and replicating the methodology is clearly desirable. At present we must take the average of the two predictions for each pending site and wait for the facts to verify or disprove our predictions.

TABLE 7. PREDICTIONS OF SITE OUTCOME BASED ON REGRESSION COEFFICIENTS TIMES SITE DESCRIPTOR VALUES AND ON CORRELATION BETWEEN PROFILES

Pending Site	Outcome Predictions			
	1	2	3	4
Trojan				
Profile correlation	.90	.89	.96*	.93
Regression model	.4*			
Summary prediction		(*)		
Calvert Cliffs				
Profile correlation	.77	.82	.93*	.83
Regression model		2.2*		
Summary prediction			(*)	
Brown's Ferry				
Profile correlation	.55	.46	.69*	.59
Regression model	.9*			
Summary prediction		(*)		
Midland-1				
Profile correlation	.97*	.93	.86	.97*
Regression model				3.7*
Summary prediction			(*)	
J. M. Farley				
Profile correlation	.57	.54	.79*	.63
Regression model		1.5*		
Summary prediction			(*)	
Shoreham Station-1				
Profile correlation	.94	.99*	.88	.92
Regression model	1.3*			
Summary prediction		(*)		

* Marks the most probable outcome for each estimation procedure. The summary prediction (*) represents the average of the profile and regression predictions.

Gaming and Simulation in the Service of Social Impact Assessment: An Exploration

Joseph D. Ben-Dak
School for International Training

I. Introduction

The potential of the future is a consequence of the public policy of today, hence the necessity of developing techniques that adequately analyze the consequence of public policy. Social impact assessment utilizes the kinds of methodologies which can project the future while taking into consideration the parameters of the present. This paper focuses on one class of these methodologies, gaming, simulation and simulation gaming. It concludes that simulation gaming holds the greater promise for social impact assessment.

Simulation gaming can be explained by defining each of its components:

1. Gaming is the structuring of interactions between role players;

2. Simulation is information manipulation--particularly in the form of computer operations--on models or sets of models that extract meaningful relations from the real world;

3. Simulation gaming is the merger of gaming with information manipulation in such a way as to be applied to research and/or training (see Ray and Duke 1968: 145).

We will not discuss here the general arguments for and against simulation and gaming (see Inbar and Stoll 1927; Coplin 1968). A brief review of the principal uses of each method for social impact research will be presented, however.

Gaming and simulation belong to a family of social science modeling which does not truly differ from the methodologies utilized in the other sciences, since results are reproducible. Their usefulness for social impact studies lies in their effectively dealing with social impact components. Specifically, these methodologies can be used to (1) sharpen and refine key decisions, (2) reveal the full array of consequences of decisions and non-decisions (i.e., lack of action), (3) assess the probability of consequences, and (4) define future conditions which are likely to necessitate new decisions. Other components of social impact such as cost-benefit considerations can also be subjected to these methodologies; thus the social aspects as well as the physical aspects of planned change (or expected change) can be studied. Taking all aspects together allows the proper attention to be given to the sequence of <u>all significant</u> decisions and consequences involved in a <u>realistic</u> decision tree.

Furthermore, the actual mechanics of doing research by simulation or gaming have inherent advantages for social impact assessment. In simulation or gaming, the computer or the social group of players free the assessment from the researcher's frame of reference. Although a basic original input is supplied by the researcher, no further intervention is necessary since the process unfolds unaided. In gaming, for example, roles, interrelationship of roles, and scenarios are first defined. Then the researcher, or "gamer," must address the question of rules and prohibitions. After that, everything which is not explicitly ruled out may unfold. In simulation the emphasis is less on <u>relations</u> and their processes than on models of encompassing information. Here again, all meaningful possible impacts must be discerned by the researcher. The natural relationship between human beings guarantees in gaming the process of <u>socially grounded</u> impact assessment; in simulation it is the consistent tidiness of the computer that will guarantee the processing of all of the available data. Contrast survey research where the researcher is burdened to the point of inertia by information in the form of discrete data bits and/or his expectations regarding the results. Other researchers working with him will tend to be influenced by him, will be less <u>efficient</u> than the computer, and will be less <u>involved</u> than an active participant in a game. Prior traditional research may be used in conjunction with these methodologies, as long as it only provides inputs into the conceptualization of impacts and does not a priori determine the possible outcomes of the research.

Social impact assessment, very much part of the new social sciences, emerges from an epoch where the quest for systematic and microscopic insight into bits of data provided the optimal approach to knowledge. Two particular biases have limited that approach. One of these is expressed as: "We cannot know the outcome of a given process if such a process has never unfolded in the past." The other lies in the methodology which focuses on the accumulation of knowledge about individual impact components. Social impact assessment must choose methods which promise better comprehension of totally new and undefined impacts, and which (while increasing awareness of the details of any given impact) must consider the array of all possible impacts.

> Rather than the identification of the whole being achieved through the firm establishment of particles, the reverse is the case; the complex being more certainly known than the elements, and neither of course being known incorrigibly. (Campbell 1966)

II. Current Practices in Gaming and Simulation

Most available approaches fall into the category of simulation <u>or</u> gaming; few efforts have attempted to maximize the benefits of both. Table 1 summarizes examples drawn from current gaming efforts; Table 2 those from current simulation. Much simulation work exists in engineering-related fields such as air pollution, transportation, in some branches of energy policy, and particularly in water resources and solid waste management (for example, Anderson and Maass 1971; Asken, Yem and Hull 1971; Helferich, Hoffner and Gee 1972). Gaming approaches have been even more broadly applied to group decision making of many types (Ben-Dak 1969a, 1972; Boocock and Coleman 1966; Boocock and Schild 1968; Gamson 1966; Inbar 1966; Kelman 1972; Raser 1969; Smoker 1971; Waskow 1969), and for training to perform in impacted environments (Abt 1964; Anundsen and Londgren 1972; Ben-Dak 1970; Coplin 1968; Duke and Meier 1966; Environmental Protection Agency 1972a and 1974; Environmetrics 1971a; Feldt 1972; Ray and Duke 1968; and Wahi and Peterson 1972). In the few cases where simulation has been combined with a gaming procedure, training was again a general objective (Boston College 1961; Environmental Pro-

TABLE 1: SOCIAL IMPACT IN CURRENT GAMING

REAL WORLD SITUATION	PROCESS INVOLVING GAMING (example)	SOCIAL IMPACT DETERMINED (example)	SOURCE
Internation Relations	Warring Coalitions	War Decisions Made	Abt (1964)
Arab-Israeli Relations	Superpower Manipulation	Reconciliation Scenarios Identified	Ben-Dak (1970, 1972)
Personal Strategies Learning	Social (Primary) Relations	Better Learning Explored	Boocock and Coleman (1966) Boocock and Schild (1968)
City and National Politics	Leadership, Compliance, etc.	Change in Power Occurred	Coplin (1968)
Dyadic Behavior	Group Representation	Bargaining Behavior Predicted	Druckman (1966)
Satisfaction/Consumption Standards	Economic Explanation	Economic Theories Evaluated	Elder and Pendley (1966)
Community (City) Process	Land Use	Ownership and Pressures Manifested	Feldt (1972)
Physical Conflict	Retaliation	Punishment and Abstention Predicted	Friedell (1968)
Interest Groups Societal	Conflicting Coalitions	Societal Welfare Interpreted	Gamson (1966)
Community Leadership	Natural Disasters	Training in Coping and Coordination	Inbar (1966)
Waste Management	Sanitary Conditions	Effective Decisions Realized	Wahl and Peterson (1972)
Community Learning	Running Simulation Exercises	Broadcasting Affected	Gray (1969)

TABLE 2. SOCIAL IMPACT IN CURRENT SIMULATION

REAL WORLD SITUATION	SIMULATED PROCESS	SOCIAL IMPACT DETERMINED	SOURCE
Market Conditions	Competing Responses	Market Responses Linked	Amstutz (1967)
Irrigation Planning	Water Supply and Agricultural Production	Farm Income Affected	Anderson and Maass (1971)
Drought Variation	Comparative Critical Drought	Community Needs Identified	Asken, Yem and Hull (1971)
City Trends	Urban Crises	Multi-Faceted Trends Identified	Forrester (1969)
City Services	Ambulance Services	Emergency Needs Answered	Gordon and Zelin (1968)
Peasant Community	Information Diffusion	Information Availability Differentiated	Hanneman (1969); Hanneman and Carroll (1969)
Urban Waste	City Waste Parameters	Solid Waste Managed	Helferich, Hoffner and Gee (1972)
International Process	International Interaction	Multi-Faceted Trends Identified	Smoker (1968)
Global Trends	Ultimate Growth	Limits Diagnosed	Meadows and others (1972)

TABLE 3: POTENTIAL GAIN FROM SIMULATION/GAMING FOR SOCIAL IMPACT DECISIONS

POSSIBLE (NEGATIVE) SOCIAL IMPACT	DECISION EXPECTED MODIFIABLE SOCIAL IMPACT	TYPICAL MODEL-BUILDING METHODOLOGY	SIMULATION OUTPUT	GAMING OUTPUT
Delay in Service, Queuing	Service Capacity/Priorities/Rules	Queuing, Sequencing	Alternative Timetables	Alternative Services, Priorities
Amortization, Overuse of Facilities	Timing of Maintenance/Repair	Optimization	Different Use Patterns	Different Facilities
Overuse, Underuse of Resources	Timing of Production/Extraction/Refurbishing	Replacement	Prolonging Strategies	New Resources
Lack of Storage of Items for Future Use	Extent of Storage/Orders/Renewal	Inventory	Reconstituted Storage	Alternative Storage (Location)
Lack of Allocation of Resources to Activities	Demand/Supply/Priorities	Mathematical Programming	New Allocation Rules	Alternative Activities/Resources
Non-Functioning Marketplace Distribution	Price Constraints/Market Regulations/Subsidy	Input-Output	Redistribution	Other Markets' Impact
Lack of Information to Foster Decision	Investment in Information Acquisitions	Decision Trees	Differentiated Amounts/Efforts	New Linkages/Sources
Competition and/or (Rancorous) Conflict	Conflict Management/Resolution Strategy	Game Theory	Preference Rules	Differentiated Consequences

tection Agency 1972a; Office of Planning and Evaluation, 1975; Shure and Meeker, 1970; Smoker, 1968).

Training aside, however, the benefit for policy making that can be derived in combining simulation and gaming goes to the very nature of developing realistic and significant policy alternatives. For example, gaming in areas such as city and national politics, dyadic behavior, city land use, and physical conflict and retailiation can contribute directly to aspects of simulated city trends, city services, information networking and city resources management. Table 3 demonstrates how simulation _and_ gaming can complement "normal" social impact assessment techniques in related contexts. Drawing on the types of decisions for which models have been developed (Environmental Protection Agency 1974), the Table illustrates what _additional_ gain can accrue to the policy planner.

III. The Particular Promise of Gaming

Games have been argued to be of value, given our research directive. They are said to be conducive to the conception of new wholes, be of future relevance, and, since they are a quasi-experimental method, are implemented in an adequately controlled environment (Waskow 1969: 97). Accordingly, the idea of discovery of new wholes of the future is very attractive. Snyder (in Guetzkow 1963) and Smoker (1968) are among many who have applied this idea to improving a given social reality (see Sawyer and Guetzkow 1965: 513). As Smoker (1968: 17) observes,

> All the validity studies so far surveyed take the correspondence between simulation and "reality" as a measure of validity of the simulation. The "real world" is regarded as an attempt to demonstrate or show or reveal what the real world is like. If there is a lack of correspondence, then the model world is altered until correspondence with the real world is achieved. It is possible to take the complementary position and to evaluate the validity of the "real world" relative to the "model world" incorporated in a simulation. In such a case the model world is regarded as an attempt to demonstrate or show or reveal the way the real world could be or should be, and differences between the two worlds are rectified by changing the real world through social and political action towards the image of the model. Such an approach is not only relevant for social change towards desired futures, it incorporates a conception of social science somewhat different from the "realist" position of telling the way it is. It relates to the concept of action research.

Partial implementation of this approach has led to the pursuit of ideas pertinent to certain predictions of conditions of a peace system in place of a conflict system in interpersonal, intergroup or international relations. Brody's (1963) use of the Inter-Nation Simulation to test predictions regarding the spread of nuclear weapons to dependent actors in a cold war situation, with "results that have been substantially confirmed by later events in the real world" (see Flook 1970: 183) is an example. This has been designed primarily in international relations but reflects strongly what has been labelled here the desired research directive.

Put simply, in gaming social relations, scholars point out that the probability of creating new "wholes" is rather high. The recognition first of patterns and then recognition of what the sub-units of those patterns are make gaming an "enhancing" laboratory for knowing a plethora of possible futures. Campbell conceives of the participants in a gaming laboratory as confronting a collection of fragments, bits of discrete data, each of which is uninterpretable and then suddenly being able to see the entire pattern or context (Campbell, 1968). Several researchers have established that games especially serve well for teaching this kind of knowledge. Participants demonstrated solid graps of roles, images, strategies, empathy for the situation, and, what is especially crucial, a feeling of potency (see Boocock and Coleman 1966; Boocock and Schild 1968; Guetzknow and others 1963).

Using this ability to detect patterns for the purposes of research does not mean only getting participants to acquire knowledge of a pattern that a simulator previously has stipulated or transferred, however; it means, ideally, getting participants to identify "patterns" which a simulator wishes them to identify, yet which he himself could not have known beforehand either in "whole" form or through all the pattern's components. This is, of course, the particular promise of gaming for our purposes.

Gaming as a method applicable to social science forecasting has been highlighted by numerous scholars (for typical general treatments see Rapoport 1966; Raser 1969; Waskow 1969; Guetzkow 1968). Regardless of its clear potential for social impact assessment, gaming is still a field in its embryonic stage (for some exceptions see Ben-Dak 1969a; Gamson 1968; Feldt 1972; Inbar 1966; House and Patterson 1972; Ray and Duke 1968). Excellent introductory texts for the construction of games do exist. Of these, the following represent the best, in our opinion, for purposes of gaming in the context of social impact assessment: Anundsen and Londgren (1972); Boocock and Coleman (1966); Boocock and Schild (1968); Environmetrics (1971); Inbar and Stoll (1972); and Peston and Coddington (1967).

Given these perspectives, several steps appear necessary to create a game for purposes of analysis or training in social impact assessment:

1. Roles and actors must be determined. Any group or individual who can affect the outcome of a public policy through a decision or series of decisions can be represented in the game. The game is meant only to include part of all those who can influence the unfolding process in the given society. Hence an early conceptuzlization of prominent and would-be prominent decision-makers is called for. We define "actors" as groups or institutions that arrive at a collective decision. Each "actor" is composed of several "roles." The simulator must choose all significant actors in the "effecting" sector, i.e., the actors whose actions include the origination, formulation and implementation of the public policy. Equally important is the inclusion of actors significantly affected or affectable. Examples for "effecting" actors could be the Federal Railway Administration. Within the FRA, roles could be Administrator, Associate Administrator and Minority (Black Representative. The affected community could include actors such as White Midwest Community, Black Southern Community, Black Lobbying Groups interest in transportation and A Mixed Community. For each of these actors there can be three roles: (1) Leader of the Majority, (2) Leader of the Minority and (3) the Actors' In-House Expert on Transportation. The game can focus on the process of negotiating a Federal Railway Law and the impact of the negotiation on the legislative process and on communities. We could also get a close look at coalition formation in the context of transportation. The game can go even farther, to the designation and implementation of new

railroads or different uses of existing networks. Each of these potentials may necessitate adding more actors and roles, e.g., Congress, Department of Transportation, etc. To the extent that the simulator pleases these all can be provided as his input to the game. This formulation indicates immediately the basic richness of the gaming approach. We start with a basic definition of the pre-impact social situation, and by specifying who <u>will interact</u> we may be able to observe closely all relations that may be important in our SIA but that in real life may be inaccessible.

2. Each actor as well as each role must have a goal and an associated yardstick of success. A game to be a game is based usually on a certain mode of competitiveness. Each role taker must know what is to be achieved and how. Goals may or may not be compatible, given simulator's consideration of what is objective reality and what is to be learned. Actors' goals may be sums of goals associated with the constituent roles or may be independent. For example, the goal of FRA may be to provide adequate railroad services to all communities that need it. The yardstick of success may be the number of communities connected to the railway network, <u>or</u> the number of communities that have inadequate transportation facilities that get connected to the network, <u>or</u> the number of people served, <u>or</u> the number of disadvantaged members of communities <u>or</u> disadvantaged communities that get connected. The game rules must include a timetable denoting when measurements are to be taken, and by whom.

3. Each role, and sometimes each actor, must have access to resources and rules about their utilization. Types of resources and their quantities must be spelled out by the analyst so as to provide a completely coherent picture of what can be used by the role taker to achieve the goal and other objectives dictated by the game rhythm. For our purposes it would be important to assign to each role tangible resources. Tangible resources include access to equipment, money, materials, etc. Intangible resources include such things as reputation, general concept of power, personal integrity or community tranquility. The game may make it possible to observe the ramifications of underuse or overuse of resources such as reputation in very much the same way we analyze the social impact of technology.

4. Each actor, and sometimes each role, must be permitted to interact with others. Rules must therefore be provided. Clearly there is nothing unique about this process except that it can induce or constrain, explicitly or implicitly, the occurrence of certain interactions. Here the challenge for SIA is to benefit from the fundamental aspect of gaming: anything that is not explicitly forbidden can be tried. While this observation is particularly important for interaction among actors (and roles), it holds value for all else that can "happen" in the game. Thus, the analyst must carefully define his constraints so that all that may happen in the game may also happen in the real world, other things being equal.

5. All important factors outside the role-taker's decisions and actions that will affect the outcome must be taken into consideration. In the SIA game the need to refer to external factors is to be interpreted primarily in terms of factors outside the effecting and affected actors' behaviors. For example, should the analyst decide to allow for chance factors, he must spell that out. The game must include a representation of all factors not controlled by the game players to insure validity and reliability to its results.

Analytically, games have at least five positive features: (1) self-judgment, (2) involvement, (3) causal imputation, (4) behavioral representation and (5) access to high risk and long-term impact situations.

1. Games are self-judging situations. Such a feature is instrumental in avoiding "authority reactions" and defensiveness by the participants. Gaming simulates roles, not people, and can benefit from participation by those who are actually involved in the project under review. In contrast, non-gaming evaluation utilizes judgments by others of one's motivation. Gaming frees decision makers to participate in social impact research in their roles or other roles. Thus, they build on authentic experience. Decision makers are more likely to contribute to games than to other research situations since the evaluation--to the extent the game is an evaluation--is of ROLES.

2. Since the consequences of moves and decisions can be immediately observed by the players, games generate a high degree of involvement.

3. The question of causality is an unresolved issue in all social science research. Games are unique in that they provide participants with the experience of a causal process. Caution must be exercised in causal imputation because the consequences may not be valid for real world processes; the game may have its idiosyncratic logic. This caution applies to all other predictive methods as well, however. In any case, hypotheses about causality can be generated in games that could not be duplicated by any other method.

4. In the game, it is behavior rather than mere verbal intent which is simulated. Gaming offers the researcher an access to action. Even when actions are simple and well-studied, their realization in games may bring about fresh insights.

5. Some phenomena are extremely difficult to study except by gaming. For example, the social consequences of natural disasters and environmental hazards are nearly impossible to study as they happen because emergency needs do and should take precedence. Gaming offers an ideal laboratory--and often the only one--to test hazardous futures and examine closely unusual events and impacts, as in Michael Inbar's (1966) simulation of community response to disaster. A related advantage of gaming may be termed the "telescoping of time." Social consequences that may take years to unfold in real life can be generated in a few rounds of game play.

IV. The Particular Promise of Simulation

The principal advantage of simulation in SIA is its demand for explicitness and specificity of the research questions. A simulator cannot capitalize on any built-in theory of social impact or social science to construct his instrument. As a social impact model is built and is gradually translated into a working simulation, methodological rigor increases.

Simulation as a method in SIA has been described and applied by many scholars in virtually all public policy areas. A typical example is the Airport Simulation used for training Immigration and Naturalization Service officers (Office of Planning and Evaluation 1975). Some trends in the United States, particularly in the Federal sector, have been summarized in the introductory guide produced by the Environmental Protection Agency (1974). Most of the literature still treats social impact as a marginal aspect of forecasting or as an obvious and not too distinct part of general futures modelling, however. Among the approaches to simulation that deal more directly with social impact analysis, the two texts that seem most pertinent to our argument are Anderson and Maass (1971) and Naylor (1971). Introductory texts useful but not specific to simulation in the service of SIA include Amstutz (1967), Ableson (1968), Dutton and Starbuck (1971), Emshoff and Sisson (1970), and Meisel and Gnugnolli (1972). Looking at the type of procedures surveyed in most simulations that apply directly or indirectly to our purposes, the following steps appear necessary in the understanding of a simulation study:

1. Operating realities of the system must be studied. A thorough system analysis--the known actions, consequences and causal relationships within the given boundaries of time and space--is critical to the development of an effective and economical simulation (Dutton and Starbuck 1971: 123). These determine what are feasible objectives for the simulation and may indicate where more data collection is necessary or, alternatively, which assumptions must be made in order to simulate the system as it is. The very necessity to document social impact antecedents and manifestations may be the best test of whether a simulation is necessary. This rigorous exercise may point the way to simpler social impact predictions, avoiding the need for a simulation study altogether.

2. Specific objectives of the simulation must be determined. The simulator must be able to specify the unique problem or process to be simulated and the purpose for which the study is generated. The scope of the simulation should be <u>bounded</u> by expected benefit to be derived. Determining specific objectives for the simulation leads to acquiring necessary additional data and becoming aware of relationships employed or assumed.

3. A model must be developed and tested. The simulation model may be atomistic (composed of one self-contained, multi-stage model) or modular (wherein each phase may call on a self-contained subroutine), or it may be a combination of the two. "Development" of a model includes the drawing of flow diagrams in a manner that will lead to a manual or some "common sense" testing of the model and its conversion to a computer program.

Computer languages aid in this double process. The most common simulation languages are SIMSCRIPT, GPSS, CSMP (see Emshoff and Sisson 1970), and DYNAMO (Forrester 1969). The latter has been amply tested on continuous and interlinked economic and social processes. Originally developed for engineering projections, CSMP can be used for simulation of social or economic impacts that are well defined. GPSS can be used for discrete processes (e.g., traffic impact). SIMSCRIPT is the only language among those mentioned here which represents a primary analysis-oriented model. The other three can be utilized also for the decision maker's needs, and do not entail much dependency on the programmer. They may therefore present a certain advantage for the social impact assessor.

4. The model must be fully programmed, tested via the computer and "debugged." These operations must bring the model to a point where the data, logic, instructions, and translation of the relationships between components represent the desired world (mostly, the real world) to the desired degree. The simulator may find the need to test-run the program several times in order to rid it of various internal incoherencies or conversion-based errors.

5. The perfected programmed model must run and when necessary rerun, so that full results can be available for evaluation. In SIA, simulations can provide only

provisional answers; no single run of any model can be made to determine a social impact. This step is different from the previous one in that what is required is the testing of perfectly _satisfactory_ models that are explicitly different, not merely the further "perfection" of a given model.

In summary, the following are **major advantages of simulation for social impact researchers.**

1. Simulations are the only practical options for a large class of social studies typified by many computational permutations and indeterminate relationships. Social impact research can benefit from available methodologies that utilize mathematical and/or formal modelling. Social consequences, responses, cross-impacts and the like can be studied by linear programming, game theory, Monte Carlo systems, queuing theories and a plethora of statistical approaches. Very often social impact problems cannot be abstracted to a simple mathematical formulation, however. On the other hand, simulation allows the researcher to test a great number of situations incorporating available information, manipulate the weights assigned to factors, consider possible answers and speculations with regard to missing data and thereby produce an approximation to objective reality that would be otherwise impossible.

2. Simulations generate outputs that save time and energy in decision making. By forcing the researcher to engage in boundary setting and problem formulation, simulations can assist in clarifying the analytic problem for SIA. Once the nature of their antecedents has been defined and fed into the machine, impacts can be set to unfold as computer permutations. Through model testing there is a higher likelihood that errors in planning and undesirable consequences will meet early detection. The positive redundance in simulation models enables the researcher to re-examine inputs, modifying slightly the givens and/or testing and retesting assumptions.

3. Finally, whether one is dealing with complex or simple modelling, in simulation it is the formalization that counts: a parsimonious language that can be retrieved and applied at will, and with minimum need to translate.

V. _Costs in Gaming and Simulation_
A cursory review of the applications of the above described methodologies to SIA leads to the following observations:

1. The procedures we described in general terms are normally not sufficiently detailed in empirical work so that reproduction is possible. Our suggestions are merely a point of departure.

2. The advantages we highlighted for each of the methodologies are generally not sufficiently understood or utilized in empirical mapping of social impacts.

3. The disadvantages of methodologies used have not been actively considered; they have **resulted in an undesirable** cost-effectiveness ratio between output and investment in many of the studies we cited.

The last observation requires elaboration. Simulation and gaming are both costly methodologies. In developing and running a simulation strategy, one must consider these costs (Dutton and Starbuck 1972: 125):

1. Analysis and model building;

2. Participation of general and functional management;

3. Programming and debugging;

4. Clerical workers and keypunch operators;

5. Computer running time;

6. Updating the simulation, if it is to be reused.

Some of these items, particularly analysis and programming time, can become very costly. Since general purpose simulators are still in very limited use, further disadvantages must be noted (Meisel and Gnugnoli 1972: 5):

7. Computer simulations use scarce and expensive resources;

8. Require fast, high capacity computers;

9. Take a long time to develop;

10. May hide critical assumptions;

11. May require extensive field studies.

While the gaming component normally requires less investment in machinery, it may cost more in facilities as well as in some of the cost categories mentioned above. Clearly, its greatest cost is buying participants and simulators' time. Cost-benefit ratios can only be assessed when benefits are also fully identified.

VI. Potential Applications of Simulation Gaming

Having considered the current practice of simulation and gaming and their respective costs and benefits, we turn now to two areas where development and application of simulation gaming techniques appear especially promising.

1. *Urban and relocation impacts*: Urban problems, and relationships between physical location and relocation generally appear to be an area in which simulation gaming is becoming more prominent. It is also one of the few fields in which the growth of strictly gaming vehicles led to same-problem simulation gaming techniques. For example, the Community Land Use Game (CLUG) is a manually-operated table game. Its players include industrialists, businessmen, home-builders and residents. Social impacts reproduced and assessed include the effects of the money market, construction and renovations on urban growth (Feldt 1972). The computer-based derivatives are RIVER BASIN MODEL (Environmental Protection Agency 1972; House and Patterson 1972) and CITY MODEL (Environmetrics 1971a). The simulation component enables rigorous and manifold decisions to take place. Basically, "where good theory does not exist, interactions and decisions are gamed; whereas when good theory does exist, it is often incorporated into the simulation component of the model" (Environmental Protection Agency 1974: 195). When comparing simulation

gaming in this area to simulation-only products (e.g., Forrester 1969), one can easily see that fledgling as simulation gaming efforts still are, they are far richer in systemic knowledge of the urban scene than computer simulations alone, or gaming alone, or most other techniques available.

Capitalizing on this richness, one possible application would be in the study of community resettlement, e.g., of refugees or the poor. Assuming options of relocation and/or further investment in community institutions, the question may arise as to which will be preferable: (1) new locations, new institutions; (2) new locations, traditional institutions; (3) same locations, traditional patterns; (4) same locations, new institutions; or (5) a mixed model of a new kind. This crude decision matrix can be fruitfully explored through a gaming simulation which exploits the large body of experience and literature that would otherwise remain a residual category of knowledge.

2. Creeping or sudden breakdowns in resource availability: Natural resources in general, and particularly resources or wastes that are utilized or produced in human settlements, is a second area for creative application of simulation gaming, augmenting the current emphasis on modeling cause and effect relationships for physical systems and for optimal management. D. H. Marks (Environmental Protection Agency 1974: 133) cites the role of water and changes in its availability on the social and political system of a river basin as an area where much more interest in modelling is necessary.

> Another area where more work is needed is in dealing with the multi-objective nature of the decision making process. Better means for assessing utility functions for interest groups, for displaying alternatives and for recognizing points at which some agreement can be reached are important from the viewpoint of implementation.

In situations of natural resource depletion or the risk of nuclear accident, a similar problem appears, though perhaps with differing weights assigned to the early warning signals. When Inbar (1966) created his Disaster Game to train community decision makers for emergency preparedness, he could be satisfied with gaming only since variables were few and objectives simple. Natural resource "disasters" are mostly much more complicated technically. The potential for creeping, latent breakdowns exist both in the technology and in human behavior. Social aspects that must be included range from consumer perceptions through key decision makers' value systems to terrorists' designs and their related action probabilities. The dearth of knowledge in these areas and the lack of promise from most alternative methods justifies greater investment in simulation gaming.

VII. Conclusion

Gaming, a group based capability to conceive of manifold "wholes," can be enriched if participants are trained to utilize simulation. If game participants "consult" simulation, their environment will become increasingly geared toward producing reliable and insightful social impact projections. The ideal way to realize this program is:

1. To prepare for gaming utilizing simulation as a resource;

2. To utilize simulation while gaming is going on;

3. To consult simulation whenever a **projection is made or a decision** is suggested during gaming and at closing sessions;

4. To manipulate data and engage in post-gaming analysis utilizing simulation.

Once this is done systematically, much of what constitutes social impact research can be accomplished with a high degree of precision and comprehension. The following possibilities are illustrative:

- Cost-benefit analysis and the larger picture: Determining appropriate level of reasonable inclusion of community action and resources can be a time-consuming process if simulation is not utilized, and less imaginative if human interaction is excluded which gaming could provide.

- Selected methodologies pertinent to current special fields, e.g., environmental impact assessment and the social impact assessment of natural resource development, must remain flexible and open while improving in rigor and precision. Simulation and gaming offer a unique openness for this assessment component.

- Grounded theory construction in social impact assessment: the limits and prospects of existing models can be developed by simulation that manipulates models and gaming that employs interaction.

- Community impact assessment; Methodological approaches can be facilitated by gaming and simulation on this level.

- Community social profile: Cost-effective methodology geared to determine baseline data and community response can be advanced by simulation manipulation and gaming guidance.

- Quantification of social impact data: While the implications of quantification can be clarified by simulation, gaming can enhance judgment on what constitutes benefit.

- Social indicators: The construction of valid and reliable indicators on micro and macro levels can be assisted by combining gaming with simulation.

- Intended and unintended consequences: Assessment of second-order consequences can benefit by varying the weighting of relevant factors and the "telescoping of time."

- Social forecasting methods: Comprehensive assessment of whole future projections can be evaluated for consistency and completeness through simulation and gaming techniques.

- The use of scenarios in projecting impacts: Step-by-step approaches to the creation of meaningful "wholes" can be explored in simulation and gaming.

Social impact analysis of cultural futures: How to conceive of
future projects in differing cultural contexts can be answered
effectively by gaming that utilizes associated simulation.

All of these are propositions which should be tested by social impact research in
order to establish the potential benefits of this approach.

Bibliography

Abelson, R. P. 1968 "Simulation of Social Behavior," Vol. II, pp. 274-356 in G.
    Lindzey and E. Aronson (eds.) Handbook of Social Psychology. London: Addison-Wesley.

Abt, C. C. 1964 "War Gaming," International Science and Technology, 32, pp. 29-37,
    96-98.

Amstutz, A. E. 1967 Computer Simulation of Competitive Market Response. Cambridge,
    MA: M.I.T. Press.

Anderson, R. L. and A. Maass 1971 "A Simulation of Irrigation Systems: The Effect
    of Water Supply and Operating Rules on Production and Income on Irrigated
    Farms." Fort Collins, CO: Economic Research Service, U. S. Department of
    Agriculture.

Anundsen, Dristin and Nilo Landgren 1972 "Can You Put a Simulation Model to Work
    in a Real Community?" Innovation 29 (March).

Asken, A. J., W. W. Yem and W. A. Hull 1971 "A Comparative Study of Critical
    Drought Simulation." Water Resource Research 7, pp. 52-62.

Ben-Dak, J. D. 1969 "Simulating International Behavior with Particular Reference
    to Disarmament Problems: An Introductory Bibliography Inventory." Proceedings
    of the International School on Disarmament and Arms Control, pp. 247-260.
    Trieste: Instituto Nazionale Fisica Nucleare.

Ben-Dak, J. D. 1969 "Social Exchange in Simulation Gaming: Strategic Linkages in
    Research on Conflict Resolution," pp. 261-302, Proceedings of the International
    School on Disarmament and Arms Control. Trieste: Instituto Nazionale Fisica
    Nucleare.

Ben-Dak, J. D. 1970 "A Social Simulation Strategy for Researching Arab-Israeli
    Relations, Proceedings of the Ninth Symposium of the National Gaming Council.
    Washington, D. C.: Environmetrics.

Ben-Dak, J. D. 1972 "Some Directions for Research toward Peaceful Arab-Israeli
    Relations: Analysis of Past Events and Gaming Simulation of the Future."
    Journal of Conflict Resolution, 16 (June) pp. 281-295).

Boocock, S. and J. S. Coleman 1966 "Games with Simulated Environments in Learning."
    Sociology of Education 39, 3.

Boocock, S. and E. O. Schild 1968 Simulation Games in Learning. Beverley Hills, CA: Sage.

Boston College Seminar Research Bureau 1961 Travel in the Boston Region 1959-1980, Vol. II: Trip Distribution Procedures. Boston: Boston College.

Brody, R. A. 1963 Some Systematic Effects of the Spread of Nuclear Weapons Technology: A Study Through Simulation of a Multi-Nuclear Future, Journal of Conflict Resolution, 7, 4, (December).

Campbell, D. T. 1966 "Pattern Matching as an Essential in Distal Knowing," in H. R. Hammond (ed.) The Psychology of Egon Brunswick. New York: Holt, Rinehart and Winston.

Coplin, W. D. (ed.) 1968 Simulation in the Study of Politics. Chicago: Markham.

Druckman, D. 1966 Dogmatism, Pre-Negotiation Experience, and Simulated Group Representation as Determinants of Dyadic Behavior in a Bargaining Situation. Unpublished doctoral dissertation. Evanston, IL: Northwestern University.

Duke, Richard and Richard L. Meier 1966 "Gaming Simulation for Urban Planning." Journal of the American Institute of Planners, 32 (January) pp. 3-17.

Dutton, John M., and William H. Starbuck 1971 Computer Simulation of Human Behavior. New York: John Wiley.

Elder, C. D. and R. E. Pendley 1966 An Analysis of Consumption Standards and Validator Satisfaction in the Inter-Nation Simulation in Terms of Contemporary Economic Theory and Data. Evanston, IL: Northwestern University.

Emshoff, J. R. and R. L. Sisson 1970 Design and Use of Computer Simulation Models. New York: McMillan.

Environmental Protection Agency 1972. The River Basin Model. 14 vols. Water Polution Control Research Series 16110 FRU 12/71. Washington, DC: U.S. Government Printing Office.

Environmental Protection Agency 1972a APEX:Air Polution Exercise. 21 vols. Washington, DC: Office of Manpower Development.

Environmental Protection Agency 1974 A Guide to Models in Governmental Planning and Operations. Washington, DC: Office of Research and Development.

Environmetrics 1971 State-of-the-Art of Urban Gaming Models. Springfield, VA: National Technical Information Service.

Environmetrics 1971a City Model Players' Manual. Washington, DC: Technical Analysis Division, National Bureau of Standards.

Feldt, Allan 1972 CLUG: Community Land Use Game. New York: Free Press.

Flook, A. 1970 "Simulation Studies of International Conflict." Simulation 1 (April).

Forrester, J. 1969 Urban Dynamics. Cambridge, MA: M.I.T. Press.

Friedell, Morris F. 1968 " A Laboratory Experiment in Retaliation." Journal of Conflict Resolution 12; 357-373.

Gamson, W. A. 1968 Power and Discontent. Homewood, IL: Dorsey Press.

Gamson, W. A. 1966 SIMSOC: Simulated Society. New York: Free Press.

Gordon, G. and K. Zelin 1968 "A Simulation Study of Emergency Ambulance Service in New York City." Report No. 320-2935. New York, NY: IBM Scientific Center.

Gray, J. 1969 "The Broadcasting Game and Simulation Exercises." Conference paper, Birmingham, England (January).

Guetzkow, H. 1968 "Some Correspondences between Simulations and Realities in International Relations," in M. Kaplan (ed.), New Approaches to International Relations. New York: St. Martin's Press.

Guetzkow H. and others 1963 Simulation in International Relations. Englewood Cliffs, NJ: Prentice-Hall.

Hanneman, G. J. 1969 A Computer Simulation of Information Diffusion in a Peasant Community. Unpublished master's thesis. East Lansing: Michigan State University.

Hanneman, G. J. and T. W. Carroll 1969 SINDI 1: Simulation of Information Diffusion in a Peasant Community. East Lansing: Michigan State University Project on Diffusion of Innovations in Rural Societies, Technical Report No. 7.

Helferich, O. K., V. Hoffner and D. E. Gee 1972 "Dynamic Simulation Model for Planning Solid Waste Management." Paper presented at the 19th International Meeting of the Institute of Management Sciences.

House, Peter and Philip D. Patterson (eds.) 1972 An Environmental Laboratory for the Social Sciences. Washington, DC: U.S. Environmental Protection Agency.

Inbar, M. 1966 "The Differential Impact of a Game Simulating a Community Disaster." American Behavioral Scientist 10 (June).

Inbar, M. and C. S. Stoll 1972 Simulation and Gaming in Social Science. New York: Free Press.

Kelman, H. C. 1972 "The Problem-Solving Workshop in Conflict Resolution," in F. L. Merritt (ed.), Communication in International Politics. Chicago: University of Illinois Press.

Meadows D. 1972 Limits to Growth. New York: Universe.

Meisel, Herbert and Giuliano Gnugnoli 1972 Simulation of Discrete Stochastic Systems. Chicago: Science Research Associates.

Naylor, Thomas H. 1971 Computer Simulation Experiments with Models of Economic Systems. New York: John Wiley.

Office of Planning and Evaluation 1975 User's Guide to the Airport Simulation. Washington, DC: Federal Computer Performance Evaluation and Simulation Center.

Peston, M. and A. Coddington 1967 The Elementary Ideas of Game. London: Her Majesty's Stationary Office.

Rapaport, A. 1966 "Laboratory Studies of Conflict and Cooperation," in J. R. Lanreng (ed.) Operational Research and the Social Sciences. London: Tavistock Publishing Company.

Raser, J. 1969 Simulation and Society. Englewood Cliffs, NJ: Prentice-Hall.

Ray, P. H. and R. D. Duke 1968 "The Environment of Decision-Makers in Urban Gaming Simulations," in W. Coplin (ed.) Simulation in Study of Politics. Chicago: Markham.

Sawyer, J. and H. R. Guetzkow 1965 "Bargaining and Negotiation in International Relations, H. C. Kelman (ed.) International Behavior: Social Psychological Analysis. New York: Holt, Rinehart and Winston.

Shure, G. H. and R. J. Meeker 1970 "On-Line Computer Studies of Bargaining and Negotiation Behavior." Santa Monica, CA: System Development Corporation.

Smoker, P. 1968 "The International Processes Simulation." Unpublished manuscript. Evanston, IL: Department of Political Science, Northwestern University.

Smoker, P. 1971 "Anarchism, Peace and Control: Some Ideas for Future Experiments." Paper presented to the Fourth International Peace Research Association Conference, Bled, Yugoslavia.

Wahi, P. N. and T. I. Peterson 1972 "Management Science and Gaming in Waste Management." Journal Sanitary Engineering, ASCE, 98 SA5.

Waskow, A. J. 1969 "Looking Forward: 1999," in R. Jungk and J. Galtung (eds.) Mankind 2000. London: Allen and Unwin.

V Assessment

Logically, the "assessment" step means solving the difference equation between profile projections "with and without" a planned intervention. Actually, a good deal of what may be construed as assessment takes place independent of formal projections. The entire arsenal of measurement techniques in the social sciences is amenable to use in the assessment of social impacts. Since numerous texts on social research methods provide easy access to these techniques, we have limited the selections in this section to articles which present innovative applications to the assessment of actual or expected social impacts.

The articles by Loundsbury and others and by James further illustrate the use of surveys in SIA. The former apply survey research to obtain general demographic and specific events information to assess community residents' attitudes toward a proposed nuclear power plant and its possible consequences. In their main report from which this article is abstracted, it was found that ". . . <u>there were virtually no major demographic differences between supporters of the plant and opponents</u>," with the single exception of sex differences. These "before" measures will be incorporated into an ongoing system of impact monitoring that follows the trajectory of development through construction to operation.

James' policy-oriented use of surveys demonstrates their utility for gauging individual response to planning alternatives, in this case for flood plain management. The impact situation assessed must also include the impacts of plan implementation. Survey research is a social technology which can furnish information on the structure of personal motives and incentives that must articulate with the planning activities of public agencies.

The next paper, by Finsterbusch, advocates the use of mini surveys in SIAs and describes a number of applications of this innovative technique. Many SIAs fail to obtain direct information from people by survey methods because of the high costs of surveys relative to other methods of information gathering. But the principle of declining marginal statistical utility of each additional survey respondent suggests that small, inexpensive surveys may provide information which is sufficiently accurate for the purpose of SIAs within budget constraints. SIAs depend mainly on univariate distributions for descriptive information. Therefore, Finsterbusch argues, surveys of small sample size are more appropriate for such studies than for multivariate analyses of the complex interrelationships of a system of variables. Accordingly, relatively small sample sizes can have high benefit-cost ratios in SIA.

Surveys are only one kind of assessment instrument, however. The section includes discussions of two others, experimental designs and the content analysis of historical records. Napier's article on experimental design utilizes surveys, but its originality lies in the experimental design framework within which surveys are utilized. Napier's paper can also be read as an argument against the standard cross-sectional analysis into which most survey work falls.

Motz emphasizes the time dimension in impact assessments through a retrospective study of the consequences of the Arkansas River Project for three small cities bordering the river. The main source of data for her analysis of differential impacts on the three cities is newspapers for 1950, 1960 and 1970. Motz describes her content analysis technique and outlines some emerging substantive findings.

Toward an Assessment of the Potential Social Impacts of a Nuclear Power Plant on a Community: Survey of Residents' Views*

John W. Lounsbury,[1] Eric Sundstrom,[1] C. Richard Schuller,[2] Thomas J. Mattingly, Jr., and Robert DeVault
Oak Ridge National Laboratory

This paper describes the results of a survey of public attitudes, perceptions, and expectations regarding a nuclear power plant now under construction near Hartsville, Tennessee, by the Tennessee Valley Authority (TVA). The survey was conducted in January and February, 1975, before construction began. The survey is part of a broad-based, longitudinal project designed to assess the social impacts of the nuclear plant. The project examines objective impacts involving governmental services, public finance, the local economy, and land use, as well as the subjective responses of individuals.

Goals of the Project
The project addresses three major goals. First, we plan to describe the social impacts of the Hartsville nuclear plant over its full cycle of development, including pre-construction, construction, and operation phases. This goal serves a second, larger goal of developing a set of methods for assessing social impacts that could be applied in other settings. Toward that end, we hope to make surveys of public views a part of the repertoire of other researchers working in the general field of social impact assessment. Our third goal is to supply data for the development of theories and models that might serve as a basis for predicting social impacts of other nuclear generating facilities and, possibly, other large-scale environmental modification projects. We hope these efforts will generate information useful in policy decisions about siting and about the amelioration of adverse social impacts.

Purposes of the Survey
As a first step in assessing the impacts of the nuclear plant, we sought to measure residents' views on a variety of topics before construction began. When TVA was

---

*This research was supported by the U.S. Energy Research and Development Administration under contract with Union Carbide Corporation.
 A more detailed description of the rationale, methods, and preliminary results appears in Schuller, et al. (1975). Other reports based on the survey include Passino and Lounsbury (1976) and Sundstrom et al. (1977). Send requests for reprints to John W. Lounsbury, Department of Psychology, University of Tennessee, Knoxville, TN 37916.
1. Consultants to Oak Ridge National Laboratory from the University of Tennessee, Knoxville.
2. Now at Battelle Human Affairs Research Center, 400 N.E. 41st St., Seattle, Washington 98105.

planning to build the facility, we expected the objective effects to be minimal, but we expected that as residents learned of plans and the actual decision to build the plant, their views and opinions might be affected. A second and primary purpose of assessing citizens' subjective responses before construction was to provide a benchmark against which to assess later social and psychological changes. To supplement data on individual, subjective responses we also plan to use other methods, such as interviews with influential members of the community, systematic observation, analysis of public documents, and tabulation of records of local agencies. Our approach is based on the philosophy of "multiple operationism" (cf. Webb et al. 1966), which calls for the use of multiple measures of variables of interest through independent procedures of measurement.

We had two main reasons for choosing a standardized survey of a random sample of residents instead of other available research techniques. (For example, we could have conducted informal, intensive interviews with selected members of the community.) First, the use of a randomly selected sample allows us to use statistical techniques to make inferences about the larger population of residents in the community. Second, a standardized interview provides quantitative data (based on structured questions).

The specific purpose of the survey was to obtain information about residents' satisfaction with their community, their perceptions about the quality of their lives, their support for or opposition to the nuclear plant, and their expectations about its effects on the community.

The Community and the Nuclear Plant

Hartsville, a town of about 2500 people, is located about 40 miles northeast of Nashville, Tennessee, in a relatively rural, unpopulated area. It is located in Trousdale County, which has a total population of about 5000 people. The proposed nuclear power plant will take about 10 years to build and will require a peak construction force of approximately 5300 workers. The plant will occupy a site of about 1900 acres of farm land. TVA estimates the cost at about $2.50 billion. There has been considerable publicity about the plant in newspapers and on radio and television.

METHODS

Sampling Procedure

A simple random sampling technique was used to select 350 adult (age 18 and over) citizens of Hartsville and the surrounding Trousdale County. To obtain a sample of 350 persons, we contacted a total of 420, with 49 persons refusing to participate and 21 persons for whom a suitable interview time could not be arranged. The median age of the people surveyed was 46. The average number of grades completed was 11; 49% were male, 9% Black, and 79% were married. Seventy-four percent were employed, mainly as salesmen, managers, clerks, farmers, and craftsmen.

Administration of the Survey

The survey was conducted between January 21 and February 16, 1975 using trained, local residents (all females) as interviewers. Each interview was conducted in the home of the respondent and lasted approximately one hour. Respondents were paid $5.00 for their participation.

Contents of the Interview Schedule

The survey considered nine general topics:

1. Demographic information.

2. Satisfaction with neighborhoods and the community.

3. Satisfaction with services available in the community.

4. Personal life satisfaction.

5. Attitudes toward the nuclear plant and toward TVA.

6. Perceived likelihood and desirability of events that might accompany construction and operation of the plant.

7. Factual knowledge about nuclear power.

8. Sources of information about the nuclear plant.

9. Use of specific geographical regions of the community for shopping, socializing, working, recreation, and other activities.

The following sections describe findings associated with all but the last three of these topics. We have organized the findings into three sections--the first presents data on the perceived quality of life; the second presents data on expected effects on the community; and the third describes the distribution of opposition and support of the nuclear plant and the correlates of support and opposition.

FINDINGS RELATED TO THE PERCEIVED QUALITY OF LIFE

We chose to examine indicators of the perceived quality of life for several reasons. First, such indicators can be used to assess impacts of environmental change on residents, and therefore contribute to the total picture of the impacts of a change. In fact, for the average citizen, his or her own reactions to changes in the community are probably a good deal more important than many objective indicators of impact such as changes in taxes or population. For example, the influx of construction workers into the community may mean nothing to a person whose residence and neighborhood are unaffected. But for someone who experiences a loss of privacy created by an influx of new people in his neighborhood, the resulting discomfort is important and may be directly related to the actual number of new people introduced into the community as a result of the construction of the nuclear plant.

Another reason for focusing on the indicators of perceived quality of life, noted by Andrews and Withey (1973), is that changes in the subjective quality of life may help researchers understand objective changes. For example, an increase in the percentage of people who leave Hartsville may be related to the perception of Hartsville as an increasingly crowded, unfriendly place to live. Also, exclusive reliance on objective indicators such as rates of out-migration may mask significant social and psychological impacts. For example, the option of moving to another town is unavailable to some segments of the population (e.g., senior citizens). But it would still be a significant impact if a person's satisfaction with neighborhood and community decreased sharply, even though the person did not move away.

Satisfaction with the Community
To assess general satisfaction with Hartsville and/or Trousdale County, we asked "Overall, how do you feel about this town or county as a place to live?" Over 70% of the respondents said their community was an "excellent" or a "good" place to live, 25% rated it "average," and only 3% rated it as "below average" or "poor." These responses indicate a high degree of satisfaction with the community.

Respondents were also asked what they liked and disliked about living in the Hartsville-Trousdale County area, and the reasons for their views. About 40% of the respondents said they liked the friendliness of the people and the closeness of the community; 21% mentioned the rural, uncrowded, small-town atmosphere. Other "likes" emphasized the quiet and peacefulness of the area. Eighty-eight percent of the respondents mentioned no "dislikes." Things most frequency mentioned as "dislikes" were lack of recreational and cultural facilities (4% of the respondents) and a lack of jobs (2% of respondents).

Another question regarding findings about Hartsville concerns the changes people said they would make in Hartsville if they could. Responses included more recreational facilities (23%), more job opportunities (18%), improvements in schools (16%), and improvements in the political system (10%). (No other response was mentioned by more than 10% of the sample).

Ratings of Neighborhoods

We sought a more specific characterization of the quality of life through ratings of neighborhoods. Respondents were shown ten pairs of adjectives, including "Friendly"/"Unfriendly," "Quiet"/"Noisy," and "Crowded"/"Uncrowded" separated by 7-step scales in the format of the semantic differential (Heise, 1967).

Neighborhoods were rated as extremely "friendly" and "pleasant" with over three-fourths of the respondents marking the most extreme point on the scale. The average respondent rated his or her neighborhood as stable, quiet, well kept, uncrowded, and inhabited by familiar, similar people.

For many respondents, positive attitudes toward their neighborhoods were related to feelings about their own homes. In response to another question, over 20% indicated that what they liked about their home was the friendly people living nearby and the high quality of the neighborhood. Other positive features of homes included convenience to stores, churches, and other services (45%) and specific attributes of the house (41%).

Satisfaction with Services

In research on perceived quality of life in communities, a recurring theme is the importance of public and private services (Lansing, Marans and Zehner 1970). In our survey, respondents were asked how satisfied they were with 17 services, including police protection, the school system, shopping, work opportunities, and recreational facilities. Each was rated on a five-point scale from "very satisfied" to "very unsatisfied" (scored as 1.0 to 5.0).

Respondents expressed considerable satisfaction with telephone service, fire protection, grocery stores, water supplies, the school system, and public streets and highways. They were least satisfied with housing availability, parks and playgrounds (there are none in Trousdale County), job opportunities, movie theaters, and restaurants.

Some of the services residents rated as deficient are likely to be most heavily affected by the influx of a large construction force. Housing was seen as inadequate for the present population. The few recreational areas and restaurants in the area were designed for far smaller numbers of patrons than would be expected if a sizable fraction of the peak construction force (5300 people) uses the facilities.

Personal Life Satisfaction

Another item was designed to tap respondents' satisfaction with their own lives. Based on a measure developed by Cantril (1965), an eleven-step "ladder" was used, with the top indicating "the best possible life" and the bottom "the worst possible life." With 10 representing the top "rung," the average response was 6.7 (SD = 2.05); 35% of the respondents chose one of the top three "rungs."

Summary of Perceived Quality of Life

A fairly consistent picture emerges from the data: most respondents were very satisfied with the quality of life. Hartsville and Trousdale County appear to share many characteristics of small, stable rural communities. Residents saw their environments as slow-moving, peaceful, and relaxing. They had few complaints about the community in general or the things it has to offer.

As the nuclear plant is constructed, it is difficult to anticipate the consequences for the quality of life in the community. However, a rapid influx of workers could disrupt much of what the residents of the community value.

RESIDENTS' EXPECTATIONS ABOUT THE EFFECTS OF THE NUCLEAR PLANT ON THE COMMUNITY

One question on the summary was designed to elicit the respondent's global evaluation: "In general do you think the proposed power plant project will be a good thing for Hartsville or not?" Sixty-seven percent answered "definitely" or "probably" yes, 24% answered "definitely" or "probably" no, and 9% expressed no opinion. Respondents were next asked "Why do you say this?" The reasons most frequently given emphasized economic impacts on the community, such as more jobs, increased business, and economic growth. Table 1 summarizes the most frequent reasons for those who said that the proposed plant would be a good thing and those who said it would not be a good thing for Hartsville.

As another means to assess Trousdale Countians' concerns about the nuclear plant, we asked an open-ended question: "If the power plant is built, what things, if any, do you think you would worry about when it is operating?" Respondents could mention as many concerns as they wished, but few mentioned more than one. In fact, 44% of the respondents said they would have no worries at all. Of the categories of concerns mentioned, the two most frequent were radiation hazards (24% of respondents) and safety and sabotage-related concerns (10% of respondents).

Following the open-ended questions, the survey gave a list of 24 potential effects of the plant on the community. The instructions to respondents were: "If TVA were to built the power plant here in Hartsville, a number of things might change in the community while the plant is being built or after it goes into operation. I am going to give you a list of things that some people have said might happen. I want you to tell me how likely each of these is." Responses were given on a five-point scale ranging from "very likely" (1) to "very unlikely" (5). Respondents were also asked to indicate which items they "would not like to see happen." Table 2 shows the percent of respondents who estimated each potential impact as "likely" or "very likely" and the percent of respondents who "would not like to see" the event occur. At least one-fourth of the respondents thought accidents and sabotage of the plant, air and water pollution, and radiation hazards were likely to occur, even though these events were seen as undesirable. Events associated with economic growth were seen as likely by over half of the respondents, and were very seldom named as things respondents "would not like to see happen."

Table 1
Respondents' Reasons for Saying That the Nuclear Plant
Would or Would Not Be "Good for Hartsville"

Response	Percent of Respondents Who Answered "Good Thing" or "Unsure"
Potential Benefits for Hartsville (N = 227)	
More jobs in the area	39%
"Economic growth"	25
Increased local business	16
Cheaper electricity	15
More money for local people	12
More industry	11
New people in the area	10
Other	24

Response	Percent of Respondents Who Answered "Not a Good Thing"
Potential Costs for Hartsville (N = 81)	
Too many people	38%
Strain on public schools	27
Plant safety and security	23
Economic boom and bust phenomena	22
Radiation hazards	20
Changes in land-use pattern	19
Strain on law enforcement	12
Housing shortages	10
Strain on traffic congestion	9
Ecological impact	5

(Source: Schuller et al., 1975 p. 49).

Note: Respondents could give as many reasons as they desired.

To examine the inter-relations among the potential affects, we performed a factor analysis (see Sundstrom et al., in press). We used a principal components analysis with varimax rotation (Fruchter, 1954) and extracted all factors with eigenvalues greater than 1.0. As shown in Table 2, five factors emerged. (An effect was placed in the factor for which it had the highest loading; all but three were greater than .50). We named the first factor <u>Hazards</u>. It accounted for 26% of the common variance and included radiation hazards, accidents or sabotage at the plant, water or air pollution, and increased noise. The second factor, <u>Economic Growth</u>, accounted for 12% of the variance and included industrial development, more public entertainment, better pay, meeting new people, increased business, more jobs, and dating with workers. The third factor, named <u>Lower Cost of Living</u>, included lower taxes, cheap electricity, and community stability. The fourth factor, <u>Social Disruption</u>, consisted of crowding, congestion, crime, and drug problems in the schools. The last factor, <u>Community Visibility</u>, referred to public recognition of the town and increased tourism. These groups of potential effects were used in assessing correlates of support and opposition of the nuclear plant.

Table 2
Respondents' Estimates of the Likelihood and Desirability
of 24 Potential Effects of the Nuclear Plant on Hartsville

Potential Effects of Nuclear Plant (Grouped Through Factor Analysis)	Percent of Respondents who Estimated the Effect "Likely" or "Very Likely"	Mean Estimate of Likelihood for Group of Potential Effects[a]	Percent of Respondents who "Would not like to see" the effect occur
Hazards			
Radiation	27	2.9	92
Accidents/sabotage	33	"Perhaps"	95
Air pollution	38		94
Water pollution	39		92
Increased noise[b]	59		84
Economic Growth			
More jobs	84		2
Better pay	62	2.2	1
Increased business	89	"Likely"	2
Industrial development	65		3
More public entertainment	52		3
Dating with workers	58		24
Meet new people[b]	93		2
Lower Cost of Living			
Community stays same	21	2.8	11
Lower taxes	9	"Perhaps"	2
Cheap electricity	23		1
Social Disruption			
Traffic congestion	71		79
Crowding/shopping areas	68	2.2	55
Crowding/schools	81	"Likely"	88
Increased crime	57		96
Crowding/rec. areas	58		59
Drugs/schools[b]	67		97
Community Visibility			
Public recognition	86	2.0	4
More taverns and bars	69	"Likely"	71
More tourists	71		11

[a] "Very likely" = 1.0 and "Very unlikely" = 5.0
[b] Factor loadings less than .50

LEVELS AND CORRELATES OF OPPOSITION AND SUPPORT FOR CONSTRUCTION OF THE PLANT

Distribution of Support and Opposition of the Facility

The key question in our survey for measuring the opposition and support of the nuclear plant asked, if it were up to them, would they permit construction of the TVA power plant near Hartsville. As shown in Table 3, one-fourth of the respondents opposed construction of the nuclear plant, while nearly two-thirds favored it.

Table 3
Responses to the Question, "If it were up to you, would you permit construction of the TVA power plant near Hartsville?"

Response	Number of Respondents	Percent
Definitely yes	147	44%
Probably yes	69	21
Don't know--not sure	33	10
Probably no	28	8
Definitely no	55	17
	N = 332	

Correlates of Support and Opposition of the Facility

To examine the question of whether support or opposition of the plant is associated with other variables tapped in our survey, we scored responses to the "permit construction" question on a five-point scale from 1 (definitely yes) to 5 (definitely no), and calculated correlation coefficients with 18 other variables from the survey, including demographic factors, measures of the perceived quality of life, and perceived likelihood of potential effects of the facility. As shown in Table 4, we found modest but significant correlations for four of the demographic variables; opposition to construction of the plant was significantly related to being female, Caucasian, having more years of education, and having lived longer at the current address. None of the four indicators of the perceived quality of life was correlated with opposition of the plant. However, the six variables related to expectations about the plant were all correlated highly and significantly with opposition to the plant. Opposition to the plant was significantly related to not viewing the plant as a good thing for Hartsville. Opposition was associated with relatively high estimates of the likelihood of Hazards and Social Disruption, and relatively low estimates of the likelihood of Economic Growth, Lower Costs, and Community Visibility. In brief, opponents tended more to expect undesirable effects; supporters tended more to expect desirable effects.

Table 4
Correlates of Opposition to Construction
of the Proposed Plant in Hartsville

Variable	Correlation[a]
Sex (1 = male, 2 = female)	.18**
Age	.09
Race (1 = Caucasian, 2 = Black)	-.17**
Marital Status (1 = married, 2 = single)	.05
Number of Grades Completed	.11*
Employment Status (1 = employed, 2 = not employed)	.06
Number of years lived in Hartsville	.09
Number of years lived at current address	.14*
General satisfaction with Hartsville as a place to live	.07
Global attitude toward one's neighborhood	.05
Global satisfaction with public and community services	.01
Current personal life satisfaction	.02
Perception of the plant as a good thing for Hartsville	-.84**
Perceived Likelihood of Hazards (1 = "very likely")	-.61**
Perceived Likelihood of Economic Growth	.52**
Perceived Likelihood of Lower Cost of Living	.17**
Perceived Likelihood of Social Disruption	-.46**
Perceived Likelihood of Community Visibility	.24**

a. Pearson Product-Moment Correlation Coefficients (Guilford and Fruchter 1973) where 1 indicates strongest support and 5 indicates strongest opposition.

*$p < .05$

**$p < .01$

SUMMARY AND CONCLUSIONS

The findings of this survey indicate that before construction of the nuclear plant the residents of Hartsville are relatively satisfied with life in their community and with their personal life-spaces. On the other hand, they expect a number of undesirable effects such as pollution, radiation hazards, traffic congestion, and crowding in schools. However, they also expect desirable effects such as more jobs, increased business and better pay. The desirable effects may outweigh the undesirable ones in decisions about plant acceptance. Only one-fourth of our sample said that they would not permit construction of the plant if it were up to them. Opposition was significantly related to expectations about effects of the plant as well as to certain demographic variables.

PLANS FOR FUTURE RESEARCH

In the next survey of these same people we will discover whether the current levels of opposition to and support for the plant are maintained. We will also expand our set of questions regarding expectations about various impacts and use a more sensitive measure of the desirability of various outcomes. When coupled with the present set of findings, the next survey will permit us to begin to monitor changes in social impacts. We will also begin to analyze the ability of community residents to correctly anticipate various outcomes and consistently evaluate the desirability of these outcomes.

References

Andrews, F. M. and S. Withey (1974) "Developing Measures of Perceived Life Quality: Results from Several National Surveys." Social Indicators Research, 1, 1-26.

Cantril, H. (1965) The Pattern of Human Concerns. New Brunswick, N.J.: Rutgers University Press.

Fruchter, B. (1954) Introduction to Factor Analysis. New York: D. Van Nostrand.

Guilford, J. P. and B. Fruchter (1973) Fundamental Statistics in Psychology and Education. New York: McGraw-Hill.

Heise, D. R. (1967) The semantic differential and attitude research. In G. F. Sommers (Ed.) Attitude Measurement, pp. 235-251. Chicago: Rand McNally.

Lansing, J. B., R. W. Marans and R. B. Zehner (1970) Planned Residential Environments. Ann Arbor: Institute for Social Research, University of Michigan.

Passino, E. M. and J. W. Lounsbury. Sex differences in opposition to and support for construction of a proposed nuclear power plant. In L. M. Ward et al. (Eds). The Behavioral Basis of Design: Selected Papers, pp. 180-184. Stroudsburg, VA: Dowden, Hutchinson, and Ross, 1976.

Schuller, C. Richard and others (1975) Citizens' Views about the Proposed Hartsville Nuclear Plant: A Preliminary Report of Potential Social Impacts. ORNL-RUS-3. Oak Ridge, TN: Oak Ridge National Laboratory.

Sundstrom, E., J. W. Lounsbury, C. R. Schuller, J. R. Fowler, and T. J. Mattingly. (1977) Community attitudes toward a nuclear generating facility as a function of expected outcomes. Journal of Social Psychology. (In press).

Webb, E. J. and other (1966) Unobtrusive Measures: Nonreactive Measures in the Social Sciences. Chicago: Rand McNally.

Appendix

Sample Questions from the Survey

16. Now I am going to read you a list of services which are available in most towns and ask you to tell me how satisfied you are with the services presently avaliable in Hartsville. Again, I would like you to pick your responses from this card please.

HAND R CARD 2				CIRCLE RESPONSE	
	(Very Satisfied) VS	(Satisfied) S	(Not Sure) NS	(Unsatisfied) U	(Very Unsatisfied) VU
a. Restaurants.......	VS	S	NS	U	VU
b. Grocery Stores ...	VS	S	NS	U	VU
c. Movie Theaters ...	VS	S	NS	U	VU
d. Variety Stores ...	VS	S	NS	U	VU
e. Police Protection..	VS	S	NS	U	VU
f. Job Opportunities..	VS	S	NS	U	VU
g. Streets/Highways ..	VS	S	NS	U	VU
h. Parks/Playgrounds..	VS	S	NS	U	VU
i. Fire Service	VS	S	NS	U	VU
j. Telephone.......	VS	S	NS	U	VU
k. Medical Care	VS	S	NS	U	VU
l. Sewage	VS	S	NS	U	VU
m. Water Supply	VS	S	NS	U	VU
n. Zoning Laws......	VS	S	NS	U	VU
o. Availability of Housing........	VS	S	NS	U	VU
p. Garbage Disposal ..	VS	S	NS	U	VU
q. School System. ...	VS	S	NS	U	VU

TO INTERVIEWER: RESPONDENT MAY MENTION THAT HE/SHE IS CONCERNED MORE ABOUT GARBAGE DISPOSAL THAN PICK-UP AND THEREFORE GIVE AN UNCLEAR ANSWER. EMPHASIZE THAT YOU WANT AN OVERALL OPINION, BUT NOTE ANY SPECIFIC REFERENCES HE/SHE MAY MAKE.

GIVE RESPONDENT CARD #6

25. Here is a picture of a ladder. Suppose we say that the top of the ladder (pointing) represents the best possible life for you and the botton (pointing) respresents the worst possible life for you.

   a. Where on the ladder (moving finger rapidly up and down ladder) do you think you will be <u>five years from now</u>?

      Step Number_____

   b. Where on the ladder would you say you stood <u>five years ago</u>?

      Step Number_____

   c. And where on the ladder do you feel you personally stand at the <u>present</u> time?

      Step Number_____

10
9
8
7
6
5
4
3
2
1
0

28. If TVA were to build the power plant here in Hartsville, a number of things might change in the community while the plant is being built or after it goes into operation. I am going to give you a list of things that some people have said might happen. I want you to tell me how likely each of these is, picking your response from this card.

| GIVE RESPONDENT CARD #7 | | CIRCLE RESPONSE |

Scale
Very likely (VL)
Likely (L)
Perhaps (P)
Unlikely (UL)
Very Unlikely (VU)

	Very Likely (VL)	Likely (L)	Perhaps (P)	Unlikely (U)	Very Unlikely (VU)
Increased noise	VL	L	P	U	VU
Opportunity to meet new people	VL	L	P	U	VU
Increased business	VL	L	P	U	VU
Water pollution	VL	L	P	U	VU
Community stays pretty much the same	VL	L	P	U	VU
Radiation hazards	VL	L	P	U	VU
Increased crime	VL	L	P	U	VU
Lower taxes	VL	L	P	U	VU
More tourists	VL	L	P	U	VU
Better pay	VL	L	P	U	VU
Air pollution	VL	L	P	U	VU
Cheaper electricity	VL	L	P	U	VU
Dating with workers	VL	L	P	U	VU
Crowding in recreational areas	VL	L	P	U	VU
Industrial development	VL	L	P	U	VU
Traffic congestion	VL	L	P	U	VU
Overcrowding in schools	VL	L	P	U	VU
More public entertainment (bowling alleys, theaters, etc.)	VL	L	P	U	VU
More taverns and bars	VL	L	P	U	VU
Drug problems in the schools	VL	L	P	U	VU
Public recognition of the town	VL	L	P	U	VU
Crowding in shopping area	VL	L	P	U	VU
Accidents or sabotage at the plant	VL	L	P	U	VU
More jobs	VL	L	P	U	VU

HAND LIST 2 TO RESPONDENT. DO NOT GIVE THE RESPONDENT THE SURVEY FORM.

A Strategy for Using Survey Questionnaires in Planning Nonstructural Flood Control Programs

L. Douglas James
Utah State University

Introduction
A wide variety of measures can be used to reduce flood damages, provide water supplies, control water quality, or achieve other water resources management purposes. A measure is classified as structural if it changes the physical system in order to alter the pattern of water flow or as nonstructural if it changes human response in order to increase benefit or reduce harm from a given pattern of flow. A measure is classified as individual if a person can undertake it on his own or as group if collective or governmental action is more appropriate.

This double two-way classification of measures may be illustrated in the alternative approaches to flood control. The major individual nonstructural adjustment is for a property manager to avoid development in or to reduce use of a recognized flood prone area. The major individual structural measure is to flood proof buildings to keep water outside. The widely used group structural measures are to provide storage reservoirs or to enlarge drainageways to contain flood peaks. The principal group nonstructural measures are governmental efforts to induce individuals to respond to flood hazards in a manner that promotes the overall public interest.

Planning a group nonstructural flood control program begins with an analysis based on economic, social well-being, and environmental criteria (Water Resources Council 1973) to determine what use of flood plains by the private sector is in the public interest. Implementation of the selected uses then proceeds not through the direct construction governmental agencies use for structural measures but rather through indirect means to encourage those uses by the private sector. The second step in formulating a nonstructural program is thus to devise a combination of means that will be effective in inducing people to make the selected use of flood plains. This paper presents an approach for performing this second step of devising suitable means at a time when the overall state of the art is still in its infancy.

Flood Control Measures and Implementation Means
The three principal individual flood control measures (other than emergency activity during a flood event) are (1) flood proofing or other modifications to existing buildings to reduce susceptibility to flood damage, (2) design and construction of new buildings in a manner that will minimize susceptibility to flood damage, and (3) land development patterns with less damage-prone property on the flood plain. Seven means that government can use to get individuals to employ these measures are listed with their intended effects and obstacles to their success in Table 1.

TABLE 1. GOVERNMENT MEANS FOR PROMOTING INDIVIDUAL FLOOD CONTROL MEASURES

Means	Intended Effect	Obstacles
1. Disseminate information on flood hazard.	People who know of the hazard will be motivated to employ individual measures, and data on the degree of hazard permits better measure design.	Information not received, not reviewed, or not understood. Understood information used to pursue goals that are not in the public interest.
2. Disseminate information on adverse external or ecological effects of flood plain occupancy.	People who understand these effects will be motivated to avoid actions that cause them. This can complement risk as a reason to avoid flood plain development.	Same as for flood hazard information but greater variation in understanding and goals is likely.
3. Use taxes or other charges to penalize "inappropriate" individual activity.	A more direct financial incentive will induce greater employment of individual measures.	Difficult to set fair rates and to obtain political approval. Places burden on low income groups that cannot afford individual measures.
4. Provide expert advice on the design of individual measures.	People with ready access to information on their range of alternatives and of the details for cost effective designs will select more effective individual measures.	Advised action may be too costly for property manager to implement. People may not understand the technical information or have different goals than the experts providing the advice.
5. Enact and enforce land use and building code regulations.	People will comply with these statutes.	Financial burden for a program of general benefit is concentrated on flood plain property owners. Compliance and enforcement grows lax without a continuing consensus on the wisdom of the regulations.
6. Subsidize financing of individual measures.	People can afford measures that are in the public interest but not economical from their personal viewpoint. Financing is provided for those without cash in hand.	Program is costly to finance. Political approval may be difficult. Public money may be wasted if measures are not maintained. Subsidy may encourage flood plain occupancy.
7. Purchase hazard areas for recreation or natural uses.	Public ownership will eliminate private flood plain development. The land can be used to provide recreation opportunities and preserve valuable natural areas.	Purchase is very costly. Condemnation may be difficult or impossible.

A preliminary judgmental determination of the effectiveness of these means for promoting individual flood control measures is provided in the three classifications of Table 2. In some situations (marked P), some use of the means is considered essential if the measure is to work at all. Other means (marked S) were judged as not essential to getting individuals to use a measure but as capable of adding substantially to its effectiveness. Still other means (marked N) were judged as not applicable for inducing implementation of a given measure. For an elaboration of these judgments see James (1975).

TABLE 2. APPLICABILITY OF AVAILABLE MEANS IN IMPLEMENTING DESIRED MEASURES

	Measures		
	Flood Proofing	Flood Proofed Construction	Land Development
Flood Hazard Information	P	P	P
Ecological Information	N	S	S
Penalties, Taxes, or Charges	S	S	P
Expert Advice	P	P	N
Regulatory Measures	P	P	P
Financial Help	P	S	N
Purchase and Conserve	N	N	S

Notation: P - Some use of the means is essential to success of the measure.
S - Use of the means can substantially add to effectiveness of the measure.
N - Use of the means is not applicable in implementing the measure.

Local Factors Determining Effectiveness of Implementation Means

One would also logically expect a given means to be more effective in inducing a given measure in one local setting than in another. The formulation of an effective group nonstructural flood control program thus requires (1) identification of the important factors for predicting how people in a given setting will respond to the various means, (2) measurement of those factors in that setting, (3) establishment of a relationship between measured factor values and the nature and extent of the response, and (4) use of that relationship to compare and decide among alternative combinations of means. The potentially relevant factors may include physical characteristics of the flood plain, characteristics of the population and decision-making institutions within the total community, and characteristics of individuals who live on the flood plain.

This study began by hypothesizing and examining potentially important factors (James 1974). In the preliminary screening, pilot field data were used to identify factors particularly associated with community and individual response to implementation means, and Table 2 was used to identify means appropriate for promoting given measures (James 1974; James, Benke and Ragsdale 1975). The screening reduced eleven hypothesized physical characteristics to the three listed in Table 3 as the most strongly related to the success of the implementation means essential to getting individuals to employ the measures. Recent flood experiences are a major factor for motivating communities to undertake nonstructural programs and individuals to employ remedial measures (James, Laurent and Hill 1971: 128-31). Easy flood plain identification also enhances layman understanding of and community support for the program. The size and shape of the flood plain are important to recreational and environmental uses.

TABLE 3. LIST OF PHYSICAL FACTORS AFFECTING RESPONSE TO IMPLEMENTATION MEANS

1. Recent flood history
   a. Number of events in which water entered the main floor of at least one building during the last seven years.
   b. Number of years since a flood larger than a 20-year event.

2. Ease of identifying flood prone areas
   a. A distinct break in relief at the edge of the flood plain.
   b. Absence of natural levees along the stream.

3. Size, shape, and location of flood plain areas
   a. Width of flood plain (100-year).
   b. Slope of flood plain land.

The 18 characteristics of the total community hypothesized as potentially important were reduced to the first six shown in Table 4. The 24 hypothesized characteristics of the flood plain occupants were reduced to the six shown on the bottom half of Table 4. For an extended discussion of these variables see James, Laurent and Hill (1971).

Measurement of Factors
If information on the factors listed in Tables 3 and 4 is to be used to formulate a group nonstructural flood control program for a given community, the factors must be defined so that they can be measured. The physical factors are readily measured from streamflow records and topographic maps. The community and individual factors might be estimated by various indirect methods or by various forms of contact with the individuals involved. The method developed here is estimation from questionnaires answered by random samples of community citizens and flood plain occupants respectively.

A questionnaire (see Appendix) was developed for this purpose from analysis of relationships among responses to a much longer questionnaire. The process was one of listing many items thought likely to influence a person's perception of and attitudes toward flood hazard and of items on degree of flood hazard experienced and adjustments to that hazard (James, Laurent and Hill 1971), analyzing the questionnaire responses for perception and attitude items that correlate closely with adjustment method, and grouping items that correlate with a given adjustment but not too highly with one another into scales of factor intensity (James 1974). The questionnaire contains those items needed to scale these factors. Groups of questions are used to scale each item in order to reduce the bias caused as individuals react out of character in responding to particular items and to gauge intensity of feeling through response consistency. Table 4 cumulates scaling for the six community factors and the six factors for flood plain residents.

Relationship Between Factors and Response
Following the reasoning used in forming Table 2, one would also logically expect a given factor to be more helpful in predicting the success of one means than the success of another. Definite determination of how well these factors serve to predict how well a given means will work in a given setting would require data on how individuals represented by known sets of factor scores are responding to means

TABLE 4. FACTORS AFFECTING RESPONSE TO IMPLEMENTATION MEANS

Community Factors	Questions[a]	Total Points[c]
1. Recognition of Flooding as a Community Problem	11,14,15,56(2)	5
2. Environmental Concern within Community	9, (23,28,32,26), (23,24,35, 51(2)	5
3. Community Acceptance of		
Channelization	65(3), 67(3)	6
Land Use Regulation	64(3), 66(3)	6
Reservoirs	61(3), 63(3)	6
Financial Aid to Residents	62(3), 68(3)	6
4. Expertise of Local Government	[b]	3
5. Willingness of Community to Increase Taxes to Help Solve Flood Problems	(20,21,24,27,31,37)(3)	3
6. Propensity to Rely on Government to Solve Flood Problems	15,64(2), 68(2)	5

Flood Plain Resident Factors		
1. Time and Inclination to Individual Action	(49,50), 53, (19,22,26,28,33)(3),60	6
2. Seclusion More Important than Good Access and Low Price as a Reason for Flood Plain Occupancy	(41,44,47)(3), (39,42,46,48)(3)	6
3. Flood Plain Resident Sympathy for		
C Channelization	65(3), 67(3)	6
Land Use Regulation	64(3), 66(3)	6
Reservoirs	61(3), 63(3)	6
Financial Aid to Residents	62(3), 68(3)	6
4. Propensity to Rely on Government to Solve Flood Problems	15,64(2), 68(2)	5
5. Perceived Personal Benefits from a Flood Control Program	15,59A(4), 59B(4)	9
6. Perceived Personal Loss if Denied the Opportunity of Living near the Stream	10(2), 54, (32,38)(3), (41,44)(3)	9

[a]Questions are from appendix. Several numbers in parenthesis indicate questions used as a group. A single number in parenthesis indicates a question contributing more than one point.

[b]Factor not assessed from questionnaire.

[c]Total number of scaled points. Factor scores are divided by this number so that they will read from 0 to 1.

Note: More detailed scaling information is provided in James (1975).

employed in their area. Such data could then be used to structure a model to predict the probability with which a given individual of known factor scores would respond to given means with a given individual measure. The individual predictions could be grouped to predict the distribution of responses over a total population.

A judgmental determination of important factor-means relationships is provided in Table 5. The reasoning used to compile the table can be illustrated by examining the column headed "regulatory Measures." The individual's philosophy on whether it is right for government to tell him how to use his property and his perception that he is indeed suffering significant losses were judged to be the most important determinants (marked D in Table 5) as to whether or not a regulatory program will succeed. If local residents experience no flood damages over long periods of time, both flood plain residents and enforcement officials become lax in respecting the regulations, particularly if the residents have strong convictions that government has no right to be regulating them in the first place.

While hard data are still lacking, Table 5 provides a starting point for assessing the various implementation means. Further study is needed for more precise definition of the important factors, to develop better factor measurement methods, and to develop a better understanding of the relative strength of the various factors in influencing response to the various means.

Case Study Application to Noonday Creek

The physical, community, and individual factors were evaluated as part of planning a flood control program for a portion of the Noonday Creek flood plain, Cobb County, Metropolitan Atlanta, Georgia. The selected portion includes 2.74 stream miles and approximately 300 acres in the 100-year flood plain. The flood prone area is coming under development pressures, being largely surrounded by single family, middle class housing. The hazard area itself is still largely undeveloped even though some homes have been built on its fringes. The 100-year flood peak from the 26.3-square mile drainage area is about 5400 cfs. As to the three physical factors,

1. a. No flood waters have entered buildings in the last seven years.
   b. Eleven years have passed since the last 20-year flood.
2. a. No break in relief occurs at the flood plain fringes.
   b. There are no natural levees.
3. a. The 900-foot wide flood plain is large for such a small stream.
   b. The flood plain is very flat with an average slope of 0.0005.

While the recommended practice is for the community factors to be evaluated for the specific local political jurisdiction responsible for the area, the time and cost limitations for this study dictated scaling the community factors from responses to a questionnaire previously distributed throughout Metropolitan Atlanta (James 1974), and Cobb County is considered reasonably representative of the larger area. Average values for each factor for the community are in Table 6.

The Noonday flood plain occupants were surveyed by leaving questionnaires and stamped, self-addressed envelopes at their homes and later phoning to request cooperation through filling it out. Scores for each of the six factors for flood plain residents were calculated from each response, and the averages and standard deviations are reported in Table 7.

TABLE 5. APPLICABILITY OF PHYSICAL, COMMUNITY, AND INDIVIDUAL FACTORS TO PREDICTING RESPONSE TO IMPLEMENTATION MEANS

	Implementation Means						
	Flood Hazard Information	Ecological Information	Penalties, Taxes, or Charges	Expert Advice	Regulatory Measures	Financial Help	Purchase and Conserve
Physical Factors							
Recent flood history	M	-	S	M	M	S	M
Ease of identification	S	-	D	S	-	D	-
Size and shape							D
Community Factors							
Recognition of flood problem	D	-	-	D	S	M	S
Environmental concern	-	M	-	-	S	-	D
Acceptance of means	-	M	D	-	M	S	-
Local expertise	-	-	M	D	-	-	-
Willingness to tax	-	-	-	M	-	D	M
Philosophy on responsibility	-	-	-	S	S	S	-
Individual Factors							
Inclination toward individual action	D	-	M	D	-	D	-
Seclusion v. access	-	S	-	S	M	-	D
Sympathy for program	-	-	M	-	M	M	-
Philosophy on responsibility	-	-	D	-	D	-	-
Personal benefits	D	-	-	D	-	S	-
Personal losses	-	-	M	-	D	-	D

Notation: D - Factor is likely to be a determining influence on whether the means will succeed.
M - Factor is likely to be a major influence on how well the means will succeed.
S - Factor is expected to have a significant influence on how well the means will succeed.
- - Factor is not expected to have a significant influence on the success of the means.

TABLE 6. ESTIMATED VALUES OF COMMUNITY FACTORS FOR RESIDENTS
OF THE METROPOLITAN ATLANTA COMMUNITY

No.	Factor	Direction	Value
1	Recognition of flooding	Toward increasing recognition	.12
2	Environmental concern	Toward increasing concern	.43
3a	Acceptance of channelization	Toward favoring measure	.56
3b	Acceptance of land use regulation	Toward favoring measure	.66
3c	Acceptance of financial aid	Toward favoring measure	.44
4	Expertise of local government	Toward greater expertise	n.a.
5	Willingness to tax	Toward greater willingness	.45
6	Public v. private responsibility	Toward greater public responsibility	.55

Source: 111 returns from 300 questionnaires mailed to occupants of single family residents living inside the Atlanta perimeter highway.

TABLE 7. ESTIMATED VALUES OF FLOOD PLAIN RESIDENT FACTORS FOR
RESIDENTS OF THE NOONDAY CREEK FLOOD PLAIN

No.	Factor	Direction	Noonday Ck. m	s
1	Time and inclination	Greater inclination	0.43	0.15
2	Faith in ability	Greater confidence	0.60	0.20
3	Seclusion v. access	More seclusion	0.53	0.15
4a	Sympathy for channelization	Favoring measure	0.57	0.19
4b	Sympathy for land use regulation	Favoring measure	0.86	0.16
4c	Sympathy for financial aid	Favoring measure	0.59	0.28
5	Willingness to conform	More willing	0.95	0.10
6	Public v. private	Greater public	0.68	0.07
7	Personal benefits	Greater benefits	0.13	0.18
8	Personal losses	Streamside advantage	0.70	0.09

Sources: 20 returns from 75 questionnaires left at homes of occupants of identified 100-year flood plain.

Note: Means and standard deviations are normalized to convert from scales reading from 0 to varying maximum values to scales reading from 0 to 1.

An economic analysis of the situation estimated that flood damages would average about $45,000 annually over the next 10 years and that the greatest net benefit from a remedial program would be to flood proof buildings to the 100-year flood elevation (James, Benke and Ragsdale 1975). A second analysis examined preserving the 10-year flood plain in an undeveloped state as an alternative and found the average annual cost to be only $1600 higher. The flooding outside the 10-year flood plain is too shallow to justify development restrictions on economic grounds.

These two approaches were then compared in terms of ease of implementation as suggested by the survey results. The first program consists primarily of flood proofing future construction in the 100-year flood plain. Table 2 shows the three means (marked P) that a local government must implement in order to achieve flood proof construction. Table 5 then lists the factors important in assessing the likely success of these means.

Table 5 shows that the success of a program of disseminating flood hazard information in reducing damages requires that the people of the community be sufficiently convinced that they have a real problem for their leadership to commit the necessary resources and that the people responsible for flood plain property perceive that they will benefit from flood proofing and be inclined to make a personal effort to do so. For the community factor, Table 6 has the relatively low value of 0.12 for recognition of flooding as a problem by community residents. While this suggests greater difficulty in getting local government to adopt and provide continuing support to flood control programs than one would expect with a higher value, the level of recognition required for any given level of community effort is not known. Therefore, the following discussion can suggest trends but not come to firm conclusions. For the two primary individual factors, Table 7 shows a low level of inclination toward individual measures and a very low perception of personal benefits on the part of people now living on the Noonday flood plain.

With respect to providing expert advice, Table 5 indicates all of the requirements for a successful program to be the same as for flood hazard information dissemination. Also required is the expertise for doing so on the part of local government, and Cobb County officials have not had much experience with flood proofing.

Finally with respect to enacting flood proofing into building codes, Table 5 shows the primary factors to be the philosophy toward such regulation on the part of flood plain residents and the personal hardship those residents expect to result from compliance. Table 7 shows an acceptance of the principle of regulation on the part of Noonday flood plain residents but also a strong sense of personal hardship should they be denied use of their flood plain property. Overall, the indicators of response to the necessary implementation means are unfavorable omens for the success of a program to flood proof new construction.

For getting individuals to flood proof homes already constructed in the hazard area, Table 2 suggests the same three means plus financial help to the homeowners. Table 6 shows financial aid to meet with greater opposition within the community than does any other measure studied. Again the social data are unfavorable for a dependable flood proofing program.

The second possibility is to adjust land use as a flood control measure. Table 2 shows the primary implementation means to be providing hazard information, penalizing nonconforming land uses, and adopting land use regulations. Providing hazard information was reviewd above. With respect to penalties, Table 5 indicates the determining factors as physical ease of identification of the hazard area, acceptance of the means by the community, and the philosophy toward such regulation on the part of the flood plain residents. The second physical factor makes the Noonday flood plain rather hard for the public to identify. Table 6 shows land use regulation to be the best accepted flood control measure by the community, and Table 7 indicates acceptance of regulation in principle by flood plain residents. The perceived personal hardship of not being allowed to live in the flood plain is a negative factor, but its impact is mitigated by the fact that most respondents live in the fringes of the flood plain that would not be affected by the land use restrictions. Overall, the results are more favorable for land use adjustment than for flood proofing.

In summary, most of the flood control benefits can be achieved by preventing further urban development in the flood plain. Some additional net benefits can be achieved by flood proofing existing structures. While the survey results suggest that flood proofing probably will not be effectively used by flood plain residents as a whole, a number of individual residents may be able and willing to use effective flood proofing measures.

Summary

If a local government is to have an effective nonstructural flood control program, the people of the community must recognize the problem to the degree required to support effective implementation means. The people who manage flood plain property and who will thus have to implement the individual measures must recognize that they have a problem, be amenable to becoming active in solving it, and be sympathetic to the solutions proposed by the community. This paper presents a questionnaire and a set of tables for using responses to that questionnaire to scale factor scores that provide the required information about community and flood plain residents. At the present state of the art, the items combined in scaling a given factor, the list of factors used, the relationship between factor values and the responses to a given means, and the expected effectiveness of the means in inducing a desired individual measure are all poorly defined. Much more work is needed to strengthen the overall methodology by collecting and evaluating experience data and modifying the approach as needed.

Acknowledgments

The work on which this paper is based was supported as Project No. B-082-GA by the Environmental Resources Center of the Georgia Institute of Technology and by the office of Water Research and Technology of the U. S. Department of the Interior as authorized under the Water Resources Research Act of 1964 (P.L. 88-379).

References

James, L. D., E. A. Laurent and D. W. Hill (1971) The Flood Plain as a Residential Choice: Resident Attitudes and Perceptions and Their Implications to Flood Plain Management Policy. Environmental Resources Center Report No. ERC-0671. Atlanta: Georgia Institute of Technology.

James, L. D. (1973) "Surveys Required to Design Nonstructural Measures," Journal of the Hydraulics Division, ASCE, 99, HY10, 1823-,836.

James, L. D. (1974) The Use of Questionnaires in Collecting Information for Urban Flood Control Planning. Environmental Resources Center Report No. ERC-0274. Atlanta: Georgia Institute of Technology.

James, L. D., A. C. Benke and H. L. Ragsdale (1975) Integration of Hydrologic, Economic, Ecologic, Social, and Well-Being Factors in Planning Flood Control Measures for Urban Streams. Environmental Resources Center Report No. ERC-0375. Atlanta: Georgia Institute of Technology.

James, L. D. (1975) "Formulation of Nonstructural Flood Control Programs," Water Resources Bulletin, 11, 4 (August), 688-705.

U. S. Water Resources Council (1973) "Water Related Land Resources: Establishment of Principles and Standards for Planning," September 10, 38, 174, Part III, Federal Register, 24778-24869.

APPENDIX

WE ARE INTERESTED IN WHAT THE PEOPLE IN THE ATLANTA AREA THINK ABOUT CERTAIN PUBLIC MATTERS. THE INFORMATION YOU GIVE US WILL BE COMPLETELY CONFIDENTIAL. WE WILL BE COLLECTING INFORMATION FROM SEVERAL HUNDRED PEOPLE AND THERE IS NO WAY FOR US TO IDENTIFY YOUR REPLY FROM THE RETURN ENVELOPE.

A. GENERAL INFORMATION.

1. Sex: _____ Male _____ Female
2. How long have you lived at this location? _____ years
3. How old is your residence? _____ years
4. In what category does your age fit?
   a) _____ under 21   d) _____ 45–54
   b) _____ 22–34   e) _____ 55–64
   c) _____ 35–44   f) _____ over 65
5. Please circle the highest grade of school you completed.
   a) Grades: 1, 2, 3, 4, 5, 6, 7, 8, 9, 10, 11, 12
   b) Business or Trade School: 1, 2, 3, 4
   c) College: 1, 2, 3, 4
   d) Graduate School: 1, 2, 3, 4
6. Race: _____ White _____ Black _____ Other
7. In your family or living group,
   a) _____ every adult has his own car.
   b) _____ at least one adult has his own car.
   c) _____ no one owns a car.
8. How interested are you in politics?
   a) _____ very much   c) _____ only slightly
   b) _____ somewhat   d) _____ not at all
9. To which of the following types of organizations do you belong?
   a) Fraternal (Elks, Eastern Star, etc.) _____ belong
   b) Professional (Occupational societies, unions) _____ belong
   c) Civic or Service (Lions, Neighborhood Club, etc.) _____ belong
   d) Conservation (Georgia Conservancy, etc.) _____ belong
10. In general, how do you feel about living conditions in your neighborhood? Would you say that it is:
    a) _____ an excellent place to live
    b) _____ a fairly good place to live
    c) _____ a poor place to live
    d) _____ a very bad place to live
11. What do you consider the most serious problem in your neighborhood?
    a) ____ schools   c) ____ play areas   e) ____ traffic
    b) ____ crime   d) ____ flooding   f) ____ other
12. With respect to neighborhood problems, have you ever:
    a) _____ signed a petition
    b) _____ talked to local officials
    c) _____ done neither
13. Which did you do first?
    a) _____ signed a petition
    b) _____ talked to local officials
    c) _____ did neither
14. Have you attended any meetings to discuss important problems facing this area of town and neighborhood?
    _____ yes   _____ no
    If so, list the major problems discussed at these meetings:
    _____
    _____
    _____
15. With respect to which problems did you sign a petition or talk to local officials (you may check more than one)?
    a) _____ schools   d) _____ flooding
    b) _____ crime   e) _____ traffic
    c) _____ play areas   f) _____ other _____
16. If you signed a petition or talked to local officials concerning one of the above problems, were you happy with the actions they took?
    _____ yes   _____ no
    Briefly explain your feelings on the official actions: _____
    _____
    _____
    _____
    _____
17. If you were to take a neighborhood problem to a county official, would you expect him to be most likely to:
    a) _____ Understand your problem and to do what he could.
    b) _____ Listen to your problem but avoid doing anything.
    c) _____ Ignore you or dismiss you as soon as he could.

B. THE FOLLOWING STATEMENTS HAVE BEEN GIVEN TO LARGE NUMBERS OF PEOPLE THROUGHOUT THE COUNTRY. THESE ARE ALL MATTERS OF OPINION: THERE ARE NO RIGHT OR WRONG ANSWERS. PLEASE INDICATE THE EXTENT TO WHICH YOU AGREE OR DISAGREE WITH EACH STATEMENT PLEASE GIVE YOUR OPINION ON EVERY STATEMENT. DO NOT WORRY LONG OVER AN INDIVIDUAL QUESTION AS IT IS YOUR FIRST IMPRESSION, YOUR IMMEDIATE "FEELINGS" ABOUT THE STATEMENT THAT WE ARE AFTER. PLEASE MARK THE STATEMENTS AS FOLLOWS: PLACE 1 BY THE STATEMENT IF YOU AGREE STRONGLY WITH IT; 2 IF YOU AGREE SOMEWHAT; 3 IF YOU DISAGREE SOMEWHAT; AND 4 IF YOU DISAGREE STRONGLY.

18. If a person doesn't care how an election comes out, he shouldn't vote on it. _____
19. If you think about too many facts when making up your mind about things, you get lost. _____
20. It is wrong for any government to tax more in order to provide more services than it now provides. _____
21. In the future, necessary increases in government expenses must be met by doing something else than increasing taxes. _____
22. People who take too many risks lose out in the long run. _____
23. It is the people who should do something about water problems. _____

24. We should try every other possible means of paying the government's bills before we consider raising taxes. _____

25. There is nothing to be gained by political activity. _____

26. It is very difficult to have a very firm opinion about such things as government, freedom, and the general welfare. _____

27. The solution to most social problems will be achieved when taxes go down. _____

28. Nature has a way to solve water problems before they get serious. _____

29. To discuss and try to change opinions that one has is not quite to my liking. _____

30. A good many elections aren't important enough to bother with. _____

31. There is something wrong with a government that cannot keep its budget balanced. _____

32. It is real important to me to have a stream or lake near where I live. _____

33. There wouldn't be many problems if we would just stick to our principles and quit getting things confused with so many facts. _____

34. It isn't so important to vote when you know your party doesn't have any chance to win. _____

35. The air should not be polluted. _____

36. Mankind has a right to free and unlimited use of water. _____

37. Raising taxes is almost always unnecessary. _____

38. The natural environment around your home has not been adequately preserved. _____

C. IF FOR SOME REASON YOU WERE TO BEGIN LOOKING FOR ANOTHER PLACE TO LIVE IN THE ATLANTA AREA, HOW IMPORTANT OR UNIMPORTANT WOULD THE FOLLOWING ITEMS BE IN MAKING YOUR CHOICE? PLACE 1 BY THE ITEM IF IT IS NOT IMPORTANT AT ALL; 2 IF IT IS SOMEWHAT UNIMPORTANT; 3 IF IT IS SOMEWHAT IMPORTANT; AND 4 IF IT IS VERY IMPORTANT.

39. Close to work. _____
40. Nice neighbors. _____
41. Natural woodsy area. _____
42. Low price. _____
43. Prestige Neighborhood. _____
44. Lots of space in yard or lot. _____
45. Nice appearing building or home. _____
46. Close to schools. _____
47. Secluded and private. _____
48. Close to shopping. _____

D. NATURAL HAZARD EXPERIENCES AND OPINIONS.

49. Are you scared or frightened of earthquakes?
    a) _____ a lot   b) _____ some   c) _____ none

50. Are you scared or frightened of floods?
    a) _____ a lot   b) _____ some   c) _____ none

51. Are you scared or frightened of pollution?
    a) _____ a lot   b) _____ some   c) _____ none

52. Had you ever had any experience with floods before moving into your present home?
    a) _____ yes   b) _____ no

53. Did you know about flooding or drainage problems in this area when you decided to move here?
    a) _____ yes   b) _____ no

54. Knowing what you know now, would you move here again if you had it to do over again?
    a) _____ yes   b) _____ no

55. Suppose that flooding became more severe around here in the coming years. In your opinion, would the principal cause be more rainfall than there had been in the past?
    a) _____ yes   b) _____ no

56. Has there been any flooding in this neighborhood while you have been living here?
    a) _____ yes   b) _____ no
    (If you answer no, skip to question 60)

57. How did you find out about flooding in this area?
    a) ___ real estate agent   c) ___ personal inspection of property
    b) ___ neighbors   d) ___ other _____

58. Did this information about flooding bother you any?
    a) ____ a lot   b) ____ some   c) ____ a little   d) ____ none

59. If your home or yard has been damaged by flooding or poor drainage:
    A. Has the damage been
       a) _____ very serious   c) _____ moderate
       b) _____ serious   d) _____ slight
    B. Has the water been (you may check more than one):
       a) _____ in the yard   b) _____ in the basement
                                    c) _____ on the main floor of the house

60. Have you spent any of your own money to protect your home or other property from future flood damage?
    a) _____ yes   b) _____ no

E. HOW DO YOU FEEL ABOUT EACH OF THESE POSSIBLE ACTIONS WITH RESPECT TO CREEKS IN YOUR NEIGHBORHOOD. MARK THE ACTION WITH 1 IF YOU STRONGLY FAVOR IT; 2 IF YOU FAVOR IT SOMEWHAT; 3 IF YOU OPPOSE IT SOMEWHAT; AND 4 IF YOU OPPOSE IT STRONGLY.

61. Build upstream surface reservoirs which could be used to retain excess water when flooding threatened. _____

62. People who live in flood prone areas should pay whatever costs are required to solve their problems. _____

63. Preserve free flowing character of local streams. _____

64. Have the local governments regulate upstream tributary land use to reduce effects on flooding of future developments. _____

65. Deepen, widen, or line the creek channel. _____

66. Permit upstream development to take place even though it may aggravate downstream flooding. _____

67. Leave the creek channels as they are. _____

68. Have the government provide financial aid to relocate families in flooded areas. _____

The Use of Mini Surveys in Social Impact Assessments

Kurt Finsterbusch
University of Maryland

Mini surveys (sample sizes from 20 to 80) are ideally suited to the needs of social impact assessment (SIA). They are inexpensive, quick, easy to conduct and often enormously informative. They can not produce a high degree of certainty, however. But SIAs have different data requirements than research articles for the social science community. The latter generally use precise and abundant original data on a narrow field of investigation. SIAs use all available or easily produced data on a wide range of impacts. They seek to provide information for choosing between policy alternatives, while basic research aims at greater scientific precision. Mini surveys may be sufficient for deciding between policy alternatives, even though high levels of certainty are not obtained.

Most social scientists would feel uncomfortable using surveys on small samples. It goes against their methodological training, which is oriented to establishing certainty of findings. Among social scientists, only psychoanalysts and clinical psychologists commonly report on findings drawn from small samples. In-depth interviews with a score of subjects are the basis for many of their generalizations. Some fields of investigation outside of the social sciences also do not have biases against studies involving 20 to 80 cases. Medical research reports cover a range from thousands of cases to just a few, for example.

Unlike social scientists, sponsors of social impact assessments tend to discount large-scale sample surveys. Their argument generally is a simple cost-benefit one. According to this view, large-scale surveys are very costly compared to other data generating techniques and their results are of questionable utility, especially in estimating potential impacts. But surveys provide important information which cannot be obtained through any other means, and should be used in most SIAs. The survey sample may have to be small to keep costs low. These mini surveys will be less conclusive than large sample surveys, but for the purposes of many SIAs their accuracy may be sufficient. The accuracy (narrowness of the confidence band) of surveys increases at a lesser rate than the cost of increasing sample size. In our judgment, mini surveys are highly cost-effective.

It should be noted that the mini survey is more useful for generating descriptive information than for analyzing relationships between variables. The small sample prevents complex multivariate analysis, but it is adequate for rough estimations of univariate distributions and some simple two-variable relationships. SIAs depend mainly on univariate distributions and, therefore, have much to gain from mini surveys.

In this paper we propose four uses of mini surveys in SIAs: estimating parameters, correcting expert opinions, applying previous findings and performing stepwise analyses. Large sample surveys can be used in these four ways but mini surveys may be sufficient as well as efficient.

1. _Parameter Estimation_

Since parameter estimation involves univariate distributions, small samples often can provide enough precision for decision making purposes. In general, most people's minds are not trained to handle precise percentages. One tends to understand 27% to mean a substantial minority and 31% to mean the same thing (unless the two numbers are being compared. Under 11% means very few, 41-59% means about half, 60-89% means a substantial majority, and 90% and over means almost all. The cutting points for these categories vary from person to person and from subject to subject; we do not tend to think in terms of precise percentages. This is especially true of categories which are important to policy decisions. Here mini surveys may provide information sufficiently accurate for policy decision purposes.

The use of small rather than large samples requires a new style of reporting results. Normally findings are indicated by point estimates, but with mini surveys they should be presented in terms of confidence intervals because those give the most accurate picture of the kind of knowledge being produced. With small samples one has little confidence in point estimates but great confidence that the population parameter lies within the identified confidence interval. Figure 1 presents the 95 percent confidence bands for proportions for various sample sizes. As the sample size gets smaller, the confidence bands get larger. As the confidence band gets larger, the point estimate becomes less important and the confidence interval becomes more important to the interpretation of the results and, therefore, should be the finding reported. Notice the great difference between the confidence intervals for samples of 8 and 40, but the small difference between the confidence intervals for samples of 40 and 100 and for samples of 100 and 1000. If the sample proportion is .5 for a sample of 40, one can be 95 percent confident that the population proportion is between .34 and .66. While this is disturbingly large, increasing the sample to 100 only narrows the confidence band to between .40 and .60. An additional 900 respondents would only narrow the confidence band to between .47 and .53. Obviously, there is declining marginal utility of additions to the sample size. This principle lies behind the cost-effectiveness of mini surveys in SIA.

It is important to remember that the accuracy (represented by the width of the confidence interval) of the point estimate is only one source of uncertainty in the survey results. The degree to which verbal responses to questions truly reflect attitudes, identify impacts, accurately report past actions and indicate future actions is uncertain to an unknown degree. Reliability is additionally jeopardized when potential policies are being evaluated, because the respondents must answer questions dealing with hypothetical future situations. In the light of these uncertainties, it is incongruous to achieve a high level of certainty about the accuracy of point estimates. Only when the meaning of the point estimate is fairly certain does accuracy become very important. The mini survey usually generates information of a quality that is appropriate to the SIA study situation.

Some have concluded on the basis of such considerations as these that surveys are of little value in most SIAs. Their alternative is to rely on experts' opinions, a very questionable procedure when hypothesizing about people's attitudes and actions. Often the best solution is to combine both methods using Bayesian statistics as described below.

2. _Modifying Expert Opinions with Mini Surveys_

Experts are often called upon to predict what people in specified situations

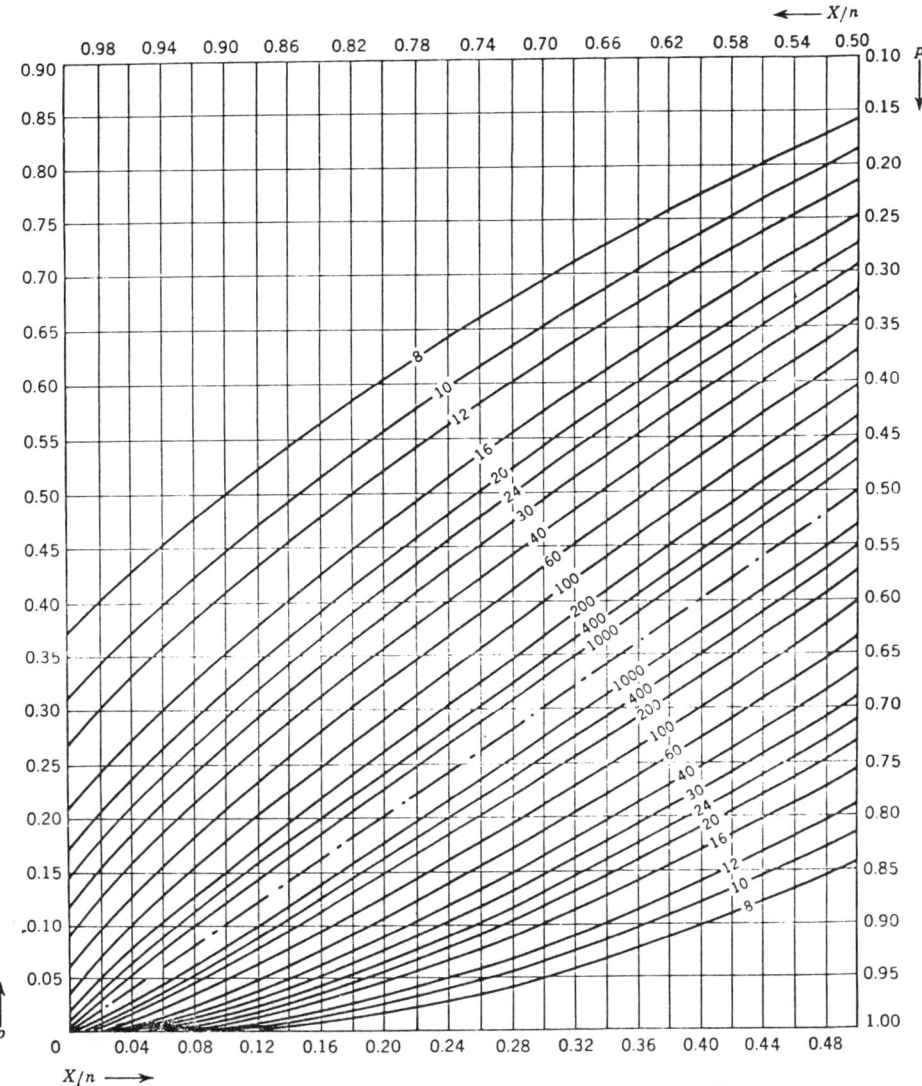

Figure 1. Ninety-five Percent Confidence Bands for Proportions of Various Sample Sizes. The numbers printed along the curves indicate the sample size n. If for a given value of the abscissa X/n, p_A and p_B are the ordinates read from (or interpolated between) the appropriate lower and upper curves, and $\Pr(p_A \leq p \leq p_B) \leq 1 - 2\alpha$.

Source: E. S. Pearson and H. O. Hartley, Biometrika Tables for Statisticians, Vol. 1. Cambridge: Cambridge University Press, 1966.

are likely to do. Their expertise may be based on familiarity with many of the people involved or on general knowledge of the outcome of similar situations. The experts' predictions will appear to be very reasonable, but frequently they are wide of the mark. Every effort should be made therefore to arrive at comparable predictions by alternative methods. Confidence in predictions increases when several methods produce similar results, and this is where mini surveys can play a useful role. People should be asked how they will react and what they will do. Their answers should not be accepted as completely reliable, but neither should they be ignored. When a full-scale survey is out of the question a mini survey should be used to check, correct, and modify the experts' opinions.

The practice of using mini surveys in conjunction with the use of experts is at a very early stage of development and no single procedure has been demonstrated as superior. We will suggest a number of options for combining the two types of information. The survey results, it should be remembered, are in the range of .95 confidence intervals.

The first, and the simplist, way to combine the mini survey with experts' opinions is to give the survey results to the experts to take into account in making their estimates. The main difficulty with this procedure is the generally faulty assumption that the experts know how to evaluate the reliability and statistical significance of the survey results. We have seen some experts "not care what the survey says" and others be intimidated by the survey results. Usually the former had a well-defined opinion prior to the survey results and the latter were more uncertain in their opinions. Social scientists are masters at constructing sensible explanations for survey results, no matter how they turn out. For this reason it is important to have the experts **give their predictions before seeing** the survey results.

The second and most complex method for combining the mini survey with experts' opinions is by means of Bayesian statistics.[1] The experts' opinions constitute the prior probabilities and the mini survey provides the data whose likelihood is computed, given those opinions. The Bayesian formula then computes posterior probabilities which take into account both the experts' opinions and the mini survey results. In the process the analyst must choose a precedure for weighting the two types of information and all of the possible procedures contain an element of arbitrariness.

The third method for combining experts' opinion and mini surveys is by making the former equivalent to a survey. The experts' opinions must be collected into a single estimate and stated in terms of a .95 confidence interval; i.e., the experts determine the confidence interval in which they have .95 confidence. The result is then treated the same as a survey having the same confidence interval and combined with the mini survey using normal statistical procedures (Finsterbusch 1975: Appendix B).

3. <u>The Application of Previous Findings</u>
When reliable methods of observation are utilized research knowledge should cumulate, reducing the need for primary data collection in each new research

---

1. For a fuller treatment see Finsterbusch (1976).

situation. At the moment too little effort is devoted to synthesizing and codifying SIAs, so that the research literature is disorganized and inconvenient to use. We foresee the day, however, when frequently repeated policy actions (e.g., the construction of highways, resevoirs, industrial plants, power plants, urban renewal and residential developments) are predictably related to a standard cycle of population, housing, employment and transportation changes and higher-order consequences. In each new study the standard pattern of changes can routinely be used as the analyst's initial hypotheses. The research effort can then concentrate on predicting how the new situation will differ from the standard pattern, and this is an ideal role for the mini survey.

Many aspects of SIAs need not start from zero but can capitalize on previous research. As discussed above if the policy action is a frequently repeated event most of its consequences can be anticipated on the basis of an analytical review of previous cases. Even relatively unique events like building a submarine base can have standard effects like residential displacements for which a literature exists.

If substantial knowledge has cumulated on a frequent policy and its impacts, one may be tempted to forego additional research altogether. This is inadviseable however since every case is somewhat unique, and general findings must be fitted to the specifics of the case. The mini survey can quickly determine some of the unique social features of the situation and thereby guide the application of previous findings to the specific case.

An example of highway impacts can illustrate this use of mini surveys. Previous research indicates that the net economic impacts on households displaced by highways is slightly positive, due to the policy of additive payments which enable occupants of substandard housing to move into standard housing, and renters to become owners, and owners to obtain comparable housing. The mini survey can determine whether people understand the additive payment policy, the percent who will take advantage of it, and how they will use it.

More importantly, previous research indicates that most people prefer not being displaced even if they can slightly upgrade their housing in the process. Displacement ruptures close social ties and severs people from their familiar surroundings. For some people the change is traumatic and their grief for the old home, surroundings and social ties can last several years. The depth of sorrow is related to age, length of tenure, stability of the neighborhood, minority status, etc. There are situations, however, where a good number of people want to move-- some want to move to a better neighborhood and some want to move away from a neighborhood which has changed character in ways which do not suit them. A mini survey would find out much about the extent of the social and psychological hardships that displacement would cause along alternative highway routes. Much of the story can be told from the literature on displacement, but on-site interviewing is necessary for an accurate understanding of the impacts of displacement in the specific situation.

4. <u>The Use of Mini Surveys in Stepwise Analyses</u>

A unique feature of mini surveys is their adaptibility to a dynamic research procedure. Full scale surveys are generally one-shot affairs that involve a linear research design, as follows:

1. Define problem and develop hypotheses.
2. Specify indicators and construct the survey instrument.
3. Pretest to make sure the questions "work."
4. Interview
5. Code, keypunch, and create data files.
6. Compute parameters and analyze data.
7. Report results.

Panel and trend analyses study change through time by comparing two or more time-ordered cross-sections of the target population. Generally, the later wave of interviews is largely determined in the original research design. The panel or trend studies may be more elaborate than single surveys but they are generally designed in the same linear mode; findings from the first wave are often not used for raising new hypotheses and redesigning the questionnaire to pursue new leads and areas of interest.

We are proposing a dynamic mode of survey analysis which utilizes the first wave findings in the design of the second wave interview instrument. For example, instead of a one-shot survey of 120 respondents with subsequent analysis, we recommend interviewing thirty respondents, analyzing the responses, redesigning the questionnaire to follow new leads (continuing useful questions throughout all waves), interviewing another thirty respondents, analyzing the responses, redesigning the questionnaire, etc. until four waves of thirty interviews are completed and analyzed. The basic idea is to dynamically integrate field work, questionnaire construction, and analysis. In this manner learning and feedback can occur throughout the study. Blind alleys are discovered and dropped early and profitable avenues are vigorously pursued. One should not have to write an add-on proposal to find out what could have been learned initially had a dynamic mode of survey analysis been used.

Summary and Conclusion

This article has identified four important uses for mini surveys in SIAs. First, mini surveys can estimate population parameters within broad confidence intervals. Mini surveys are less precise in measuring parameters than full-scale surveys but they often are adequate for policy making purposes. Second, mini surveys can be used to corroborate or modify the opinions of experts which play a large role in many SIAs. Third, mini surveys can provide valuable information on the social characteristics of the impacted population and determine the applicability of previous research findings to the subject situation. Finally, mini surveys can be used in a dynamic research mode well adapted to the needs of SIAs. We are not advocating the substitution of mini surveys for full-scale surveys. We are advocating several uses of mini surveys when full-scale surveys are prohibited by considerations of time and cost.

References

Finsterbusch, Kurt (1976) "The Mini Survey: An Underemployed Research Tool," Social Science Research, Vol. 5, (March), pp. 81-93.

Finsterbusch, Kurt (1975) A Methodology for Analyzing Analysis of Social Impacts of Public Policies. Vienna, VA: BDM Corporation.

Methodologies for Assessing the Social Impact of Projects Necessitating Forced Relocation of Rural People

Ted L. Napier
Ohio State University

Social scientists in recent years have been seeking new methodologies which will hopefully provide a relatively easy means of assessing the social impact of planned socioenvironmental change. While the development of new research techniques is a highly desirable goal and should be encouraged, the problem of social impact assessment is not so much a lack of appropriate methodologies as it is the use made for evaluative purposes of existing methodologies. As Heberlein (1973) observes, social scientists could play a much more useful role in policy making if the research methodologies employed were more closely aligned to the general methodological norms of social research. The major purpose of this paper is to discuss some of the methodological techniques which I have used in social impact evaluation studies conducted in rural areas. A brief example of research using the techniques discussed is offered to demonstrate how a quasi-experimental design may be applied to social impact assessment.

RESEARCH DESIGNS

The existing social impact literature clearly shows that cross-sectional designs using single case study groups are still prevalent in impact evaluation research. If the goal of an assessment is to measure the social impact of a development stimulus, isolating that effect from the influence of extraneous forces within and outside the community is of major concern. A single case study taken at one point in time does little to isolate the development impact. The apparent community response may be due to forces long in existence before the development stimulus was introduced. Moreover, to evaluate the social impact of planned development, or any other type of change for that matter, there must be a basis for controlled comparison.

Longitudinal and quasi-experimental research designs meet these conditions for evaluating social impacts. One type of longitudinal design involves repeated observations on a panel of respondents (Napier and Wharton 1974). Certain development projects do not lend themselves to the panel approach, however. In the case of a major reservoir project, for example, many long-term residents may elect to sever relationships with the affected group and move away. Moreover, in-migrants during and after the construction stages of the project form part of the reconstituted interaction framework of the group (Munch and Campbell 1963). In situations where panel design may not be sensitive to real changes taking place, periodic sample surveys may be conducted and the data sets compared between the various time periods (Napier and Wright 1975).

Attitudinal Studies

An area of significant research emphasis in recent years has been attitudinal studies (Yoesting and Burkhead 1971; Napier 1971; Napier and Wright 1975; Burdge and Ludtke 1970; Wilkinson 1966; Peterson and Ross 1971; Dasgupta 1967) of socio-environment development. The first step in attitude scale construction should be the development of a mini-theory relative to each scale, from which concepts may be derived to form the construct being measured. Scale items may then be formulated from the concepts used within the mini-theory to develop a tentative attitude scale. Once the scale items for each variable to be measured have been constructed, the tentative scales should be submitted to a group of "experts" who are knowledgeable about the phenomena under investigation. Their role is to review the scale items for relevance, wording, response set (patterned responses) and ease of understanding.

The next step is to pretest the scales using a group with characteristics similar to the universe to be sampled. While a pretest is expensive and time-consuming, the additional effort is easily justified if analysis of pretest data should indicate that the measurement instruments are defective. New scales could then be constructed before the final data collection. Extensive statistical analysis of the pretest data is necessary to determine the reliability of the scales. Either item or factor analysis is appropriate for evaluating the constructed scales. Items that are shown to be uncorrelated with other items may be removed from the scale thus reducing the length of the questionnaire and increasing the likelihood of response. Once the scales have been reformulated and administered, the data generated from the sample should be subjected to the same statistical procedures (item or factor analysis) to further test reliability. The final step in the process is the determination of factor scores (Nie and others 1975: 487-490), summing the individual scale items to produce scale scores for each respondent. The resulting data set may then be used for various types of data analysis--multiple correlation and regression analysis, analysis of variance and so forth.

Factor Analysis

While I have relied heavily upon item analysis in the past, data from a recent study have been analyzed with factor analysis and the resultant factors have been shown to explain a large portion of the variance within the data set. Yoesting and Burkhead (1971) effectively used factor analysis in a study oriented toward recreation and pollution in Iowa. While their items did not load very well together and the variance explained was small, subsequent research has shown this technique to have considerable potential for index construction.

Factor analysis should provide social impact assessors with an excellent tool for reducing the number of variables with which we must work. The resultant factor scores may be computed for each respondent and treated as observations. The individual observations may then be used as independent or dependent variables for other statistical purposes. A most promising methodology for social impact studies is the combined use of factor analysis and path analysis (an extension of regression analysis). By this means several variables (25 for example) may be reduced to a very few (5 for example) and the resultant index scores used to build path models, assuming the factors are theoretically cogent and the amount of variance explained by the factors in the total data set is high.

Problems of Sampling in Rural Areas

A major problem for social impact assessors, especially for those interested in evaluating social impact in non-metropolitan communities, is drawing a representative sample from a rural population. Determining community interaction boundaries (Munch and Campbell 1963) in order to establish the sampling universe can be assisted by the use of local informants. In several of my studies, local people were able to demarcate the boundaries very clearly. Comments that residents on one side of a particular road were not part of "our" community while people on the opposite side were part of the "we" group were quite common. If personal interviews are the primary data collection technique, telephone directories prove to be of little value in locating addresses. I have effectively used a modified systematic sampling technique which involves the random selection of highways from detailed county maps provided by the state highway department. A systematic sample using the Kth occupied residence is then drawn. Comparison of the sample characteristics with known references, such as township or county data, provides a means of checking the representativeness of the sample drawn. Social impact assessors who have not encountered commercial directories of rural counties should explore the possibilities of using them where available. The commercial directories have names and addresses of nearly every resident in the county. They are rather expensive, however, ranging from $50 to $75 per county.

Data Collection among Dispersed Populations

Most social impact assessors either use secondary data or rely upon primary data which are most often collected by mailed questionnaire or some form of personal interview (telephone or in-depth personal interview using open-ended or structured instruments). Due to budgetary restraints, the sample drawn on the personal interview basis is often small. A technique that I and several colleagues have used with excellent results is a "drop-off, pick-up later" method. This technique consists of an interviewer approaching the selected respondent, explaining the basic purpose of the study and receiving a commitment to participate. The second step is to briefly explain the questionnaire and leave it with the respondent to be collected at a designated future time. When the interviewer returns to collect the questionnaire he/she scans the responses and provides a debriefing period to probe for additional information or to answer questions. The time involved in securing a completed schedule is quite small and the thoroughness in completing the questions has been excellent.

Comparison of questionnaires completed using the personal interview and the "drop-off method" reveals few significant differences either in the structured or unstructured responses, except that more extensive written responses to open-ended questions have resulted from the "drop-off" method. Respondents also tend to be more willing to provide education and income information using the "drop-off" method as opposed to verbal responses to such sensitive questions. The refusal rates are about 10 percent for the "drop-off" system, against 15-20 percent for verbal interviews. The reason most often given for refusing a verbal interview is the inconvenience of time, whereas with the "drop-off" method respondents can complete the schedule at their own pace and chosen time. Mailed questionnaires have generally produced a return rate of only 25-35 percent. While the drop-off technique is quite effective, care must be taken that respondents are able to understand the questions without someone present to explain them. A slight variation on this technique is to leave a self-addressed, stamped envelope for mailing back the completed questionnaire, but the rate of non-returns is higher than the "drop-off, pick-up later" technique.

Example of Social Impact Assessment in Rural Areas: A Case of Watershed Development

A brief example will demonstrate how the methodologies noted above have been used to study the impact of forced relocation upon rural groups (Napier 1971; 1972; 1974). The stimulus for the population displacement was the construction of large water impoundment projects. A quasi-experimental research design was employed using static group comparisons (cross-sectional data sets) with control groups (Campbell and Stanely 1963: 12-16). Four communities affected by watershed development were selected as the experimental groups and two nonaffected communities were chosen as control groups. Two of the affected communities were in the initial stages of population relocation while the relocation in the other two affected communities had been completed. The two control communities were not directly affected by forced relocation of population. Two of the affected communities and one of the control communities were located in central Ohio, and the remaining communities were located in the southwestern portion of West Virginia. The control groups were selected by comparing secondary data from numerous sources (census, biographies, etc.) for all experimental groups and "matching" the experimental groups with an appropriate control group. A control group was selected from each state to control for possible cultural differences.

The decision was made to operationalize variables to be used in the study in terms of attitude scales. Mini-theories were constructed for each construct to be measured and pretests conducted. The scales were reformulated and submitted to selected informants within community groups affected by lake construction. Item analysis techniques were used to determine reliability.

The modified systematic random sampling technique noted above was used for sample selection. The interviewers were trained in the use of the questionnaire and instructed to interview an adult member of every 4th occupied dwelling, with the first home selected at random. If an interview were denied, the adjacent dwelling was selected until an interview was granted, at which time the original 4th dwelling procedure was reinstated. Both relocated and nonrelocated people were personally interviewed. The data set was analyzed using analysis of variance, regression analysis (Napier 1971) and path analysis (Napier and Wright 1975).

The research design used in this and subsequent studies provides a means of evaluating the effect of the stimulus (forced relocation) through a comparative analysis. The experimental groups were compared with the appropriate control group to determine if significant differences were identifiable (effect of the stimulus). The initial shock and post shock groups were compared to determine whether or not the stage of development (initial disruption period versus community after relocation has taken place) had any identifiable effect upon the attitudes of the affected groups. The grouped data were then disaggregated into relocated and nonrelocated subgroups and comparisons made within communities (West Virginia initial shock relocated and nonrelocated groups were compared, for example) to determine whether or not being relocated had any effect upon the attitudes of the sample.

The quasi-experimental design provided considerable flexibility for empirically testing the effect of several factors. The major problems with the design are the cost of such research efforts and the difficulty in "matching" the experimental groups with appropriate control groups. Several communities must be studied simultaneously and the data bases become somewhat large, but the rewards in terms of causal analysis are well worth the cost and effort.

SUMMARY

A research process has been discussed using social impact assessment of rural projects requiring forced relocation as the focus. It is my contention that existing research methodologies are quite adequate for assessing social impact, but that many studies which claim to measure social impact do not really evaluate the effects of development change. Quasi-experimental and longitudinal research designs are offered as being more productive methods for evaluation research. Research design is the most critical factor in the determining whether or not the social impact of development projects is being measured.

References

Burdge, Rabel and Richard L. Ludtke (1970) "Factors Affecting Relocation in Response to Reservoir Development." Research Report No. 29. Lexington: Water Resources Institute, University of Kentucky.

Campbell, Donald T. and Julian C. Stanley (1966) Experimental and Quasi-Experimental Designs for Research. Chicago: Rand-McNally.

Dasgupta, Satadol (1967) "Attitudes of Local Residents Toward Watershed Development." Preliminary Report No. 18. State College: Water Resources Research Institute, Mississippi State University.

Heberlein, Thomas A. (1973) "Methodological Strategies for Evaluating the Effects of Water Resources on Social Well-Being and Quality of Life," pp. 89-100 in Wade H. Andrews and others (eds.), The Social Well-Being and Quality of Life Dimension in Water Resource Planning and Development. Logan: Institute for Social Science Research on Natural Resources, Utah State University.

Munch, Peter and Robert Campbell (1963) "Interaction and Collective Identification in a Rural Locality," Rural Sociology, 28, 1 (March), 18-34.

Napier, Ted L. (1971) The Impact of Water Resource Development Upon Local Rural Communities: Adjustment Factors to Rapid Change. Unpublished doctoral dissertation. Columbus: Department of Sociology, The Ohio State University.

Napier, Ted L. (1972) "Social-Psychological Response to Forced Relocation Due to Watershed Development," Water Resources Bulletin, 8, 4, (August), 784-794.

Napier, Ted L. (1974) "An Analysis of the Social Impact of Water Resource Development and Subsequent Forced Relocation of Population Upon Rural Community Groups: An Attitudinal Study." Economic and Sociology Studies No. 513. Columbus: Department of Agricultural Economics and Rural Sociology, The Ohio State University.

Napier, Ted L. and Carol Wharton (1974) "The Expanded Food and Nutrition Education Program: An Experiment in Behavior Change." Bulletin 1070, Wooster: Ohio Agricultural Research and Development Center.

Napier, Ted L. and Cathy Wright (1974) "An Evaluation of Forced Relocation of Population Due to Rural Community Development." Bulletin No. 1073, Wooster: Ohio Agricultural Research and Development Center.

Napier, Ted L. and Cathy Wright (1975) "A Longitudinal Analysis of the Attitudinal Response of Rural People to Natural Resource Development: A Case Study of the Impact of Water Resource Development." Economic and Sociology Series No. 517. Columbus: Department of Agricultural Economics and Rural Sociology, The Ohio State University.

Nie, Norman H. and others (1975) Statistical Package for the Social Sciences. 2nd ed. New York: McGraw-Hill.

Peterson, John H. and Peggy J. Ross (1971) "Changing Attitudes Toward Watershed Development." State College: Water Resource Research Institute, Mississippi State University.

Wilkinson, Kenneth (1966) "Local Action and Acceptance of Watershed Development." State College: Water Resource Research Institute, Mississippi State University.

Yoesting, Dean and Dan L. Burkhead (1971) "Sociological Aspects of Water-Based Recreation in Iowa." Ames: Iowa State Water Resources Research Institute.

Toward Assessing Social Impacts: The Diachronic Analysis of Newspaper Contents*

Anabelle Bender Motz
The American University

The recency of development of the field of social impact assessment has led a number of persons engaged in discussing methodologies to assert a need for the study of long-term impacts of projects on communities. Implicit in the recognition of this need is the desirability of considering project impacts from the time the project is officially initiated to a few years after its completion. This report is based on another point of departure, namely, the environmental conditions and the interactions between community members and actual or potential project-related groups from the inception of the project through the post-project phase are of significance in any attempts to assess social impacts. Underlying this view are several assumptions:

1. The life of a community as a community may or may not parallel the lives of its constituent populations. Its life is an ever-evolving, continuous process of interpersonal and group interactions which are cooperative and conflicting. The community's survival or demise is distinctive from the lives of individuals or subgroups that compose it.

2. The history of the development of a project may reveal "impacts" on the community prior to project construction or completion which may be of great significance to the life of the community. Such early impacts may be of comparable--or greater--significance to the community than construction and/or post-construction impacts.

3. Change is inherent in the life cycle of individuals and communities. Therefore, deliberate innovation in the form of a project must be viewed in relation to other changes occurring at the same time.

4. Archival data may be successfully utilized for diachronic analysis of social impacts on community life.

The aim herein is to report on the usage of content analysis[1] of archival data as a research procedure in order to find out what happens in small-sized cities when technological changes are introduced. The project identifiable as a change-inducing agent is the McClellan-Kerr Multiple Purpose Arkansas River Project (here-

---

*The research reported here is part of a larger social impact study of the Arkansas River area. The research is supported by the Institute for Water Resources, U.S. Army Corps of Engineers. I wish to thank Dr. Austin Van der Slice of American University for his helpful suggestions.

after referred to as the MKP), whose major purposes are flood control, hydroelectric power, and navigation. Three small cities bordering the river were selected for an exploratory, longitudinal study aimed at the formulation of a research strategy. Interest is directed to identifying what has happened to the lives of these <u>communities qua communities</u> over a thirty-year period (1940-1970) spanning preconstruction, construction, and postconstruction phases.

The cities are Ozark and Dardanelle in Arkansas and Sallisaw in Oklahoma. They present a picture of marked similarities. They are small (all with populations under 5,000 in 1970). They are located on, or in proximity to, the Arkansas River. And they are very much the same in terms of a number of population characteristics noted in the U.S. Census. Today these cities are linked to one another by two highways (U.S. 64 and I-40). They have the opportunity for another type of linkage—the navigable Arkansas River. Yet the potential of the river as a link between these communities or as a link to the world does not appear to have been realized in the same way in each of the cities. Dardanelle alone has a port where barges to or from Tulsa and Little Rock stop to load and unload their commodities. Sallisaw and Ozark showed no visible signs of such contacts by 1970.

Since the 1800s these three cities and their environs have experienced severe flood problems. For years, the Federal government has been asked to step into the situation and control the rampaging waters. Finally, in 1946, legislation was passed which would relieve the populations residing along the banks of the 450 mile stretch of the Arkansas River between Tulsa and Little Rock from the constant threat of floods. The project was made possible by the coalition of commercial and industrial interests (particularly utilities) and local landowners, farmers, and city people. The corporate and commercial interests saw the advantages in a navigable river and hydroelectric power; the others, the small town and rural people, were eager to protect their farmlands and cities from the floodwaters.

In the first phase of the river development project, reservoirs, locks, and dams were built. Later navigability was made possible. Finally, local people—responding as communities or individuals—built ports for barges hauling loads to and from places as far away as Japan or as near as the Kansas wheat fields. In 1971, President Nixon officiated at the formal opening of one of the most expensive Army Corps of Engineers' projects to date—the McClellan-Kerr Multiple Purpose Arkansas River Project.

Ideally, this project provides a unique laboratory for tracing the development of a Federal program from the planning stage to its implementation. It affords an opportunity to see the evolution of the communities over time—and to detect the confluence of events and happenings that took place and caused social changes. With approximately one hundred small communities within a ten-mile radius of the river and two great metropoli at either end—Tulsa, Oklahoma and Little Rock, Arkansas—the research eye is provided with exciting challenges for the conduct of <u>ex post facto</u> social impact studies—including the challenge to develop research methods.

Prompted by these opportunities, I designed a project that had two goals: (1) to attempt to ascertain impacts of the MKP from its conception through its actualization on small cities, and (2) to design a methodology which identifies variables that may supplement ones generally employed in social impact assessment.

The decision was made to use what Norman K. Denzin (1970) refers to as "a triangulation of methodologies," namely, the usage of diverse methods in order to approximate one's goals. The procedure was to conduct diachronic case studies of the three cities using archival resources: records of public hearings conducted by the U.S. Army Corps of Engineers, the contents of Dun and Bradstreet's Reference Books (which provide recommended credit ratings of business and industrial firms), U.S. Census data, local newspapers, histories of the states or portions of them, and economic and other reports of the counties and the area.

In the following pages, attention is focused on one of these resources--the weekly newspaper.[2] Following presentation of techniques for content analysis, a brief indication of the kinds of data that were found will be given. Finally, the utility of the content analysis techniques for social impact assessment will be discussed.

Technique for Content Analysis
Development of Technique: Although Federal aid for floor control of the Arkansas River had been sought since the last century, it was only in the 1940s that authorizing legislation was passed. Therefore, a first step was to learn about a small city and its relationship to the problems of the River. To accomplish this, microfilms of the newspaper of one of the sample cities were obtained. Virtually every issue of the paper from 1943-1948 was studied. As a result of this careful perusal, two sets of content analysis guidelines were developed: Guideline Form I dealt with leaders, social and economic organizations, information about the MKP, and community issues. Guideline Form II provided a careful tallying of all news items and ads appearing in the papers.

The review of the papers of the forties led to the decision to select for sample analysis newspapers from the first two weeks of the year, the last two weeks of June, the first two of July, and the last two weeks of December.[3] The logic for this selection was to include both "presumed typical weeks," i.e., second week after a holiday in winter and summer, and "atypical weeks," i.e., holiday weeks. In order to be able to compare data with those obtained from the U.S. Census, Dun and Bradstreet and other sourses, the papers for study were to be from 1950, 1960 and 1970.

Content Analysis Forms: The schema for analyzing the contents of the newspapers was devised so as to provide a picture of the sample cities over thirty years. It was designed to include categories that would (a) enable comparison between the decades; (b) provide comparable information about the three sample cities; (c) allow for recording of idiosyncratic information (i.e., information that appeared repeatedly in only one city's papers or in a given decade); and (d) allow for quantification if possible.

> Guideline Form I: The instruction sheet was designed primarily to enable the noting of interactional patterns and processes and to provide a more complete picture of each city in terms of specific personalities, events, and places. It consisted of the following major categories:
>
> a. Business establishments: Each business mentioned three or more times in the newspaper(s) was listed. Ownership, event reported, references to other persons or organizations, and mobility were recorded.

b. Community leaders: Each person mentioned more than twice in the newspaper(s) was listed. Here, personal data along with the event reported, references to other persons or organizations, and mobility were recorded.

c. Voluntary associations or organizations that met locally and/or involved local or nearby people: A list of associations or organizations, their locations, purpose, officers and members, and interactions with other organizations or between individuals was maintained.

d. Issues and interests of the city: A record was maintained of situations calling for decision-making or that appeared to involve an element of community conflict. The issue, persons involved, and outcome were recorded.

e. Outlying communities that submitted news columns: A listing--by issue and decade--was maintained of items headlined by the name of a nearby community.[4]

f. References to the Arkansas River flooding and projects: The event, persons involved, and organizations mentioned were noted.

In each of the above instances, whenever a newspaper item was recorded, the city and newspaper date were indicated.

Guideline Form II: In order to analyze the complete contents of each of the sample newspapers, each item was tallied in categories that had been developed after intensive reading of Dardanelle papers. I devised the categories and established criteria for inclusion of any article in a given category. The categories were then pretested by a colleague and were subsequently employed by the three persons who tallied the newspaper items. Since the bulk of the news stories were about persons and events in the sample cities, much of the newspaper content went into subcategories of a major category referred to as "Local." As shown in Table 1, the other major categories were "Locality and Non-Sample City Stories," i.e., stories about communities and places outside of the sample city, "Advertisements," and "Pictures." A coding system of numbering was adopted so that additional categories or subcategories could easily be added as necessary.

<u>Using the content analysis forms</u>: To facilitate usage of the technique, coders were given the Guideline Forms. They included the following:

a. A glossary indicating the major categories and a brief explanation of the kinds of articles that should be tallied in each;

b. A tally sheet with the major categories and numbers of subcategories; and

c. Cross-tab sheets for organizations and persons.

TABLE 1: SELECTED SAMPLE CATEGORIES FOR NEWSPAPER CONTENT ANALYSIS

I. LOCAL

    A. Personally-Oriented Stories
        1. Individual participation outside sample city
        2. Vital statistics

    B. Organizations
        1. Internal organizational activities
        2. Notices, announcements of meetings
        3. Joint meetings
        4. External club activities
        5. Inter-club activities

    C. Social Problems
        1. Crime
        2. Poverty

    D. Community Development
        1. Long-term services
        2. Arkansas River developments

    E. Social Institutions
        1. Economic
        2. Political
        3. Religious

II. LOCALITY OR NON-SAMPLE CITY STORIES

    A. Locality
        1. Personal incident items
        2. Economic-agricultural

    B. State

    C. Outside--canned features

III. ADVERTISEMENTS

    A. Local

    B. Consumer Product Ads or Mail-Order Ads

IV. PICTURES

Researchers with different degrees of familiarity with the project and instruments applied the techniques to the sample cities. (After minimal instruction, an assistant with very limited knowledge of the study was able to code the materials expeditiously.) As a check on reliability, two or three coders tallied the same newspaper issue on occasion. Steps in developing procedures for the content analysis of newspapers and other archival materials are recapitulated in Table 2.

Relevance to Social Impact Assessment

The described technique for the content analysis of the newspapers of three small cities makes a contribution to social impact assessment in a variety of ways. Firstly, it enables the researcher to reconstruct the community before, during, or after the technological change. Secondly, the diachronic approach utilized also helps to make changes over time apparent and to differentiate between short-term and long-term factors relating to the impacting agent and the life of the city. Thirdly, the application of a standardized procedure to the three sample cities made comparison between them possible. And finally, content analysis of newspapers served to test the validity of data and findings from other sources. In turn, these other sources provided checks on the validity of newspaper findings. The following paragraphs discuss each of these points more fully.

Constructing community: Content analysis of newspapers provides an answer to the researcher's question, "How can a picture of the life of a city be obtained in order to see how a change agent 'fits' into it and impacts upon it?" The answer helps to provide a basis for pre- and post-project interpretations. Through content analysis of entire newspaper issues, the researcher is provided with a picture of the life of a city as well as with its component elements and interaction processes at any given point in time. Guideline Form I provided the dynamics of the latter; Guideline Form II facilitated identifying major institutions and the pattern of their relations. Form I was particularly valuable in revealing community leadership and the social stratification of the sample cities.

A picture of a community is important to the social impact assessor whether undertaking a pre-project or post-project assessment. It is crucial to be able to indicate the course of community involvement with a project and the segments of the population aware of it as well as those whom the researcher perceives as being affected. By having a picture of the community's organization and concerns, the researcher was in a better position to ascertain the role of the changed waterway in the life of the city. It provided a basis for before-project and post-project analysis.

A finding drawn from study of one of the Arkansas communities serves to illustrate this. The data indicated that leadership was vested in the Chamber of Commerce (rather than in the official local governing body). Their contacts reinforced through memberships in social and religious groups, the leaders acted together in fostering river development in a way similar to many other public issues. The cohesiveness of this leadership group over the years--and its receptivity to river development--appears to have been important in the subsequent relations with the project and the city's port development.

This finding suggests the hypothesis that any given community is likely to have a "typical" way of responding to change agents whether they be technological or

TABLE 2. STEPS IN THE DEVELOPMENT OF PROCEDURES FOR THE CONTENT ANALYSIS OF ARCHIVAL MATERIALS

1. Assess <u>purpose</u> and needs of the researchers.

    (a) Why are the researchers interested in the material?
    (b) What do they hope to learn by doing a content analysis?

2. Select sample city (cities).

3. Find out what newspaper(s) would be available for analysis (including back issues).

4. Determine time span to be covered, e.g., 20 years, 10 years.

5. Determine the number of issues and which ones will constitute the sample.

6. Read copies of earliest and latest issues and attempt to devise categories.

7. Test categories on several papers from the earliest and most recent periods.

8. Use flexible numbering system for categories.

    Example:
	1.0.	Educational items
	1.1	High school news
	1.1.1	High school "cultural activities"
	1.1.2	High school student-teacher relations
	1.1.2.1	Cooperative situations
	1.1.2.2	Conflict situations
	1.2	College/University news
	2.0	Population characteristics

9. Develop a guide sheet that clearly explains types of content/category.

10. Devise tally sheets which include space for recording date of issues, publisher, ed., no. of pages, and other pertinent information.

social. Its general pattern of response can be predicted from knowlege of its past actions.

Comparative analysis: By analyzing the newspapers with the same sets of categories and allowing for the addition of other ones to note a particular city's variance, the similarities and differences between the communities became apparent. Comparison in this way led to the important insight that though these three small cities shared many demographic characteristics, their social structures and interaction patterns were not the same. Two of the cities that resembled each other with regard to these factors tended to respond similarly to the proposed and constructed MKP; the other responded differently.

In addition, by viewing the three cities in relationship to one another over time (as well as by viewing each city separately over time), differences in patterns of change could be traced and compared. The content analysis, taken together with data from other sources, led the researcher to formulate abstract types of small cities and to hypothesize the differences in their reactions to change agents.

Validation of research procedures: Ascertaining whether data sources are reliable and whether findings are valid is facilitated by a triangulation of methods. The use of the newspaper as a source of information and the development of the techniques appropriate to it served as a basis for substantiating data and hypotheses generated through alternative sources (namely, Dun and Bradstreet, the U.S. Census, public hearings, reports and other materials). It was found that the researchers arrived at similar hunches independently when focusing on a distinct source and that the data tended to be consistent.

Conclusion

The analysis of the newspapers of three small cities along the Arkansas River provided a source of data about the lives of these communities over time. The data served to clarify the skeletal information from other sources. Further, when related to these other sources, they provided a fuller picture of the past and present in the small city. The usage of the newspapers was particularly valuable in the development of the following theses:

1. A combination of factors--historical experiences in relationship to the river, community leadership (e.g., visible vs. non-visible leaders, small business vs. professional or bureaucratic leaders), and the presence of locally-owned and controlled vs. externally-owned and controlled businesses or industries--are associated with response to the MKP.

2. The part that the river and the MKP play in the lives of the communities *qua* communities varies in terms of:

    - The timing of the project in relationship to other occurrences in the community.

    - The types of issues perceived by community leaders, e.g., the perceptions of community leaders who see their own futures positively or negatively affected by a project may lead them to define situations as issues and lead to community conflict or to intensified cohesion.

- The perceived functions of the MKP, e.g., navigation, recreation.

3. Community cohesion is suggested in the newspapers by the relationship of a sample city to the immediately surrounding area and to the state and nation (e.g., the more locally-oriented the news, the greater the likelihood of allegiance to the total community), and the degree and nature of interaction between voluntary associations within the community (e.g., organizations uniting for the performance of instrumental and social functions that are not performed by other institutions are likely to foster community cohesion).

4. Content analysis facilitates the identification of social and technological changes that occur more or less simultaneously and the evaluation of their relative importance as perceived by community leaders and the public.

At a more general level, the in-depth acquaintanceship with the three cities made possible through content analysis and amplified through other resources (i.e., public hearings, Dun and Bradstreet Reference Books, and the U.S. Census), has been suggestive of an important direction for future research. Since the purpose of this report is to focus on the newspaper analyses, two of the broader implications of findings acquired from the combined resources will merely be suggested below.

The first develops from finding that although the sample cities *appear* very much alike in terms of certain selected objective characteristics, each has a unique history during the course of which each has developed a specific type of social structure and style of living--its "social climate." People, activities, technological innovations, or what have you, get sifted, sorted, tempered, and rejected or accepted within the framework of the city's social climate. In turn, these mediating processes serve to perpetuate and modify the city's social climate.

A second implication follows from the first. It is that the "social climate" of a city may be a significant variable that more acutely differentiates responses to technological change and their social impacts than the usual socioeconomic variables. The nature of the impact a proposed change may have on a community is dependent upon the history of the social relationships and social structure within the community. Even if the proposed environmental change is rejected, it may have an impact on the city's social climate.

The foregoing has implications for social impact assessors and for policy makers. Content analysis of newspapers provides a valuable source of information about a city which enables viewing social impacts in terms of total communities. It highlights the need for the social impact assessor and the decision-maker to consider the temporal and spatial parameters of the city under study. It directs attention to the "total city" and to factors that appear to be conducive to its survival as a city over time. The diachronic analyses of newspapers enable the researcher to perceive of a city in terms of processes of becoming so that city *qua* city, community *qua* community, may be envisaged as having a course of development and/or survival that is something other than the sum of its parts.[5]

Footnotes

1. In its broadest sense, the term "content analysis" is used to refer to any interpretation of the contents of written materials. Promoted by the pioneering work of Lasswell, social scientists use the term to mean objective and systematic techniques for analyzing symbols embodied in communications. The techniques attempt to develop categories which isolate specific words, phrases, or sentences that may then be counted, or to categorize ideas or themes in a way that lends them to numerical treatment. Criteria for identifying ideas or patterns of expression and the like within a given communication are indicated and a descriptive analysis or interpretation is made. Thus, a content analysis may be quantitative or qualitative.

2. The acute awareness that social scientists have of biases that enter into the research act applies to newspaper analyses. These range from biases that may be attributed to the publishing of the paper to the technicalities of data-gathering. It is impossible to know how the editor performs his gatekeeping functions* in the selection of what news is printed, and the extent and type of readership the newspaper has as an indicator of its influence. Technical difficulties encountered in this study included: variations in number of columns and size and length of paper; missing pages; small, inserted pages of ads blocking out other ads or stories on occasion. The biases of the researcher also enter into analysis of the papers. One obvious problem was the lack of acquaintance with the many names and places which the editor assumed all readers must be familiar with. Further, it was difficult to determine the significance of an event or a person in the life of the city. (E.g., are cited public figures "powerful" or simply socially prominent?) The researcher views the paper from a different cultural frame of reference and in a different time period from the reader's when the paper was "hot off the press." In addition for the researcher there are technical problems ranging from film accessibility to the strain of prolonged usage of microfilm. Hopefully, cognizance of the problems associated with the usage of content analysis of newspapers helps one to avert some pitfalls.

3. Presumably, the Fourth of July holiday and the Christmas season would reveal community activities at their peaks; the post-holiday seasons would provide the more usual activities in the community. The June-July issues would enable following through some of the stories over a four-week period. Further, since July 1 marks the beginning of a new fiscal year, the assumption was made that some financial information of importance might be disclosed at that time. Logical and highly practical considerations account for the selection of the first two weeks of the year and the last

---

* David Manning White (1964) uses the term "gatekeeper" to refer to the "gates" through which a news story flows in the process of being selected for publication or elimination. Usually it is an editor who decides what constitutes "good" copy.

two; the logical rationale was that this provided annual coverage; the highly practical basis for the decision was that the microfilm rolls generally ended with the last issue of the year!

4. The columns contained personal and social information, e.g., an anniversary celebration, the addition of a new room to a private home, a family's trip. The stories, apparently reproduced just as they had been submitted by a writer from an outlying community, were headlined by the name of the community.

    In order to have some indication of the frequency and amount of space devoted to news from neighboring places, a tally was recorded for every five inches about a single place. The assumption was made that the longer the column, the greater the affiliation between the outlying community and the sample city. Of course, the writing facility of the volunteer informant may have been a factor.

5. An extensive discussion of the typology and scenarios that originated from the use of archival data in the study of these three small cities appears in the author's report, "A Research Strategy for Social Impact Assessment: A Tale of Three Cities" (1975).

References

Denzin, N. K. (1970) The Research Act: A Theoretical Introduction to Sociological Methods. Chicago: Aldine.

Holsti, O. R. (1969) Content Analysis for the Social Sciences and Humanities. Reading, MA: Addison-Wesley.

James, Robert W. (1958) "A Technique for Describing Community Structure through Newspaper Analysis," Social Forces, 37 (December), 102-9.

Kovach, John (1976) "Community Institutional Structures and Social Change: A Community Study of Sallisaw, Oklahoma, 1950-1970. Unpublished masters thesis. Washington, DC: The American University.

Lasswell, H. D. (1949) Language of Politics. Policy Sciences Foundation.

Motz, A. B. (1975) "A Research Strategy for Social Impact Assessment: A Tale of Three Cities." Institute for Water Resources, Fort Belvoir, VA: U.S. Army Engineer Institute for Water Resources, July. (review draft)

White, David Manning (1964) "The 'Gatekeeper': A Case Study in the Selection of News," pp. 160-73 in L. A. Dexter and D. M. White (eds.), People, Society, and Mass Communications. New York: Free Press.

VI Evaluation

Policymakers must make decisions. Social impact assessments can provide the information necessary to increase the social benefits and reduce the social costs of these decisions. To be useful for decisions, however, SIAs must not only assess impacts but must also evaluate them. This is extremely difficult to do because incomparable variables must be compared. A satisfactory medium of exchange which can be used to compare social utilities for non market values is not currently available. Until such a discovery, social factors either are not weighted relative to each other or some group, e.g., a sample of citizens or planners, is asked to weigh them.

The selections in this section are concerned with the problem of evaluation. Some attempt to evaluate the desirability of public projects. Others describe methods for obtaining evaluations from publics or planners or tell how SIA can serve affected parties in advancing their interests in the politics of the decision making process.

As an analytical task, evaluation is based on values and is inevitably subjective. Social impact assessors may identify better and worse alternative policies, but they can only do so in a subjective way--based on someone's definition of "better" and "worse". Frequently researchers are unaware of the role of values in their policy recommendations. They think of themselves as objective and interested only in the good of society. They expect all unbiased people to agree with their evaluating procedures. Other analysts present as much impact data as possible for the alternatives but avoid the heavily subjective task of recommending an alternative. A quite different approach is being advocated in this book and is expressed in several articles in this section. We propose that evaluation is an integral component of SIAs and that evaluative procedures be described and justified.

Some values are so widely adhered to that they are safe evaluative criteria. Examples are health, income, jobs, safety, housing, nourishment, education, recreation, and most other quality of life dimensions. Few people would disagree that health is better than sickness and many other quality of life indicators enjoy the same consensus. At the same time there is no consensus on the relative rankings of the various quality of life dimensions. Without being presumptuous, therefore, SIAs can indicate that various impacts are positive or negative because of the way that they affect the quality of life of people. But how can a SIA arrive at a total quality of life score for alternative policies? For aggregation the dimensions must be weighted, and the choice of a weighting scheme is inevitably somewhat arbitrary. One procedure which has the merit of being relatively democratic is to ascertain the evaluations by the community and interested parties of the alternative policies. Though we recommend this procedure as a general rule, we recognize that the public does not necessarily choose the "best" alternative. Nevertheless the attitudes of groups, organizations, and the general public toward the alternatives should be reported in the SIA. Decision makers, especially politicians, need to know where people stand when they make their decisions.

The article by Willeke presents a comprehensive review of methods for identifying publics (affected parties), including geographic, demographic, historical and comparative analyses; analysis of associations; and field interviews.

Following Willeke are two articles which report on evaluations of specific projects that used innovative evaluative designs and/or methods. Gregori and others describe how they evaluated a residential development policy by identifying planners' assumptions about the public's likely behavior and then collecting data to test these assumptions. Most of the assumptions turn out to be erroneous and modifications of the policy are recommended which better suit the public's values and behavior. Their work shows how the analysis of people's values may be important to designing effective policies.

The paper by Heder and Francis describes an innovative technique for surfacing and describing people's values as they relate to the redevelopment of the Harvard Square area. They imaginatively use workshops to determine how residents and users perceive and utilize the Harvard Square area. Valuable inputs to the development plans for Harvard Square are derived from their study which could not have been obtained from less intensive methods. Clearly, when workshops are conducted effectively, they are a valuable tool for the evaluation of public policies.

The next two papers describe computer-based methods for examining value systems. Johnson's procedure explicates people's weights for impact dimensions, and Kawamura and Malone's procedure interacts a working group with a computer program to determine the hierarchy in a system of values. Johnson describes a method for explicating policy-relevant values and their relative weights. The method is called "policy capturing" and is likely to find use in a wide range of policy analyses. The respondent is given a number of scenarios of future states involving several dimensions and is asked to rank them. In so doing he/she articulates his/her value system. When these rankings are computer analyzed the value system is explicated through the determination of the weighting coefficient for each dimension.

Kawamura and Malone present a computer-based method called Interpretive Structural Modeling for groups to structure their goals for complex problem solving. It may be most useful in explicating the hierarchy of goals of government agencies as represented by agency personnel, but it can be used to structure or map the objectives of any policy-relevant group.

The last two papers examine factors which can improve the benefits of public involvement and social impact assessments on agency actions. They provide guidance for improving the communication at these interfaces. The importance of their objective cannot be overemphasized, because the final test of SIAs must be the kind of influence that they have on policy decisions.

316   Evaluation

The paper by Hornback provides some valuable suggestions for ways to overcome obstacles to communication between the action agency and the public. The prejudices and values of both the agency and the public are reviewed and then taken into account in devising a strategy for achieving public involvement in policy decisions which is useful to the agency in planning effective programs.

The final paper by Llewellyn reports on a study of the social and environmental effects of alternative highway locations for the Federal Highway Administration. The researchers became concerned that the study would not be utilized by the state highway departments for which it was intended. The study plan was therefore revised to include extensive interviews with state highway planners about their information needs. The results of this study form the basis for a number of suggestions on how to make SIAs more valuable to users. As experienced assessors can attest, the packaging and form of the SIA can be as important as the soundness of its substance. Llewellyn's observations can contribute to the effectiveness of SIAs by improving their presentation to decision makers.

Identifying Publics in Social Impact Assessment*

Gene E. Willeke
Georgia Institute of Technology

From direct field experience, most planners have learned that the public is not a unitary mass. Similarly, researchers have developed the concepts of audience segments (in communication research) and market segments (in market research). These terms refer to identifiable, but not necessarily socially connected, groups having similar behavior patterns relative to communication in the first case and a marketable product in the second. With few exceptions, both audience and market segments are defined in terms of demographic and geographic characteristics. Having accepted the plurality of publics, the planner is then faced with the tasks of identifying, describing, and communicating with those publics.

PURPOSE

The principal reasons for identifying publics are so that potential effects on these groups may be assessed and so the groups may, if they wish, become involved in the planning process. Whether or not certain segments of the public wish to be involved in planning does not negate the need for a thoroughgoing effort to identify each relevant segment, however. For those unable or unwilling to become involved, the planner must more explicitly search for effects since they do not have a spokesperson or advocate as do those segments which can speak for themselves.

Many planners consider the silent public as the really important segment. Those holding such views look upon organized, vocal groups as minorities who don't speak for many people and whose views, therefore, should be given little consideration. True, vocal and active groups have usually adopted such a role because they perceive themselves to be acutely affected by a proposed action. As Ragan (1974) points out, however, such groups can be effective surrogates for the general public. Moreover, an organized surrogate group can usually bear the cost of full participation--do the necessary research, present the case to responsible decisionmakers, and muster the necessary political support.

COMPONENTS OF IDENTIFICATION

Because there are many publics, there are many ways of defining and describing them. Identification methods vary in degree of specificity from very broad, amorphous categories to discrete units. In general, identification should be brief enough to be manageable and complete enough to be useful. The following three

---

*The work on which this report is based was partially supported by the Environmental Resources Center and the Graduate Program in City Planning, Georgia Institute of Technology, and by the Office of Water Research and Technology, U.S. Department of the Interior as authorized under the Water Resources Act of 1964 (P. L. 88-379).

components may be used as a starting point.

Location
One approach to public segment identification is location. In water resource planning, for example, segments may have a definite geographic locale: those living inside the project boundaries, those living in a flood plain, those living below a dam, those living on either side of a river, or those living around a lake. Other public segments may not have a specific geographic location but derive their significance to planning from some other characteristic. For those segments, a part of the identification process is to explicitly recognize those characteristics which do relate to project planning.

Interests
A segment of the public identified as having some relevance to planning would ordinarily have some particular interest in the outcome of project planning. To some extent, the interest of an identified segment would be known to the planner. For completeness and accuracy, an explicit statement of interest should be secured from the segment, however. This statement need not be complete at the early stage of identification.

This step in identification has ultimate importance _to the segment itself_ because the segment has been assisted in clarifying its role in relation to the nature of the anticipated effects. It is important _to the planner_ because he knows why a segment is becoming involved and what some of the issues of concern to it are. It is important _to the other participants_ because they can know the relationship of each segment to the planning process and because segments with common interests can work together. Also, conflicting interests may be more easily determined at an early stage when there is more opportunity for conflict resolution.

Social Characteristics
In order to involve effectively some segment of the public in the planning process, it is desirable to know something of the social characteristics of the segment. Since a public segment may or may not be a social group, one of the first social characteristics to be determined is whether a _social group_ exists. Where the segment does comprise a social group, its goals, history, boundaries, reasons for existence, size, structure, mode of organization and operation, and communication patterns may be determined.

Attributes of a population such as age, sex, race, education, income, and occupation are commonly referred to as demographic characteristics. While the amount of information they convey about segments of the public is obviously limited, much of public works planning is oriented toward use of highly aggregated demographic data as primary components of project or program development. As in the case of audience and market segments, some public segments are defined almost entirely in terms of demographic characteristics. The elderly; the young; low, high, or middle income strata; racial, ethnic, religious and occupational groups are all examples of public segments defined in terms of demographic characteristics. Demographic characteristics often are used as proxies or surrogates for other cultural traits. Thus, low income people in a small city may mostly reside in a particular territory, belong to certain voluntary associations such as churches and community groups, and share common problems. Communication behavior may be quite similar among most members of a segment defined in demographic terms. (Indeed, marketers of consumer products stake much of their advertising budget on the belief that this is the case.)

THE PRACTICE OF IDENTIFYING PUBLICS

The methods for identifying publics may be classified as self-identification (with or without staff intervention), third party identification, and staff identification. In general, a mix of all three approaches would be appropriate to any given public participation program.

Self-Identification
In public works planning, there has customarily been some opportunity for self-identification, either of groups or individuals. While these provisions vary considerably, ranging across petition, appeal, public hearing, election, suit, protest, and publicity, laws at all levels of government usually afford some means by which a citizen or group may enter the planning process.

The laws governing citizen-initiated access mechanisms are so variable from place to place that citizens may be unaware of what must be done to intervene in governmental action. This, of course, applies primarily to such mechanisms as petition, appeal, public hearing, and suit. For example, a Vermont statute (Ann. Tit. 10, Secs. 1100-1105, Supp. 1971) provides that adoption of rules for municipal shoreland zoning be considered at public hearing on a petition of ten freemen. To use such a statutory provision a citizen needs to know what a freeman is, the form of the required petition, and what kind of action might be taken as a result of public hearing.

Citizens may identify themselves by corresponding, by letter or telephone, with the planning agency or a related agency and/or by appearing at public meetings. The usefulness of such means can be expanded with little effort and cost. A toll-free telephone number may be established for those who would prefer to communicate by telephone. Radio and television announcements may be used to publicize the willingness and desire on the part of the planner to have people identify themselves. In recent years, radio and television programs operating in a two-way communication mode have been initiated. Listeners may telephone directly to the station and talk on the air with a moderator or panelist. While not ordinarily used for this purpose, this "talk-back" format could be adapted to identify interested parties. An important ingredient in facilitating self-identification approaches is the use of multiple channels of communication to and from the public so that maximum opportunity for self-identification is afforded and so that the publics have a number of ways to self-identify themselves with little cost and effort.

Third Party Identification
Third party identification is much like self-identification except that it is done by a third party, such as a citizen advisory committee. One purpose of citizen committees is to identify those groups and individuals who should be involved in planning or who are likely to be affected by proposed plan alternatives. This principle can be extended further, of course. Any person who is aware of the planning effort and knows of some other individual or group that should be involved may identify that person or group to the planner.

Staff Identification

The planner plays the role of facilitator in both the self-identification and third party identification approaches. In staff identification, on the other hand, nearly all the work involved in identifying publics is done by the planning staff itself. The principal techniques and approaches to staff identification are described below, with some appraisal of their effectiveness and appropriateness in public works planning.

METHODS OF IDENTIFYING PUBLICS

Analysis of Associations

Analysis of associations is a process of consulting available lists of organized groups and picking out those which appear to have possible interest in being involved. The groups then are contacted and queried about their interest. Analysis of associations is always an appropriate method of beginning to identify publics. It is fast and inexpensive, and prompts thought about possible interested and affected groups. Moreover, it provides a guide to the general social organization of the area, however approximate and incomplete.

Lists of associations are usually available in any community, though such lists are almost always incomplete. The Yellow Pages of the telephone directory, the Chamber of Commerce, newspaper lists, and city and county directories are all ready sources. Going beyond these are lists available from direct mail services on a national and state basis, sorted by ZIP code and categorized by type of association.

A recent tendency in some public works studies, especially those conducted by the Federal Government, is the use of standard categories of publics. In the Atlanta Water Resources Management Study, for example, three levels of publics were used: "all major units of government," special interest organizations, and local public interest groups.

Developing a good, accurate mailing or correspondence list is an essential part of a public involvement program and, as it is developed, is a partial means of identifying publics. To be really effective, it needs to be regularly updated and categorized in a fashion permitting easy use, e.g., so that mailings can be made to selected persons or groups on the list. The computer is a useful tool for handling mailing lists.

There is a considerable risk in assuming that the mailing or correspondence list *is* the identification of publics. In a recent study done for the U.S. Army Corps of Engineers, it was found that most lists are over 70 percent dominated by governmental interests (Ragan 1974). Their purpose was primarily for notification of public meetings. While it is acknowledged that a list of those interested in and affected by water resource plans normally includes a number of public agencies, their importance as publics should not be exaggerated. Identification is more than naming; it implies learning about the characteristics and concerns of identified segments.

Geographic Analysis

Geographic analysis involves the study of maps and photographs to determine areas that should be singled out for special attention in the planning process. As mentioned earlier, flood plain dwellers, those downstream from a dam or sewage treatment plant, those displaced by a reservoir, etc., are obvious groups to be identified from map studies. Other groups that may be identified by geographic analysis are those who live in proximity to the proposed project site or program area. Ordinarily, those closest to a project have the most interest, though this is not always the case.

Demographic Analysis
Demographic analysis may be used alone or in combination with geographic analysis. When it is used alone, a public is defined as that group of persons having a given set of demographic characteristics. When used in combination with geographic analysis, as is usually the case, one might look for those territories which contain unusually high percentages of elderly, non-white, middle income, or any other demographic characteristics of interest. By this approach, subareas are redefined and a project or program is analyzed in terms of the effects on groups of persons with given demographic characteristics who reside within those areas.

Demographic analysis can ordinarily be done without extensive interaction with the public. This has the advantage of speed and low cost, but it has the disadvantage that no public contacts are made until the study is completed.

Historical Analysis
Most public projects and programs have a history, documented by reports, correspondence files, and newspaper accounts. Reference to such data can provide a means of discerning what the various publics have been in the past, relative to project issues. Some planning agencies make extensive use of clipping files; newspapers also keep such files, but they are not always open to the public. Libraries may likewise keep such files on particular projects.

Comparative Analysis
A fruitful source of information about publics is the record of studies and projects in closely related fields, such as housing, water resources, land use, forestry, outdoor recreation, and transportation. The public hearing transcripts, clippings, reports, and correspondence files on such studies may yield information about groups who would be interested in a given planning effort. In doing comparative analysis, interviews with the study managers should be conducted in addition to simply reviewing documentary materials. Such interviews give insight into the contemporary situation, rather than what the situation may have been a few years ago (Arnstein 1974).

Field Interviews
The field interview has been much discussed as a method of identifying publics. There are essentially two methods used in field interview work. The best known is often referred to as the "snowball technique," in which the planner begins by interviewing a group of people known to have some interest in the topic and asking them to identify others likely to be interested. Those persons are subsequently interviewed and asked the same question and the process is repeated until no more new names are received.

Much of the reported work on the snowball technique has concentrated on "influentials" or opinion leaders as part of examinations of decision making and "power structure." While this is certainly an important part of those who should likely be involved, it is by no means the only segment. Essentially the same methods could be employed with people not ordinarily considered part of the "influential" group. Snowball techniques will identify most readily those persons who have in the past been interested in and/or influential in a particular issue area. It will not easily identify persons who are not well-known but who have a legitimate interest in participating.

There is a definite advantage to doing snowball interviews in such a manner that the planner gets more detailed information about publics. Indeed, this type of field interviewing should be used to increase understanding of social structure and planning issues, uncover data sources, and ascertain something about goals, objectives, and problems.

The other approach to field interviews concentrates more on understanding the community and its problems than identifying publics. As the community and its problems are studied, publics are identified as a matter of course.

Selecting the Mix of Methods

Not all the techniques described above should necessarily be used in any one planning study. Rather, those techniques should be selected which are appropriate to a given planning situation. The difficulty in identifying publics lies more in the practice than in the availability of methods and theory. Variations in local culture, in the personalities of the practitioners, and in the planning situation require a somewhat different strategy for identifying publics in each planning effort. It would be rare, however, to find a situation in which one of the three general approaches was inappropriate. Self-selection and staff identification are clearly appropriate anywhere, though not all the specific techniques under these general approaches are. Although highly cost-effective, third-party identification is probably the most underused of the three approaches. The really important point is that explicit consideration be given to identifying publics and that a strategy for doing it be developed. In the absence of such a strategy, there will be the possibility of gaps, surprises, and an inability to effectively communicate with some publics.

CONCLUDING REMARKS

At each stage of the planning process, the planner should be able to identify in some form those groups of people who in some way are likely to be affected or impacted by the proposed project or program. As the planning progresses the identified groups will change, but even at the very beginning the planner should have some idea about the nature of probable impacts and, therefore, the groups affected.

Examples of groups that could be identified in this way include those who would gain or lose economically, those physically in the path of some project element, and communities whose pattern of activity would likely be changed in some way. In part, these groups would be recognized from economic, demographic, or geographic studies. Others would be recognized from staff discussion. An alert group of planners sensitive to the local social-political-economic situation should be able to acquire a good deal of knowledge of relevant publics just by being observant and by thinking about the probable consequences of proposed actions (Wenrich 1974).

Analysis of affected publics should be part of any attempt to identify publics. Indeed, it should also be part of any planning effort. After all, planning seeks to reduce adverse effects and increase beneficial effects to various segments of the public. If these groups are not brought into the planning study in some way, it is doubtful the full planning job can be done.

Finally, it is important to re-emphasize that identifying publics is only one part, albeit an important part, of social impact assessment. That, in turn, is only one part of the entire planning process. We must seek to fully integrate all the parts into a meaningful and useful whole.

References

Arnstein, Sherry R. (1974) Personal communications.

Ragan, James F., Jr. (1974) Public Participation in Water Resources Planning: An Evaluation of the Programs of 15 Corps of Engineers Districts. Fort Belvoir, VA: U.S. Army Engineer Institute for Water Resources, July (review draft).

Wenrich, J. William (1974) Personal communication.

Evaluation of a Proposed Residential Development Policy

Harry E. Gregori, Elliot B. Reiff,
D'Ann L. Roche, William M. Rohe,
John L. Street, and Lawrence A. Swanson
Pennsylvania State University

ABSTRACT

Evaluations in planning traditionally come after the fact. This paper, however, describes an evaluation of a proposed residential development policy and sets forth a model of how such policies may be assessed prior to their implementation. The major purpose of the research was to assess the validity of the assumptions concerning the effect of facilities on neighborhood interaction, the effect of heterogeneity of population on neighborhood interaction, and the kinds of neighborhood features which affect moving decisions. The methodology developed for this study involved the extensive collection of survey and demographic data. Several assumptions of the policy were found to be invalid, and the policy has been modified to reflect these findings. Policy hypothesis testing as described in this paper is an important tool in designing policies which have the greatest likelihood of achieving their goals.

Formal evaluations can come in three places in the planning process. The first is in determining the need for a plan, and involves assessing the present conditions and placing a value on their desirability. These ratings of desirability usually concern some judgment of how various conditions affect quality of life. If it appears that there is a need for improvement and resources are available, a plan may be developed.

Once a plan is developed, a formal pre-implementation evaluation may be designed to project and judge the intended effectiveness and general consequences of the plan if implemented. Many different programs and policies have either failed to accomplish their objectives or have generated a variety of unanticipated negative side effects. The purpose of pre-implementation evaluation is to identify the conceptual shortcomings that can cause such problems.

A final or post hoc evaluation may occur after the plan has been implemented and its impacts on the area are manifest. The effort is directed at assessing and judging the full range of effects occurring as a result of the program or policy. This information may then be compared to the projected effects and used to modify the original policy or provide inputs into future policies.

The most common form of evaluation is this third type. A plan is generally considered to be a success when its goals have been attained. Conversely, when they have not been attained, the failure is often attributed to inappropriate strategies of implementation. When new strategies are developed they often are based upon the original conceptual framework of the plan. The goals and the assumptions utilized in deriving the objectives from the goals remain unquestioned.

Assumptions are made in the planning process in both the statement of goals and in the derivation of objectives from goals. For the purposes of this paper, goal statements are considered to be value judgments which are not subject to evaluation. The derivation of objectives, however, is a reflection of the decision maker's perception of the functioning of the system to be modified by the plan. This is subject to test.

This paper suggests that in addition to this problem of inappropriate strategies of implementation, other problems can occur even earlier in the planning process. The assumptions used to derive the objectives from the goals may be faulty. An important step in the planning process should consist of an assessment of these assumptions. This procedure will be called policy hypothesis testing; an example is presented in this paper.

Policy Hypothesis Testing
In recent years, a number of techniques for assessing the social and environmental impact of plans have been suggested (Leopold 1971; Isard 1973; Wolf 1974). These usually involve the development of a list of attributes potentially affected by a policy or plan along with a method for weighting and combining them. Ideally, both positive and negative impacts of alternative plans or policies are assessed and compared. The most desirable is then selected for implementation. Thus, impact assessment involves an examination and comparison of alternative strategies. A complementary approach to impact assessment is policy hypothesis testing. This would involve the examination of the assumptions upon which the alternative strategies are based.

This approach is particularly relevant to analyzing social policies, given the generally poor understanding of social behavior. In many instances there is little empirical evidence to suggest the social consequences of a particular strategy. Moreover, there may well be considerable variation in the response of different socioeconomic and cultural groups to various social policies. For example, many planned communities have been concerned with including a variety of social groups and have emphasized the role played by a central set of facilities in generating a sense of identity in the area and in fostering social interaction and integration. This relationship has not been empirically verified, however, and the effectiveness of such a plan may vary depending on the characteristics of the groups involved.

Policy hypothesis testing can be viewed as a combination of applied and basic research. It may provide both an indication of the general response to a social policy and more specific information concerning the interaction of the policy with the subgroups involved. Wholey (quoted in Wolf 1974) states that "every policy decision represents not an ultimate solution but a hypothesis; ...success lies in testing and applying the results of tests of policy hypotheses."

Centre Region Neighborhood Policy

The aim of this study was to evaluate the assumptions inherent in a neighborhood residential policy as it was being developed in the conventional way. Local planners perceived that strip development, long commuting distances, absence of neighborhood parks, etc. were detrimental to the quality of life in the area. They proposed a policy to alleviate these problems.

The geographical area in which this study was carried out is the Centre Region of Centre County, Pennsylvania. The Centre Region is composed of five contiguous townships, a borough, and the main campus of the Pennsylvania State University. The University is the socioeconomic focus of the area. The housing structure of the region is oriented toward the student population (apartments) and the professional staff affiliated with the University (single family homes). Fourteen thousand students live off campus. Of the twelve thousand employees of the Pennsylvania State University, seven thousand reside in the Centre Region. A majority of blue collar and clerical employees at the University and at nearby industries live outside the Region, however, commuting up to one hour to work. Residential neighborhoods in the Centre Region tend to be populated exclusively by one of three groups: white collar workers, blue collar workers, or students. Thus, one of the major aims of the proposed policy was increased spatial integration of blue collar workers, students, and white collar workers within the Region.

The proposed policy made two major assumptions derived from planning dogma. The first related to the belief that all those who work in the Region would prefer to live close to their work but could not do so because of housing costs. The assumed value of social heterogeneity led to the conceptual design of neighborhoods which would allow various socioeconomic groups to live side by side in harmony.

This task was contingent upon the planners' second assumption. It was assumed that neighborhood design has an important role to play in individual satisfaction and social integration within the neighborhood. This can best be summarized by a statement elicited through discussions with the planners.

> Integrated physical design of a neighborhood and its facilities will promote a safe, healthy, convenient, identifiable residential environment and will result in positive social interaction among its residents.

The planning staff perceived that the presence of neighborhood facilities would lead to greater social interaction among members of the neighborhood. Also, the existence of a sense of neighborhood was expected to engender a civic spirit and prevent the onset of anomie.

Another part of this assumption was that the presence of heterogeneous groups within a neighborhood would lead to friendship formation among individuals of the various groups--the so-called "equal status contact hypothesis." An interaction was assumed to occur between this process and demand for housing in the area. Overcoming the mutual aversion of the various socioeconomic groups would be difficult at first. The planners assumed that as the initial neighborhoods developed and grew, so would intergroup contacts and friendships. As a result, those who were considering a move to the Region would be attracted rather than repulsed by the chance to live in these heterogeneous neighborhoods with integrated physical design.

The planners who developed this policy recognized that there were assumptions inherent in the proposed program. A search of the literature convinced the authors that many of these assumptions were, in fact, questionable. Furthermore, the generalization of findings (which either supported or refuted the assumptions) from any other setting to the Centre Region is a procedure which is fraught with difficulties. Every locale has its idiosyncracies in terms of population characteristics, housing, job market, and saliency of the neighborhood. It was thus determined that a study should be conducted to resolve the doubts as to what impact the policy would have on this particular planning area.

Neighborhood Evaluation Model

The evaluation group's involvement in the planning process began (at the planners' invitation) after the original neighborhood policy had been developed. This study was concerned with analyzing one particular policy rather than conforming to the rational model of planning which suggests that alternative policies be evaluated and compared. Alternative policies were considered by the planning staff before the evaluation group's involvement, and these considerations were beyond the group's mandate.

The first step in the evaluation process, shown in Figure 1, was to identify the assumptions implicit in the neighborhood policy. These were then discussed with the planning staff. The outcome of these discussions resulted in three areas of focus. Assumptions concerning the social effects of propinquity, facility use, and length of journey to work and house location were selected for study. An extensive literature review of these three areas was conducted leading to the formulation of policy hypotheses to be subsequently tested.

Preexisting demographic data on each of the neighborhoods were acquired from the planning commission, the county tax assessor's office, and local school districts. This information was used to develop profiles of neighborhood characteristics including income homogeneity, homogeneity of house type, age of neighborhood, plannedness of neighborhood and facilities within the neighborhood.

A stratified random sample of students, Centre Region residents, and residents of surrounding areas was used to collect information on respondents' perceptions of their neighborhood and neighbors. Information was collected on the friendliness of neighbors, sense of community within the neighborhood, use of neighborhood facilities, and the boundaries of the area which the respondent considered to be his neighborhood.

Conceptually, the demographic data contained the independent variables of neighborhood characteristics while the dependent variables of individual responses to the environment were obtained from the survey. The data were subjected to causal analysis with the intent of determining the effects of various neighborhood characteristics (e.g. the provision of facilities, density, etc.) on social behavior and satisfaction (e.g. interaction, facility use, etc.). This information was then used to evaluate the assumptions of the policy and recommendations for revision were submitted to the Planning Commission.

Results

The results of the analysis demonstrated that some of the planners' assumptions were unwarranted. It was found that respondents would choose to live in their

FIGURE 1. NEIGHBORHOOD EVALUATION MODEL

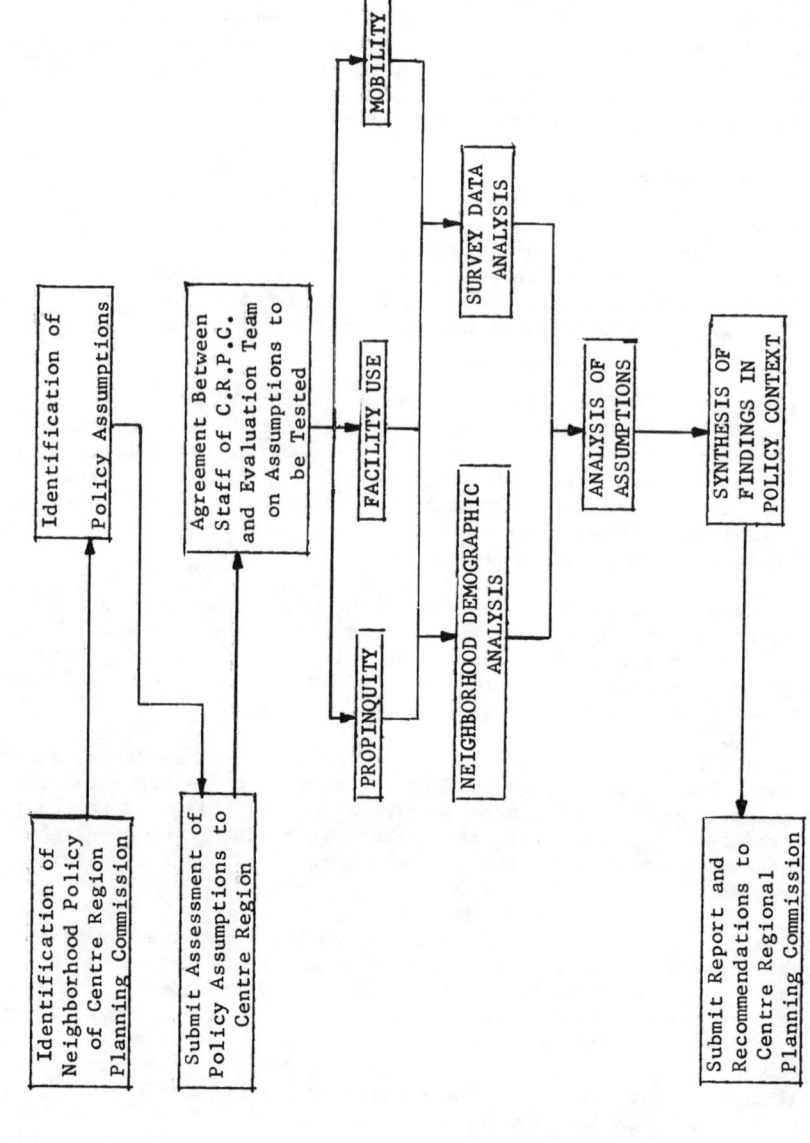

328

current jurisdiction over any other location in the country. Those living outside the Centre Region expressed a desire not to live within the Region due to their perception of higher crime rates, drug problems, and crowding relative to their current locale.

Respondents were not concerned about the length of their journey to work. Few respondents mentioned it as an important factor in selecting their present residence. The reasons for residential location cited by nonresidents of the Centre Region related to positive feelings that they had for the area in which they lived. Many had lived in the same area all of their lives. These results implied that the demand in the Centre Region for blue collar housing which the policy was designed to accommodate was smaller than anticipated.

The second set of hypotheses dealt with the role of integrated physical design in promoting friendliness, sense of community, and neighborhood satisfaction. A planner assigned a score for integrated physical design to each neighborhood in the Centre Region. Statistically significant differences were found in reported friendliness and neighborhood identification between neighborhoods with high and low integrated physical design scores. However, the physical design of the neighborhood had little apparent effect on interaction, sense of community, and satisfaction with the neighborhood.

There was a large discrepancy between the size of neighborhoods as defined by the planners and as perceived by residents. The latter group tended to conceive of the neighborhood as a one or two block area surrounding their home, while the planners conceived of the neighborhood as an area of sufficient population to support an elementary school. The planners perceived many facilities to be neighborhood oriented which the residents of the area viewed as serving the general public. Thus, the facilities could not perform their integrative function at the neighborhood level. The provision of local neighborhood facilities was, therefore, found to be an ineffective approach toward promoting friendliness and the other objectives of the policy.

A significant pattern uncovered in the study showed that University students were very different from nonstudents (regardless of their location) in terms of visiting patterns, sense of community, perceptions of the area, and satisfaction. Nonstudents throughout the county were similar on all of these response measures. The planners had not been aware of the scope of differences between students and nonstudents. They had assumed the major differences to be between Centre Region residents and nonresidents.

Conclusions
The policy proposed by the planners seemed to have inherent defects in that the assumptions upon which it was predicated were shown to be unwarranted. Residents living outside the Centre Region did not have a strong desire to move closer to work. Integrated physical design was not shown to be effective in promoting behaviors the planners wished to foster. This pattern conforms to the pattern generally reported by other researchers. Finally, regardless of neighborhood characteristics, students were basically different from nonstudents and had different needs and desires vis-à-vis neighborhood design.

The results of this evaluation were presented to the Centre Regional Planning Commission and resulted in modification of the original policy. The new policy emphasis recognized the need for diversity of neighborhood types to accommodate a variety of individual needs and placed less emphasis on the integrative effects of physical design.

Recommendations

The utility of the method of policy hypothesis testing has been demonstrated. A policy with small chance of success has been modified to reflect the needs of the populace, rather than the normative assumptions of the planning profession. Many policies carry within them such a set of assumptions. It is only by testing these assumptions that their validity can be assessed, thereby avoiding costly mistakes.

If policies can be evaluated before they become plans, the social scientist is in a stronger position to have an impact for two reasons. First, the input occurs earlier in the planning process, and therefore has less inertia to overcome. Second, by dealing only with the behavioral assumptions of policies, the evaluator is not open to charges of lack of knowledge about costs, scheduling, regulations, etc. as when evaluating a concrete plan. In effect, he is playing in his own ballpark by his own rules.

Finally, there is one other implication of policy hypothesis testing. By facilitating the explicit statement of goals and testing of assumptions before implementation, post hoc evaluation becomes a more meaningful tool both for decision makers and theory builders. Evaluators will have access to baseline data and process oriented information which will allow them to assess whether the plan or the assumptions were in error, a distinction which is crucial to effective evaluation.

Bibliography

Gans, H. J. (1968) People and Plans. New York: Basic Books.

Hartman, C. W. (1972) "Social Values and Housing Orientations," pp. 304-315 in G. Bell and J. Tyrwhitt (eds.), Human Identity in the Urban Environment. Baltimore, MD: Penguin.

Isard, W. (1972) Ecologic-Economic Analysis for Regional Development. New York: Free Press.

Leopold, L. B. and others (1971) "A Procedure for Evaluating Environmental Impact." Geological Survey Circular 645. Washington, DC: U. S. Department of the Interior.

Studer, R. G. (1969) "The Dynamics of Behavior-Contingent Systems," pp. 55-70 in G. Broadbent and A. Ward, (eds.), Portsmouth College of Technology Symposium on Design Methods. Portsmouth, England, London.

Wolf, C. P. (1971) "Social Import Assessment: The State of the Art," pp. 1-44 in C. P. Wolf (ed.), Social Impact Assessment. Milwaukee, WI: Environmental Design Research Association.

Quality of Life Assessment: The Harvard Square Planning Workshops

Lajos Heder and Mark Francis
Moore-Heder Architects and Planners

This paper will present techniques of environmental assessment and community participation developed as part of the Harvard Square Urban Ecology Project at M.I.T. Ths focus of the research is on the quality of urban life, a major concern of urban planners and impact assessors in recent years. While several social researchers have attempted to identify indicators of quality of life (Finsterbusch and others 1975) and to quantify their dimensions (Dalkey and Rourke 1971), little attention has been devoted to the qualitative assessment of the everyday activities and attitudes of city residents. Factors of urban settings which form community activity patterns, user attitudes and community desires are often discounted in the traditional planning or impact assessment process due to their alledged unquantifiable nature. The Harvard Square Urban Ecology Project,[1] an ongoing, action-research effort based at the Laboratory of Architecture and Planning at M.I.T., has developed and tested techniques based on user participation in group workshop situations which proved successful in assessing many basic quality of life issues.

WORKSHOP OBJECTIVES

The Harvard Square Planning Workshops were designed to help groups of interested lay citizens in translating their subjective needs and concerns about the environment into practical planning policy recommendations on the desired future of Harvard Square. Specific tools were provided in the workshops to facilitate the process of defining user activities and attitudes, particularly the Harvard Square Planning Workbook (Heder, Karen and Francis 1974). The Workbook consisted of background information organized to provide easily understood planning information and several exercises such as activity mapping. The workshop techniques, which grew out of our previous studies in "urban ecology" at M.I.T., were designed first to help people in clarifying and expressing their individual needs and desires to others in a group, and then to collectively translate these into planning policy and implementation.

THE URBAN ECOLOGY OF HARVARD SQUARE

Harvard Square in Cambridge is a complex public place. It serves a variety of purposes: local and regional shopping, transportation interchange, neighborhood

---

1. The project team consisted of Lajos Heder, Project Director; Mark Francis and Victor Karen, Research Assistants, and Steve Townsend and Libby Siefel, Special Project Assistants.

center and world crossroads. There is a wide range of users and settings in Harvard Square, and its diversity makes it an urban center of unique excitement mixed with growing conflicts.

Much of the theoretical interest that led us to the Harvard Square project is rooted in our search for techniques by which to plan for a richness and diversity in the urban environment. Pressures for increased land development, rising rents, and growing traffic and parking problems have begun to pose a threat to the diversity in Harvard Square by gradually eliminating many of the less competitive uses. Tourist-oriented attractions and fast food chains have begun to replace older businesses and many local residents feel squeezed out of Harvard Square. The proposed Kennedy Library Complex increased many local residents' fears that the quality of life in Harvard Square was threatened (Francis 1975). In one sense we saw the workshops as a vehicle to define the balance among the various components of the diverse Harvard Square environment. The intent was to have Cambridge residents, who themselves are a part of this ecology, define their own place in it, understand its other human and physical dimensions, and negotiate with one another toward a workable balance.

WORKSHOP STRUCTURE

A total of seven workshops were held with Cambridge neighborhood residents whose neighborhoods abut Harvard Square. Workshop participants were selected from three different neighborhoods, with each neighborhood group devoting either two full Saturdays or four evenings (judged by the study team to be the maximum time commitment the participants could make). Twelve to fourteen workshop participants were selected from each neighborhood group by a process which chose willing participants by age, occupation and location of residence. The overall schedule of workshop events and tasks is shown in Figure 1. Results of the workshops were summarized by the project team, fed back to workshop participants, and submitted to local officials as community-based policy recommendations. The workshop results were then incorporated into the comprehensive Policy Plan for Harvard Square prepared by the Harvard Square Development Task Force, a body composed of local representatives from the various citizen and business groups appointed by the City Manager in 1972.

ENVIRONMENTAL ASSESSMENT TECHNIQUES USED IN WORKSHOPS

Four major types of techniques were tested in the workshops: (1) <u>Individual Mapping</u>, (2) <u>Activity Sets</u>, (3) <u>Awareness Exercises</u>, and (4) <u>Group Policy Exercises</u>. These techniques paralleled several stages of assessment designed into the workshops: individual perception and recording; group discussion and evaluation of issues; understanding of background information and constraints; and formulation of planning policy recommendations. The workshop sessions were held in a space with various planning data and analyses displayed on the walls. As the discussions proceeded the participants' ideas were recorded, adding new information to the prepared exhibit. The major techniques and their results can briefly be described as follows:

INDIVIDUAL MAPPING:
Several types of mapping exercises were used in the workshops to record each participant's individual uses of and attitudes toward the various settings within Harvard Square, as well as to form a composite group picture of the area. The

FIGURE 1. SCHEDULE OF WORKSHOPS

1st Session
4 hours
	Introduction, coffee
	Recording of Personal Maps
	   DISCUSSION ON USE PATTERNS, LIKES & DISLIKES
	   SUMMARY MAP FOR GROUP
	
	Presentation of Activity Set Descriptions
	   Video tape, Questions

Walk in Harvard Square - lunch or drink

2nd Session
4 hours
	Questionnaires on Existing Activity Set Use
	   SUMMARY AND DISCUSSION
	
	Review of Activity Set Trends
	   Questionnaire-Activity Set-Changes
	   SUMMARY AND DISCUSSION OF CHANGES

SUMMARY MAP - AREAS OF CONCERN

Walk Harvard Square, look, note, talk with your friends and neighbors

3rd Session
5 hours
	DISPLAY AND DISCUSS MAP from our own group <u>and</u> other groups
	
	POLICIES TO REGULATE PRIVATE DEVELOPMENT
	   Information, Clarification
	   DEVELOPMENT POLICY MAP
	
	Coffee Break
	
	STREETS, SIDEWALKS AND PUBLIC SPACES
	   Information, Clarification
	   PUBLIC ACTION POLICY MAP

Walk in Harvard Square - lunch or drink

4th Session
3 hours
	ENVIRONMENTAL IMPROVEMENTS
	   Hopes and dreams beyond solving the problems
	
	DISCUSSION, IMAGINING, DREAMING
	
	IMPROVEMENTS POLICY MAP
	
	   GROUP DECISION: Do we need any more sessions?
	                            Work sessions with other groups?

CELEBRATION with all groups at conclusion of workshops

first mapping exercise was a free-form exercise similar to the cognitive mapping techniques used by Kevin Lynch (1960) in his studies of residents' perceptions of Boston, Jersy City and Los Angeles. Prior to the first session, each of the workshop participants was asked to prepare a personal map, noting the places used most often, and movements through the Square. An example of one participant's map for the first exercise is shown in Figure 2. The first free-form mapping exercise succeeded as a method of familarizing workshop participants with one another but not as a method for composing an overall use map of the Square.

The second and third mapping techniques proved much more useful in assembling group use of and attitudes toward the Harvard Square environment. The second exercise asked workshop participants to draw the boundaries of what they consider to be the edge of the Harvard Square area; the third had participants locate on a map provided for them in the Workbook those areas they used more than once a week and the areas most liked and disliked by the residents. The third exercise was done on a very detailed map prepared by the project team which deliniated the Harvard Square area down to the interior spaces of ground-level shops (see Figure 3).

ACTIVITY SETS

The analysis of the Harvard Square area by Activity Sets was a descriptive technique developed by the project team. Its purpose was to assist the participants in bridging between their subjective assessments of the environment and the formulation of planning policies.

This technique was developed in response to the inadequacy of traditional techniques in planning for expressing the richness and diversity that are primary values of Harvard Square. These traditional techniques rely on comparatively large-scale descriptions of land use and activity, such as census tracts. The resulting policies tend to be insensitive to smaller-scale diversity. For instance, the zoning for Harvard Square defines a single undifferentiated Business District with uniform controls. The already visible results have been the gradual elimination of activity elements such as older, community-oriented businesses in favor of the narrower range of more competitive uses. The workshop participants clearly perceived this trend and wanted to counteract it. The language of "Activity Sets" enabled them to formulate this objective in terms of potential planning and zoning policies.

Techniques for assessing the ecological status and interaction of Activity Sets grew out of Roger Barker's work on "behavior settings" and the application of ecological principles to large-scale land use planning, best exemplified by Ian McHarg's _Design with Nature_. Activity Sets identify the combined nature of places and mixes of activity which contribute to diversity in various settings. Twelve Activity Sets were selected to describe Harvard Square: (1) City Center, (2) Town Square, (3) Special Shopping, (4) Student-Public, (5) Social Niches, (6) Public Open Space, (7) Tourist Area, (8) Private Office, (9) Semi-Public Institution, (10) Harvard University, (11) Residential Neighborhoods, and (12) Ambiguous Areas. In the context of the workshop, the various Activity Sets (as defined by the project team) were presented in the form of a half-hour video tape which provided visual examples of the settings as well as describing their distinctive character-

Quality of Life Assessment   335

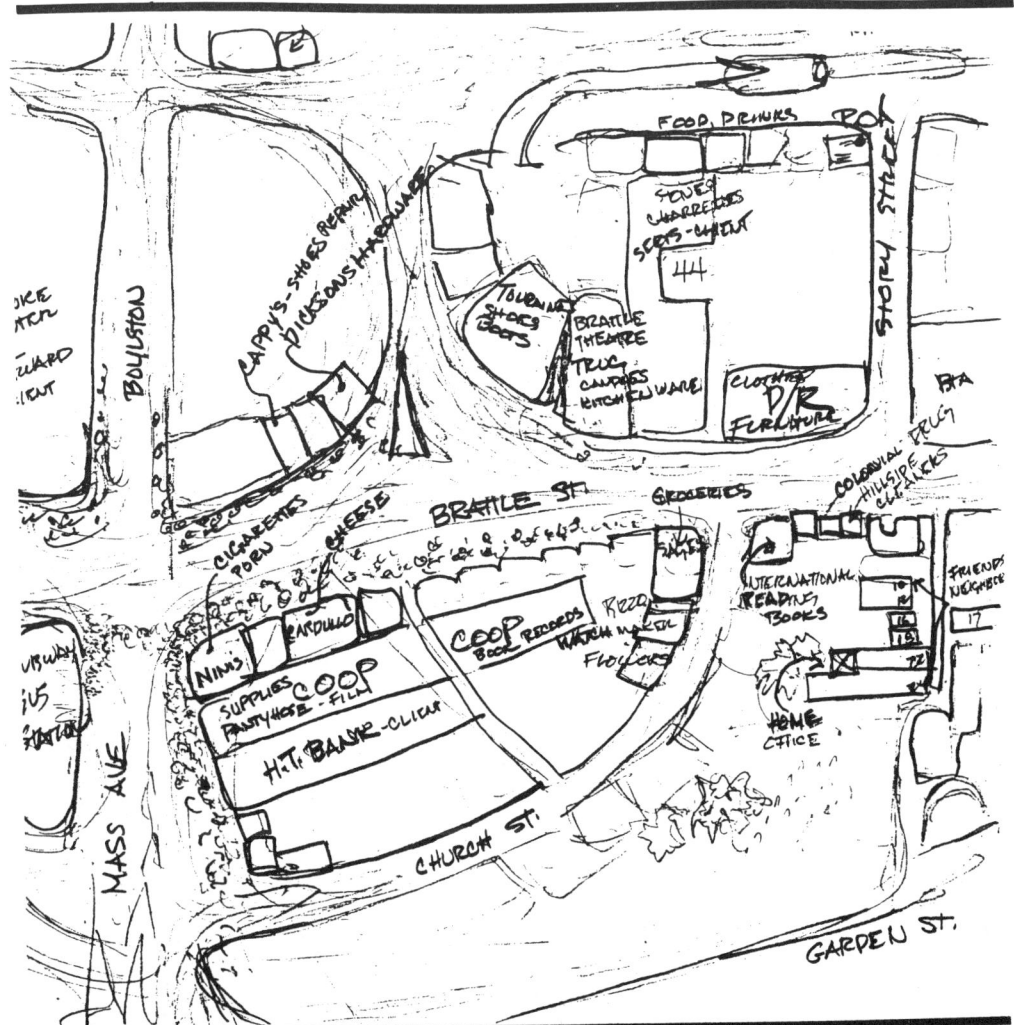

FIGURE 2.   FREE-FORM MAPPING EXAMPLE

336 Lajos Heder and Mark Francis

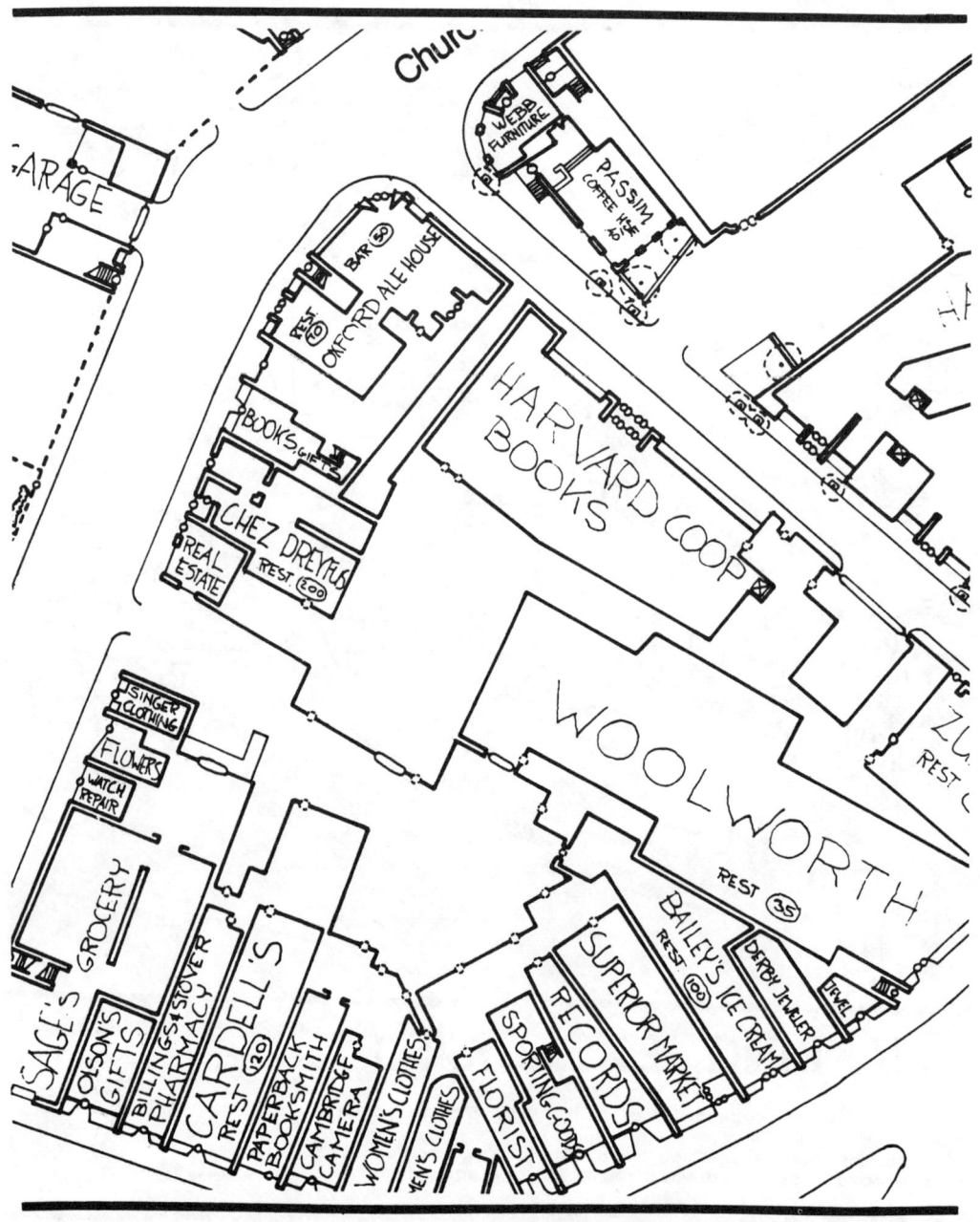

FIGURE 3. DETAIL OF HARVARD SQUARE BASE MAP

istics. After viewing the video tape, participants discussed their reaction to the
Activity Sets and described their individual use of and attitudes toward each of
them. The interrelations among Activity Sets were stressed, including competition
between activities and the capacity of particular settings. The likely impact of
existing pressures such as traffic and redevelopment was considered for each
Activity Set.

Some of the Activity Set vocabulary proved too complex for workshop participants on
first hearing, but by the following session many of the concepts resurfaced in debating policy alternatives. The type of environmental analysis possible with the
Activity Set vocabulary matched closely lay peoples' experience of the environment.
It allowed them to evaluate the environment and alternative planning policies in
a way that was both personal and yet suggested specific planning policy and action.

AWARENESS EXERCISES

Another technique used in the workshops was an environmental awareness exercise
developed by landscape architect Lawrence Halprin for similar workshop groups
(Halprin and Burns 1974). Participants were asked to take a "scored" or preplanned walk through Harvard Square, observe each Activity Set and record their
personal reactions. This was accomplished during a lunch break and participants
shared their reactions with the entire group upon returning. The "Activity Set"
walk proved to be quite successful in forcing more detailed discussion about the
quality and composition of the Square. Most importantly, the walk proved to be
a further learning exercise which contributed to the second half of the workshop--
the group policy sessions.

GROUP POLICY EXERCISES

Drawing from the experiences of the previous exercises, more detailed work sessions
were conducted to translate participants' subjective feelings into concrete criteria for Harvard Square planning policy and impact assessment. Workshop participants were divided into small working groups of three to four people, with one
person from the project team assisting each group. The groups then each spent
several hours discussing three main policy areas: (1) Policies for Regulating
Private Development, (2) Policies for Streets, Sidewalks, Parking, and other Public
Spaces, and (3) Ideas for General Environmental Improvements.

The group work sessions were supplied with background materials consisting of
maps, analysis drawings and Workbook information. Each group made choices between
various policy and issue options in two ways. First, Policy Lists were recorded
on large newsprint sheets. Secondly, Policy Plans were made by each group to
spatially define those areas of concern to the group. In the case of the Private
Development Regulations, areas were defined by the group that should be preserved,
rehabilitated or allotted to new development. In the Public Space group, areas of
desired street closing and pedestrian improvements were delineated. An example of
one of the Policy Plans developed in the work groups is shown in Figure 4.

Throughout these discussions an effort was made to face rather than to avoid the
more difficult choices and tradeoffs. The interrelationships between various
decisions were stressed by the background materials and the project team members.

338 Lajos Heder and Mark Francis

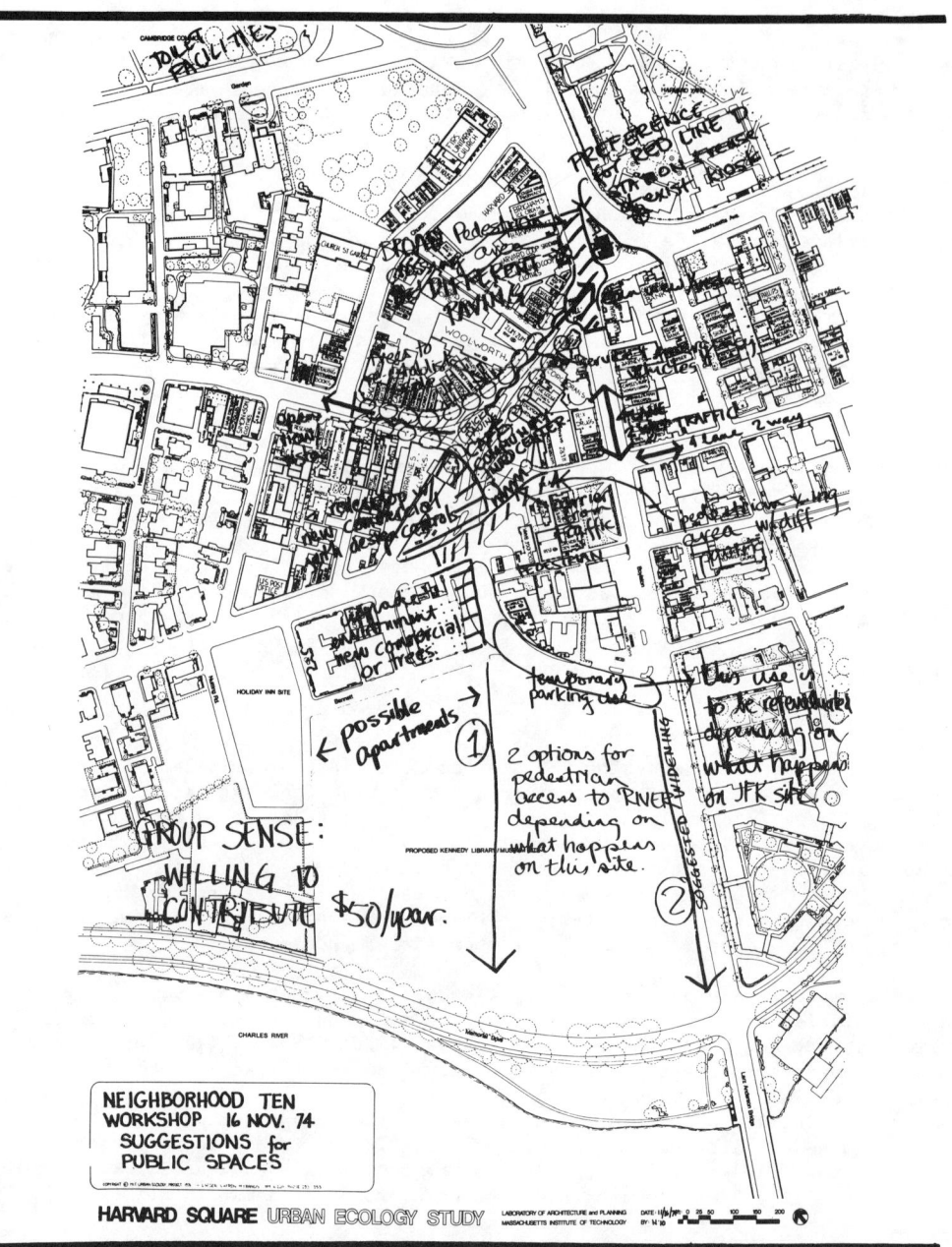

FIGURE 4. WORKGROUP POLICY PLAN

The participants came to realize that less traffic could also mean limiting access for themselves, that limiting development might also make it hard to invest in improvements, etc. They debated and negotiated these points and devised some highly inventive solutions to difficult problems. The careful preparation leading up to these sessions was well worth the effort; the results produced here were remarkable.

On completion of the lists and plans, each group presented its findings to the entire workshop group and discussions took place among the participants on the implications of the choices. The final event of the workshop was reaching group concensus on those policy suggestions which should be submitted to city officials and the Harvard Square Development Task Force. In one of the neighborhoods, the members of the Workshop organized a follow-up meeting for the Neighborhood Association in which they presented their recommendations and held their own workgroup discussions. The larger meeting--about 50 people attended--enthusiastically supported the recommendations.

CONCLUSIONS

While the Harvard Square Workshops and the materials which supported them were custom-designed to fit the unique features of the Harvard Square environment, the techniques used in the Workshops appear to have utility for assessment and planning efforts in other settings. Used in the context of the Workshop process, these techniques generated two types of useful products. First, the maps and policy lists produced in the work groups provided important recommendations for decisions facing Harvard Square officials. Second, the techniques and workshop process produced groups of active citizens attached to local neighborhood associations who continue to participate in the political activities associated with Harvard Square planning efforts.

The Workshops achieved their success because people were available from the various constituent groups to seriously consider, debate, and resolve environmental policy issues. The fact that Harvard Square represents significant resources as well as major problems contributed to the excitement and productivity; such workshops in a deprived situation could prove to be futile unless they opened up clear access to new resources. The participation of stable, often long-term, residents insured a follow-up of the politices through implementation. The particular scenario of the Harvard Square Planning Workshops would be most applicable to other situations where these resources and conditions are also present.

In summary, the Harvard Square Planning Workshops demonstrated that the needs and attitudes of individuals in a community can be assessed to determine the effective quality of life in cities. The Workshops also showed that with professional support this assessment can be translated by the community itself into policy decisions to effectively guide the future of a complex urban environment.

References

Dalkey, N. and D. Rourke (1971) The Delphi Procedure and Rating Quality of Life Factors: Experimental Assessment of Delphi Procedures with Group Values. Santa Monica, CA: Rand Corporation.

Finsterbusch, K. and others (1975) "A Methodology for the Analysis of Social Impacts." Vienna, VA: BDM Corporation, May.

Francis, M. (1975) "Urban Impact Assessment and Community Involvement: The Case of the John Fitzgerald Kennedy Library," Environment and Behavior (September), 373-404.

Halprin, L. and J. Burns (1975) Taking Part: A Workshop Approach to Collective Creativity. Cambridge, MA: M.I.T. Press

Heder, L., V. Karen, V. and M. Francis (1974) The Harvard Square Planning Workbook. Cambridge, MA: Laboratory of Architecture and Planning, M.I.T., 1974.

Lynch, K. (1960) The Image of the City. Cambridge, MA: M.I.T. Press.

Policy Capturing in Energy

Jean M. Johnson*
National Science Foundation

Policy capturing is a normative forecasting device useful for areas of uncertainty in planning where no "best" scientific answer is clearly available. Normative forecasting is based on <u>evaluating</u> desirable futures from an array of realistic alternatives, and <u>exploring</u> policies that will help arrive at those preferred conditions (Gabor 1964). Normative, or value-based decision making, rather than predictive forecasting,[1] is necessary for many responses to national energy issues. Current unresolved issues the society as a whole must come to terms with are:

1. The "appropriate" Federal intervention in the energy situation;

2. The level of uncertainty or risk the society should tolerate regarding dependence on a nonrenewable energy source;

3. "Desirable" energy use growth rates;

4. "Acceptable" environmental degradation; and

5. An "equitable" energy distribution system.

<u>"Appropriate" Federal Intervention</u>
An array of policy interventions have been advocated as "appropriate" Federal roles in the energy crisis:

<u>Command and control</u>: Robert Heilbroner (1974) and others have suggested a command and control approach as the only viable solution to scarcity of resources and the growing global population. In this role, the Federal government would, through legislation, regulations, quotas and monetary policy, divert energy and resources to high priority needs and away from wasteful uses. The Federal role would be one of an energy traffic policeman.

<u>Technological</u>: Alvin Weinberg (1973) believes that "the Faustian bargain is worth it" and that nuclear production should be accelerated to increase energy and maintain lifestyle despite risks involved. In this role, the Federal government would be a technologist, allocating R&D funding to the development of improved extraction and conversion technology for conventional sources, capital investment for the high

---

*Any opinions, findings, conclusions and recommendations are those of the author and do not necessarily reflect the views of the National Science Foundation.

1. Predictive forecasting is based on quantitative data (e.g., trend extrapolation of energy use growth rate) and current patterns of knowledge, technology and social institutions.

technology of unconventional energy sources, and more efficient equipment and engines for end-use energy conservation.

Economic: E. J. Mishan's work has suggested the inclusion of the full social and environmental costs in benefit-cost analyses. In the role of a broker, the Federal government would assure that the full external environmental and social costs are included in the price of energy-recovery cost for strip-mined land, rental cost of land until fully reclaimed, desulphurization equipment, mine health and safety costs, ash disposal, water cooling and esthetic costs. A rise in energy price would prevent waste, while denying some users a minimum level of consumption.

Social: Lewis Mumford (1974) has advocated adaption to a less energy intensive lifestyle as a more human approach, since high energy use fosters machine-like qualities in humans. The Federal role would be that of demonstrating and providing information on alternative options for less energy intensive buildings, industrial processes and transportation systems. In this role the Federal government assumes the role of a teacher, and voluntary action is taken on the part of citizens and industries to selectively adopt those lifestyle changes and equipment modifications they choose.

Some energy planners consider high risk-taking as appropriate for a high level of existence, while others consider high technology and energy intensity a disastrous path for organic life and human society.

"Desirable" energy growth rates are also debated. For some, securing energy supplies to maintain and accelerate past high energy use is considered essential for individual well-being, employment, and industrial and agricultural needs (Hobby 1974). For others (Freeman 1974), a reduction in energy intensive production and transportation is desirable.

Policy Capturing
Tradeoffs must be made among preferred social, political, economic and environmental policy options. Policy capturing is a normative planning methodology which can determine the tradeoffs which policy makers, special interest groups, and concerned citizens are willing to make. In policy capturing, one is presented an array of alternative futures and asked to rank order and scale them according to individual preferences. Figure 1 shows two representative scenarios. The alternative futures are about 25 mini-scenarios written in a narrative form and including various conditions of the future which can be scaled on a dimension of greater or less. The dimension of energy intensity taps attitudes toward scarcity and continually rising per capita consumption. The dimension of risk taps the uncertainty and social disruption that will occur to life and security if energy becomes scarce. The dimension of environment taps the environmental quality in terms of noise, air, and water pollution and degradation of the landscape. The dimension of social cohesiveness taps the degree of equity in the distribution of the energy budget. Since no scenario is optimal, one's policy is "captured" by determining the tradeoffs one is willing to make among preferred conditions in the future (e.g., how much reduction in environmental quality one is willing to live with in the future if there is equitable distribution of energy).

Policy capturing requires about one hour to read the scenarios and to rank and scale them according to what is considered desirable. Multiple linear regression analysis is applied to the scale of values each individual assigns to the 25 scenarios.

Figure 1: Two Representative Scenarios

A. This national energy situation was to a large extent influenced by political groups which attempted a scientific management approach to energy production and consumption. To assure proper uses of this vital national resource, energy was rationed to major end-use sectors. Wasteful energy uses were discouraged and efficient uses promoted.

The material well-being of the nation is considered below expectations, with an energy consumption at 350 million Btu per capita.

There is a low level of risk to the society if energy is reduced. The decrease in uncertainties has occurred from allocating energy away from energy intensive products, decentralized farming, and widespread availability of public transportation.

The environment is considerably more degraded than that of the 1970s, since extensive strip mining was required for increasing domestic energy supplies.

The distribution of energy in the society is skewed in favor of the upper classes. Lack of services to the poor of inner cities severely constrains their energy consumption.

SUMMARY OF LIFESTYLE - YEAR 2000

Federal Role		Energy Intensity	Risk	Environment	Social Cohesiveness Population - Total Energy
Regulator	60%	(Million			Lower 1/3 = 10%
Technologist	10%	Btu)	Low	-50%	Middle 1/3 = 40%
Economist	20%	350			Upper 1/3 = 50%
Teacher	10%				

B. This national energy situation was to a large extent influenced by technological innovations which increased energy supplies through nuclear fast breeder reactor plants and allowed continual economic growth.

There has been a continually improved standard of living since the 1970s, reflecting a 2% annual increase in energy consumption. Energy intensity is 400 million Btu per capita.

There exists a high level of risk and uncertainty in the society. Since there is a totally energized food production system, a loss in energy availability (e.g., a nuclear plant shutdown) would severely curtail food distribution in the society.

The nation has avoided scarring the landscape from fossil fuel extraction. The society does not perceive a potential high environmental threat, however, through radioactive material and risk of plant explosion.

Figure 1. (continued)

SUMMARY OF LIFESTYLE - YEAR 2000

Federal Role		Energy Intensity	Risk	Environment	Social Cohesiveness Population - Total Energy	
Regulator	20%	(Million Btu) 400	High	-20%	Lower 1/3	= 25%
Technologist	60%				Middle 1/3	= 35%
Economist	10%				Upper 1/3	= 40%
Teacher	10%					

The equation is of the following form:

$$Y_j = a_o + a_1x_1 + a_2x_2 + a_3x_3 + a_4x_4 + a_5x_5 + e$$

where Y = scaled values for each subject (j)

a_o = constant

x_1 = appropriate Federal role

x_2 = energy intensity per capita

x_3 = risk

x_4 = environment

x_5 = equity of energy distribution (social cohesiveness)

a_1-a_5 = regression weights on each of the independent variables (x_o)

e = error term.

Regression coefficients are derived for each of the independent variables. The present policy capturing instrument has not been administered to a stratified random sample of Americans or to an adequate sample size that would allow for generalizations about alternative energy policies of various sectors of society. It has, however, been used successfully with a wide variety of groups, e.g., housewives, engineers, students, coal miners, and environmental lobbyists.

Three examples of results are given on the next page (Table 1) as an illustration of the types of information which could be obtained.

The general pattern of concern of citizens in Morgantown, West Virginia was the equitable distribution of energy. This was the most "grass-roots" section of the sample, and they are obviously concerned about rising prices of energy and the rights of the poor to an adequate energy budget. Coal researchers of the U. S. Bureau of Mines were most often concerned about the improvement of the environment in the future and the prevention of strong Federal control of production and consumption. Energy researchers in Texas were often concerned about maintaining a high

Table 1. Illustrative Policy Capturing Results

	Federal Role	Energy Intensity	Risk	Environment	Cohesion
Citizen in a coal mining town of West Virginia	.26	.52	-.54	.26	.64
Member of the U.S. Bureau of Mines in Minneapolis	.32	.19	.03	.87	.31
Energy specialist on the Governor's Energy Advisory Council, State of Texas	-.25	.56	.02	.06	-.40

level of energy use and opposed to equitable distribution of energy. This may reflect the situation of a high energy producing state which would prefer to keep energy supplies for its energy intensive petrochemical and refinery industries.

Policy capturing may provide some obvious information, such as that poor people prefer equitable distribution of energy, and that Texas prefers to maintain its intensive industrial energy use. But policy capturing may also provide insights into national issues which are currently in debate (e.g., an appropriate Federal role in energy shortages). No person in the sample, regardless of his background in energy, preferred government control of production and consumption as a desirable alternative future for the United States. A broad-based sample of citizen option through policy capturing would provide important information to the Congress as well as to Federal agencies engaged in analysis of energy policy.

Limitations of Policy Capturing
Policy capturing has been used for several years without including constraints or consequences in alternative futures. Realistic scenarios should be generated from a dynamic model of the problem situation, however. The aggregated variables selected for the description of lifestyles related to energy use are only as good as the structural analysis which has preceeded the design of the policy capturing instrument.

Policy capturing should revolve around a defined problem. The main system variables, their definition, scope, and structural relationship, must be addressed in a dynamic modeling procedure. This analysis was not performed for the policy capturing instrument described. The aggregated variables were selected by the author from a synthesis of political and social issues described in current research and publication in energy (Johnson 1973; 1974).

All future scenarios presented in a policy capturing instrument should be the result of plausible policy interventions in the present system. Optimal scenarios with no social costs should not be included in the array of possible alternatives. If an energy situation is described in terms of all favorable conditions, then some qualitative dimension has been excluded from consideration. For example, if the State of Texas envisions that accelerating its energy intensive petrochemical and refinery industries will provide all pluses in the future in terms of employment, individual well-being, and maintenance of industrial and agricultural production, then there is some social costs and disbenefits of energy intensity which are being excluded from the model of the energy situation in Texas. What will be the long term consequences of being totally dependent on a nonrenewable resource? What are the short-term social costs of attempting to keep 40% of the national supply of the petroleum and natural gas produced in Texas for its own end-uses?

Benefits of Policy Capturing

Policy capturing instruments provide a method for handling quantitative variables which can be scaled on a dimension of greater or less. It is an easily administered and analyzed participation technique which can highlight issues of national concern and conflicting interest, and it can provide an individual insight into his policy. If a decion-maker gives great weight to efficiency and technological progress to the exclusion of all social, ecological and economic benefits and costs, the analysis of his policy will provide important information on his mode of thinking. Policy capturing avoids asking people to rate individual variables in isolation. Scenarios--snapshots of alternative futures--can include several dimensions for a more realistic appraisal of the future.

References

Freeman, S. Davis (1974) Paper presented at the National Science Foundation Energy Seminars, Washington, DC, June.

Gabor, Dennis (1974) Inventing the Future. New York: Alfred A. Knopf.

Heilbroner, Robert L. (1974) An Inquiry into the Human Prospect. New York: W. W. Norton.

Hobby, W. P. (1974) Memorandum to the Governor's Energy Advisory Council, State of Texas, September.

Johnson, Jean M. (1973) "Preliminary Review and Analysis of Global Energy Policy Issues." Washington, DC: National Science Foundation.

Johnson, Jean M. (1974) Societal and Political Implications of the Energy Crisis. Arlington, VA: Forecasting International, April.

Mumford, Lewis (1974) Paper presented at the National Academy of Sciences Energy Forum, Washington, DC, January.

Weinberg, Alvin (1973) "Can Man Live with Fission? A Prospectus." Paper presented at the Living with the Atom Conference. Washington, DC: Smithsonian Institution, June.

Probing Complexity in Social Systems Through Interpretive Structural Modeling*

Kazuhiko Kawamura
Battelle Columbus Laboratories
David W. Malone
The American University

This paper presents the outline of a conceptual framework of a methodology for dealing with complexity in societal problem solving and an overview of a technique called "interpretive structural modeling" (ISM), which has been found to be very effective in helping people deal with complex issues. Emphasis is placed upon system structuring and "human" aspects. An illustrative ISM application to goal structuring is discussed.

Introduction
The study of complex societal problems has become increasingly important as such issues as energy have become critical. Engineers have been successful in solving complex technical problems, but they are also constantly being reminded that systems that involve nature, man, society, and technology are very different from those that are purely technological. Tools and techniques they developed can't be applied to societal issues directly. As Linstone (1974) has stated, in societal problem solving "system structure is far more important than system state, which means that the nature of the interrelationships among elements is much more critical than the precision of the input data." In the following sections we will describe an approach for establishing system structure in societal problem solving.

A Perspective on Complexity
A simple "systems framework" for dealing with complexity can be established using only three concepts: elements, relations, and structures. Here <u>elements</u> are nouns or noun phrases, <u>relations</u> are verbs or verb phrases. A <u>structure</u> is a representation of the interaction pattern imposed over a set of elements by a specific relation. Examples of these primitive concepts are contained in Table 1. Note that more than one relation may be applied to any given set of elements (e.g., see "variables").

To apply this simple framework to societal problem solving we have to recognize the nature of "complexity," which can be summarized as follows:

$$\text{Complex issues involve} \begin{Bmatrix} \text{many} \\ \text{unclear} \\ \text{incomplete} \\ \text{controversial} \\ \cdots \end{Bmatrix} \text{sets of} \begin{Bmatrix} \text{elements} \\ \text{relations} \\ \text{structures} \end{Bmatrix}.$$

---
*The authors have benefitted greatly from the writings and counsel of Dr. John N. Warfield.

TABLE 1. ILLUSTRATIVE EXAMPLES OF ELEMENTS, RELATIONS, AND STRUCTURES

Elements	Relations	Resulting Structure
People	"... reports to ..."	Organization Chart
Objectives	"... supports ..."	Intent Structure (Objectives Tree)
Variables	"... is a function of ..." "... is relevant to ..."	Mathematical Model Relevance Tree
Trends	"... influences ..."	Trend Interaction Diagram
Activities	"... precedes... "	PERT Diagram or Flow Chart

From this perspective, analysis of complex issues can be thought of as being characterized by three phases:

Extraction -- identifying and defining sets of elements and appropriate relations.

Exploration -- systematically examining selected subsets of elements to discover the structures imposed by selected relations.

Resolution -- devising action plans, or revising the perception of the issue context or lists of elements and relations, based upon the results of the exploration activities.

One consequence of complexity is that individuals from different institutions and different disciplinary backgrounds are likely to generate different element sets and relations and may even assign different priorities for concern among commonly recognized or accepted elements or relations. Any specific techniques for dealing with complexity in the social sciences must be made operational within such an environment.

Methodology Development

In dealing with complex issues, we have two principal sets of concerns. First, the techniques employed within the methodology should be sufficiently robust to deal with the full complexity of the issue; and second, careful attention should be given to the task of establishing and maintaining adequate communications among various parties to the issue. These concerns and the systems framework of the previous section provided the impetus for establishment of a more explicit framework within which to develop methodology for dealing in a systematic way with complex social issues (Kawamura and Malone 1975). The logical flow of the process is suggested in Figure 1, where explicit attention is paid to the need for establishing goals and objectives acceptable to the various parties at interest.

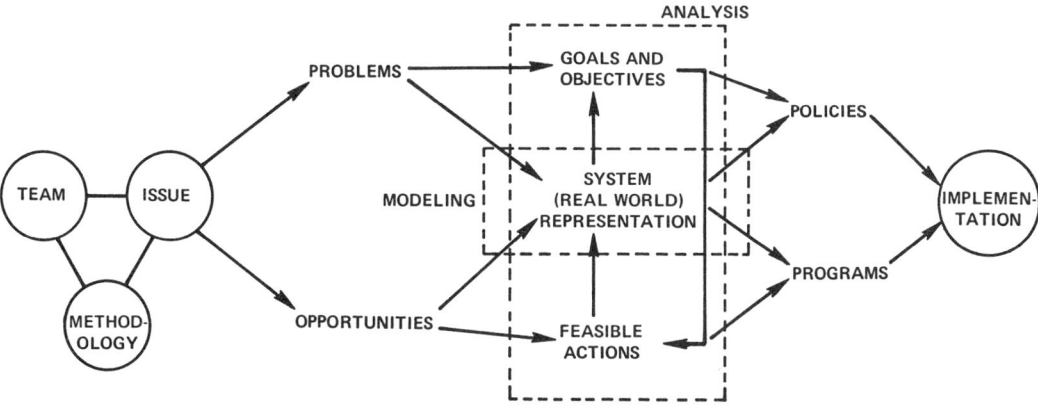

FIGURE 1. THE LOGICAL FLOW DIAGRAM OF COMPREHENSIVE POLICY AND PROGRAM PLANNING

This logical process model can be executed temporally in a number of ways. For example, the framework of Figure 1 could be used as a crude taxonomic structure in the extraction phase to guide the generation of lists of problems, opportunities, etc. The exploration phase could then be characterized by activities which are commonly labelled "modeling" or "analysis." The resolution phase would then consist of identifying and implementing specific policies and programs. Alternatively, Figure 1 could be used as a <u>communications</u> device to rationalize one or more small group workshops to deal with specific pieces of the overall process. For example, a group could be assembled solely for the purpose of generating shared perspectives on the list of problems embedded in a particular issue.

<u>Interpretive Structural Modeling: A Technique to Help People Deal with Complexity</u>
Kane (1972) suggests that there are two broad classes of methodologies used for analyzing complex systems, the arithmetic and the geometric. The arithmetic methodologies deal with specific numerical values, tend to make precise, time-specific predictions, and are generally concerned with optimization of a few select parameters. For example, Forrester-type system dynamics and input/output models belong to this class. They can be best used to analyze systems where elements and their interrelationships are fairly well defined. The geometric methodologies are primarily concerned with the structure and form rather than precise numerical specification. They are implicit in that they tend to be verbal or mental images and are utilized heuristically. Therefore, they are best used for a broader social understanding of a problem.

"Interpretive structural modeling" (ISM) is a computer-aided geometric methodology which facilitates the generation of a hierarchical structure based upon a set of elements and a transitive relationship among them (Warfield 1974). People are responsible for making all subjective judgments, beginning with the specification of an appropriate set of elements and a relational statement, while a computer is used in an unobtrusive manner for ordering questions and for performing and displaying the results and implications of the judgmental decisions involved in answering the questions. Thus, users do not need to understand the mathematics involved to comprehend the logic of the procedure.[1] The fundamental concepts of the ISM process (see Figure 2) involve the following:

- Issue Context

- Element Set

- Relational Clause

- Directed Graph or Digraph

- Interpretive Structural Model

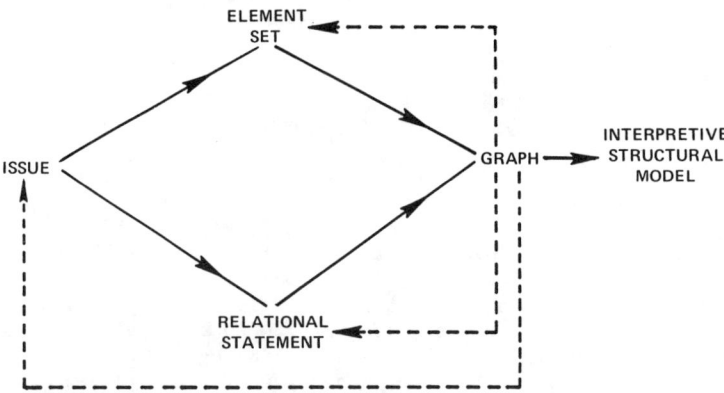

FIGURE 2. BASIC CONCEPTUAL ELEMENTS AND OPERATIONS INVOLVED IN THE ISM TECHNIQUE. (Dotted lines indicate possible feedback and iteration of the process.)

The <u>issue context</u> is a statement of general concern which is widely accepted and promulgated. For example: What can we do about the energy crisis? How should we conduct a social impact assessment of a project? It is from this issue context that ISM users must derive a pertinent <u>element set</u>. The methodological framework of Figure 1 suggests some types of elements that might be considered, i.e., "problems," "goals," etc. Examples of elements also appeared in Table 1.

The <u>relational clause</u> expresses a possible transitive relationship among the elements. Thus, in conducting an ISM exercise, the users are subjected to a series of questions in the form "Is element A related to element B?" or similar questions appropriate to the context of the problem situation being addressed.

The <u>digraph</u> is the primary product to be derived from the process. It is a directed graph whose nodes represent the original set of elements and whose lines indicate the presence of relationships established by the consensus opinions of the users. The digraph is synthesized by the computer from the responses of the user group. After the digraph is examined by the users for completeness and/or possible

---

[1]. A formal description of ISM is found in Malone (1975).

reinterpretation of relational links, it is used to produce the interpretive structural model.

The _interpretive structural model_ is the final documentation that records the results of applying the ISM technique to a specific issue context. It is derived from the digraph by introducing appropriate interpretive symbols and/or notation to form a structural model reflecting the user-established relationships among the original set of elements.

Application of ISM Technique: Goals and Objectives Structuring

It is widely accepted that values and subjective judgments play a major role in societal problem solving. When a team or group approach is required, any methodology must incorporate these "human" aspects. This is exactly where ISM has been most effective to date (Baldwin 1975). At the early stages of research or planning, in dealing with concepts or situations which are difficult to describe quantitatively, or when attempting to establish broad participation in the identification of important variables for later analysis, ISM provides a relaxed yet structured experience for a small group of interested and knowledgeable persons.

We often admire the individual whose style of choosing and acting seems to be based upon a well-defined set of objectives. However, if he happens to be in a position to decide within his own mind what the objectives are for a group and retains the power to make decisions on the basis of those objectives, we often complain. The identification and structuring of collectively held goals and objectives become more and more important and difficult as the number of parties involved becomes larger and the issue becomes more complex.

By identifying as clearly and concisely as possible the principal objectives of the various parties at interest, and by attempting to arrange them in a mutual support structure, it is possible to generate a simple graphical display which can serve as a focus for communication and debate. Further, if there is participation by some of the principal parties at interest in the phrasing of the objectives statements and in the creation of the support structure, there tends to be a commitment on the part of the principals to the activities which follow.

The problems resulting from the lack of communication among governmental agencies have been discussed by Hart and Malone (1974). They applied ISM to obtain a representation of the goals and objectives structure for the Ohio Environmental Protection Agency, shown in Figure 3. Kawamura and Malone (1975a) demonstrated the utility of objectives setting in a systematic planning and decision-making methodology. Finally, although in a slightly different context, Waller (1975) used ISM to assist the City Council of Cedar Falls, Iowa, in setting investment priorities among a specific set of capital investment projects. In this case, a noncomputerized version of ISM was used.

Conclusions

ISM has been found a useful technique for assisting small (4-12 people) groups at the early stages of research or planning. In this role, for a small investment of time and resources, it can help to identify important elements, to identify alternative options, and to qualitatively evaluate them. In particular, ISM is especially useful in setting goals and objectives.

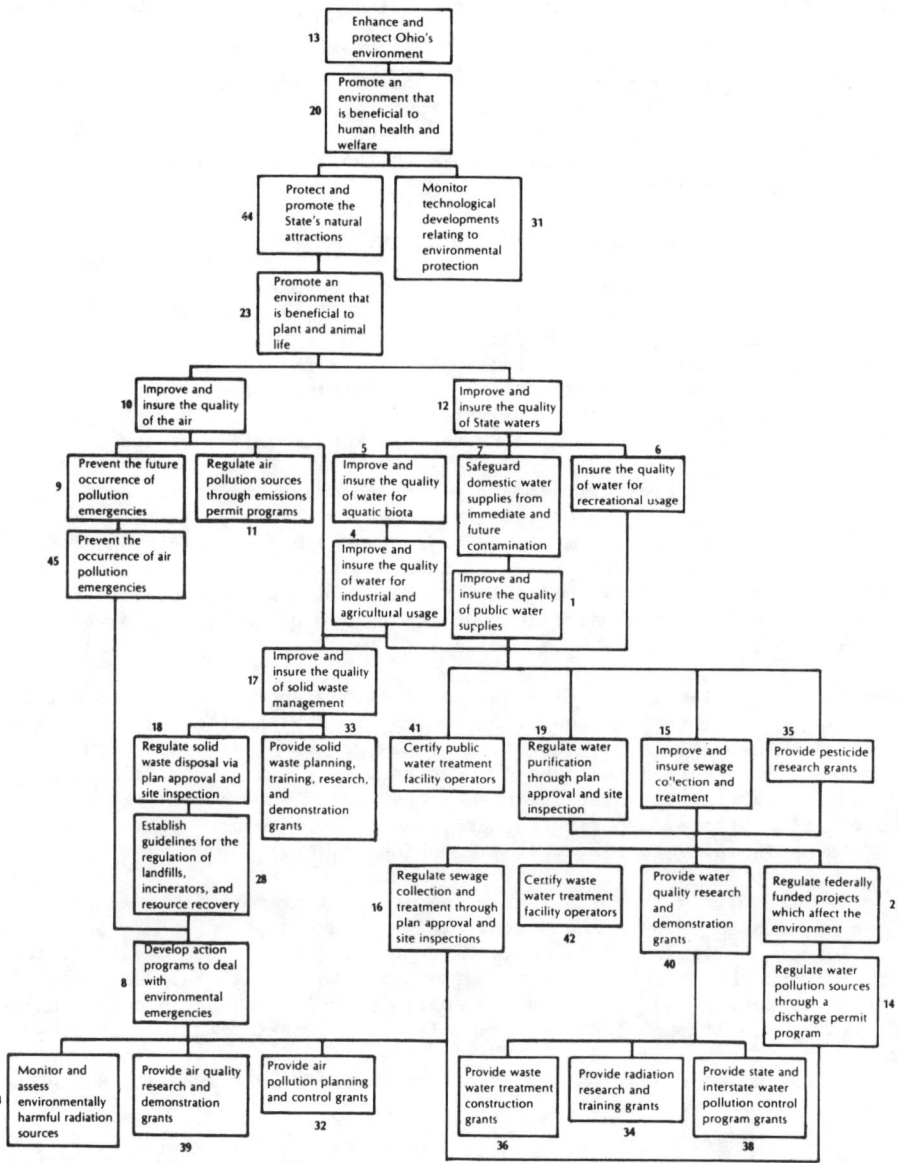

FIGURE 3. AN EXAMPLE OF AN INTERPRETIVE STRUCTURAL MODEL: OHIO EPA GOALS AND OBJECTIVES HIERARCHY. Objective statements appearing lower in the hierarchy are considered to "support" achievement of higher-level objectives to which they are attached.

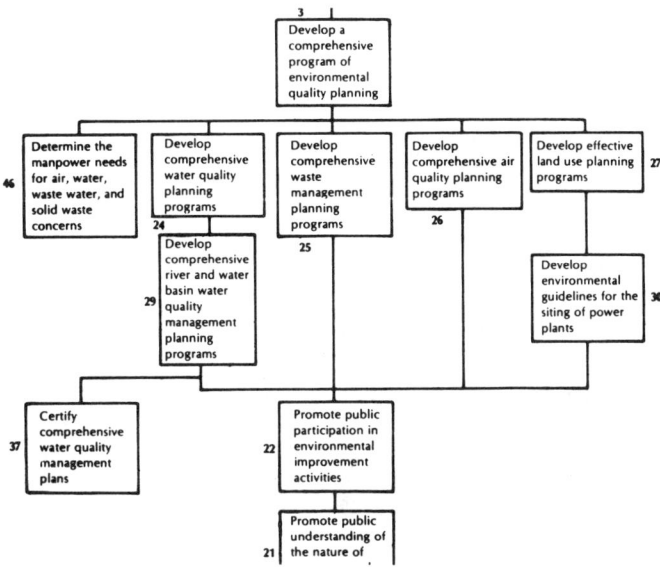

FIGURE 3 continued

Unlike many simulation models which are run by highly skilled "experts" and which involve an elaborate language, ISM is simple in its operation and can be used by people with little computer and/or mathematics knowledge to obtain a broader understanding of a complex social problem. It also provides an excellent medium for communication between experts and decision makers. Finally, unlike such other participatory methodologies as delphi, ISM will provide a hierarchical structure for any problem.

References

Baldwin, Maynard M. (ed.) (1975) Portraits of Complexity: Applications of Systems Methodologies to Societal Problems. Columbus, OH: Battelle Memorial Institute, June.

Hart, William L. and David W. Malone (1975) "Goal Setting for a State Environmental Agency," pp. 89-94 in Maynard M. Baldwin (ed.), Portraits of Complexity: Applications of Systems Methodologies to Societal Problems. Columbus, OH: Battelle Memorial Institute, June.

Kane, Julius (1972) "A Primer for a New Cross-Impact Language--KSIM," Technological Forecasting and Social Change, 4, 2, 129-42.

Kawamura, Kazuhiko and David W. Malone (1975) "Strategies for Conducting Issue-Focused Workshops as an Aid to Program and Policy Planning." Columbus, OH: Battelle Columbus Laboratories, 24 March.

Kawamura, Kazuhiko and David W. Malone (1975a) "Structural Objectives in a Systematic Decision-Making Methodology." Paper presented at the 6th Modeling and Simulation Conference, Pittsburgh, PA, April.

Linstone, Harold A. (1974) "Planning: Toy or Tool?" IEEE Spectrum, (April), 42-49.

Malone, David W. (1975) "An Introduction to the Application of Interpretive Structural Modeling," Proceedings of the IEEE, 63, 3 (March), 397-404.

Waller, Robert J. (1975) "An Application of Interpretive Structural Modeling to Priority Setting in Urban Systems Development," pp. 104-8 in Maynard M. Baldwin (ed.), Portraits of Complexity: Applications of Systems Methodologies to Societal Problems. Columbus, OH; Battelle Memorial Institute, June.

Warfield, John N. (1974) Structuring Complex Systems. Columbus, OH: Battelle Memorial Institute, April.

Overcoming Obstacles to Agency and Public Involvement: A Program and Its Methods*

Kenneth E. Hornback
National Park Service

Since the growth of grass roots political activism during the 1960s and the enactment of legislation defining elements of citizen participation in public administration, citizens have acquired and used the power to interrupt the machinery of government whenever they feel their interests have been ignored by decisionmakers. The problem of legally or politically interrupted planning efforts is resolved, partially, by the involvement of people in the process of planning. This involvement must itself be a process if it is not to turn the planning effort into chaos. Impromptu citizen involvement programs and traditional public hearings do not enable consensus formation and problem resolution. Effective public involvement requires conscious efforts by members of the public and public officials because of a variety of obstacles to such relationships.

The Nature of the Problem
Public involvement in public administration is hindered by general fears and beliefs about the authenticity of public meetings. The general public is often skeptical about the sincerity of officials at public meetings and the reality of opportunities for involvement presented to them (Spiegel 1971; Arnstein 1969). Similarly, public officials often fear the public and are frustrated by the demands frequently placed on the officials by individuals attending public meetings (Wengert 1971; Burke 1968).

The Citizen's Perspective
General suspicions of conspiracy are often directed toward public officials and agency actions by the general public. Public involvement efforts have both grown out of and been caught up in the recent climate of distrust and suspicion of government following the Watergate affair and other political controversies of the early 1970s. Heberline (1975) has offered an inventory of some common complaints by the public:

1. Those groups which complain the most are served, while those who are quiet, unorganized, or inexpressive may be ignored.
2. The views of organized groups seem to be given more weight than opinions of unorganized interests.
3. The citizen often must initiate the inquiry.

---

*The author wishes to acknowledge the valuable criticisms and suggestions offered on earlier versions of this paper by Dr. Harvey Fleet and Ms. Kay Roush of the Denver Service Center, National Park Service. The views expressed here are those of the author and do not involve approval nor disapproval by the National Park Service.

4. When the agency initiates public involvement, the meetings are too formal. The agency defines the procedure and information to be aired. Public concern is channeled and controlled to avoid threatening challenges to the agency position.
5. Public involvement takes place after decisions have been made.
6. Agency public meetings tend to "snow" the public with jargon and technical material to suppress the expression of fundamental concerns.
7. There is little feedback concerning the impact of suggestions on the agency.
8. Because participation is erratic, "there is always the feeling that options are being quietly dropped into the deep bogs of the bureaucracy while the citizen is still waiting to make comment."

Such attitudes partially account for the public's lack of interest in civic affairs even when events have considerable importance to their lives (Bultena 1974).

The Agency Official's Perspective

For a variety of reasons, public officials are also hesitant to engage in frank disclosure of plans and decisions (Wengert 1971). The following are examples of beliefs that serve as barriers to public involvement from the perspective of the agency official.

1. Public involvement is unnecessary if the agency is simply carrying out the actions already approved by elected officials.
2. Public involvement reduces the agency's freedom to exercise discretionary action.
3. Public involvement adds information that makes the job more difficult.
4. There is no clear way to reduce the volume of information provided by the public and translate it into decisionmaking source material.
5. Public involvement invariably requires greater disclosure of facts than would be required otherwise; there is seldom adequate staff or funding to provide for this demand.
6. The demands for explanations are threats to the professional expertise of the agency staff.
7. The agency must respond to public involvement according to majority opinion.
8. The people who come to public meetings are only concerned with what is in it for them personally.
9. Only the "politicized" public comes to meetings; the general public stays home, trusting the agency to define and implement the public interest.
10. Local interests demand a share in decisionmaking, a position that conflicts with existing requirements to operate in the general public interest.
11. The interested public does not represent the public that the agency serves.

When such beliefs are coupled with the fact that few agency people have both professional expertise and the skills required for public forum diplomacy, a formidable argument against open and frank public involvement can be made.

This paper argues that the removal of obstacles to public involvement depends on changing the nature of the relationship that exists between the public and the agency and, consequently, changing the nature of the roles played by public officials and members of the public.

The traditional public hearing may be regarded as an example of a situation which is not conducive to public involvement, for the following reasons:

1. Public hearings generally occur only once during the planning effort, usually at the end of the effort.
2. Hearings generally adopt a format of adversary confrontation—either the agency presents its plan to the public and receives reactions to the presentation, or citizen advocates present their solutions or challenges to the agency which "hears" this presentation with tape recorders and/or stenotypers.
3. Hearings tend to be ritualized, legalistic, formal ceremonies which intimidate the citizen rather than encourage the presentation of concerns and ideas.
4. Hearings only serve a legal purpose insofar as planning efforts or decisions are not contingent upon the satisfaction of some goal by the hearing itself.

More effective public involvement might be based on the following considerations:

1. In order to develop informed plans and decisions, an appreciation of the characteristics, concerns and problems of people living in the area to be affected must be gained at the earliest possible point in the planning or decisionmaking process.
2. In order to integrate public concerns and perspectives into the plan or decision, periodic meetings must be held as substantial thresholds in planning or decisionmaking are met.
3. In order to avoid continuing delays in problem resolution, public involvement must become more task specific and narrowly focused as plans become more precise. This gradually declining flexibility implies two responsibilities for the agency: exhaustive recruitment of publics via the mass media (and other means), and person-to-person communication about involvement opportunities with persons who might be impacted by possible alternative actions.
4. In order to develop a cumulative effort at plan resolution, public meetings must be purposeful—the meetings must accomplish some task upon which the enterprise of planning or decisionmaking is dependent.

A Program
If public involvement is to be effective, rather than a mere ritual, stages of plan development must be contingent upon reaching some degree of mutual understanding with the public at every stage in planning. This involves both presenting

the public with information relative to the task and requesting from the public informational material (judgments, concerns, opinions, and knowledge related to the task). Information received from the public must be reducible so that it can be integrated into the decisionmaking process. Such a program might resemble the following:

Phase 1: Identification of goals. At the earliest point in the process of problem solving, the nature of the planning problem to be faced should be shared with the public (see Figure 1). Their concerns and remarks about the problem and suggestions about possible solutions can serve to better define the scope of work that will have to be undertaken. The public can help identify limiting factors. Common local knowledge can help prevent inadvertent errors and save time in basic resource studies by complementing agency expertise. The more that is known about the problem early in the planning process, the more likely that important facts or possibilities will not be overlooked.

The desires of the general public must be constrained, however, by the same legal considerations that bear on the agency. In addition, fiscal and administrative conditions may further limit the efforts of the agency. These limitations must be fully explained to the public. Failure to openly disclose both opportunities and constraints can serve as grounds for "conspiracy theories" about influences on planning which can ruin the problem solving effort. The first phase, therefore, addresses the task of problem definition and delimitation and results in a better conception of goals to be accomplished by the plan.

Phase 2: Options review. Options are different specific actions which serve to accomplish goals developed in Phase 1. There may be one or more different ways to accomplish any single goal. Options should be reviewed by the public to make sure they exhaust the possibilities within the constraints which have been established. The public can help identify those options which may be disruptive to the community and give concreteness to options abstractly defined. Public concern is collected in the form of reasoning for or against any specific option. Amendments to existing options or entirely new options can be added at this time. A dossier of reasoning and amendments is compiled for each option. The contents of the dossier can be used to develop new ways to arrive at the goals or modifications to existing concepts. The dossier can suggest new areas of information which should be developed or provide a basis for establishing mitigating actions to reduce undesired effects of an option under consideration. The dossier contents may provide sufficient grounds for the elimination of an option altogether. The dossier is a valuable tool for both social impact assessment and decision-making.

Phase 3: Alternatives review. Alternatives are combinations of options grouped to make a compatible set of actions. The public's reasoning for or against options (collected in Phase 2) is added to other pertinent basic data (economic, demographic, natural resource, etc.) and becomes part of the criteria for narrowing down the available options. The remaining options (alternatives) become the action ingredients of the environmental assessment. The alternatives review phase is a review of the environmental assessment.

The method of gathering public commentary for or against the alternatives is the same as that used in Phase 2. The public comments are used as a source of information on impacts and their assessment as viewed by the involved public. Such

FIGURE 1. PLAN DEVELOPMENT BY PUBLIC-AGENCY DIALOGUE

Phase	Public Task	Agency Task
		Problem detection and program initiation
1	Problem Elaboration (adding public goals and concerns)	
		Problem review and revision, options development
2	Options review	
		Reduction of option list, preparation of environmental assessment
3	Alternatives review	
		Selection of proposed action, preparation of draft environmental report
4	Review of draft environmental report	
		Preparation of final environmental report
5	Document review	
6	Court contest ← or →	Plan implementation

comments may also help refine existing alternatives. Collecting early public commentary on the environmental assessment is desirable in order to give both the agency and the public time to review the document and suggest tentative objections and/or unresolved problems. Such suggestions are tentative because of the complexity likely to be contained in the assessment document and the persistent problem of finding the clearest, most accurate mode of expression. The option/alternative review steps are separated to prevent problems due to the hasty aggregation of actions which often result in the wholesale rejection of plans--the "throwing the baby out with the bathwater" syndrome.

The remaining phases (4-6) of public involvement are the conventional hearings on the draft and final Environmental Impact Reports. If public involvement in Phases 1-3 has been actively cultivated to this point, the recommended action will come as no surprise to the public concerned with the planning effort. Undoubtedly, the proposal will not suit everyone, but all will have had an opportunity to influence their neighbors and inform the planners of their thinking on matters relevent to them. Moreover, the information provided by the public will have been used by the planning staff.

Methods

While a variety of techniques and how-to-do-it guides are available (e.g. Hendee and others 1973), the number of techniques which do not require special expertise and skillful, coordinated administration is small. Two techniques which do not require special expertise are the "self-administered small group workshop" and the "workbook completion method." These two techniques are based on the following assumptions: people who come to public meetings need an opportunity to discover their neighbors' views and to better form their own opinions; people who come to public meetings are capable of interpersonal political negotiation with others; and, people who come to public meetings are willing and able to help the agency discover the common public interest. The methods to be discussed are simply improved ways to exchange information between the agency and the public. However, the methods require a level of involvement from the public which is more demanding than is characteristic of conventional public hearings. The methods also require a commitment by public administrators to a process and a relationship with the public to which officials are effectively insulated in the hearings context.

The self-administered small group workshop (Phase 1 method). This method is a variation of the Nominal Group Method and various delphi decision making exercises. The workshop involves problem solving and consensus identification steps. Participants are concerned citizens responding to media announcements of agency planning activities and workshops in the project area. (Some have advocated random sampling to assure representativeness but the normative attractiveness of town meeting democracy tends to obscure the basic question of how the public interest is best determined; see Wengert 1971: 28; Dahl 1956: 90.) The procedures are fully translated onto a set of instruction cards which are handed to a participant who is asked to initiate the process by randomly selecting a moderator for the small group of which the person is a member. By the end of the workshop the goal of the small group is to identify ten common concerns they agree the planning effort should address. A version of the procedure is explained in the work of Delbecq and Van De Ven (1971; 1972; 1975) but modifications are required to make the process self-guiding and appropriate to the character of politically formed groups (persons who respond to appeals for citizen viewpoints because of common, but not identical, concern with an issue of some community importance).

The agenda for this type of meeting includes a brief introduction to the planning problem; identification of constraints on the scope of work; explanation of the workshop procedure, emphasizing that this method enables more people to express their concerns as well as establishing a forum for the identification of common goals; adjourning to the small groups; the workshop; reassembling for presentations of the goal lists (10 objectives for each small group).

Field experience suggests that the self-administered workshop method can easily be followed by untrained persons without internal dissention and with only occasional additional assistance by agency staff. In fact, agency staff can expect to be asked to excuse themselves from the workshops while the participants work out their common concerns. Rather than feeling helpless and unorganized (as in a randomly assembled public at hearings), the small groups gain a sense of purpose as they develop ideas and present them formally to the agency at the end of the meeting. Such a creative method of problem identification provides a basis for continuing public interest in the planning effort. Diffusion of public interest in the planning effort can also be expected. The process is not ritualistic but in fact commits the agency to pursue certain objectives as defined by the concerned public.

Subsequent to the Phase 1 public meeting, the goal lists provided by each small group are merged and compared to legal, administrative, and fiscal limitations. Any goals which must be eliminated because of such constraints are identified and a report to the public is prepared and mailed to workshop participants and other interested parties that have come to the attention of the agency (including related governmental agencies). Such reports or "planning newsletters" provide valuable resumes of the workshop accomplishment and serve to identify possible misunderstanding between the public and the agency over the scope of the planning task. Copies of all "planning newsletters" should be provided to persons wishing to become involved in the planning process at later times to help them catch up to the pace set by persons involved from the beginning. This practice helps overcome the tendency of some to feel that planning accomplishments can be turned back to fundamental issues which have been already resolved by initial public involvement (for a related discussion see Jordan's (1973) comments on the "exhaustion of remedies doctrine").

The workbook completion method (Phase 2 and 3 method). This method is based on the need for a systematic organization of information provided by the public. Tape recordings, flip charts, and stenographic transcriptions all fail to deliver an organized body of information to public officials. Expensive and time consuming content analysis is generally not programmed into planning endeavors. The workbook is a simple way to organize the information provided by the public. Each page of the workbook is devoted to a single option. Three entry spaces are provided following the option statement: reasons for the option, reasons against the option, and amendments to the option. After all the options for any goal are listed, an additional page is inserted where entirely new options can be explained.

The agenda for Phase 2 and 3 meetings, which use the workbook completion method, includes a brief introduction to the planning problem and a review of how the plan has evolved to this point via earlier public involvement and the explanation of viewpoints and values that people want their neighbors and the agency to recognize and consider.

The public is encouraged to use the workbook to state their reasons for or against any idea of concern to them. Everyone is encouraged <u>not</u> to fill in their workbooks until they have had a chance to hear what their neighbors have to say, however. Many people will not be able to make up their minds on important issues by the end of the meeting. The workbooks may be taken home so people can consult with their friends, family, or neighbors. Additional workbooks are available upon request. A time limit for the submission of notebooks is set and mailers are provided to those who wish to fill in their workbooks later.

The workbook completion method provides information about the actions under consideration in a way which is usable--it gives reasons for and against each option; it gives a general indicator of the level of concern for each option; it gives a general indicator of the bias of concern (degree of favor, disfavor, or controversiality); it serves to identify new ideas and variations on old ideas and thereby expands the inventory of possibilities for problem solving.

<u>The Nature of the Solution</u>
Overcoming the obstacles to agency-public involvement can be facilitated by improved methods of communicating information as well as by the application of methods suited to the changing processes of planning and public concern. Such procedural improvements over the conventional public hearing confrontation can help to eliminate the myths that hinder public involvement, e.g. the idea that the agency is the enemy of the public or vice versa. Frank and open public involvement can create a planning process which improves the chances of discovering and delivering action consistent with the public interest.

References

Arnstein, Sherry R. (1969) "A Ladder of Citizen Participation," Journal of the American Institute of Planners, 35 (July), 216-24.

Bultena, Gordon (1974) "Dynamics of Agency-Public Relations in Water Resources Planning," pp. 125-49 in Donald R. Field, James C. Barron and Burl F. Long (eds.), Water and Community Development: Social and Economic Perspectives. Ann Arbor, MI: Ann Arbor Science Publishers.

Burke, Edward M. (1968) "Citizen Participation Strategies," Journal of the American Institute of Planners, 34 (September), 287-93.

Dahl, Robert A. (1956) Preface to Democratic Theory. Chicago: University of Chicago Press.

Delbecq, Andre L. and Andrew H. Van De Ven (1971) "A Group Process Model for Problem Identification and Program Planning," Journal of Applied Behavioral Science, 7, 4, 466-92.

Heberline, Thomas (1975) "Principles of Public Involvement: A Primer for Park Service Planners and Managers." Madison: Department of Rural Sociology, University of Wisconsin.

Hendee, John C. and others (1973) "Public Involvement and the Forest Service." Washington, D.C.: Forest Service, U. S. Department of Agriculture.

Jordan, Robert E. (1973) "Alternatives under NEPA: Toward an Accommodation," Ecology Law Quarterly, 3, 4 (Fall), 722-23.

Spiegel, Hans B. C. (1971) "Citizen Participation in Federal Programs." Journal of Voluntary Action Research Monograph 1.

Van De Ven, Andrew H. (1975) Group Decision Making and Effectiveness: An Experimental Study. Kent, OH: Kent State University Press.

Van De Ven, Andrew H. and Andre L. Delbecq (1972) "The Nominal Group as a Research Instrument for Exploratory Health Studies," American Journal of Public Health, (March), 337-42.

Wengert, Norman (1971) "Public Participation in Water Planning: A Critique of Theory, Doctrine and Practice," Water Resources Bulletin, 7, 1, 26-32.

Social Impact Assessment: A Survey of Highway Planners*

Lynn G. Llewellyn
United States Fish and Wildlife Services

"Satisfying client needs" is one of the most frequently encountered slogans in the field of management consulting. Indeed, it is a rare research proposal which does not describe in glowing terms the unique capacity of the writer's firm to provide solutions to the most complex problems. Modesty is a trait seldom encountered in management consulting; yet most firms have much to be modest about, particularly with respect to meeting user needs.

The experience of transportation planners in this regard is no different from that of officials in other agencies across all levels of government: consultants are often perceived as "unresponsive," their performance is lackluster, and what they produce is of little value in the decision-making process. Ironically, the failure of applied researchers to work closely with those individuals who ultimately use their products, and to comprehend fully the problems of day-to-day operations, has probably contributed as much as anything else to a general lack of confidence in consultant performance.

The purpose of this discussion is not to hurl brickbats at management consultants (although a comprehensive evaluation of their track record is long overdue); rather, it is to discuss briefly one method of identifying user needs which was utilized in the development of a social impact assessment sourcebook for state highway planners. The technique itself is neither new nor unique; however, when combined with other means of collecting data, it can serve as an important communication channel between researchers and client groups.

In the sections which follow an attempt is made to (1) review the history of a study that the National Bureau of Standards conducted for the Federal Highway Administration, (2) describe a series of informal interviews with highway planners representing nine states, and (3) summarize social assessment needs, problem areas, and gaps in information as perceived by highway department representatives.

METHOD

Background
In 1973, at the direct request of the Federal Highway Administration (FHWA), the Technical Analysis Division of the National Bureau of Standards began a 26-month

---

* The interviews on which this study was based have been discussed more extensively in Llewellyn and others (1975). In contrast to the earlier paper this account is focused primarily on the problem of meeting user needs.

study of the social and environmental effects of alternative highway locations. Following the completion of a comprehensive evaluation of the research literature on highway impacts (Llewellyn 1974), it quickly became clear that the technical approach stipulated in the contract with FHWA would not greatly benefit decision-makers outside the Federal Government. To be more specific, what we had proposed differed but slightly from countless other highway impact studies which relied heavily on the results of mail-out surveys. Even more disturbing was the absence of information on who would use the survey data, how the data would be used, and for what purpose.

After several discussions with the sponsor a revised work plan was developed. Two changes are worth mentioning. First, we were in general agreement that the survey should be deleted from the plan and much greater emphasis given to the development of a package of social impact assessment techniques which would be combined in a sourcebook. FHWA Policy and Procedure Memorandum 90-4, which enjoined the development and implementation of state highway action plans, provided strong support for a vigorous state highway department effort in the area of social impact assessment. The second major change was the result of our uneasiness about the backgrounds, capabilities, and information needs of those highway department officials responsible for social forecasting under PPM 90-4. We clearly did not want to conduct our study in an atmosphere of uncertainty nor run the strong risk that the final product could not be implemented by the people it was designed to assist. Hence, permission was requested to conduct a series of informal interviews with highway planners representing nine states--one in each of the FHWA regions--to obtain an understanding of **prospective sourcebook users and their** information needs.

Procedure

The sample of nine state highway departments was selected jointly by the project team and the sponsor. Time and budgetary constraints precluded a random selection of interview sites; however, by choosing one state within each FHWA region it was still possible to control for variables such as degree of urbanization, geography, attitudes toward transportation alternatives, and the like.

Formal contacts with the states were initiated by FHWA in Washington, D.C. The FHWA regional offices were first notified of our plans; they in turn contacted the appropriate District Planning Engineer and his office arranged the time and place of the interviews once approval was granted by the states. It is interesting to note that although the procedure just described is normally followed in situations where state highway department participation is requested, in some instances the purpose of our interviews was misinterpreted. After the first two interviews we made certain that state officials understood clearly why we were there, who we specifically wanted to see, and the proposed content of the discussions. Better rapport was obtained once officials recognized that there was to be no evaluation of department performance and the names of the states we visited would not be disclosed in any future publication.

In order to minimize disruption to on-going department activities, the interviews were conducted in small groups rather than individually. Those in attendance generally included officials concerned with social impact assessment, environmental quality, community involvement, highway location and right-of-way. Whenever possible, we also specifically requested the presence of highway sociologists working at the project level; they frequently provided the best information on day-to-day problems and prevented the discussions from becoming too lofty and theoretical. The interviews usually lasted from 2-4 hours except in a few instances where it was necessary to hold discussion groups in different locations. Tape recorders were not used during the interviews because of the potential inhibitory effect on participants, particularly those who might be ill at ease in the presence of Federal Government employees. Thus, we decided in advance to use at least two experienced interviewers at each session to maintain the continuity of discussions but, more importantly, to insure that all the relevant data would be recorded.

In retrospect, it seems clear that there were numerous disadvantages inherent in group vs. individual interviews. Perhaps the most serious problem was the occasional tendency of highway department division chiefs to dominate discussions, especially when controversial questions were raised. As a result staff and project level personnel may not have responded as openly as they might have had the interviews been conducted differently. For the most part, however, there was little reluctance to discuss sensitive issues; in fact, the presence of several department staff often prompted a lively debate on key questions. Given the limitations of time and budget there is little doubt that the data collected through multiple group interviews far surpassed what we might have been able to obtain from telephone conversations or impersonal mail questionnaires. The fact that the Federal Government was actively <u>seeking</u> advice from the states, rather than <u>telling</u> them what to do, was a pleasant change for transportation officials.

RESULTS

<u>Personal Limitations</u>
One of the first steps in meeting client needs is to learn as much as possible about the "user" himself--his background, education, capabilities, and the like. This area of questioning was of particular significance to us in designing the proposed social impact assessment sourcebook. How much training in the social sciences could we expect to find within each highway department, and at what level should the sourcebook be written?

The interview data suggested considerable variation in academic training and practical experience among department personnel. A few states could point to social psychologists or sociologists with advanced degrees; most were not so fortunate, however. Responsibility for social impact assessment was frequently assigned to personnel with undergraduate degrees in the social sciences, sometimes to liberal arts majors and engineers with little or no training in social research methods.[1]

---

1. While the absence of social science expertise is not necessarily a cause for alarm, situations do arise which deserve the attention of professionally trained individuals. For example, occasionally highway departments perform research that, to the public, has an aura of scientific respectability which is totally undeserved. During one of the site visits a community preference survey was drafted by department personnel who lacked the most rudimentary background in questionnaire design and administration; yet the results of the survey were to be used as the basis for decisions which might profoundly affect the quality of life of numerous individuals.

In an effort to improve social forecasting procedures highway departments in a few localities were either enrolling engineers in courses designed to make them more cognizant of social problems or were seeking assistance from outside consultants.

Another factor affecting the availability of social scientists is tight money. Several departments mentioned that severe budgetary limitations precluded the hiring of additional sociologists to comply with the requirements for interdisciplinary teams specified in state action plans. Moreover, in some instances the modest salaries paid to government employees prevented certain states from retaining high quality specialists for more than a few months. Faced with these difficulties highway department spokesmen cited the need for short-cut methods of research and social analysis which could be performed by a small staff. Most of the departments interviewed felt that they did not have enough social scientists on board to cover all the projects requiring some form of social impact assessment.

Current Social Assessment Techniques and Guidelines
A second area of inquiry essential to the determination of user needs had to do with the range of social impact assessment techniques, guidelines and definitions currently employed by highway departments. As might be expected, the interview data indicated as much variation in impact assessment techniques as we found in the types of people performing the assessments. Generally speaking, states which maintained a strong, in-house social science capability were also more likely to be using relatively sophisticated techniques, e.g., community profiles, neighborhood social interaction indices, and various types of surveys. A majority of the departments had used census tapes at one time or another, but most highway planners felt that census data either became obsolete too quickly or were not particularly helpful except for large-scale social analysis.

It was also interesting to find that guidelines and definitions related to social impact assessment had not yet been formulated in the states comprising our sample. For some planners all impacts had a "social" component; for others, the word "environmental" could just as easily substitute for social; still others argued that any "social cost" could ultimately be reduced to a monetary value. In essence, each state had a different perception of "social," which, in the absence of uniform Federal guidelines, governed the types of effects selected for in-depth treatment. One of the few impacts mentioned by all the states was "displacement and relocation;" however, concern was generally limited to the economic aspects of relocation, e.g., availability of comparably priced replacement housing, effects on relocated businesses, etc. Unfortunately, there was little awareness among planners of the grief syndrome described by Fried (1963) or, more importantly, of the mounting evidence that sudden dislocation correlates with accelerated morbidity among the elderly (Pastalan 1973; Johnson and Burdge 1974).

Gaps in Information
The disturbing lack of awareness of the socio-psychological consequences of involuntary dislocation is closely related to another facet of user needs--gaps in information, both known and unknown. To clarify this point somewhat, the diverse experiences of highway planners have underscored a number of areas related to social forecasting which are ambiguous, unclear, or defy coverage because of a lack of solid data. Planners seem to be cognizant of most of these information gaps; sometimes, however, they simply are unaware of data which might affect decisions on specific highway locations and designs. Consider, for example, the

effects of highway-related noise on reading achievement (Glass, Cohen, and Singer 1973) and classroom interaction (Ward and Suedfeld 1973). By compiling a list of information gaps which planners could identify, we hoped to accomplish three objectives: (1) develop a crude but useful set of information priorities; (2) determine which problem areas were common to a majority of states, and which were specific to only one or two localities; and (3) provide some insights on social impact categories not commonly understood by most highway planners.

The gaps in information identified by highway planners were generally concerned with two problem areas: the nature of social effects and the desire for specific techniques with which to measure social impacts. No attempt will be made to discuss all the information needs collected during the interviews; nevertheless, it might be instructive to mention a few areas where assistance was requested.

The Nature of Social Effects
As indicated earlier, every department visited was uncertain about the meaning of "social impact." Most of the officials we interviewed expressed the urgent need for an operational definition of "social," one that delineates the boundaries of the concept yet is easily understood by both those who draft and those who review environmental impact statements. A number of respondents suggested that simply identifying key social impacts--that is, promoting greater awareness of their significance among department personnel--would be an important contribution to highway planning. Beyond these general needs, some specific areas of concern related to social impacts are listed below:

- Timing of effects: How long are social impacts likely to last? What are the major short-range, imminent effects of highways? What types of social impacts are characteristic of the construction phase of highway projects?

- Location of effects: What types of social impacts typically occur in rural communities? How are neighborhoods defined and delineated? What types of communities do residents desire? What are their transportation goals? What range of alternative futures might be predicted for communities as the result of new or improved highways? How does a new highway facility affect the boundaries of social service delivery systems?

- Consequences of social disruption: How does a new or improved highway affect the individual? What happens to the people who remain in the vicinity of a new highway? How does a relocatee once more become part of the social structure of the community? What is the effect of road closures on small businesses? What changes occur to community organizations and small formal groups as the result of new highways?

- Impacts related to construction alternatives: What happens if the decision is made not to build a facility? How are adverse impacts mitigated? What are the positive and negative consequences of mitigation procedures? How does the location of a highway change the priorities of various classes of impacts, for example, social vs. environmental?

Impact Assessment Technique

Although the discussion of techniques was focused primarily on the proposed social impact assessment sourcebook, some of the needs expressed by highway planners may prove useful to consultants contemplating similar endeavors. In this vein perhaps the most frequently expressed admonition was to keep the presentation simple, straightforward, and free of "philosophy." It was further suggested that we (1) use small volumes (one for each technique) rather than one large volume because a bulky, unwieldy appearance is disconcerting; (2) provide step-by-step procedures including check lists, numerous examples of applications, a system for weighting impacts, and suggestions regarding appropriate situations in which to use each technique; and (3) include a comprehensive literature review on social impacts and a volume covering the construction and administration of surveys for those individuals who have had limited experience in this field. Highway planners expressed the hope that an outgrowth of the current interest in social impact assessment might be a demand for standardized data; at present, social data are often collected on the basis of administrative fiat with little transferability from one situation to another.

DISCUSSION

This paper has briefly described a systematic attempt to identify the needs of highway planners with respect to social impact assessment and to incorporate the advice of practitioners in the conceptual development of a research product. The question remains, however, as to the success (or failure) of the effort and how success should be measured. Various criteria which might be used include the sourcebook's _acceptance_ by the states, its _applicability_ in a wide range of situations, and the extent to which it contributes to greater _awareness_ and better _understanding_ of social effects. It may be, however, that the best index of success is whether "better understanding" is then translated into attitudinal and behavioral change; that is, will the adverse social impacts which have sometimes occurred in the **past** be prevented in the future? Some of the factors which influence these indices of success are worthy of further discussion.

There are two ways of viewing user needs. One school of thought maintains that nobody is in a better position to judge what he needs than the practitioner himself. Conversely, it can be argued that, if the user knew what he wanted, he wouldn't be asking for help; hence, it is the consultant's job to tell the client what his needs are, and then to satisfy them. In all likelihood there are times when both philosophies apply, specific circumstances dictating how much support to give each one.

On the basis of the information we obtained in the field, much of the displeasure with the performance of consultants had to do with their failure to comprehend the operational problems of the highway department and their propensity for developing products on the basis of armchair logic rather than scientific method. Our first goal in developing the sourcebook was to establish credibility, i.e., write it in a manner acceptable to the states. Thus, to avoid repeating previous mistakes, we placed greater reliance on the needs identified by highway planners, and less on our own preconceptions about social impact assessment. From the standpoint of format and overall content of the sourcebook, we were reasonably successful; as suggested, a separate volume was devoted to each impact assessment technique, a modified **literature review and a manual on survey techniques were included**, and considerable stress was placed on areas of application. Unquestionably, we were less successful in other areas. For instance, we found that you cannot provide step-by-step procedures, and numerous examples of application, and still keep a volume short. By striving too hard for brevity there is a greater risk of superficiality, and this we did not want to happen.

The wide variation from state to state with respect to social science capability and sophistication made level of presentation a problem. One approach would have been to search for the lowest common denominator in order to make certain that all the procedures provided in the sourcebook could be used by personnel who might have only minimal training in research methods. Unfortunately, however, states with a strong social science capability would have derived little benefit from this treatment. For this reason we included two techniques--associative group analysis (Szalay 1975) and the judgmental impact matrix (Schofer, Peterson, and Gemmel 1975) --which, while demanding, have distinct advantages over some of the more traditional impact assessment methods. Both techniques are relatively **unobtrusive and can be** used in situations where direct methods (e.g., mail surveys) might be impractical. In contrast, most of the other techniques contained in the sourcebook do not require the same degree of training.

In sum, it seems likely that some but not all of the volumes on social impact assessment methodology will be acceptable to a majority of highway departments. Their applicability and the degree to which they enhance awareness of social effects will have to stand the test of time. We feel that the process of developing operationally useful impact assessment techniques has to be iterative and tailored to meet the needs of each individual department. Those techniques that do not appear useful should be discarded; those that do should be tested, modified, re-tested and refined until a satisfactory impact assessment procedure is developed.

Earlier it was suggested that the ultimate criterion of the sourcebook's success would be its ability to bring about positive change in the decision-making process, particularly the avoidance of negative impacts of highway construction. Certainly, it would be **presumptuous to conclude that any social impact assessment** sourcebook is the last word on the subject. There have been similar efforts before; undoubtedly, many others will follow this one. The best we can hope for is that the sourcebook will provide some guidance to state highway departments which do not currently maintain a strong social science capability. As we learned from the interviews, change cannot take place until critical information requirements are satisfied. Thus far, dissemination of information to the people working at the project level has not been very effective.

Assuming for the moment that the barriers to effective communication are removed, and that the essential elements of "social" information required by planners are translated into adequate assessments of highway construction impacts, what are some of the other factors which will affect decisions? One of these has to be the political climate in the state. If the Governor lets it be known that "highways <u>will</u> be constructed, and the sooner the better," then the no-build alternative is no longer a viable option and potential adverse social impacts will probably be discounted.

Similarly, although there is growing awareness of the social consequences of new and improved highways, a number of departments are still staffed with "hard-liners." To convince these individuals that social variables should be considered in the decision-making process will be a difficult task. Highway departments are not monolithic; however, it should be remembered that the departmental reward system has not changed fundamentally. Personnel are still judged on their ability to facilitate the process of building highways.

A third factor that must be taken into account is the highway department's relationship with the public. The Council on Environmental Quality (CEQ) has noted that one of the biggest complaints from citizen groups is that the highway department will not answer their questions. In some areas the public is becoming well versed in the techniques used for impact assessment, social as well as environmental. However, citizens in other localities, particularly rural communities, have no real conception of the changes which may occur as the result of new highway construction. Many have a sense of powerlessness and do not feel that they can influence decision-making. Thus, it seems especially important that materials such as the sourcebook be made available to the general public. Community groups constitute a different set of potential users whose information needs are seldom taken into account. If the general public is provided the same opportunity afforded government agencies to become better informed about social impacts and those techniques which might be used to measure them, the danger of potential misuse of an impact assessment sourcebook will be substantially reduced.

REFERENCES

Fried, M. (1963) "Grieving for a Lost Home," pp. 151-171 in L. J. Duhl (ed.), The Urban Condition. New York: Basic Books.

Glass, D. C., S. Cohen and J. E. Singer (1973) "Urban Din Fogs the Brain," Psychology Today, 6, 12, 94-99.

Johnson, S. and R. J. Burdge (1974) "Social Impact Statements: A Tentative Methodology," 69-84 in C. P. Wolf (ed.) Social Impact Assessment. Milwaukee, WI: Environmental Design Research Association.

Llewellyn, L. G. (1974) "The Social Impact of Urban Highways, pp. 89-108 in C. P. Wolf (ed.) Social Impact Assessment. Milwaukee, WI: Environmental Design Research Association.

Llewellyn, L. G. and others (1975) "The Role of Social Impact Assessment in Highway Planning," Environment and Behavior, 7, 3 (September), 285-306.

Pastalan, L. A. (1973) "Involuntary Environmental Relocation: Death and Survival," 410-415 in E. H. Steinfeld (chm.), Action Research in Man-Environment Relations. Environmental Design Research. Vol. 2. Stroudsburg, PA: Dowden, Hutchinson, and Ross.

Schofer, J. L., R. S. Gemmel, and G. L. Peterson (1976) The Judgmental Impact Matrix Approach: A Framework for Evaluating the Social and Environmental Impacts of Transportation Alternatives. Vol. 8 in L. Llewellyn, C. Goodman and G. Hare (eds.) Social Impact Assessment: A Sourcebook for Highway Planners. Washington, D.C.: Federal Highway Administration.

Szalay, L. B. (1976) "Associative Group Analysis," Vol. VI in L. Llewellyn, C. Goodman, and G. Hare (eds.) Social Impact Assessment: A Sourcebook for Highway Planners. Washington, D.C.: Federal Highway Administration.

Ward, L. M. and P. Suedfeld (1973) "Human Response to Highway Noise," Environmental Research, 6, 306-326.

VII Epilogue

The epilogue by Peterson and Gemmall emphasizes the evaluative function of SIA and the political nature of evaluation. They object to SIAs which are designed to inform top decision makers. Rather, they argue, the three major objectives of impact assessment are: "(1) clarifying for each player (affected party) all of the factual issues that are of concern to him; (2) improving his skills and opportunities to play the game; and (3) helping identify which issues and disagreements are ideological or value-related (and hence not resolvable through known or knowable facts) and, in particular, helping to identify areas of mutual utility, thus facilitating cooperation where possible." In other words, the SIA is to facilitate the political process of decision making by informing all affected parties. But to do this fairly politics must become a part of the control and direction of the assessment process. The authors see the choices about what is to be studied as political choices. It is from this perspective that the authors extensively criticize the current state of the art in SIA.

Social Impact Assessment: Comments on the State of the Art

George L. Peterson and Robert S. Gemmell
Northwestern University

Introduction
In the process of our accumulation of wealth-producing tools and machines, we have accumulated social and environmental complexity that may already have exceeded the capability of our forethought. For every action taken in the name of social progress there is an intricate cascade of reactions, and a pricetag for someone or some group. During the past decade, society has voiced, in the form of environmental quality legislation and public opposition to numerous proposed projects, unwillingness to accept blindly the "hidden costs" that are commonly associated with the things we do. Projects such as urban freeways or power generating stations which have previously been judged beneficial until proven detrimental now seem to be regarded conversely by the public. As a result, forethought with regard to indirect consequences as well as direct purposes is being demanded in the form of an environmental impact statement. In the midst of this public clamor for clarification of the environmental consequences, we have seen the recent emergence of the broader notion of social impact assessment, or the clarification of the social and human meaning of the consequences of projects, programs and technologies that our apparently **short-sighted forethought is creating**. This presents no **small** challenge, for no one seems to know quite how to do it.

The viability of impact assessment is based on two premises: (1) that the future (or alternative futures) can be predicted, and (2) that those who are concerned about alternative futures in the context of a proposed project or technology will understand the assessment and respond by modifying the decisions they might otherwise have made. The complexity of impact processes may invalidate the first premise and the plurality of the sociopolitical decision process may invalidate the second.

The purposes of this paper are three in number: (1) to try to define the problems inherent in impact assessment, (2) to criticize the current state of the art of impact assessment, and (3) to define some performance specifications that may help to guide future efforts and, perhaps, spur a little progress toward more valid and efficient methodology.

Statement of the Problem
Apparently, the problem of impact assessment is regarded under the law as the preparation of an environmental impact statement (EIS), the purpose of which is to identify and publicize consequences of a proposed action. The word "environment" means much more than physical things; most assessment efforts at least attempt to be concerned with social, economic, political, and human things as well as with conditions of air, water, and land. We all want to know exactly

what we are getting when we buy a freeway or a nuclear power plant and that we all pay a fair share. The major problems thus include: (1) externalities, (2) unexpected or subtle consequences, (3) irreversible and uncompensatable damages, and (4) distribution of costs and benefits in all of these categories as well as costs and benefits, which are the purposes for which the thing is being perpetrated.

To clarify these issues for even the simplest public works project is to lengthen one's stride vastly beyond the current state of the art. This must be recognized. In the selection of alternative futures, society asks for rational forethought which, to begin with, requires a scientific explanation of the processes by which the future is generated. If these processes can be understood, theories can be applied to specific projects to expose the impacts. This should not be done simply in general terms, but in very detailed terms with respect to quality, quantity, time and place. Unfortunately, the scientific explanations frequently are not available, and each project thus looms as an overwhelming problem in original research, rather than the application of known theories or existing methods to a specific case. We cannot rely on "intuitive" or "judgmental" insights either, without the invention of valid methodology for synthesizing the insights of many individuals into a comprehensive whole. Even if the science were not deficient, and the problem were simply one of applying known theories and valid methods to specific cases, how do we ascertain that we have dealt with every conceivable consequence likely to be of significant concern to someone and that we have dealt with it at an appropriate level of detail?

Perhaps one of the most important obstacles to successful impact assessment is a failure to recognize and allow for the pluralistic nature of the public decision process. The urban planning "profession" has recently come to realize that it is trying to use methods based on the assumption of "planning from the top down." Given that the public decision process is pluralistic, one way to approach the goal of better decision making is to improve the individual decision through better information, on the one hand, and better skill at playing the same, on the other. The challenges, then, in impact assessment are: (1) clarifying for each player all of the factual issues that are of concern to him; (2) improving his skills and opportunities to play the game; and (3) helping to identify which issues and disagreements are ideological or value-related (and hence not resolvable through known or knowable facts) and, in particular, helping to identify areas of mutual utility, thus facilitating cooperation where possible. We can't insure that a fully informed and politically adept society will optimize social welfare, but the decisions certainly will be better than those made by a society with ignorant and politically inept participants.

Still the problem statement is incomplete. Not everyone needs to know the same things, and what one person is concerned about may be irrelevant to another. How does the impact assessor know which issues must be clarified? Most budgets are ridiculously lean, so he can't expose every conceivable fact. Perhaps the answer lies in pluralistic impact assessment methodologies. This suggests abandonment of the notion of an impact assessor in favor of an impact assessment process where multidisciplinary teams work more or less together in pluralistic ways to cover the many facets of impact. May we expand this concept to incorporate citizen teams or perhaps expert-citizen interactive relationships which would define the areas of concern via some form of educational negotiation? The technical clarifications then could operate on the issues identified.

Thus, we redefined the problem. Instead of focusing on an impact statement, we have called for enlightenment of the decision process. In the place of or in addition to the environmental expert team, we have called for a pluralistic inquiry process. As an extension of the public hearing, we have called for enhancement of political skill and opportunity for all individuals who will be affected significantly by the proposed project. These are not new ideas, but their reemphasis may help to define the impact assessment problem.

Stated differently, it is probably a mistake to assume that the impact problem will be solved when we perfect the art of preparing impact statements. There is the notion that decisions (and progress) are being delayed because our impact statements are incomplete, illegible, controversial, or otherwise ineffective. This may be true, but the argument implies that THE IMPACT STATEMENT is the best way to approach the problem of improved public decisions regarding technological interventions. It may not be even a good way, let alone the best way, and even if it were the best way, we simply do not have the means to prepare GOOD impact statements for things like nuclear power technology. If GOOD statements could be prepared in such cases, debate could focus on ideological or policy issues rather than substantive ones, but at present much of the debate is centered in factual matters that are, in theory, concerned with knowable things.

While it would be irresponsible to suggest the best way to approach the problem, we do propose that a better way is to regard impact statements as factual inputs to a pluralistic process. Everybody who knows anything about the problem tries to get his knowledge into the mill. Competent scientists are commissioned to do their best formal work on the subject, and improved institutional frameworks are set up to allow the articulation of concerns, the identification of specific questions, and the exchange and distribution of available information. Then, we all slug it out in the political arena. This is how it is done, and it is probably better to recognize the fact than to dream wistfully about the ultimate impact statement methodology. The process is a much richer one than we are capable of inventing by way of formal methodology, and is probably much safer in the long run by virtue of its richness and diversity. Let us focus attention on how to get better facts into the mill and how to get the mill to be more effective in the exchange of ideas and the diffusion of information. The decisions may never be perfect, but there may not be a better way.

SOME SPECIFIC CRITICISMS

Recognizing the plural nature of the process by which impacts really are evaluated, let us turn to some specific criticisms of the current state of the art by which the (alleged) factual inputs are being generated and diffused into that process.

<u>Information vs. Evaluation</u>
Is the impact assessment supposed to present information or make decisions? If it is supposed to make decisions--that is, if it is supposed to evaluate the goodness or badness of the predicted consequences of a project or if it is to select among several alternative plans--then the social welfare function has to be made explicit. This is probably impossible except in very special cases.

It seems more reasonable to view the impact assessment as a clarifier of facts toward a more enlightened pluralism. Yet, many impact statements contain conclusions about which impacts are desirable, which are undesirable, and which are unacceptable. Who makes these decisions, and what criteria are used? Are the conclusions ad hoc value judgments, or do they arise from a priori criteria and standards that have been accepted through due process as public policy? Where such standards and criteria have been established, evaluation is justified; but where they do not exist, the technical experts should not be so arrogant as to impose their own values unless such value judgments are clearly identified as such. The facts should be presented and the evaluation should be arrived at politically.

Technical vs. Political Matters

We will define technical matters as those which are concerned with known or knowable facts, and political matters as those that deal with ideological problems. Conflicts arising from technical questions can, in theory, be resolved by the scientific method, given sufficient resources. Conflicts arising from ideological questions, i.e., regarding what is good or moral or fair or ethical, cannot be resolved by the scientific method, no matter what the resources. Thus, the exposure of alternative futures resulting from alternative courses of action would seem to be a technical problem, while evaluation of the relative desirability of those futures would seem to be a political problem.

Why, then, is there so much controversy over apparently technical things that should be resolvable through research, expert testimony, and the scientific method? It is because the "facts" are only more or less certain, because they are based on more or less evidence, from more or less credible sources and are more or less comprehendable. Presumably, if the true risks associated with nuclear power generation are known, the decision problem is the political one of willingness to accept those risks. But that truly political question has been intermingled with and often obscured by uncertainty about the validity of reported risk levels. As a consequence, efforts are made to resolve, in the political arena, the validity of "facts" as well as the level of acceptable risk.

In concept, the EIS is a clarification of facts, but it is political in at least two ways: (1) with regard to what questions have been addressed and the relative allocation of emphasis among questions, and (2) with regard to the level of confidence people have in its findings. Thus, it cannot be regarded as the clarifier of consequences attendant on a proposed project, but rather as one of many inputs to players in the game. Many people disagree with the accepted utility of science and expert testimony insofar as impact assessment is concerned. Such people make decisions on the basis of intuition rather than rational calculation and weighing of evidence. Indeed, in some situations, the more facts and figures that are available, the less capable is the decision-maker to process the information effectively and incorporate any of the information in his decision-making.

Fact or Fantasy?

It has been our experience that certain kinds of impacts can be predicted with reasonable confidence and evaluated by means of legally established standards. For example, the noise generated by a proposed freeway, the likelihood of flooding in a proposed new town, or the effect of groundwater extraction on the subsurface reservoir can be predicted fairly well. But even these "clear-cut" technical issues are not without controversy and possible error. Does the 100-year flood plain include pockets of localized ponding during periods of intense precipitation? How extensive is the historical record on which the flood plain is estimated? What effects will increasing urbanization have on the watershed over the next several decades, and where and at what rates will urbanization take place?

Clearly, there is a sizeable portion of probabilistic estimation and, unless studiously avoided, outright speculation in even the most well developed areas of impact prediction. What can we say for those areas that are not so well developed? Impact statements are replete with speculative reasoning either because resource limitations prevent rigorous examination or because facts and valid methods are not available, or both. Frequently the speculator is not even well trained in the field about which he is speculating. While it is not wrong for him to speculate--indeed, that privilege belongs to everyone--such speculation should not be institutionalized in the sacred cannon of the EIS. If it is included, it should be clearly identified for what it is.

Impact statements generally give the impression that they are attacking the problem of predicting futures. Credibility and clarity suffer because the mission to be predictive generally leads to the appearance of knowledgable prediction in areas of genuine uncertainty. Such "predictions" actually are guesses, opinions, and speculations. These may be intermixed with predictions based on reasonable information, where the risks can be assessed and scientific confidence is quite good. The result is either a tendency to give undue credibility to questionable guesses or to discredit valid information. Where uncertainty exists, it needs to be identified and exposed. The existence of uncertainty is, itself, an important fact to be considered.

Predictions vs. Decisions

Too often we are concerned with predicting things that we might better be controlling. The impacts of major public projects, for example, tend to be modified by numerous intervening variables. Many of these intervening variables are tied to policy variables that are more or less subject to control. On the one hand, a major intervention can be expected to generate impacts, and the impact task would be trying to predict these consequences. On the other hand, a major intervention can be expected to generate opportunities to manage the future, and then the impact task would be equally concerned with trying to identify these opportunities.

Reaction or Design?

One of the biggest current failings of impact statement preparation is that the whole process is a _reaction_. Perhaps this is built into the way the legislation is written, but it inhibits the effectiveness of the effort. In order to be efficient, the process by which alternative courses of action are identified or designed should incorporate a self-organizing sensitivity to the consequences that are likely to be of public concern. A common assumption presently being made is that such sensitivity is already a part of the design process and that the subsequent impact statement affords a public review to insure that no important feature has been missed. We would argue, however, that such public review would be more effective and more helpful if it were to occur on a continuing basis throughout the design process. What is needed, then, is a way to integrate impact prediction with design, so that the design itself is responsive to the same criteria that are being applied in generating the impact statement _reaction_.

Half-Vast Evaluation of Vast Projects

While we do not wish to offend others who may have engaged in responsible efforts to prepare impact statements, it has been our experience that multi-million dollar projects that would affect millions of people in profound ways tend to have only token resources devoted to the prediction of their impacts. For example, one project that anticipated an expenditure of about a hundred million dollars per year for about fifty years was allocated only sixty thousand dollars or so for the evaluation of economic, social and environmental impacts. While it was only a planning study having no immediate prospects of implementation, the budget ratio was not atypical. In another case one person was expected to do a complete impact statement for a new town of 60,000 people in six weeks. If we are serious about clarifying the consequences of proposed projects, we must be prepared to commit substantial amounts of money in the process--although in some cases where large budgets have been available, the money went largely for redundant superficiality and nice looking bindings.

To Inform, to Confuse, or to Divert the Public?

Apparently, one purpose of impact prediction is to increase the probability that all participants in the pluralistic public decision process will be well enough informed to defend and pursue their interests rationally. This presents some problems; projects such as urban freeways, new towns, or nuclear power plants are so technical and massive in impact that the ordinary citizen is not able to identify easily those aspects that relate to him, and his education is not sufficiently specialized to allow him to understand the processes that are involved. An impact statement is generally a comprehensive document consisting of hundreds (sometimes thousands) of pages written in technical terms and in very tedious style. Surely, there must be a better way to inform people. It could be argued that such matters should be left to technocrats who are elected or appointed and paid to read the ponderous documents and defend the interests of the public. This can be a dangerous route unless mechanisms are included to ensure that the technocrats are responsive to the values of the people they are supposed to represent. As has been shown repeatedly, technical decision makers tend to use different evaluative criteria than their clients, even though they are trying to be sensitive and responsive.

This leads us to an even more serious and basic problem: are the significant issues being addressed in the impact statements? Most are written according to legislative and administrative guidelines which aim at being general and comprehensive. The critical issues of local concern are often treated only superficially, if at all. Whose values are being served thereby? How can we be sure that the important issues of local concern have been given adequate treatment? Perhaps there should be a citizen participant role built into the impact prediction methodology so that members of the public can become more effectively informed and so that the guidelines can be tailored to address the important public concerns. Too many impact statements are designed to serve bureaucratic goals only.

Illogical Taxonomy

A common mistake is to treat impacts such as effects on water quality, changes in industrial production, and population migration as commensurate dimensions of impact--as though they can be compared and somehow weighed in relative importance. In fact, the physical change in water quality will have an effect on industrial production, which may, in turn, bring about shifts in migration patterns. True, it is interesting and perhaps important to know that these things are happening; but each measurement of impact ought to be embedded in a proper framework that shows how the several measures relate to each other. Impact assessment should not be aimed at eradicating disjointed symptoms. Rather, it should be aimed at solving the problems that produce the symptoms.

A functional taxonomy of dimensions of impact should be based on how these variables participate in the impact process. Water quality is of concern <u>because</u> it affects the efficacy of human activities and our ability to maintain desirable states of being. We might want to look at impact in terms of changes in the physical condition of the environment; or we might want to describe it in terms of changes in economic processes or social organization; or we might want to look at changes in personal satisfaction with the quality of life. But these perspectives must be recognized as different slices from the impact process, at different points along the sequence of events from project to person.

In an early (1969) effort to prepare an impact statement for a proposed highway, one of the authors assembled a team of "experts" from several disciplines, recognizing that the impact problem was multi-faceted. After many months of trying to come up with answers, the team began to recognize one of the sources of their frustrations: they didn't understand what the questions were. There was no logical framework or structure within which to make organized inquiry. (It didn't matter in that case, however, because it became apparent that the whole effort was window dressing; the bureaucrats in question were more concerned that there was visible effort made to predict impacts than they were with the prediction of the impacts.)

Out of this and other efforts has emerged a realization that the best framework for asking questions is one that is based on an understanding of the process by which the impacts occur. Unfortunately, the impact processes are not understood well, except in a few very specialized areas, and the result is that the questions are poorly defined. Poorly defined questions can only lead to poor answers.

This lack of theoretically-based structure causes each impact evaluation project to resemble an original research endeavor. Major research effort is required, in most cases, to find out what the questions are and to organize them in a meaningful way. Then, major research effort is required to come up with answers. For some kinds of questions, answers simply are not available, and operating budgets cannot be expected to support the level of research that would be needed. We might argue that the needed research is a legitimate cost of the project. If you can't afford the research needed for proper clarification of consequences, perhaps you can't afford the project. But that is not how things are done.

<u>Intervening Variables and Dynamic Processes</u>
Related to the distribution question and further emphasizing the complicatedness of impact processes is the fact that the same thing behaves differently in different situations. A study of the impacts of urban freeways in Chicago (Wang, Peterson and Schofer 1975) found that the introduction of a freeway tended to stimulate the growth of a growing area and accelerate the decline of a declining area. We suspect the existence of many such intervening processes and question the capability for predicting such things <u>a priori</u>. The difficulty with impact statements in this regard is that they tend to deal with first-order effects such as noise, pollution, land consumption, etc., but give little or no attention to the dynamic processes that are thereby set into motion. These dynamic processes of change are

probably of more importance to social welfare than the first-order changes; but impact statements are almost exclusively devoted to lists of such changes, and even these lists are uneven in depth and detail. Often they are grossly superficial.

Who, Where, and When?

In a recent study of the long term effects of a tornado (Russell 1975), it was demonstrated that poor people are much slower to recover than rich people. During the years following such a disaster, the poor people who are displaced have a harder time getting settled back down, while relatively rich people get settled rather quickly. Apparently, when you jiggle the cart, there are a lot of people in precarious positions who fall off and can't get back on again. Construction of an urban freeway is similar in some ways to the occurrence of an urban tornado, and it is to be expected that there are social and ethnic differences in the distribution of the consequences of freeways and other such disruptive projects. There are political questions here, and perhaps a political resolution of the problem would ultimately decide that people with a weak grip ought to be jiggled off, but we doubt it. Unfortunately, that is what is happening in many cases, by default and without explicit policy decision, because distributional issues are not being effectively exposed in impact statements. Furthermore, the people who are in the greatest danger of getting toppled from the cart are the ones who are least likely to read the impact statements, least able to understand them, and most apt to find that their particular interests are not even addressed in the inquiry.

To some extent this is a political issue, not a technical one, but a good way to get political resolution is to expose the problem. That is the purpose of the environmental impact statement: to catalyze political resolution by exposing problems and clarifying issues for _all_ concerned parties. As a consequence, distributional questions are of critical importance. It is the interests of the "cliff-hangers" that are most in need of attention, because even with perfect technical clarification of their impact-related concerns, these people face the further obstacle of uneven distribution of power and responsiveness in the political process itself.

The Unfortunate Predisposition

Mission-oriented governmental agencies often tend to produce environmental impact statements that are aimed more at selling projects than at exposing impacts. When negative aspects are identified, they tend to be surrounded by mollifying speculations and softening explanations. Even a well-intentioned technocrat working for a large governmental agency finds it very difficult to push his candid, negative appraisals through the bureaucratic filters if the prevailing predisposition toward the project is a favorable one. On the other hand, steel traps spring shut with alarming swiftness at the slightest hint of flaw in a project toward which the bureaucracy has a negative predisposition.

Even more scathing arguments can be aimed at the special interest groups who, for one reason or another, are strongly opposed to a given project. They seem more inclined to discredit source than to address substance. On a budget of $60,000 you do the best you can to expose the impacts, and the client bureaucracy gets mad because you don't come up with the right conclusions. The political sharks discredit the whole project because you can't do anything worthwhile on $60,000, or you have used methodology that is "obviously" not good. The impact analyst is in a position not unlike that of a divorce lawyer, except that he doesn't get paid that much. Again, these are political problems that may not be solvable, but they help to set the stage on which impact assessment is played; if methodology and theory are to do the job, they must be capable of performing under such circumstances.

Predisposition about a project and its impacts need not always be something to be struggled against. It might be an embryonic manifestation of policy. If the technical impact assessor comes to conclusions that are viewed with disfavor by the client agency because of predisposition, it need not be concluded that the predisposition is wrong and the assessor is right. If the "agency" position is an expression of the opinions or prejudices of one or two individuals, perhaps the environmental professional is right and the agency is wrong. If the predisposition is an as yet unformalized expression of policy (i.e., public preference) that is emerging from diverse pluralism, perhaps the agency is right. Which is more valid-- a conclusion arrived at through formal and informal negotiations among many individuals, or a conclusion that is the product of rational inquiry by a small group of environmental professionals? It is tempting to assume that rationalism is more valid than pluralism but, as we have shown, impact assessment is an art, not a science, and the alleged "rationalism" may be no more rational than the pluralism. Indeed, it may be simply a less diversified pluralism and, for that reason, less likely to arrive at valid conclusions.

If You Can't Do It, Ignore It?

To a certain extent sciences have developed in response to the level of demand for answers. This has been particularly true in modern times of war effort and space exploration. It might be said that answers and methods for getting answers tend to be most available for the most important questions. However, there may be some very important problems of critical concern to individuals, but where the nature of the problem is such that demand for answers is not well articulated. Industrial organizations and war efforts tend to generate very articulate demands, backed by impressive sums of money for research. Individual concerns for environmental quality tend to be inarticulate because of ignorance and the diffuse nature of the problem. So, there may be some important areas of concern for which answers and methods are poorly developed due to an inability of the demand to express itself effectively. For some other problem areas, the poor development results from the complexity and obscurity of the underlying processes.

There is an unfortunate tendency to base formal evaluations on those questions that can be answered effectively, and to ignore or give only lip service to the remainder. The standard methodology is to treat such factors "judgmentally," but formalized procedures for incorporating judgments into impact statements are not well developed. This is in spite of the fact that some well-developed methods for extracting judgments from individuals and groups are available. Indeed, with limited funds, an organized framework of pluralistic judgment may be the best way to prepare an impact statement, provided enough points of view are included (Schofer, Gemmell and Peterson 1976).

Too Many Pieces in Too Many Places

A lot of what we call impact assessment is like putting together a difficult jigsaw puzzle. The pieces of the puzzle are spread all over the place. Some reside in obscure scientific journals in the form of esoteric articles that have not been translated from jargonese to meaningful facts and concepts. Other pieces are cooking in the minds of scientists and have not been articulated as formal theories, facts, or propositions. Still other pieces are missing altogether, and we don't know from the start which pieces are missing or what the final picture is supposed to look like. Some pieces are common knowledge and are nicely identified in practical how-to-do-it handbooks of standard procedure. Each project seems to be an impossible task. Somebody should get it all together in a set of volumes, but until that is done each impact statement will continue to suffer from uneven rigor and missing pieces that might well be available someplace.

Because the impact assessment institution now tends to put the project and its advocates in the position of being guilty until proven innocent, unanswerable questions tend to be regarded as admissions of guilt. Find a question or feature for which innocence cannot be proven, and the project may be hung up indefinitely and perhaps even abandoned. Even well-intentioned environmental professionals can often be observed raising all kinds of trivial questions about a project, thereby causing the project sponsors to spend large sums of money to find answers of questionable usefulness. Too often these are questions that would not be asked by a competent professional in the area of concern, because he would recognize them as insignificant or unreasonable. For example, to criticize a proposed new town on the grounds that the plan is not innovative from an energy viewpoint may be valid, but not necessarily reasonable. If the market and institutional framework are such that the developer cannot be competitive if he addresses the energy question "properly," and if he is not to receive subsidies for investment in energy innovation, it seems unreasonable to expect him to commit financial suicide. The standard practice in subdivision design is deficient with regard to energy questions, and what is really being asked is for the developer to underwrite the cost of original research before he is to be allowed to build his new town. There may be environmental guilt in his proposal, but whose guilt is it? Is it the fault of the developer, or is it the fault of the institutional framework of the society? Does it matter whose "fault" it is if there is a better way than what is being proposed?

We can't answer these questions, but there is at least one way that unreasonable or insignificant questions may have an undesirable consequence. The project may be pushed beyond the point of cost-effectiveness with subsequent abandonment or bankruptcy. If that happens, is the absence of the project better than if it had been implemented? The impact of impact assessment needs to be assessed. Such a project might have been cost-effective if so much effort had not been misguided by the naivete of the impact assessors.

Answers or Games?

The literature on impact assessment methodology seems to be concerned primarily with answers as the direct product of the method. For example, if we had better theories and models of impact processes, we could develop methodology that calculates quantitative estimates of impacts, given quantitative descriptions of alternatives. Carried to the extreme, such methods might become "backward-seeking"; that is, given a quantitative specification of the desired future, calculate deductively via the process model the quantitative characteristics of the optimal alternative.

These are nice ideas, and research should continue to strive in these directions. In the meantime--and there is likely to be a lot of "meantime"--impacts will need to be assessed for a lot of practical situations. There is a need for alternative methodology. The pluralistic "game" would seem to be a promising alternative, and more emphasis should be placed on this approach. Impact matrices that produce meaningful answers would be nice, but impact matrices embedded in a gaming framework for the purpose of producing more knowledgable participants in the preparation of an impact statement may be more reasonable for the present.

Almost everyone agrees that impact assessment should be a team effort, because the problems transcend the areas of competence and mental capacities of any one person. The disagreements arise about who should be involved and how the team effort should be orchestrated and conducted. Teams are hard to work with. They tend to devote inordinate amounts of time philosophizing and jumping around like popping corn. What kinds of mechanisms would facilitate the utilization of a team in the estimation of impacts?

If answerable questions can be identified, they can be assigned to individuals and groups for answering. Before the answering can be done effectively, however, the questions must be understood. In the case of most projects, the alternatives tend to be complex, and the problems of learning what the alternatives are is not simple. The impact processes also tend to be complex, and different people tend to have different bits and pieces of the puzzle. Also, it is seldom clear from the outset what the areas of concern are.

A methodology that has the appearance of being directed toward answers, perhaps based on preliminary notions about what the questions are and how the impact processes work, can be a productive way to get a team into the problem. It can be used as a catalytic and educational game that initially pushes participants to answer given questions in rather structured ways, i.e., by means of judgmental matrices, etc., but which encourages questioning of the question. This will stimulate modification of the questions as well as of the conceptualized process. At the same time the participants will be educating themselves interactively about the alternatives as well as about the questions, the processes, and the pieces of the puzzle brought by other members of the group. To do this effectively, there has to be a structured framework for interaction. Many possibilities are available such as various modifications of "delphi" techniques. The technique, whatever it is, needs to be embedded in a framework (Peterson, Schofer and Gemmell 1974; Schofer, Gemmell and Peterson 1975).

SUGGESTED AREAS OF IMPROVEMENT

The foregoing discussion has pointed out deficiencies in the art of social impact assessment, with special reference to the institution known as the "Environmental Impact Statement." It may be redundant to turn now to suggested areas of improvement, because the improvements we would like to suggest are implicit in the criticisms that have been raised. It would be more constructive at this point to specify the steps that must be taken to achieve improvement, but, in most cases, research must precede such recommendations. This section may thus be regarded as a concluding summary that turns attention from a rather negative examination of what is wrong to a positive concern for the directions we should be going. These directions are the following:

1. Clear identification in the impact assessment process of which issues are technical and which are political, and proper delegation of issues to appropriate institutions.

2. Recognition that even the best technical answers to questions that properly fall into the technical domain have a finite level of confidence associated with them as determined by the ability of the reader to comprehend the technical facts and the methods by which they were derived and/or the level of credibility enjoyed by the technical source in the reader's mind. (The implication of this is that "truth" is not necessarily established in the eyes of the public by perfecting the technical state of the art of impact assessment.)

3. Elimination, to the fullest extent possible, of speculative reasoning, especially where the effect of such reasoning is to prejudice the response of the reader to the issues in question. Speculative reasoning may be appropriate in the form of identification of plausible outcomes under conditions of uncertainty, but such "plausible outcomes" should not be presented as "probable" or "likely" outcomes in the absence of ability to specify the level of likelihood with some degree of confidence.

4. Recognition of the pluralistic nature of the public decision process and appropriate adjustment of the institutional roles of social impact assessment.

5. Increased emphasis on identification of opportunities to control alternative futures by appropriate management of the impacts of proposed projects (as opposed to exclusive preoccupation with the role of predicting alternative futures).

6. Better integration of social impact assessment with the processes and/or institutions which design alternative projects, so that assessment participates in the evolution of the design and is not merely a reaction to it.

7. Better assessment of the consequences of incompetent or superficial social impact assessment and more appropriate levels of investment (usually much higher) in the social impact assessment job, with consequent charging of the assessment cost to the project and inclusion of these costs in the evaluative decisions.

8. More emphasis on clear, concise, simple, relevant, informative and useful communication with the public on impact issues.

9. Better examination of the processes by which impacts are originated and transmitted throughout society. This will lead to more logical taxonomies of variables, more legible and rigorous exposure of impacts, more meaningful identification of questions, and improved ability to deal with dynamic, spatial and distributional problems. It will also assist in identification of

intervening processes and variables that seem to limit the generality of findings.

10. Particular attention to the question of social distribution of impacts.

11. Improvement of technical methods and substantive knowledge in areas of inquiry now frequently neglected because they are difficult to deal with. In particular, there is a need and opportunity to develop judgmental and perceptual methods for dealing quantitatively with the perceived environment and the public environment. Methodology is available (but seldom used) for dealing with subjective and intangible aspects of impacts as well as for dealing judgmentally with technical phenomena for which formal scientific explanations have not yet appeared (Peterson, Schofer and Gemmell 1974; Schofer, Gemmell and Peterson 1976).

12. More effort to review, collect, and correlate available knowledge and method from the many obscure places where it tends all too often to reside unnoticed.

13. Better judgment with regard to what to emphasize in the impact assessment. This must include more responsiveness to the concerns of the affected interest groups, perhaps via participatory processes. It must also include less concern for the trivial and irrelevant.

14. More emphasis on the impact assessment methodology as an educational gaming process of a pluralistic nature, the product of which is more informed and skillful players of pluralism, as opposed to the view that the product is a formal document known as the "Environmental Impact Statement" which provides the answers to questions about the impacts of the projects. Efforts to develop the ultimate impact assessment methodology in purely technical information terms will fall short of what is expected and needed from social impact assessment.

15. Finally, less use of the "Environmental Impact Statement" as propaganda intended to predispose the public in a given direction, and more use of it, where appropriate and in appropriate ways, as an informational lubricant that helps public pluralism to arrive at better decisions by enlightening the players.

References

Peterson, George L., Joseph L. Schofer and Robert S. Gemmell (1974) "Multidisciplinary, Design-Interactive Evaluation of Large-Scale Projects," pp. 251-72 in Charles C. Lozar (ed.), Methods and Measures Vol. 5 Milwaukee, WI.: Environmental Design Research Association.

Russell, Stuart H. (1975) An Analysis of Residential Stability Following a Natural Disaster. Unpublished master's thesis. Evanston, IL.: Department of Civil Engineering, Northwestern University.

Schofer, Joseph L., Robert S. Gemmell and George L. Peterson (1975) "The Judgmental Impact Matrix Approach: A Framework for Evaluating the Social and Environmental Impacts of Transportation Alternatives," in L. Llewellyn, C. Goodman and G. Hare (eds.), Social Impact Assessment: A Sourcebook for Highway Planners, Vol. 8. Washington, D.C.: Federal Highway Administration.

Wang, P. K., George L. Peterson and Joseph L. Schofer (1975) "Population Change: An Indicator of Highway Impact," **Transportation Engineering Journal**, ASCE, 101, TE3 (August), 491-504.